The Formation of a
Provincial Nobility

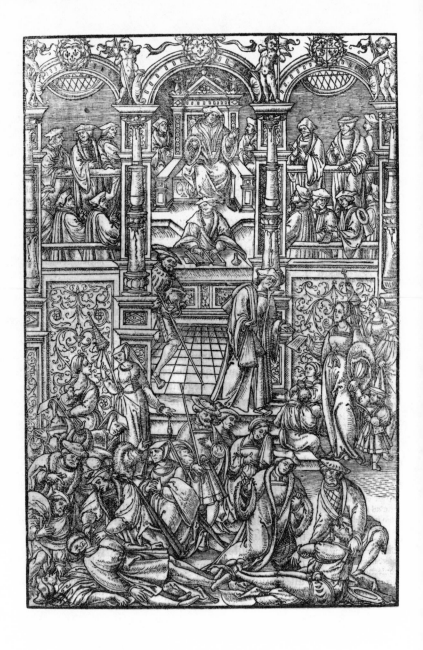

The Formation of a
Provincial Nobility

THE MAGISTRATES OF THE PARLEMENT
OF ROUEN, 1499-1610

By Jonathan Dewald

PRINCETON UNIVERSITY PRESS
PRINCETON, NEW JERSEY

[*Frontispiece*] The judge and his society:
from *Praxis criminis persequendi* . . .
Joanne Millaeo Boio authore (Paris, 1541).
Bibliothèque Nationale, Paris

For C.J.D.

PREFACE

THIS study was begun in 1971, as a doctoral dissertation for the University of California, Berkeley. Its completion has been possible only because of the help and encouragement I have received since then. My debts are, first, to institutions. A Special Career Fellowship from the University of California, Berkeley, supported the initial phases of research and writing. Later grants from the School of Humanities of the University of California, Irvine, and from the Regents of the University of California permitted further research in France. Most of the research was carried out at the Archives Départementales of the Seine-Maritime and of the Eure. Their staffs were remarkably helpful, despite the difficulty of many of my requests.

My debts to individuals are larger and more complex. Gene Brucker and Natalie Zemon Davis directed the project as a dissertation, and have continued since to offer suggestions and encouragement. I am obliged to them for much more than the sum of their specific kindnesses: reverberations from their scholarship and teaching are to be found throughout this book. At Berkeley, Richard Herr and Randolph Starn also commented on portions of the dissertation and made valuable suggestions. At Irvine I have profited from discussions with a number of colleagues: in particular I would like to thank Joyce Appleby, Karl Hufbauer, and Michael Johnson. Several other scholars have commented on earlier formulations of the ideas presented here. William Beik, Duncan Foley, George Huppert, Robert Kingdon, Bridget O'Laughlin, Nancy Lyman Roelker, and Christopher Stocker have all forced me to rethink parts of this study and have suggested valuable lines of inquiry. Philip Benedict has read in their entirety two versions of this study. As well as indicating a number of corrections and improvements, he has generously shared with me his extensive knowledge of Rouennais history and sources. Carolyn Dewald has read still more versions. I have made use of her erudition at a number of points, and the model of her own scholarship has made this a much larger inquiry than it would otherwise have been—however many issues remain incompletely resolved.

In France I have benefited from the graciousness of the Baron d'Esneval and the Comte de Caumont, who allowed me to consult their families' archives. The Comte de Caumont also made available to me his unpublished study of his family's history. Madeleine Foisil, Roland Mousnier, and Denis Richet listened patiently to my ideas and offered helpful advice. My specific disagreements with some of Professor Mousnier's interpretations are noted below. Those familiar with his work, however, will also recognize the degree to which this study stands within the broad and fruitful scholarly tradition that he has established. Jean-Pierre Bardet, whose forthcoming *thèse d'état* will be the standard work on seventeenth- and eighteenth-century Rouen, introduced me to Rouennais archives and has been a constant source of ideas and stimulation. Finally, I would like to thank a group whose help has been less easily definable, involving as it has elements of the archivistic, the intellectual, and the personal. These include Jacques Bottin, Christiane Douyère, Gérard Ermisse, Brigitte Lainé, Gérard Maudouech, Georges Mouradian, Anne Pallier, Denis Pallier, Elisabeth Smadja, and Gérard Smadja. Whatever perceptions of France as a society and culture underlie this study have been largely their doing.

J.D.

TABLE OF CONTENTS

113496

LIST OF FIGURES AND TABLES

NOTE ON MEASUREMENTS

MEASURES of capacity varied widely within upper Normandy: from one market to another, over time, and for different commodities. It is thus impossible to offer adequate equivalents for the sixteenth-century measures referred to in the text. However, the researches of G. D'Arandel de Condé allow approximate conversion of sixteenth-century to modern measures. For wheat, the most common measures were the *boisseau* and the *mine* (= six *boisseaux*). At the market of Rouen, the *boisseau* in the eighteenth century equalled 22.8 liters; at Gisors, the *boisseau* equalled 29.1 liters; at Pont de l'Arche, 36.4 liters; and at Montivilliers, 38.6 liters. (See G. D'Arandel de Condé, "Les anciennes mesures de capacité pour les grains en Seine-Maritime au XVIIIe siècle," *Revue d'Histoire Économique et Sociale*, XLVIII, 3 [1970], 305-352.)

NOTE ON MONETARY VALUES

Most of the monetary values given in what follows are set in *livres tournois*, the fictitious money of account that Frenchmen used during most of the sixteenth century; only between 1577 and 1602 was the attempt made to use a real coin, the *écu soleil*, set at an official value of 3 livres, as the unit in which prices were calculated. Only an approximation can be offered of the livre's actual value. Its value in precious metals declined steadily through the sixteenth century: from 17.96 grams of silver in 1513 to 15.62 grams in 1543, 11.79 grams in 1577, 10.98 grams in 1602, and 8.69 grams in 1636 (M. Baulant and J. Meuvret, *Prix des céréales extraits de la Mercuriale de Paris, 1520-1698*, 2 vols. [Paris, 1960], I, 249). More meaningful indications are supplied by the costs of goods and labor. At and near Rouen in the mid-sixteenth century, a cow cost between 6 and 10 livres, a sheep about 1½ livres, a pound of butter about ⅛ livre; a mason's day wages amounted to ⅕ livre between 1515 and 1546, ½ livre in 1578, and ⅘ livre in the first decade of the seventeenth century (AD Eure E1235, 8 September 1550; E1242; AD S-M 14H102; Raymond Quenedey, *L'habitation rouennaise: étude d'histoire, de géographie et d'archéologie urbaines* [Rouen, 1926], pp. 390-391).

LIST OF ABBREVIATIONS

AD Eure: Archives Départementales, Eure
AD S-M: Archives Départementales, Seine-Maritime
AN: Archives Nationales, Paris
BM: Bibliothèque Municipale, Rouen
BN: Bibliothèque Nationale, Paris
Frondeville, *Les présidents*:   Henri de Frondeville, *Les présidents du Parlement de Normandie (1499-1790)* (Paris-Rouen, 1953)
Frondeville, *Les conseillers* i: Henri de Frondeville, *Les conseillers du Parlement de Normandie au seizième siècle (1499-1594)* (Paris-Rouen, 1960)
Frondeville, *Les conseillers* ii: Henri de Frondeville, *Les conseillers du Parlement de Normandie sous Henri IV et sous Louis XIII (1594-1640)* (Paris-Rouen, 1964)
Hérit. 2:   Archives Départementales, Seine-Maritime, E, Tabellionage de Rouen, Héritages, 2e série
La Riv. Bourdet: Archives Départementales, Seine-Maritime, J, Chartrier de la Rivière Bourdet
Meubles 2:   Archives Départementales, Seine-Maritime, E, Tabellionage de Rouen, Meubles, 2e série
Reg. sec.:   Archives Départementales, Seine-Maritime, B, Parlement, Registres secrets
Tabel.:   Archives Départementales, Seine-Maritime, E, Tabellionage de Rouen
ł: *livre tournois*
s: *sou*
d: *denier*

The Formation of a
Provincial Nobility

THE *NOBLESSE DE ROBE* AS AN HISTORICAL PROBLEM

"IF I were to speak of the middle estates of this world and the low ones," wrote Philippe de Commynes, "it would take too long. It will be sufficient to speak of the high-ranking people, for it is through them that God's power and justice are made known. For if misfortunes befall a poor man or one hundred of them, no one worries about this, for it is attributed to his poverty or lack of proper care, or if he drowns or breaks his neck because no one was there to save him, people hardly talk about it."[1] For the past generation, historians of early modern France have sought to correct this long-standing historiographical bias, by directing their attention to the lives and misfortunes of the lower estates. Their efforts have been brilliantly successful, but one result has been a paradoxical distribution of our knowledge of the period. Our knowledge of "the high-ranking people" of the sixteenth and seventeenth centuries is perhaps more circumstantial and picturesque than our knowledge of the poor, but it is less often based on archival research and sophisticated method. What we know about the nobilities of early modern France (in contrast to the knowledge that Lawrence Stone and others have given us of the British aristocracy and gentry) continues largely to be based on literary sources and on a few well-known examples.[2]

[1] Samuel Kinser and Isabelle Cazeaux, eds., *The Memoirs of Philippe de Commynes*, 2 vols. (Columbia, South Carolina, 1969), I, 361.
[2] For review of recent studies of the nobility, François Billacois, "La crise de la noblesse européenne (1550-1650): Une mise au point," *Revue d'histoire moderne et contemporaine*, XXIII (April-June, 1976), 258-277. Studies of the early modern French nobility include Edouard

The present study is directed to this large gap in our knowledge of French society. It deals with the lives and properties of a provincial elite during the sixteenth and early seventeenth centuries, the magistrates who made up the Parlement of Normandy. My intention has not been to res-

---

Perroy, "Social Mobility among the French *Noblesse* in the Later Middle Ages," *Past and Present*, 21 (April, 1962), 25-38; J. Russell Major, "The Crown and the Aristocracy in Renaissance France," *The American Historical Review*, LXIX, 3 (April, 1964), 631-645; James B. Wood, "La structure sociale de la noblesse dans le bailliage de Caen et ses modifications (1463-1666)," *Annales de Normandie*, XXII, 4 (December, 1972), 331-335 (for the outline of an important study still in progress); "Demographic Pressures and Social Mobility among the Nobility of the Election of Bayeux, 1463-1666," *The Sixteenth Century Journal*, VII, 1 (April, 1977), 3-16; and "The Decline of the Nobility in Sixteenth and Early Seventeenth-Century France: Myth or Reality?" *Journal of Modern History*, XXXXVIII, 1 (March 1976); William A. Weary, "The House of La Tremouille, Fifteenth through Eighteenth Centuries: Change and Adaptation in a French Noble Family," *ibid.*, IL, 1 (March, 1977); Pierre Deyon, "A propos des rapports entre la noblesse française et la monarchie absolue pendant la première moitié du XVIIe siècle," *Revue historique*, CCXXXI (April-June, 1964), 341-356; Jean-Pierre Labatut, *Les ducs et pairs de France au XVIIe siècle. Étude sociale* (Paris, 1972); François-Charles Mougel, "La fortune des princes de Bourbon-Conty: revenus et gestion, 1655-1791," *Revue d'histoire moderne et contemporaine*, XVIII (January-March, 1971), 30-49. Because of the issues surrounding the French Revolution, more attention has been given to the eighteenth-century nobility than to that of earlier periods. See especially Robert Forster, *The Nobility of Toulouse in the Eighteenth Century* (Baltimore, 1960) and *The House of Saulx-Tavanes. Versailles and Burgundy, 1700-1830* (Baltimore, 1971); and Jean Meyer, *La noblesse de Bretagne au XVIIIe siècle*, 2 vols. (Paris, 1966). Two studies directed specifically to the *noblesse de robe* have also been of particular importance as models for the present study: Roland Mousnier, *La vénalité des offices sous Henri IV et Louis XIII* (2nd ed., Paris, 1971), which deals with some of the individuals considered here but in very different ways; and François Bluche, *Les magistrats du Parlement de Paris au XVIIIe siècle (1715-1771)* (Paris, 1960). For discussion of the distortions which reliance on literary sources has introduced into studies of the sixteenth- and seventeenth-century nobility, see Daniel Dessert, review of Labatut, *Les ducs et pairs*, *Annales. Economies*,

urrect Commynes' belief that the workings of history can most profitably be seen in the fortunes of the great. On the contrary, the study derives from a belief that the rich were as often as the poor the objects of large historical forces, and that literary accounts are equally misleading about both groups. Similar kinds of analysis need to be applied to both.

The Norman *parlementaires* offer substantial advantages for such an approach. They formed a sufficiently numerous group for some forms of statistical analysis: at its foundation, in 1499,[3] the Parlement included thirty-five members, and by 1610 its members numbered eighty-six. Further, in contrast to the military nobility, the *noblesse d'épée*, who were divided by subtle and often imperceptible differences of family antiquity, standing at court, and wealth, the *parle-*

Sociétés, Civilisations, XXXI, 4 (July-August, 1976), 850-851; Julian Dent, review of Davis Bitton, *The French Nobility in Crisis, Renaissance Quarterly*, XXIV, 2 (Summer, 1971), 244-247; and Jean Meyer, "Un problème mal posé: la noblesse pauvre. L'exemple breton au XVIIIe siècle," *Revue d'histoire moderne et contemporaine*, XVIII (April-June, 1971), 161-188. It will be apparent how much the methods used in the present study owe to the works of Forster, Meyer, and to Lawrence Stone, *The Crisis of the Aristocracy, 1558-1641* (Oxford, 1965). This book was written before the appearance of Robert Harding's excellent study, *Anatomy of a Power Elite. The Provincial Governors of Early Modern France* (New Haven, 1978). Although mainly concerned with the high aristocracy, this study offers a view of the French landed elite that in many ways is similar to the one presented here.

[3] Before the Parlement's foundation, the ultimate judicial authority in Normandy had been the Echiquier, a court that combined elements of provincial independence and Parisian control. Leading aristocrats and ecclesiastics sat by right in the Echiquier, and were supposed to pronounce on questions of Norman law. Ultimate authority, though, was held by a group of royal judges sent from Paris; their domination of this supposedly provincial institution was a source of frequent complaints. In the fifteenth century the Echiquier was in full decay, meeting irregularly and for only a few days; the Parlement's foundation thus responded to widespread demands for more efficient judicial institutions. See A. Floquet, *Histoire du Parlement de Normandie*, 7 vols. (Rouen, 1840-1842), I.

mentaires formed a group with clearly defined, straightforward boundaries. Finally, because of the magistrates' relative wealth, institutionalized political role, and residence in the provincial capital, source materials concerning them are abundant and coherent.

Although sources concerning the *parlementaires* are relatively numerous, they have special qualities that deserve emphasis at the outset. Most important is their fragmentary nature. About thirty Rouennais robe families have left collections of private papers from the sixteenth century, but few of these are sufficiently extensive to permit a full view of the family over several generations or even a full view of its situation at any one moment. Contemporary statistical documents, such as tax records, are equally rare. Knowledge of most of the *parlementaires* must come from legal sources, above all from notarial contracts of marriage, inheritance division, loans, rentals, and the like. Together with the few surviving collections of private papers, such contracts supply the principal economic source employed here and the basis for most of the study's statistics, and they have determined as well the method followed in most of this investigation: that is, an effort to combine the partial but statistically coherent knowledge which notarial contracts offer of a large number of *parlementaires* with the more complete knowledge that private papers give of a handful of individuals and their families. A similar disparity applies to the study of the *parlementaires'* professional attitudes and personal sensibilities. Letters, speeches, and even personal reflections survive from a small number of the most important *parlementaires*, but for the large majority there are only occasional expressions of personal views, in notarial contracts, lawsuits, or the debates of the Parlement itself. Here too it is necessary to combine our relatively full sense of the attitudes of the few with our fragmentary knowledge of the majority—though at many points it is simply necessary to acknowledge the sources' bias in favor of the successful and important.

In certain respects the Norman *parlementaires* formed part of a national group, but their lives in many ways were dominated by the conditions of the region where they found themselves. This study is meant to be a regional and not national inquiry. The chapters which follow will sufficiently indicate the degree to which Norman geography, laws, patterns of landownership, and the like affected the magistrates' experiences. Yet it is worth emphasizing also the ways in which Normandy and Rouen, the provincial capital where the Parlement was situated, presented in acute form tendencies and problems basic to provincial society in the old regime. The province was close to Paris and felt with special severity the pressures of absolutism, but contemporaries were also impressed at the strength of provincial patriotism. Rouen itself, with its 75,000 inhabitants, its position on the Seine, and its capacity to profit from Atlantic commerce, claimed to be the second city of France and enjoyed huge commercial prosperity in the sixteenth century. But equally characteristic of the city were its large ecclesiastical establishment and its law courts, and within the province were to be found the estates of some of the most powerful French aristocrats.[4] To study the Norman *parlementaires* is thus to witness, within a confined space and under many special conditions, the interchange of these varied elements, monarchical absolutism and provincial loyalty, commercial wealth and aristocratic power.

The questions which are asked here reflect the study's basic concern to illuminate the patterns of wealth and domi-

[4] On Rouen's population and activity, see Philip Benedict, "Catholics and Huguenots in Sixteenth-Century Rouen: The Demographic Effects of the Religious Wars," *French Historical Studies*, IX, 2 (Fall, 1975), 209-234; Michel Mollat, *Le commerce maritime normand à la fin du Moyen Age* (Paris, 1952); and Michel de Bouard, ed., *Histoire de la Normandie* (Toulouse, 1970), esp. pp. 245-250, 288-299, 303-314. A forthcoming collective history of Rouen will provide further insights into Rouen's commercial dynamism. In this respect Rouen was quite unlike such other *parlementaire* cities as Dijon, Rennes, Aix, and even Toulouse, all of them heavily dominated by the law courts.

nance within a provincial society. This means, first, examining the professional training, attitudes, and activity which defined the magistracy as a group. As will become apparent, their professional mentality also had important implications for their relations to the society around them; these issues are the subject of Chapter 1. Chapter 2 deals with the group's social origins, with the processes by which its members were recruited, and with some of the attitudes which surrounded these processes. In particular, it asks how willing the magistrates were to accept new men and how rigid they believed social boundaries to be. Chapters 3, 4, and 5 deal with the various problems of *parlementaire* wealth and incomes: Chapter 3 considers the size and nature of *parlementaire* fortunes and seeks to determine the contribution which office in the Parlement made to them; Chapter 4 considers *parlementaire* landowning, as both a focus for social ties and a source of income; and Chapter 5 considers what the magistrates spent and the obstacles which expenditure posed to efforts of the families to conserve or increase their fortunes. Finally, Chapter 6 examines the magistrates' families. It investigates the role which the family played in determining professional and political positions, its economic role, and the kinds of social solidarities which it created. Although all of these chapters include substantial amounts of quantitative analysis, all of them attempt as well to convey something of what the magistrates' daily lives were like, and indeed to suggest linkages between the quantitative and the picturesque: between, for instance, the financial aspects of marriage and its emotional qualities.

By their nature many of the questions asked here require that we move beyond consideration of the *parlementaires* themselves and that we give some attention to other groups, notably to the military nobility, the *noblesse d'épée*. To understand the *parlementaires'* social origins, for instance, demands some understanding of both the patronage networks of the great aristocracy and the nobility's attitudes toward social distinction. Analysis of *parlementaire* landownership likewise requires some comparison with the practices of other large landowners, if we are to understand the causes that underlay the magistrates' successes and failures with landed property. The paucity of serious studies of the early modern nobility means that such efforts cannot be pursued with complete rigor; it has been necessary to rely on examples drawn from the Norman aristocracy, rather than on a full range of quantitative data. But it has nonetheless seemed worth presenting the answers which these examples suggest, rather than to neglect such comparative issues altogether.

The present study treats the *parlementaires* as representatives of the French landed classes during the Renaissance, as a specific instance of larger phenomena. Although such an approach is not entirely novel, it does conflict with important themes in the historiographical traditions surrounding the *noblesse de robe*. Because specific divergences between the Norman example and these historiographical traditions will receive attention at several points in the chapters which follow, some attention should be given here to the broad outlines of historians' treatment of the *noblesse de robe*. In particular it is important that some of the assumptions, implications, and ambiguities in these traditions be understood. Three areas of concern have been especially prominent. Historians have been concerned, first, with the magistrates' professional and political position, midway between the monarchy and the society it sought to control. Secondly, they have sought to understand the magistrates' social origins and to establish relationships between recruitment and attitudes. Finally, there has been an effort to understand the magistrates' economic role, and notably their impact on the structure of landowning.

Each of these problems was of considerable interest to sixteenth-century writers, and modern discussions have in many ways been shaped by their formulations. Like later historians, sixteenth-century writers noted the ambiguous political and professional role played by the *noblesse de robe*. It was from among the magistrates that the monarchy drew its most devoted servants; and both their long tradition of royal service and the absolutist tendencies of the Roman law in which they were educated suited them well for this role.[5] Yet the magistrates were also seen to be a check on the monarchy's power. To Claude de Seyssel in 1515 they represented the means by which fundamental law was preserved against the monarch's whims.[6] A half century later Etienne Pasquier took up this theme, and added to it social and historical dimensions. Though Pasquier did not argue (as some lawyers did) that the parlements antedated the monarchy itself, he did believe the Parlement of Paris to be very old and nearly equal to the monarchy in its claim to authority. It had been founded, he argued, by the early Carolingians as a way "to captivate . . . the heart and devotion of the subjects," and thus to legitimate the dynasty's assumption of power. In Pasquier's own day the parlements were still the means by which the monarchy's acts were given authority and basic agreement between monarchy and society was assured. "It is a marvelous thing," he wrote in summing up his discussion of the parlements, "that as soon as some act (*ordonnance*) has been published and approved by the Parlement, suddenly the French people agree to it without a murmur: as if this company were the bond which

[5] See, for instance, Hotman's stress on the absolutist impact of Roman law: *Francogallia*, ed. Ralph Giesey and J.H.M. Salmon (Cambridge, 1972), p. 505, discussed by Donald Kelley, *Foundations of Modern Historical Scholarship. Language, Law, and History in the French Renaissance* (New York, 1970), esp. pp. 202-211; see also Kelley's discussion of Étienne Pasquier, pp. 284-287. More generally, see J. R. Strayer, "Normandy and Languedoc," repr. in *Medieval Statecraft and the Perspectives of History* (Princeton, 1971), pp. 56-57; William Bouwsma, "Lawyers and Early Modern Culture," *The American Historical Review*, LXXVIII, 2 (April, 1973), 310-311; and Roland Mousnier, "Trevor-Roper's 'General Crisis:' Symposium," in Trevor Aston, ed., *Crisis in Europe, 1560-1660* (Garden City, 1967).

[6] Claude de Seyssel, *La monarchie de France* (ed. Jacques Poujol) (Paris, 1961), pp. 115-119.

ties the obedience of the subjects to the commands of their prince. This is of no small importance for the grandeur of our kings."[7] The Parlement of Paris had been especially effective in filling this role during the earlier Middle Ages, Pasquier believed, because of its social composition. The court had not been made up of legal specialists only, but had included many leading aristocrats. The society's most important elements had thus been amply represented and able to influence the monarchy.[8]

Such analyses of the ambiguous relations among parlements, monarchy, and society have received further dimensions from the work of Roland Mousnier on venality of office. The buying and selling of offices in the parlements and elsewhere created other tensions between the magistrates' roles: between ideals of service to the monarchy and serious legal training, for instance, and a view of office as private property, bought with an eye to social status. Although venality gave the monarchy certain means of controlling the magistrates, Mousnier argues, it also had the danger of creating a "new feudalism" of officials whose interests were quite unlike the monarchy's.[9]

[7] Etienne Pasquier, *Les mémoires et recherches de la France. Livre Premier et second* . . . (Paris, 1594), ff. 77, 99. For the idea that the parlements had existed in Julius Caesar's time, thus before the monarchy itself, see Iehan Papon, *Recueil d'arrestz notables des courtz souveraines de France* . . . (Paris, 1566), prologue. For discussion of Pasquier's methods and concerns, Kelley, *Foundations*, pp. 271-300, and George Huppert, *The Idea of Perfect History. Historical Erudition and Historical Philosophy in Renaissance France* (Urbana, 1970), pp. 28-71.

[8] Pasquier, *Les mémoires et recherches*, ff. 85-86. For contemporary repetition of this idea, see Louis D'Orléans, *Les ouvertures du Parlement* (Paris, 1607), pp. 65-66, and Bernard de La Roche Flavin, *Treze livres des Parlemens de France* . . . (Bordeaux, 1617), p. 350.

[9] Mousnier, *La vénalité des offices*, p. 53; see also pp. 83-89 for discussion of the complexities of the political attachments of officials. The problem of the venal officials' attachments to the society around them, especially to its poorer elements, is central to the debate between Mousnier and Boris Porchnev. For summaries of these issues, see J.H.M. Salmon, "Venal Office and Popular Sedition in Seven-

There has been a similar convergence of sixteenth-century opinion and modern historical analysis with regard to a second group of problems, that of the magistrates' social origins. Etienne Pasquier dealt with the issue only by implication, in his comments on the relationship between the parlements' recruitment and their political effectiveness. In the early Middle Ages, he believed, the Parlement had effectively restrained the monarchy because it included great noblemen as well as lawyers; it was less effective in this role in the sixteenth century because its social base had narrowed, to lawyers only.[10] Earlier in the century Seyssel had offered a more direct assessment of the magistrates' origins. The *noblesse de robe*, he wrote, was drawn from a "middle estate" whose most conspicuous members were financiers and officials; office was a means by which families from this milieu might rise to positions of authority and prestige, and thus formed one of those avenues of social mobility which Seyssel saw as characterizing French society.[11]

Again, historians have tended to accept these views while seeking to add further dimensions to them. Like Seyssel they have been concerned with offices as means of social mobility. Henri Drouot and Roland Mousnier, for instance, have attributed political disruption in the late sixteenth century to the growing difficulty which new families had in obtaining high offices.[12] More broadly, such historians as Fernand

teenth-Century France: A Review of a Controversy," *Past and Present*, 37 (July, 1967), 21-43, and Robert Mandrou, "Vingt ans après, les révoltes populaires dans l'historiographie française du XVIIᵉ siècle," *Revue historique*, CCXLII (1969), 29-40.

[10] Pasquier, *Les mémoires et recherches*, ff. 86-99. Cf. the view of the relationship between legal specialization and ineffectual political stances developed by Edouard Maugis, *Histoire du Parlement de Paris de l'avènement des rois Valois à la mort d'Henri IV*, 3 vols. (Paris, 1914; repr. New York, 1967), I, xiv, 270.

[11] Seyssel, *La monarchie de France*, p. 123.

[12] Henri Drouot, *Mayenne et la Bourgogne: étude sur la Ligue (1587-1596)*, 2 vols. (Paris, 1937), I, 71-72, 413-415, 425-427; Mousnier, *La vénalité des offices*, pp. 43, 83, 91-92.

Braudel and Robert Mandrou have seen the *noblesse de robe* as representing an important phase in the history of the bourgeoisie: to Braudel, the enthusiasm of merchants and financiers for offices was part of a larger process, in which bourgeois all over Europe turned away from their true commercial vocation; to Mandrou, the officials represent social "half-castes," seeking desperately but with only partial success to escape the taint of commercial origins.[13]

Much the same stress on the particular ambitions and outlook of the bourgeoisie has characterized treatment of the third set of issues to be considered here, the economic role of the *noblesse de robe*. Since the fifteenth century, wrote François de La Noue, in the 1580's, "the judges, lawyers, fiscal officials, and some merchants have been such good managers (*ménagers*) that they have lopped off a good number of [the nobility's] fiefs." The officials' success in buying landed property, he thought, was a principal reason that the nobility of his day held only half the fiefs it once had held.[14] Marc Bloch and other students of French rural history have sought to understand the roots of this success, and they have found them in the social origins of the officials. Members of the *noblesse de robe* benefited from both the commercial success and the attitudes of their bourgeois parents. They had funds which the older nobility lacked, and thus could buy large estates; they were oriented to profits rather than to military glory, and their backgrounds in commerce made them better able than the nobility to administer landed properties successfully.[15]

---

[13] Fernand Braudel, *The Mediterranean and the Mediterranean World in the Age of Philip II*, 2 vols., trans. Sian Reynolds (New York, 1972-1973), II, 725-734; Robert Mandrou, *Introduction à la France Moderne, 1500-1640* (Paris, 1961), pp. 157-158. See also Marc Bloch, *French Rural History. An Essay on its Basic Characteristics*, trans. Janet Sondheimer (Berkeley, 1966), p. 125.

[14] François de La Noue, *Discours politiques et militaires*, ed. F. E. Sutcliffe (Geneva, 1967), p. 264.

[15] Thus Bloch, *French Rural History*, pp. 124-126; Lucien Febvre, *Philippe II et la Franche Comté. Étude d'histoire politique, religieuse*

Historians have been alert to the ambiguities in this contrast of economic practices. They have stressed, for instance, the officials' eagerness in buying land to imitate the lives of the nobility; and they have shown the extent to which magistrates like noblemen considered themselves to be members of dynasties and castes, and framed their economic choices accordingly.[16] Yet, despite such nuances, the historiography of the sixteenth-century *noblesse de robe* has retained a considerable degree of coherence: bourgeois recruitment, an aggressive economic role, and an uncertain political position have been seen as closely related phenomena. Historians have understood the group's economic impact in terms of its essentially bourgeois origins; and, like Pasquier, they have found links between the group's status and its professional position. As the group sought to establish itself as a privileged order, a new nobility, its commitment to the monarchy and professional seriousness tended to diminish. As a result, an underlying theme in the historiography of the *noblesse de robe* has been that of conflict within the French upper classes: between bourgeoisie and nobility, city and country, the economically progressive and the economically backward, those profiting from the state and those under attack by it.

Much of the present study is directed to a reassessment of these oppositions. I hope to show that, when set against the realities of sixteenth-century Norman practice, those sixteenth-century concepts which have so strongly shaped

---

et sociale (2nd ed., Paris, 1970), pp. 183-198; and Roland Mousnier, "Les survivances médiévales dans la France du XVIIᵉ siècle," *XVIIᵉ Siècle*, no. 106-107 (1975), 73-78. Cf. Pierre de Saint Jacob's remark that "The archaic conceptions of the peasant (*laboureur*) lurk within the soul of the *parlementaires*": *Les paysans de la Bourgogne du Nord au dernier siècle de l'ancien régime* (Paris, 1960), p. 54.

[16] Robert Mandrou, *La France aux XVIIᵉ et XVIIIᵉ siècles* (3rd ed., Paris, 1974), pp. 83-84; Mousnier, *La vénalité des offices*, pp. 536-541, and most recently *Les institutions de la France sous la monarchie absolue, 1598-1789*, I (Paris, 1975), 47-61.

more recent discussion of the *noblesse de robe* display important uncertainties. It is not clear, for instance, that Seyssel's "middle estate" should be identified with a commercial bourgeoisie, or that aristocratic complaints about the *noblesse de robe* should be understood in terms of competition between rival classes or castes. In Normandy, indeed, a substantial fraction of the *parlementaires* was drawn from the nobility itself and very few came from Rouen's commercial bourgeoisie. The conditions of their recruitment, in fact, ensured that most of them were the dependents of the courtly aristocracy and that they continued to serve the aristocracy's interests, once appointed to office. Conflict between the *noblesse de robe* and the feudal aristocracy was equally attenuated with regard to economic attitudes and practices. The *parlementaires* experienced many of the same economic pressures as other sixteenth-century landowners, and robe families had to confront many of the same threats to their prosperity. In Normandy, in short, the *noblesse de robe* grew out of aristocratic society, rather than in opposition to it.

No claim is made here that this was the case throughout France. The claim is made here, however, that the example of Normandy can suggest useful perspectives for examining the ruling groups of other French provinces, and that the methods which have been applied to the study of the early modern working classes are as much needed for a real understanding of the privileged and wealthy.

ONE

PROFESSIONAL IDENTITY
AND PROFESSIONAL ATTACHMENTS

"So MUCH of our fine youth lives uselessly," complained the
military nobleman Blaise de Monluc, in the early 1570's,
"although these youths would be very capable of bearing
arms. Entering from time to time the Parlements of Toulouse and Bordeaux, . . . I have continually been astounded
that so many young men could thus amuse themselves in a
law court, since ordinarily youthful blood is boiling."[1]
Monluc's comments reflect the disdain with which the nobility of the sword regarded the nobility of the robe. His
comments also point to the complex reasons which underlay
the nobility's feeling. He did not complain about the low
birth or excessive powers of the magistrates; on the contrary, he was disturbed that such "fine youth," well suited
to more aristocratic pursuits, should devote themselves to so
unlikely a profession. The tension between robe and sword,
as Monluc perceived it, was not one between disparate
castes, but rather between differing professional mentalities.

Some of the issues which Monluc's comments raise—in
particular the question of whether robe and sword nobilities
were in fact distinct castes—must await consideration in
later chapters. The central question which his comments
pose concerns the nature of the special professional outlook
which membership in the magistracy created. What were
the daily professional demands that magistracy imposed?
How seriously were members of the Parlement affected by
them? What effects did their particular outlook have on

[1] Blaise de Monluc, *Commentaires, 1521-1576* (Bibliothèque de la
Pléiade, Paris, 1964), p. 345.

16

their relationship with the surrounding society? These are the questions to which the present chapter is directed.

Nearly all of the Norman magistrate's professional life took place in Rouen's Palace of Justice, a magnificent flamboyant Gothic building set in the center of the city. Construction on it was begun shortly after the Parlement's foundation, in 1499, and it was completed in the second decade of the sixteenth century. The Palace was a scene of enormous activity in the sixteenth century, in which the magistrates were only the central figures. The arcades along its first floor were filled with shops, rental from which helped to pay for the building's maintenance.[2] Book and paper sellers had regular positions in the corridors inside. A special room housed the attorneys (*procureurs*), who numbered about fifty in the later sixteenth century and who needed always to be present in case something affecting their clients arose. A more motley collection was made up by the clerks and mere "practitioners," men who lacked both legal education and office but who were ready to undertake legal chores and who usually survived as clerks for lawyers and judges. They, together with the sergeants and other lesser figures, formed the notoriously rowdy world of the *basoche*. Despite periodic repression, each year they performed satirical, sometimes scandalous, plays, and they seem to have been the leading participants in the brawls which occasionally took place in the halls of the Palace: as in 1583, when a paper seller assaulted a clerk in pursuit of an unpaid debt.[3] One of those charged with managing such

[2] A. Floquet, *Histoire du Parlement de Normandie*, 7 vols. (Rouen, 1840-1842), I, 342-348, 450; Reg. sec., 1573-1579, f. 535v; A. de Blangy, ed., *Journal de Gilles de Gouberville pour les années 1549, 1550, 1551, 1552* . . . (*Mémoires de la Société des Antiquaires de Normandie*, XXXII [Caen, 1895], pp. 64, 104, the latter concerning "la boutique d'un changeur").

[3] E. Gosselin, *Recherches sur les origines et l'histoire du théâtre à Rouen avant Pierre Corneille* (Rouen, 1868), pp. 57-61; save during periods of *parlementaire* irritation at their excesses, the basoche were

disorders, the sergeant and poetaster Jacques Sireulde, described the scene in about 1550: "Ought one to see in a Palace of Justice so many hawkers, men and women alike? So many pages and valets? So many messengers? And then there are the fruit sellers, who come whether wanted or not. . . . all of these have to be kept out to assure that the commonality stops coming to piss beneath this vault."[4] Finally there were the litigants and all those who had requests to make of the magistrates, whether as part of a lawsuit or concerning administrative matters.

The magistrates' appearance was eagerly awaited. They were expected to arrive early in the morning, usually at 6:00, clothed in the black robes that they were required to wear everywhere in the city and riding the mules that were equally the mark of their position (but which in the late sixteenth century fell victim to the new vogue for carriages).[5] The magistrates' arrival must have been an impressive sight, for this was the moment for petitioners to present their grievances or other papers. The magistrates then moved to the court's different chambers. As the court was organized in 1600, the twenty-three senior councillors made

---

allowed to present their plays in either the courtyard or the salle des procureurs of the palace, and were given an annual subsidy of 75ł from fines paid the Parlement. See also AD S-M, B, Requêtes du Palais, 7 October 1583 (for altercation within the palace); Reg. sec., January-June, 1597, ff. 16-17 (for *procureurs'* numbers and their efforts to prevent new appointments); the palace also included a *buvette*, at which the magistrates might refresh themselves (Reg. sec., 1596, f. 8v). On the *basoche* in general, and for suggestions on magistrates' relations with the *basochiens*, see Howard Graham Harvey, *The Theatre of the Basoche. The Contribution of the Law Societies to French Medieval Comedy* (Cambridge, Mass., 1941).

[4] Jacques Sireulde, *Les abus et superfluitez du Monde* . . . (Rouen, n.d. [ca. 1550]), no pagination. Sireulde was a leading member of the *basoche*, and at one point was suspended from office for mocking a magistrate in one of his carnival plays. See Gosselin, *Recherches*, pp. 49-50, and Reg. sec., 1546-1547, f. 6, for his reinstatement.

[5] BM MS Y214, ii, 69; Floquet, *Histoire du Parlement*, ii, 164-168.

up the Grand' Chambre, forty-five junior councillors made up the Chambre des Enquêtes, and eight specially designated councillors made up the Chambre des Requêtes; in addition, members of the Grand' Chambre and the Chambre des Enquêtes served on a rotating basis on the Tournelle, the court's criminal chamber, and in the Chambre de l'Édit, created by the Edict of Nantes to try cases concerning Protestants. Most of their work was devoted to appeals, cases from the province's royal and seigneurial jurisdictions, but privileged individuals and institutions might begin their cases in the Chambre des Requêtes.[6]

For some hours these chambers worked in closed session, hearing witnesses, examining documents, and voting decisions. The dominant figures in this work were the four presidents, of whom two presided over the Grand' Chambre, one over the Enquêtes, and one over the Tournelle; the three king's attorneys, who were expected to intervene whenever the king's interests seemed to be involved in a case; and the reporter, the councillor chosen by the presidents to summarize the evidence in a case, lead discussion of it, and recommend a decision. Mid-mornings on most days, litigants and their lawyers were admitted for oral arguments, usually in public sessions. Such arguments in principle were limited to the Grand' Chambre, though apparently arguments were sometimes also heard in the Chambre des Enquêtes. These were dramatic moments in the routine of the Parlement, for the closing arguments of well-known lawyers were greatly appreciated by contemporaries. "There is nothing which more greatly flatters our senses or tickles our minds than to hear a learned and eloquent lawyer argue the merits of a case," wrote the Parisian magistrate and political conspirator Louis D'Or-

[6] On the court's make-up, BM MS Martainville Y23 (Alexandre Bigot de Monville, *Traité de l'Eschiquier et Parlement de Normandie*); more generally, R. Doucet, *Les institutions de la France au XVIe siècle*, 2 vols. (Paris, 1948), I, 173-175.

léans of his former profession: "It is a marvelous thing to see him command all those present with powerful and imperious words; it is delightful to see him . . . make himself loved and admired by even those who cannot see him, and who let themselves be carried away by the power of his words." The magistrates agreed, and arranged that important visitors hear the closing arguments of famous local lawyers.[7] At the close of this dramatic and public oratory, the magistrates announced decisions in the cases which they had completed, then went home for their dinners. They reassembled for normal sessions at 2:00 and continued closed discussions for two hours. If the quantity of business demanded it, they continued in extraordinary session into the late afternoon.

Occasionally this routine was broken by closed assemblies of the chambers, called by the presidents or the king's attorneys to discuss issues of general importance, in particular political issues. Other events were still more infrequent: *mercuriales*, in which failings of the company as a whole or of individuals were discussed, examinations and receptions of new members, ceremonial events, such as the burial of a colleague (in which the court normally marched as a group) or public processions (in which they were quite reluctant to take part), and assemblies to receive the visits of important dignitaries, colleagues from other courts, subordinate judges, or city councillors. Each year's session opened on

[7] Louis D'Orléans, *Les ouvertures du parlement* (Paris, 1607), p. 336. In 1571, when the duc de Montmorency appeared before the court to begin his brief service as bailli of Rouen, "on a parlé de plaider une cause de quelque belle importance" before him (Reg. sec., 1570-1571, f. 88v). Cf. Édouard Maugis, *Histoire du Parlement de Paris de l'avénement des rois Valois à la mort d'Henri IV*, 3 vols. (Paris, 1914; repr. New York, 1967), I, 314-315. In contrast to other parlements, the Parlement of Rouen seems not to have limited oral arguments to specific days; see, for instance, Reg. sec., 1572-1574, ff. 55v-59v (litigants heard Monday, Tuesday, Thursday, Friday, and Saturday, June 1-6, 1573). Cf. Maugis, *Histoire du Parlement de Paris*, I, 283-286.

St. Martin's day, November 12th, with an address by the first president, and closed August 31st; during the court's two-month vacation, cases were heard and decided by a Chambre des Vacations, drawn by rotation from the Grand' Chambre and the Enquêtes.

All of this professional activity was carried on in a setting of explicit symbolism. Much of this symbolism was religious, as for instance the large painting of the crucifixion which hung at the front of the hall used by the Grand' Chambre and for all general meetings of the court; its purpose, according to the Toulousan *parlementaire* Bernard de La Roche Flavin, was "to cool off and hold back by this commemoration of holy things the too active and too greedy minds of the judges."[8] The theme of restraint was repeated in the costumes which the magistrates themselves ordinarily wore, everywhere save in their own houses and in the privacy of their country properties. The magistrates wore robes "the same as the priests,' " as a Norman lawyer pointed out, and this was meant to remind them and others of the special characteristics of their position: first, of the nearly sacerdotal, divinely instituted functions of the judge;[9] second, and perhaps more important, of the need for maturity and moderation in performing their tasks. To contemporaries the robes were not just reminiscent of the

[8] Bernard de La Roche Flavin, *Treze livres des parlemens de France* . . . (Bordeaux, 1617), p. 303.

[9] Josias Bérault, *La coustume reformée du Pays et Duché de Normandie* (4th ed., Rouen, 1632), p. 40. Bérault's view was that ". . . in consideration of Ulpian's description of them (magistrates) as *sacerdotes*, it would not be appropriate that *sacerdotio quodam fungentes*, and performing a sacred function, they appear to the people in profane clothing, rather than clothing distinct from that of the commonality." For the sacred character of the monarchy more generally, see Percy Schramm, *Der König von Frankreich. Das Wesen der Monarchie vom 9. zum 16. Jahrhundert*, 2 vols. (Weimar, 1960), I, 252-254, and *passim*. Cf. the rather different analysis of *parlementaire* dress given by J. H. Shennan, *The Parlement of Paris* (London, 1968,) pp. 34-35.

magistrate's closeness to the priesthood. They also called forth images of age and of retirement from active pursuits. In this sense also the magistrates' costumes were meant to symbolize and encourage mature self-restraint: precisely the qualities which Monluc found so surprising when assumed by young men.[10]

The symbolism of age was repeated in the constant stress within the Parlement, echoed throughout the magistrate's workday, on rankings according to seniority of service. Nearly everything that the magistrates did involved some affirmation of seniority. When the court took part in a procession, it marched in the order of its members' reception; when opinions were given, either on political issues or in the more typical discussions of lawsuits, the same order was followed; and the question of seniority repeatedly came up in arguments over precedence, especially between the court's two junior chambers, those of Requêtes and of Enquêtes.[11]

Such were the magistrates' daily activities and some of the meanings which those activities were commonly supposed to contain. They formed the surface of the magistrates' professional lives. To understand these professional lives more deeply, we must pose further questions, about the training and background of those who entered the magistracy and about the nature of the work they did.

The formal educational requirements for entering the Parlement were straightforward. Candidates were required to have a *licence* from one of the law schools, for the Parlement as for all positions in the royal judiciary. Normally this required about six years' study in the arts curriculum of the universities, culminating in the *licence* in arts, then the two or three years spent studying Roman law which normally were needed for the *licence* in law.[12] All of this

[10] See Philippe Ariès, *Centuries of Childhood*, trans. Robert Baldick (New York, 1962), pp. 24, 31.

[11] For instance Reg. sec., 1570-1571, ff. 70-73.

[12] See Bernard Guenée, *Tribunaux et gens de justice dans le bail-*

education could be acquired within Normandy itself, but most magistrates studied outside the province. Local institutions had never been vigorous, and were in steady decline during the sixteenth century. At Rouen there was only the Collège des Bons Enfants, which was mainly for the education of the poor and which was rarely frequented by the magistrates or their children. Both arts and law courses could be had at the University of Caen, in lower Normandy, but this too had few attractions. Charles de Bourgueville, a judge at Caen and an enthusiastic local patriot, noted in the 1580's that the university "has been as famous as any in the kingdom; but it has lacked Maecenases, princes or lords, to favor it and to maintain there famous doctors." The civil wars were especially difficult for the provincial university. Funds were inadequate and many of the endowments had been alienated. Few law professors remained in these circumstances (there were only two doctors of law in 1564), and only a few students listened to their lectures.[13]

---

liage de Senlis à la fin du moyen âge (vers 1380-vers 1550) (Paris, 1963), pp. 185ff. For law-school teaching in the mid-sixteenth century, see Donald Kelley, François Hotman. A Revolutionary's Ordeal (Princeton, 1973), pp. 27-28.

[13] Histoire de l'église cathédrale de Rouen, métropolitaine et primatiale de Normandie . . . (Rouen, 1686), 161-163; the Cardinal de Bourbon had expressed his eagerness to found a Jesuit college at Rouen as early as 1569 but the project was realized only in the 1590's (Reg. sec., 1571-1572, f. 61); Charles de Bourgueville, Les recherches et antiquitez de la province de Neustrie . . . (Caen, 1833; first published Caen, 1588), pp. 333, 376-377, 385-386. Underscoring the charitable functions of the Collège des Bons Enfants were testamentary donations from Rouen's cathedral canons and others. Thus the magistrate and canon Guillaume Tulles in 1535 left 3l to the college, "in order that they say and chant vigils of the dead at each of my [funeral] services," and to each of the bons enfants he left a bonnet worth 10 s (AD S-M, G3442; see also AD S-M, G3431, for a similar gift by the councillor and canon Guillaume Gombault). Philip Benedict has pointed out that after 1550 the status of the college's students tended to rise; see his forthcoming study of Rouen during the Wars of Religion. The marginal position of the University

Even without the disasters of the late sixteenth century, Caen would have had difficulty attracting the magistrates and their children. Caen in the sixteenth century was "two good days' travel" away from Rouen, just as far as Paris.[14] More important, it was widely accepted that education—and especially legal education—ought to involve travel, in a search for famous teachers and famous sites. Bourgueville's own career well illustrates this restlessness. "Some time after [1521], when Master Guillaume Desmares of the town of Caudebec and I were [at Caen], continuing our studies, we received the degree of bachelors; then I traveled to the universities of Angers and Poitiers, in the years 1524 and 1525. . . . There was a great deal of excitement at Poitiers [because of] two learned doctors . . . , and at Angers [there were] Masters Vallin Gizay and Anguinare Baro. And also three young and learned lecturers had been brought from Toulouse. . . . I consider myself very fortunate to have been the student of such learned men."[15]

Most magistrates apparently received cosmopolitan educations. Their studies usually began at home, with a private reading master; after a year or two of this tuition, they were sent out to a private schoolmaster, who in some cases fed and lodged them. After two or three years of such rudimentary education, at the age of about twelve, the child was sent to one of the colleges attached to the University of Paris, usually in the company of a master or *com-*

---

of Caen even during the early sixteenth century is suggested by its omission from Pantagruel's tour of French law schools.

[14] (Charles Estienne), *La Grand guide des chemins pour aller et venir par tout le royaume de France* . . . (Rouen, 1600), f. 77v, For an example of the time required for travel between lower and upper Normandy, Blangy, ed., *Journal de Gilles de Gouberville*, pp. 62-64, 125-127.

[15] Bourgueville, *Les recherches*, pp. 345-346. See also Roger Chartier, Marie-Madeleine Compère, Dominique Julia, *L'éducation en France du XVIe au XVIIIe siècle* (Paris, 1976), p. 263, for the strength of contemporaries' belief that students ought to visit several universities.

pagnon d'études sent to watch over him. His stay at the college lasted several years, during which he was expected above all to acquire a solid Latin education. Once he had finished his arts degree, the young man's travels normally began: to the famous law schools, like Bourgueville, or, with increasing frequency during the later sixteenth century, throughout Europe. Rome seems to have been an especially popular objective—so much so that Gentien Thomas, oldest son of a member of Rouen's Chambre des Comptes, sold all his linen, books, and other possessions to finance an unauthorized trip from his Parisian college to Rome. The German universities were also popular. These patterns were only slightly changed by the foundation of a Jesuit college in Rouen in the 1590's. The college did mean that, for the first time, respectable local educational institutions were available, and many magistrates did send their children there. Paris remained attractive to many, however, and extensive travel after leaving the arts course became if anything more prevalent.[16]

Contemporaries were aware, however, that such an education had disadvantages as well as certain attractions. The cosmopolitan quality of their education brought future magistrates into a wide network of acquaintance with future lawyers and judges from throughout France. Most future magistrates also achieved a solid grounding in Latin; in the critical eyes of the seventeenth century, at least, the quality of the magistrates' Latin eloquence improved markedly

[16] AD S-M, 10J13. Other examples from Reg. sec., 1572-1574, ff. 448, 541, 32; Reg. sec., 1573-1579, f. 351; BM MS Y214, II, 40-41 (for the court's acceptance of a candidate in 1544 because "several of the councillors made a favorable recommendation, having known him at the universities *dela les mers*"); AD S-M, 1F39, Abbé Maurice, *Les Romé de Fresquiennes*, p. 30; BN Cabinet de d'Hozier, 301; La Riv. Bourdet, 2916; Bourgueville, *Les recherches*, p. 346. On the development of local institutions at the end of the sixteenth century, *Histoire de l'église cathédrale de Rouen*, p. 163 (for the Collège de Bourbon) and Reg. sec., 1596-1599, f. 58v (the founding of an academy at which young men could learn horsemanship and fencing).

over the sixteenth century, probably in the direction of closer conformity to classical rather than to scholastic standards.[17] But the quality of the magistrates' legal training was haphazard, as their extensive travels would suggest. Complaints of fraud in the granting of law degrees were common in the early sixteenth century, and tended to become more frequent. The crown's periodic efforts to reform the system of legal education served only to highlight its deficiencies: as for instance the early seventeenth-century requirement that the student have studied for at least six months in the university which gave him his *licence* in the law.[18]

What the law schools provided, it appears, was some familiarity with the specific elements of Roman law, some notion of what contemporaries called the "theory" of the law, and above all an appreciation of the historical setting and meanings of the law.[19] At least in the disapproving view of some contemporaries, this last facet of legal education seemed to be growing at the expense of the more straightforward elucidation of the texts of Roman law. "These days," complained La Roche Flavin, "the young have no interest in studying the law; instead we amuse ourselves with literature (*lettres humaines*), and God knows how we make use of it." The historical study of Roman law, the so-

[17] Thus Bigot de Monville on some of his early sixteenth-century predecessors' speeches: of one, from 1523, he noted "part is in French, part in a gross Latin"; another, from the late 1530's, he described as a "harangue, part in French, part in inelegant Latin, in which are cited several very commonplace passages of holy scripture" (BM MS Martainville, Y96 ["Extraict des registres des mercuriales du parlement de Rouen"], pp. 263, 267).

[18] Guenée, *Tribunaux et gens de justice*, pp. 196-197; Alfred de Curzon, *L'enseignement du droit français dans les universités de France aux XVIIe et XVIIIe siècles* (Paris, 1920), pp. 14-15.

[19] A view of the technical competence attained by the average candidate for the magistracy is given by the court's comments as it accepted a candidate in 1552. The candidate was accepted "given that he has the terms of the law and that he has reasonably well presented the laws and chapters" (BM MS Y214, IV, 268-270).

26

called *mos Gallicus*, was in his view a "very great abuse," which ought to be driven out of the universities.[20]

No one expected the law schools to provide a further element which the magistrate would need, familiarity with legal procedure and the customary laws which governed most property transactions; throughout the sixteenth century the law schools concerned themselves only with Roman law. To meet this need, candidates were required to spend at least one year as lawyers in the Parlement before being admitted to the magistracy itself. The candidate was not expected to practice seriously. Rather, he was to visit the courts regularly, find out what he could about procedures and about local law, and continue his reading of Roman law.[21]

By this point the candidate was normally about twenty-five years old, the minimum age during most of the century for admission in the Parlement.[22] He had now to acquire letters of provision from the king, and to secure their acceptance by the Parlement. How his letters of provision were acquired varied widely from case to case, and also tended to change over the century, as the sale of offices in the Parlement became more thoroughly organized and businesslike; but all letters of provision spoke of the "good report" which the king had had of the candidate's abilities, thus implying the usefulness of influential patrons at the royal court. The final step was that of securing the approval of his future colleagues. This involved several stages. A committee of the court was first appointed to look into

[20] La Roche Flavin, *Treze livres*, pp. 263, 361-362.

[21] Thus the king's advocate in 1554: this was a period when "one frequents the courts and jurisdictions, and . . . one can have some experience of *la pratique* so that one can, in part, digest what one has learned of theory at the universities" (BM MS Y214, v, 27). See also Guenée, *Tribunaux et gens de justice*, pp. 196-197.

[22] During the reign of Henry II the minimum age was briefly raised to 30. Some violations of age regulations did occur, especially in the early seventeenth century, but they were apparently unusual—certainly less frequent than in the eighteenth century.

his training, morals, age, and, from 1543 on, Catholic ortho-
doxy. Although it was often impossible to discuss the issue
explicitly, the committee was expected to consider also the
candidate's family background and wealth, "because (in the
view of La Roche Flavin) of the problems which poverty
ordinarily brings with it, to the point of constraining *ad
turpia et ad sordes*, . . . and, what is even worse, to tumults
and seditions, so as more easily to fish in troubled waters."
Once the committee had reported favorably on him, the
candidate was required to give a Latin oration before the
assembled court, to comment on a text of Roman law, and
to respond to questions from the magistrates about his ex-
position. Having passed these trials, he was received into
office, taking an oath on the Gospels while kneeling before
the crucifixion in the Grand' Chambre.[23]

Not all candidates did well on this set of examinations.
Some of them cheated, some were accepted only grudging-
ly, and a few were rejected altogether. In the course of the
sixteenth century, moreover, the process was made steadily
easier: for example, by allowing candidates more time to
prepare their commentaries on the law.[24] However, it would
be wrong to assume that the magistrates were interested
only in the social standing and wealth of their candidates,
and that they were indifferent to the candidates' talent
and learning. On the contrary, they recognized talent clearly, and rewarded it even when mixed with low birth. In
1543, when fifteen new councillors were admitted to the
court they were ranked "according to their merits and
learning," and this procedure was followed on at least one
later occasion, in 1552.[25] The two cases are especially striking, because in each the magistrates violated the norms of
precedence that seventeenth-century *parlementaires* be-

[23] La Roche Flavin, *Treze livres*, pp. 348, 340-360. For description
of the examination at Rouen, Reg. sec., 1571-1572, f. 30r; for the
ceremony of reception, BM MS Martainville, Y23, f. 56r.

[24] Floquet, *Histoire du Parlement*, I, 380-385.

[25] BM MS Y214, II, 431, IV, 268-270.

lieved had always been absolute. The leading candidate among the fifteen admitted in 1543 was the son of an attorney (*procureur*), and in the seventeenth century his birth alone would have disqualified him from acceptance in the Parlement. In 1552, likewise, the Parlement gave precedence to the son of a lower official over the son of a president, again on the basis of superior learning.[26]

By the 1590's at the latest the Parlement's position on these matters had changed, and birth had become considerably more important than learning in settling questions of acceptance and precedence.[27] However, in the middle years of the sixteenth century, the magistrates showed in other ways the importance they attached to learning. In 1541 the court waived its right to examine the competence of a newly appointed king's attorney, because "the said [candidate] was notoriously one of the famous and learned lawyers of the Parlement of Paris." A decade later, when the court was asked for its suggestions to fill a vacant presidency, the same concern was shown. Some of the nominees were local men, but the majority were important Parisian figures: masters of requests, members of the Grand Conseil, councillors in the Parlement of Paris. Two lesser officials and a lawyer also received votes. In 1570 the magistrates sought to secure the nomination to a vacant councillorship of the humanist Louis Le Roy, "a personage well enough known from the books which he has composed and published."[28] Conversely, the court seriously resisted appointments which it thought unsuitable. In 1548 the king nominated Jacques de Bauquemare to a presidency in the court. Bauquemare had been a councillor, had several relatives in the court, and was a member of an important Rouennais

---

[26] For Jean Lallement's origins, Frondeville, *Les présidents*, p. 182; for seventeenth-century opposition to admitting sons of *procureurs*, BM MS Martainville, Y23, f. 44r. Cf. Maugis, *Histoire du Parlement de Paris*, I, 223-224.

[27] For instance, Reg. sec., 1597-1598, f. 192.

[28] BM MS Y214, II, 303-304; IV, 21; Reg. sec., 1570-1571, f. 25r.

family; some years later he became the court's first president. But in 1548 the Parlement successfully resisted his nomination. The magistrates argued that Bauquemare had inadequate experience for the position, and pointed out that when he was received as councillor in 1543 he had been ranked only third or fourth according to ability.[29]

The most important indication of the Parlement's seriousness about its legal work came after the candidate had been accepted into the company and began taking part in the preparation and deciding of cases. In the eighteenth-century parlements, it appears, most such work was left to a handful of councillors, while the large majority concerned themselves with political questions. At the Parlement of Rennes in the eighteenth century, for instance, only about one-fourth of the councillors even attended on a regular basis, and three or four assiduous councillors reported more than half of the cases which the court decided. The situation was much the same at the Parlement of Paris.[30] In sixteenth-century Rouen the distribution of judicial labor was quite different. Although some councillors were indeed more able and more diligent than others, nearly all councillors had some share in the court's work, and the leading councillors did not play too large a role. Between 1550 and 1610, it appears, the most active 25 percent of the councillors reported between 40 and 50 percent of the Parlement's cases: that is, organized the evidence, summarized its major points, indicated the legal precepts which applied, and recommended the course of action which the Parlement ought to take. This was demanding work, and it was clearly understood that several councillors were simply incapable of reporting any but the most straightforward cases. But the relatively equal distribution of these tasks among the councillors indicates that typical levels of both competence and

[29] BM MS Y214, IV, 21.

[30] Jean Meyer, *La noblesse de Bretagne au XVIIIe siècle*, 2 vols. (Paris, 1966), II, 948; François Bluche, *Les magistrats du Parlement de Paris au XVIIIe siècle, 1715-1771* (Paris, 1960), pp. 280-282.

diligence were fairly high. The magistrates took their legal tasks seriously.[31]

Given the degree of commitment which the magistrates displayed toward their professional tasks and the degree to which they were concerned with legal learning, it remains to consider the characteristics of their professional outlook, the attitudes which were bound up with their work. Contemporaries who discussed the matter were impressed with the special nature of these attitudes, which they believed set the magistrates apart from other members of the legal professions. The magistrates had gone to the same law schools as the lawyers, and had even practiced briefly, but their position gave them a special perspective on the law. Jean Papon, a Parisian judge and commentator on the decisions of the sovereign courts, expressed a common view of the *parlementaires'* special position: the Parlement of Paris, he wrote in 1566, "is composed of men of long experience, who have drawn from their experience a singular knowledge of things, which cannot be learned at the schools where the law is read. . . . [There are] a thousand secrets for the determination of all matters [of] which, unless one spends time in the court, one could spend a lifetime in the schools without encountering a single one."[32]

Three aspects of the professional mentality of the magistrates were of particular importance. First, they understood their role to be practical and political, rather than concerned with the development of legal theory; second, they worked

[31] Calculated from AD S-M, B, Parlement, Arrêts, June-August, 1520; April-May, 1550; June-July, 1550; May-July, 1580; July-August, 1580; June-July, 1610; July-August, 1610. See BM MS Martainville, Y96, p. 307, for discussion of procedures by which reporters were chosen.

[32] Iehan Papon, *Recueil d'arrestz notables des courtz souveraines de France* . . . (Paris, 1566), prologue. Cf. the similar comments of Jean Bodin, quoted by Julian Franklin, *Jean Bodin and the Sixteenth-Century Revolution in the Methodology of Law and History* (New York, 1963), pp. 63-64.

with systems of laws that were often incomplete or contradictory, and so often had to supplement them with historical example or practical and political considerations; and, third, both their political orientation and the weakness of the legal traditions they worked with tended to make them a conservative and even timid group.

Rhetorical descriptions of the magistrates' orientation to practical affairs were common. They described themselves continually as men of action, who needed knowledge as a tool, but whose main need was for practical sagacity. "For the judge," the Parlement's first president told it in 1532, "knowledge and eloquence are less needed than good morals, gravity, majesty, and decency. . . ." La Roche Flavin repeated this notion in the early seventeenth century: "Our kings do not recruit their servants at the exits of the great schools, even though such men are knowledgeable and—in their own way—wise; affairs of action strengthen the brain, contemplation enfeebles it."[33]

One reason for this emphasis on practice at the expense of theory was the secrecy of the magistrates' work. For reasons that were partly political and partly judicial, the Parlement's deliberations were supposed to be kept entirely secret. Their only public expressions were to be their decisions (*arrêts*); only when the implications of a decision were particularly unclear were these to be accompanied by brief comments directing lawyers to the interpretation which the Parlement wished them to draw from the individual case. The court's decisions, in fact, shaped the development of law within the province, but they did so in a special way: by the piling up of decisions and of what were called "maxims of the palace," brief statements of what was appropriate in procedure and argument, rather than through the development of a body of legal opinion and theory. As the magistrates told the chancellor in 1593, "the court is not in the habit of giving the reasonings for its decisions (*les*

[33] BM MS Martainville, Y96, pp. 267-268; La Roche Flavin, *Treze livres*, p. 428.

motifs de ses arrestz) unless the king demands it of his full power and authority—and in that case one of the presidents and councillors would be delegated to go before His Majesty and explain the matter to him."[34]

Opinion and theory of this kind were developed not by the judges, but by the lawyers practicing in the court. The issues which we expect to find developed in the judges' opinions in fact were developed in the lawyers' arguments, which they presented at the close of the case. In these, rather than in any statements by the magistrates, are to be found the considerations which were seen to surround the decision itself: questions of the specific case's relationship to the larger body of law, to abstract questions of morality, to social utility, and so forth. The respective roles of the magistrate and the lawyer were to be seen clearly in legal handbooks. Throughout these collections, the central figure is the practicing lawyer. When the Parlement's decision is presented, usually it is accompanied by the arguments of the opposing lawyers for the two sides of the question; these arguments represent the viewpoints between which the court decided, and were to be used in that way by future litigants. The magistrates themselves took a comparable interest in the lawyers' arguments, and sometimes had them copied out in manuscripts for their own use.[35]

Judicial secrecy was one reason for the magistrates'

---

[34] Reg. sec., 1593-1594 (Caen), f. 45r. Cf. the chancellor's comments to the Parlement in 1563, quoted by La Roche Flavin, *Treze livres*, pp. 547-548. See the discussion by Maugis, *Histoire du Parlement de Paris*, I, 269, and John P. Dawson, *The Oracles of the Law* (Ann Arbor, 1968), pp. 297-303; Dawson also discusses an exception to this policy, the reports published by the Parisian *parlementaire* Georges Louet, in 1608 (pp. 314-325).

[35] For instance, Henri Basnage, *Oeuvres* (4th ed., Rouen, 1778), *passim*. For private summaries, BM MS Y202, ff. 91-98, and BN MS français 5348. See also La Roche Flavin's comments concerning the "*advocats consultans:*" "They hold the place of the ancient Jurisconsults. . . . Their houses are virtual public oracles, to which people come from throughout the city to consult their tripod and ask their opinions" (265-266).

view of themselves as practical men who decided between legal arguments, rather than as theorists who created them. Equally important was the fact that they were far from being jurists alone. A good deal of their work was more properly political or administrative, and indeed there was a strong tendency for contemporaries to view even their legal functions in terms that were essentially political. This was true, in the first place, of much of the magistrates' daily activity. They had the responsibility for overseeing all judicial officials within the province: examining their initial suitability for office, reviewing their performance, and rebuking them for inadequacies in procedure and judgment. Likewise, the Parlement had considerable responsibility for administrative decisions within both Rouen and the province as a whole. They were involved in regulating such diverse issues as poor relief, hospitals, prices, questions of what the Protestants could and could not do, and so forth. Often these efforts were carried out in common with other representatives of the community, or were left to the attention of lower officials, but the Parlement always retained ultimate control; and its intervention was often needed in the uncertain conditions of the later sixteenth century. Finally, there were administrative commissions from the crown, which regularly used members of the court to perform widely varied functions within the province. This might include investigating the state of the University of Caen, auctioning crown lands within the province, examining the spread of heresy near Dieppe.[36]

[36] For examples of such activities, Reg. sec., 1570-1571, f. 269 (examining lower officials' conformity to royal edicts); 1573-1579, ff. 160-163 (regulating grain prices in Rouen); 1575-1576, ff. 2-3 (intervening in criminal cases that lower officials were afraid to prosecute and watching over the condition of rural churches); 1597-1598, f. 9v (responding to complaints about *"malversations"* in the province, especially oppressions of the poor by the rich); 1549-1556, f. 142 (investigating leprosaries); June-October, 1597, f. 139 (investigating taxation). For the Parlement's dealings with Rouen's poor, see Gustave Panel, ed., *Documents concernants les pauvres de Rouen extraits*

But simply to list the court's extralegal functions does not fully convey the nature of the magistrates' political role. Political conceptions dominated contemporary discussion of even their purely legal work. The aim of their judicial labors, it was argued, was the maintenance of peace and order. The Parlement's task, the first president told it in 1571, was "to restrain the passion and enterprises of those who want to oppress the people, and to restrain the people's desire to rise up." The notion that the judges held this kind of social responsibility was a widely repeated one.[37] It was to be found not only in the magistrates' own oratory, but also in their very view of themselves as senators, whose position was modelled on that of the Roman senate. It was likewise to be found in the arguments of writers like Pasquier, to the effect that the parlements' golden age had been one of non-specialist magistrates, magistrates who were simply men of dignity within the society and not trained as lawyers;[38] as both the magistrates and those who wrote about them never tired of emphasizing, learning was much less important to someone in this senatorial position than "gravity, decency, good morals."

Such views of the magistrates' tasks accorded well with a second aspect of their professional identity, the uncertainties which surrounded the law itself. The magistrates had to formulate their decisions from an extremely diverse set of traditions and sources.[39] Previous decisions and the collec-

---

des archives de l'Hôtel de Ville, 2 vols. (Paris and Rouen, 1917), I, *passim*.

[37] Reg. sec., 1549-1556, f. 33. Cf. the Parlement's letter to Henry IV on the death of the duc de Villars: "we assembled promptly in order to do whatever was necessary and appropriate to our positions to maintain everyone in obedience (*un chacun en son devoir*)"; they also urged Henry to maintain their own authority, for "this is the only means of securing obedience" (Reg. sec., June-October, 1595, f. 30v.).

[38] Étienne Pasquier, *Les mémoires et recherches de la France* (Paris, 1594), ff. 77, 85-86.

[39] The argument which follows owes much to the views of Donald

tion of "maxims of the palace" provided one of the bases for the magistrates' judicial labors; so strong was the force of such precedents, according to La Roche Flavin, that "one should never argue against the maxims, still less against the regulations [*stiles et reglements*] of the palace."[40]

The clearest source of law was the king himself, and the sixteenth century produced a large body of royal legislation. Much of this concerned procedure in the royal courts rather than the substance of the law, however, and it left large areas untouched. The same was true of the Norman customary law, which regulated such issues as inheritance, marriage, feudal rights, and so on. This was not only incomplete, but its medieval concepts often required extensive commentary before they could be applied to contemporary needs. In some measure these problems were mitigated by the revision of the custom which a commission from the Parlement completed in 1583, belatedly following the example of other provinces. This revision for the first time provided the province with a fully official version of the custom. But even the revised custom was very far from providing a complete body of legislation, and many of its provisions remained ambiguous or uncertain.

Lawyers throughout the old regime were acutely conscious of this lack of clear legislative authorities. On the one hand, argued a late-seventeenth-century lawyer, the customary law "barely suffices . . . for deciding half of the cases which must be judged"; on the other hand, "most

---

Kelley, presented most recently in "History, English Law and the Renaissance," *Past and Present*, 65 (November, 1974), 24-51. In contrast to the intellectuals whom Kelley has studied, for whom uncertainty and diversity of legal tradition were sources of stimulation, the *parlementaires* appear to have found uncertainty more paralyzing than liberating. Cf. John Langbein, *Prosecuting Crime in the Renaissance: England, Germany, France* (Cambridge, Mass., 1974), p. 249, who argues for the exceptionally solid legal knowledge of the French judges.

[40] La Roche Flavin, *Treze livres*, p. 560.

royal ordinances are more concerned with drawing up cases than with deciding them," and offered the judge small guidance.[41]

Such gaps in the royal legislation and the provincial custom left the magistrates to formulate their legal decisions from sources that were essentially historical: from Roman law, and from the examples of French history itself. Sixteenth-century jurists believed that the Roman law had been "received" in France in the reign of Charlemagne, who was thought to have brought its teachings back from his invasion of Italy. In contrast to the German experience, no formal act of reception took place, and the precise role of Roman law remained extremely ambiguous. Its authority, in Jean Papon's words, was that "of example, and not of necessity,"[42] and in the sixteenth century even that authority was increasingly questioned. The philological study of Roman law pointed out the transformations which it had undergone at the hands of Justinian's compilers and of medieval scribes. The growth of patriotic and Gallican sentiments made jurists doubtful about the value of laws that glorified Rome and Roman wisdom at the expense of native developments; constitutionalists of all kinds felt a similar reluctance to grant full authority to a law that left so little place for intermediate powers between king and people. Pragmatic conservatives like La Roche Flavin found this strain of skepticism disquieting, and urged lawyers and judges that "above all we must keep away from that new Academy . . . , so much has impudence

[41] Claude-Joseph de Ferrière, *Histoire du droit romain* (nouvelle édition, Paris, 1738), pp. 337-338.

[42] Papon, *Recueil*, prologue. See also the opinions quoted by Donald Kelley, *Foundations of Modern Historical Scholarship. Language, Law and History in the French Renaissance* (New York, 1970), pp. 198-201, 283-287. Even in areas where a formal reception of Roman law took place, as in many German states, procedures were much more affected than the substance of the law; see Georg Dahm, *Zur Rezeption des römisch-italienischen Rechts* (Darmstadt, 1960), pp. 41-45.

grown, since it has begun to give itself licence to impugn things which are certain." His complaints testify eloquently to the broad impact of the new, critical analysis of the Roman law, and of well-publicized literary debates about the relative merits of French and Roman law.[43]

Thus, although the magistrates had been educated exclusively in the theories and categories of Roman law, the exact practical uses of that law were surrounded by uncertainties. These uncertainties seem to have encouraged the magistrates in their tendency to stress the practical rather than the theoretical aspects of legal learning, and they drew the magistrates' attention also to what seemed a principal repository of practical wisdom: history. Insofar as the main elements in their professional mentality can be understood, the magistrates appear to have been intensely historical in outlook. Historical examples were of constant relevance, even in apparently technical legal issues. Lawyers who argued before the court made full use of citation of *"les vieux auteurs"* and of *"les histoires estrangeres"* to support their contentions, and these citations seem to have carried great force. Similar references fill the speeches which the magistrates made in their closed sessions, in dealing with both political and judicial questions.[44] The same concerns seem to have filled their private hours. The mid-sixteenth-century councillor Baptiste Le Chandelier concerned himself with Rouen's foundation and early years; at the end of the century, the first president Claude Groulart was undertaking researches into the early years of Frankish history, for which he made long extracts from

[43] La Roche Flavin, *Treze livres*, p. 253. For debate about the place of Roman law in sixteenth-century France, see Kelley, *Foundations of Modern Historical Scholarship*, pp. 66-76, 106-112, 189-194, 283-300, and *passim*; on the implications of such debates, see also William Bouwsma, "Lawyers and Early Modern Culture," *The American Historical Review*, LXXVIII, 2 (April, 1973), 303-327.

[44] For an especially clear example, AD S-M, B, Parlement, Registre d'Audiences, 4 May 1600. Other lawyers' *plaidoyers* are copied throughout the Registres d'Audiences.

Gregory of Tours, Paul the Deacon, Einhardt, and the like.[45] Unfortunately, no inventories of the magistrates' libraries have survived, and it is thus impossible to follow their reading in greater detail. But the library of a mid-sixteenth-century Rouennais lower court judge (the uncle of a *parlementaire*) does suggest the strength of historical concerns: together with an impressive collection of the texts and summaries of ancient history, there were the leading examples of sixteenth-century historical research (for instance, Budé's *De Asse*), and French and Latin chronicles of Scotland, France, and Venice.[46]

The absence of clearly established legal authorities, and the consequent need to turn to historical example and tradition, might have led the magistrates to a self-confident assertion of their own powers. For the most part, however, their response to this situation was quite different. To most of the issues which they confronted, the magistrates responded timidly and conservatively, with expressions of veneration of the past and aversion to any form of change. The widespread notion that the parlements had existed for as long as French history could be traced—at least to the time of Julius Caesar—was part of this outlook.[47] The magistrates expressed a similar attitude when they discussed the processes by which the law developed. Thus, Claude Groulart in 1586 argued that the customary law "acquires its force little by little and through long years of the common consent of all, or of the majority. . . . [W]e find that all introductions of new laws, even when they are founded on an appearance of great reasonableness, have been the precursors of the ruin and loss of the state."[48] This con-

[45] Noel Taillepied, *Recueil des antiquitez et singularitez de la ville de Rouen* (Rouen, 1610; first published 1587), pp. 8-9; BM MS Y202, ff. 140ff.

[46] AD S-M, E, Tabellionage de Dieppe, 1559, ff. 44-57.

[47] Papon, *Recueil*, prologue.

[48] BM MS Y202, ff. 111-112. Such views of law and legal institutions are strongly reminiscent of contemporary discussion of English law. See J.G.A. Pocock, *The Feudal Law and the Ancient Constitu-*

servative view of the law and of the dangers involved in any legal innovation was a commonplace in the magistrates' deliberations, and it found expression also in numerous ceremonial occasions: for instance, in the magistrates' insistence that they occupy exactly the same position at each entry of a newly crowned king in the city.[49]

Contemporaries were impressed with a further aspect of the magistrates' conservatism, the conservatism of the very language which they used. The "language of the palace," as contemporaries called the usages of lawyers and judges, had quickly become fossilized, and by the later sixteenth century had become a subject of mockery to all those who concerned themselves with the development of elegant French. This was not a question of making legal formulae clear and specific, as in the development of technical legal language in English. To Étienne Pasquier, at least, the failure of the "language of the palace" was a more mysterious matter of taste. "I do not know what misfortune has determined that most of us not only make no effort to use well-chosen words, but—what is even worse—because of some jealousy which runs among the lawyers, when someone does make such efforts we attribute them to affectation rather than to [a concern for] praise."[50]

A sense of the anxiety which underlay this conservatism may be gained from the letters of Claude Groulart, the court's first president. In a letter of 1599, following the settlement of the League and the peace with Spain, he wrote

---

tion. *A Study of English Historical Thought in the Seventeenth Century* (Cambridge, 1957), pp. 30-55 and *passim*. Both Pocock and Kelley, "History, English Law and the Renaissance," stress differences between French and English views of tradition.

[49] Reg. sec., 1549-1556, f. 33; see also ff. 34 (ceremonies for the burial of the Cardinal d'Amboise), and 59v (debate about cases to be argued before the king).

[50] Quoted Ferdinand Brunot, *Histoire de la langue française*, 13 vols. (2nd ed., Paris, 1966), III, 21. See Bouwsma, "Lawyers and Early Modern Culture," for a different view of the relationship of lawyers to developing vernacular culture.

one fellow official, "we live here as if in peace, but without really benefiting very much from it, either for the relief of the burdens on the people or for the reuniting of minds. These are still affected by the last sickness, which brought so much corruption that the fruits of true repose cannot be tasted, and many spirits still nourish certain discontents, which can well lead to disaster. . . . The king is the sole barrier against France returning to its unhappy state, so strong are individual interests, and no one concerns himself with the general."[51] Disorder from all levels of society had continually to be watched for, in Groulart's view. Although Henry IV's success offered some hope for a genuine restoration of health to the society, Groulart was usually less than optimistic. Commenting on the premature death of the historian and magistrate Pierre Pithou, he wrote: "For myself I consider him fortunate to have lived in such great esteem and to have governed himself in the middle of storms and tempests with much dexterity, and to have departed when there remained hardly any hope for seeing good in the state—for if on the one hand learning is a consolation, it also subjects us to a bitterness which common minds do not experience."[52]

Groulart's expressions of despair were certainly more frequent and more eloquent than those of his colleagues. But the court as a whole seems to have shared his belief that disorders within the state continually threatened, and that only the magistrates' own efforts could prevent more deterioration. Groulart at least held out no hope beyond that of preventing further decay, and in fact his pronouncements tended to become gloomier despite the apparent success of Henry IV's reign.[53]

[51] BN Fonds Dupuy, 712, f. 61r.

[52] BN Fonds Dupuy, 802, f. 140r. On Pithou's premature death, Kelley, *Foundations of Modern Historical Scholarship*, p. 257.

[53] On Groulart's central position within Rouen's *noblesse de robe*, see below, pp. 285-287. For his complaints to other Parisian figures, BN MS français, 15898, ff. 553, 560, 561, 576, 581. A different expression of a comparable pessimism is provided by *Carolii Paschalii regii*

We have analyzed here three broad elements in the magistrates' professional outlook: their political orientation, the difficulty they had in finding clear and complete legal authorities, and the timidity and conservatism with which they approached many issues. This set of attitudes is important to an understanding of a further aspect of the magistrates' position, their ties to the society around them. Three sets of relationships are of particular importance here: those with their colleagues in other courts, with the crown, and with the city and province in which they resided. All of these relationships involved considerable elements of ambiguity, but all were important in shaping the magistrates' position, both as a professional group and as a local elite.

Rouennais magistrates' ties with their colleagues in other parts of the kingdom, and notably with members of the Parlement of Paris, combined resentment and dependence. On the one hand, the Parisians enjoyed both real and honorific privileges which were denied the Rouennais. More fundamentally, it was normally to the Parlement of Paris that the crown turned when it "evoked" a case from the Parlement of Rouen: that is, when the crown decided that a case could not be impartially tried within Normandy itself, even by the supposedly sovereign Parlement, and that it should be decided by another court. Precisely because it called into question their position as the ultimate jurisdiction for all legal issues within the province, the problem of

---

in Normaniae senatu consiliarii Christianarum precum libri duo (Caen, 1592): "Only one thing . . . can restore our affairs, or nothing can. You know well enough that it is not our prudence, than which nothing is more imprudent; not our long-since worn out works; not the long-since powerless aid of men. It is prayer, which breaks through the heavens with the force of our groans. . . ."

("Una res . . . rem nobis restituere potest, aut nulla potest. Eam satis intellegis non esse prudentiam nostram, qua nihil imprudentius; non opes iamdiu attritas; non hominum auxilia iamdiu invalida. Hoc est opus pietatis, quae perrumpet coelum vi gemituum . . .") (dedication).

évocations seemed to the magistrates one of the most serious possible challenges to their authority, and it was the subject of endless complaints to the crown.[54]

However, causes of friction between Rouennais and Parisian magistrates were less important than cooperation between them. The Rouennais' sense both of the uncertainties of the law and of the fragility of political order encouraged them to seek advice from their Parisian colleagues, and they did so with striking frequency, to ask about the enforcement of sumptuary legislation, modifications of royal edicts, procedural matters, and a series of other, often trivial, matters.[55] The magistrates' eagerness not to proceed without such support testifies to the anxieties of their position; consultation served to fill the gaps left by precedent. The frequency of interchange between Rouennais and Parisian judges, however, is only to be understood in terms of the ease of movement of all kinds between Rouen and the capital. It has already been seen that the magistrates and their children usually received part of their education at Paris, and there were frequent visits to supervise lawsuits and other private business. The magistrates knew the city, often had been at school with Parisian judges, and often had relatives established in Paris.[56] The journey itself was also

[54] Thus the *procureur général*, in 1597: respect for the Parlement having diminished "because of the outrageous number and ease of evocations, all the rest of the populace falls into confusion and disorder" (Reg. sec., June-October, 1597, ff. 55-56). By this period the problem of evocations was closely linked to that of Protestantism, another cause which the *parlementaires* frequently adduced to explain popular disorders; the Rouennais magistrates' evident bias against the Protestants was a common reason for evocations, possibly the most frequent in these years. For the privileges enjoyed by the Parisians and the Rouennais' eagerness to share them, Reg. sec., 1573-1579, f. 401r.

[55] Reg. sec., 1549-1556, f. 4r (asking about the Parisians' stance on royal sumptuary legislation), 5r (about legal procedures), 55r (about ceremonies used in royal entries).

[56] For examples, Reg. sec., 1549-1556, ff. 20v, 44r, 128r, 132r, 145v. The councillor Jean Le Lieur had even been in jail in Paris (BM MS Y214, II, 171).

an easy one, even by sixteenth-century standards. Delegations sent by the Parlement to confer either with the king or with the Parisian courts traveled at a stately pace, but they were able to reach Paris within two and one-half days. It was possible to do the trip in less than two days. What this could mean was illustrated in 1552: on September 9th of that year the king's attorney announced to the Parlement that he had been called to Paris to confer with the master of the seals (*garde des sceaux*); on September 17th he was again before the Parlement, to report on his discussions. This was an extreme example, but it properly suggests the readiness with which the magistrates set out for the capital and the ease with which they might exchange views with their Parisian colleagues.[57]

Similar ambiguities dominated a far more important relationship, that between the *parlementaires* and the crown itself. At the most obvious level the magistrates were the king's officials, and both rhetoric and ceremony were used to celebrate their position as his agents. "The court and its justice," said the first president in 1550, "these are [the king] himself," and the sentiment in various forms was repeated countless times.[58] Whenever the king appeared before the Parlement, notably in the royal entries, the idea was given dramatic representation in a *lit de justice*. Before the king's arrival, a case of particular interest was chosen from among those pending; then, with the king and his entourage installed at the front of the Grand' Chambre and the Parlement watching, the two lawyers and the king's attorney presented their arguments, and the king gave his decision. Such acts, repeated with each new king who visited the city, were a conscious affirmation of the identity between crown and Parlement; with as much ceremony as possible they

[57] Reg. sec., 1549-1556, ff. 124r, 126r. For description of a typical delegation to Paris, La Riv. Bourdet, 2893.

[58] Reg. sec., 1549-1556, f. 45v. For other examples of such rhetoric, BM MS Y214, V, 73; BM MS Y202, f. 108r; Bourgueville, *Les recherches*, p. 346.

represented the parlements' position as simply agents of the crown, needed because the king could not be present everywhere.[59]

But how seriously should such rhetoric and ceremonial be taken? Historians have usually taken them less seriously than indications of antagonism between crown and parlements. The parlements, it usually has been argued, were far more attached to their interests as virtually independent corporations and to the interests of their local societies than to the crown. Since the monarchy was intent on subduing local and corporate interests, the main theme of relations between crown and parlement was one of opposition, latent at most times but occasionally erupting into direct and angry disputes. In the course of these, it is argued, the magistrates were willing even to mobilize the local populations, and to use their often violent support as a weapon against the crown.[60]

Examples in support of such a view of relations between the Parlement of Rouen and the crown are readily found. In a dramatic episode in 1540, the king—acting on reports of corruption and disobedience by the magistrates—abolished the institution altogether. Most of the councillors were reinstated within a few months, but a handful were barred from the court for three years, and one was permanently stripped of his office.[61] A much more frequent sign of discord between crown and Parlement was the court's occasional refusal to register royal legislation and its re-

[59] The *lit de justice* accompanying the Parlement's declaration of Charles IX's majority, in 1563, is described in detail by Floquet, *Histoire du Parlement*, II, 589-596.

[60] For instance, Maugis, *Histoire du Parlement de Paris*, I, 522, 547-583; William F. Church, *Constitutional Thought in Sixteenth-Century France* (Cambridge, Mass., 1941), pp. 136-155; R. Doucet, *Les institutions de la France*, I, 221-223. These views have been criticized by Christopher Stocker, "The Politics of the Parlement of Paris in 1525," *French Historical Studies*, VIII, 2 (Fall, 1973), 191-212.

[61] Floquet, *Histoire du Parlement*, II, 1-80. Even the one councillor expelled from the court was eventually reinstated, almost twenty years after his expulsion.

monstrances to the king about them. Such registration was a requirement for any royal measure to acquire full legal force within the province; according to Pasquier, this was the key to assuring the subjects' obedience to royal measures.[62] The Parlement could add or delete provisions where it thought royal measures defective, and it could refuse altogether its registration when it thought a measure especially ill-considered. Its veto power was not, however, absolute. Ultimately the king could always force registration, in the last resort by appearing himself at the Parlement in a *lit de justice*—a procedure much used in the great struggles of the eighteenth century. In the sixteenth century the king's mere insistence was enough, but measures thus accepted were registered with clear notice that this was by the king's express command.[63]

Delays, amendments, and even outright refusals to register legislation, however, should not be interpreted as signs of serious opposition between crown and Parlement. For most of the sixteenth century, they reflected, rather, the normal workings of a coherent political system. The magistrates were not expected to accept without question all of the king's legislation, because the king's will was not always his own. Courtiers and representatives of particular interests sought continually to obtain legislation in their own favor or exemptions from fundamental laws of the kingdom. The Parlement's ability to block such acts was of considerable use to the king, and he explicitly encouraged the magistrates to make use of this right. The reforming legislation of the sixteenth century included numerous such encouragements. Article 30 of the Ordinance of Orléans (1560), for instance, limited the number of offices in the judicial and financial administrations. It concluded with an admonition to the sovereign courts: "We forbid our parlements, Chambres des Comptes, and all our other officials to give any

---

[62] See above, Introduction, pp. 10-11.

[63] See Pasquier's complaints about monarch's tendencies to use these powers excessively: *Les mémoires et recherches*, ff. 97-99.

regard to letters of provision obtained contrary [to this article] by importunity or otherwise." Article 32 forbade relatives from holding office in the same sovereign court, and concluded with a similar directive: ". . . we declare void all letters of dispensation which may be obtained to the contrary, for whatever cause or reason."[64] These questions were developed in greater detail by Henry IV in an angry discussion with a delegation from the Parlement in 1609. "His Majesty," reported the first president to the assembled chambers, "is very angry with the court. He believes that the edicts which concern the good of the crown (*le bien de ses affaires*) have received little favor in this company over the last few years; on the other hand, some individuals have had greater ease [i.e., in securing the Parlement's assent] with the edicts which he has accorded them because of their importunities. Of these there have been a great number, . . . and they have been much more dangerous to the public welfare (*preiudiciables*) than those which remain to be registered—yet the court has registered them without awaiting a single command (*iussion*)."[65] Henry, the first president emphasized, was angry with the Parlement, not for resisting his will, but for undertaking the wrong kinds of resistance. In his view, the magistrates were resisting measures of benefit to the state as a whole, and letting pass without protest measures that benefited only individuals. He was not asking that the *parlementaires* give up their efforts to amend royal legislation, but that they apply them properly, for the defense of public interests and as a counterbalance to the influence of courtiers and favorites.

For the most part, relations between crown and Parlement were close in the sixteenth century. Members were repeatedly employed by the crown in administrative tasks,

---

[64] François Isambert *et al.*, *Recueil général des anciennes lois françaises* . . . (Paris, n.d.), xiv, 72-73.

[65] BM MS Y214, x, 307-308. See also BN MS français 20538, for the duc d'Aumale's efforts to secure the Parlement's approval of such a measure and the Parlement's resistance to it.

47

of the sort that in the seventeenth and eighteenth centuries would have been left entirely to masters of requests. Most impressive in the difficult conditions of the sixteenth century was the *parlementaires'* response to the crown's efforts at religious toleration. The Rouennais magistrates were nearly all intensely Catholic, and their dislike of religious toleration was considerable. Despite this, however, they followed with some zeal the crown's efforts to establish religious peace. They registered without serious delay each of the sixteenth-century edicts of toleration, and they sought to enforce them fairly. Although their sympathies tended to be Guisard, they resisted joining the Catholic political movements which the Guise sponsored until the king explicitly directed them to do so.[66] The magistrates' devotion to the crown was genuine, and led them to political positions quite at variance with their personal views.

Close relations between *parlementaires* and the crown are readily understandable in terms of what has been seen of the magistrates' professional attitudes. Given their intense fear of disorder and their frequent inability to find adequate foundation for their labors in a coherent, independent body of law, it is not surprising that they turned eagerly to the monarchy. Their fundamentally political conception of their role, their view of their function as maintaining order

[66] Reg. sec., 1595, f. 123r; BN MS français 15551, 176r, 184r, 186r; BN MS français 15905, f. 475; Floquet, *Histoire du Parlement*, II, 372, 584; III, 38-42, 76, 142-143. The Parlement's reluctance to accept the League of 1576 may be followed in Reg. sec., 1573-1579, ff. 487, 504. On January 30 the magistrates were told by Carrouges and La Meilleraye, respectively the king's lieutenant and governor in the province, to sign "*l'asotiation faicte par la noblesse*"; they replied that only with the king's express command could they do so. On February 13 Carrouges presented them with letters from the king, asserting the king's full confidence in him and urging the magistrates to sign the association; they replied that they would send a delegation to the king to learn his intentions directly. On March 5 Carrouges again urged them to sign, but the magistrates replied that they would await letters patent from the king formally instructing them to do so.

rather than interpreting the law, likewise encouraged intense belief in the monarchy.

At the close of the sixteenth century, however, this relationship between the magistrates and the crown began to change, and real hostility began to assume a considerable degree of importance. In essence, the *parlementaires* began to develop in the direction of the eighteenth-century parlements, for whom opposition to the crown was a normal political stance.[67] The most dramatic indication of this increasingly ambiguous relationship was the Parlement's response to the restoration of religious toleration after the League, in 1595. Although the Rouennais did register parts of the Edict of Nantes, they continued throughout the reign of Henry IV to resist full registration, despite enormous pressure from the king. They also made it clear that, although they might formally register most of the edict's provisions, their enforcement of religious equality would be unenthusiastic, for, as they told the king in 1609, "His Majesty's intention is to reduce [the Protestants] little by little to the Church, . . . which certainly would not happen if they were made on all points equal to the Catholics."[68] Antagonism over the crown's efforts to restore religious toleration was only one of several sources of conflict, however. The magistrates quarreled with Henry IV over taxation, over the problem of

[67] See Bluche, *Les magistrats*, pp. 282-289.

[68] BM MS Y214, x, 320. See also *ibid.*, x, 306, for the king's irritation that "after so many times having heard from his principal officials his will concerning the Edict of Nantes, which has been registered in all the other parlements of the kingdom, we persist in the modifications which we have made in it"; and *ibid.*, ix, 408, for the king's anger "because of our deliberations concerning his edict of the *commissaires examinateurs* (to inspect alienations of crown lands), concerning which His Majesty claimed to have heard all [the magistrates'] opinions. These had been so misrepresented to His Majesty that it seemed to him that we only wanted to make him contemptible and odious to his people, and [he said] that he knew well that the company was intriguing (*faisoit des monopoles*) to the detriment of his service. . . ."

49

evocations, over governmental structure, and over a series of other issues.[69] Friction between crown and Parlement continued to develop after 1610; during the years leading up to the Fronde, the Rouennais magistrates were apparently among the most fractious in the country, and they repeatedly seconded the more dramatic efforts of the Parisian *parlementaires*. "His Majesty is ready," according to a warning from the chancellor in 1609, "to move to some severity against us such as he has never yet employed against any of his parlements."[70]

This transformation in the relations between the magistrates and the crown had complex origins. As Roland Mousnier has pointed out in his examinations of judicial opposition to the crown during the seventeenth century, the initiative in these conflicts often came from the crown itself. It was the crown that insisted on bypassing normal governmental procedures, thus antagonizing officials of all kinds, and often threatening their very incomes; the crown wanted to raise higher taxes, and to raise them more efficiently, and this too led it to disregard the established rights of its own bureaucrats. In the conditions of seventeenth-century government, as Mousnier argues, it was the absolutist monarchy that was the revolutionary force, and such officials as the *parlementaires* who sought to resist change.[71]

But the Parlement's resistance to royal measures involved

[69] BN MS français 15898, f. 549r (1601? Parlement objecting to the Chambre de l'Edit); f. 588r (1605? objecting to extraordinary commissions); 598-599 (1605? obstructing sale of royal domain); Reg. sec., June-October 1597, f. 62 (objecting to the creation of new councillorships); Reg. sec., 1597-1598, f. 41 (to the evocation of a criminal case); Reg. sec., 1595, ff. 115-117 (refusing to register a fiscal edict).

[70] BM MS Y214, x, 306. On the Parlement during the years leading up to the Fronde, see A. Lloyd Moote, *The Revolt of the Judges. The Parlement of Paris and the Fronde, 1643-1652* (Princeton, 1971), pp. 56-59, and Madeleine Foisil, *La révolte des nu-pieds et les révoltes normandes de 1639* (Paris, 1970), pp. 263-264.

[71] See Roland Mousnier, "The Fronde," in Robert Forster and Jack Greene, eds., *Preconditions of Revolution in Early Modern Europe* (Baltimore, 1970), pp. 142-146.

more than simply a response to violations of tradition and established rights. Opposition also expressed those professional and political attitudes whose importance to the magistrates has been traced here, the conservatism, sense of hierarchy, and anxiety which they had expressed all through the sixteenth century. In a contorted set of arguments, the magistrates defended their opposition to royal policies on the grounds of a need to preserve order and stability; their opposition, so they argued, was aimed at preventing the outbreak of actual rebellion. Thus, the *parlementaires'* resistance to new fiscal edicts whose registration the king demanded was based on the fear that, as the king's attorney argued in 1597, "there is nothing more insupportable than the excessive charges weighing on the poor people, which are turning them away from obedience to their prince."[72] In just the same way, as the first president Claude Groulart argued in 1597, "we are taught by both modern and ancient histories that there is little hope for peace in a kingdom where there are two religions," and by this maxim he justified the magistrates' unwillingness to support a genuine system of toleration.[73] Most basically, the magistrates argued that sedition must be expected if the structure of the state itself was not respected: if, that is, the crown's use of novel expedients to replace established officials endangered the respect which the magistrate needed to maintain order. "It is under the guidance of the parlements," argued the king's attorney in 1597, "that all the king's subjects live and are restrained (*retenuz*), and once these come to be scorned, . . . because of the excessive number and the ease of evocations, the people as a whole falls into confusion and disorder."[74] As the *parlementaires* understood the situation, their resistance to the crown was part of their continuous preoccupation with maintaining order.

Were they sincere in these claims? As will be seen in later

[72] Reg. sec., January-May, 1597, ff. 98-99.
[73] *Ibid.*, ff. 42-45.
[74] Reg. sec., June-October, 1597, f. 56r.

chapters, these changes in the magistrates' political style, in the contours of what they understood to be normal responses to royal demands, coincided with important changes in their social position. The magistrates had good reasons to believe their position less assured in the early seventeenth century than it had been in the mid-sixteenth century. But a reading of their deliberations in these years also suggests the depth of their feelings about the disorder around them. They had undergone an intense experience of political disorder during the years of the League, between 1589 and 1594, when many magistrates were first able to return to their homes after five years of exile. Much more than earlier events in the civil wars, certainly much more than the St. Bartholomew's massacres, the League appears to have opened terrifying prospects to the magistrates. From their experience in the League, the magistrates drew a conviction that all forms of authority had been weakened and that habits of obedience had been lost.[75] To conserve order required a still greater effort of vigilance and the observation of established governmental forms.

Evidence that this was indeed, as the first president Claude Groulart put it, a time "so ungoverned, so full of disorder and of confusion,"[76] was seen everywhere. Conflicts between young and old councillors were one such manifestation and their incidence appears really to have been increasing. Groulart told his colleagues in 1604, follow-

[75] The magistrates themselves attributed a great deal to the facts of war and exile. When a Toulousan councillor criticized their deportment, in 1596, he was told that *"messieurs de Tholoze*, who had not had to leave their homes during the troubles, have been better able to maintain the proprieties of their position than have those who left their homes, who, because of the disruptions of the times (*licence du temps*), have given up something in formality and dignity" (Reg. sec., 1596-1599, f. 25v). See also Reg. sec., January-May, 1595, f. 3r. For more general comment on the effects of the war, see Reg. sec., 1596-1599, ff. 79-80: "an infinite number of young men returned from the war, who every day break into houses, violate women, and commit an infinite number of intolerable assaults . . ." (October, 1598).

[76] BM MS Y202, f. 119r.

ing a dispute between two of the Parlement's members, that "the honor of the whole company . . . seems to be declining hour by hour . . . ; one no longer sees any mark of the former modesty and respect which the young held for their elders, as if for their fathers. This is one of the signs of the troubles which threaten us, since the first oath that one takes on entering this company is that of honoring and respecting one's elders."[77] And the outcome of this internal disorder, so the magistrates believed, was a steady loss of respect from the people. "In these times," as the *parlementaires* were told in 1597, "the officials and justice itself [are] so badly respected and our fortunes are so poorly assured. . . ." So low was popular respect for the court, in Groulart's view, that the people were unwilling to plead their cases before it.[78]

Relations between the magistrates and the crown thus deteriorated in the late sixteenth century, after having been close through much of the century. Ironically, this change appears to have reflected a basic continuity, that of the magistrates' concern for maintaining political order and their belief that conservative methods were needed for this.

[77] BM MS Y214, x, 382. For the reality of the problem, see the chancellor's comments to the president Charles Maignart, in 1609, "that not only in matters of general import but also in private cases [the councillors] band together against one another" (La Riv. Bourdet, 2893); and the early seventeenth-century complaint by the Chambre des Enquêtes concerning "the intolerable scorn which those in the first chamber (the Grand' Chambre) have recently shown and continue to show every day . . . the usurpations which every day they commit in the division of cases" (BN Fonds Dupuy, 498, f. 153r). For the division of younger against older councillors during the League, see my article, "Magistracy and Political Opposition at Rouen: A Social Context," *The Sixteenth Century Journal*, v, 2 (October, 1974), 71, and Roland Mousnier, *La vénalité des offices sous Henri IV et Louis XIII* (2nd ed., Paris, 1971), p. 91.

[78] Reg. sec., June-October, 1597, ff. 8-9; BM MS Y202, f. 65. See also above, note 54, for the magistrates' argument that evocations were reducing the popular respect for the court and thus increasing the likelihood of political upheaval.

It was because the political events of the late sixteenth and early seventeenth centuries, the disruptions of the League in particular, so directly touched the magistrates' professional mentality that their responses to Henry IV's measures were so bitter.

As the magistrates understood the issue, their relationship with those whom they called the people—that is, with local society—was the counterpart to their relationship with the crown. This was so in complex ways, however. On the one hand, as we have seen, the magistrates believed that their position within local society depended on their relationship to the crown. If the crown did not maintain the Parlement's honor, and make clear to the populace its support for the magistrates, the result would rapidly be popular scorn for the magistrate and royal justice more generally. In this sense their ties with the crown and their ties with the people were mutually reinforcing. On the other hand, there was also a clear sense of possible contradictions between the two relationships, a sense that loyalty to the populace might come at the expense of service to the crown. Such tensions had in some form always existed, but their seriousness increased during the later sixteenth century.

What the magistrates stressed first about the relationship which they ought to have with local society was distance from it. Unless they stood apart from the populace, they would be unable to maintain the authority which seemed essential to their functions. In 1532 the councillors were told that they "ought not to drink and eat with *le commun*." In 1540 they were rebuked by the chancellor himself because "several of the company are men ordinarily giving and attending banquets, frequenting dissolute and dishonest games, and commonly associating with people of low estate (*gens de ville condition*)." "Let us be *separati et segregati a vulgo*," urged Groulart in 1595.[79]

[79] BM MS Martainville Y96, pp. 305-306; BM MS Y214, II, 204; BM MS Y202, f. 113r.

Such complaints and urgings were repeated all through the sixteenth century. Their frequency, of course, indicates that many magistrates did indeed consort with the lower classes, and the problem shows no signs of having diminished in the later years of the century. However, in some surprising ways the magistrates in fact were separate from the rest of the city's population—not merely from the "people of low estate" but from the wealthier bourgeois as well. A survey made in 1544 (for fiscal purposes, it is true) showed that fewer than half of the court's members even owned houses in the city; and many magistrates would have agreed with one councillor's claim, that he "only resides in the city of Rouen for the king's service and for the requirements of his office in the court," and that his family and principal domicile were in the countryside.[80] Even within the city, most of the magistrates resided in a small number of parishes in the center of the city. About one-fourth of them resided in the single parish of St. Laurent; about half in five other, adjoining parishes; and one-fourth in the city's remaining thirty parishes.[81]

Residential patterns in themselves affected ties to the city, for the parish was an important center of social relations. As one councillor told the court in 1597, he had had little contact with a litigant in a case before the court "save that, as neighbors and residents of the same parish, they see each other and talk occasionally, and principally in church."[82] Yet indications of more solid relations even within the parish prove surprisingly slight. One magistrate claimed that he simply never dined outside his own house;[83] and references to neighbors in the few subsisting *parlementaire* testaments are very rare.[84] Most important is the evidence of baptismal

[80] BM MS Y214, III, 125; V, 337.

[81] Residences are taken from notarial acts passed between 1600 and 1604.

[82] Reg. sec., June-October, 1597, f. 25r.

[83] Reg. sec., 1573-1579, ff. 224-225.

[84] Of eight *parlementaire* testaments, only one (from 1633) men-

records, for godparentage provided a public and ceremonial affirmation of social solidarity. The parish of St. Laurent provides a good example, for in the early seventeenth century about one-fourth of the magistrates resided there and at least one-fourth of its total population consisted of lawyers, officials, and their families. In the later sixteenth and early seventeenth centuries, *parlementaires* and members of their families took part in a very small proportion of the baptisms performed in the parish: 4 or 5 percent of the total, depending on the year, and in nearly every case as godparents for the children of colleagues in the Parlement itself or in other jurisdictions. The magistrates appear to have had little involvement with their neighbors from lower social classes.[85]

Perhaps more surprisingly, their involvement with even the city's wealthiest and most cultivated bourgeois seems to have been slight. For this group a principal expression of social solidarity was the Puy de la Conception, a confraternity which each year sponsored a poetry contest in honor of the Immaculate Conception. Although the Puy's interests were partly devotional and partly artistic, its chief concern was social. With each contest came an extravagant banquet and (on at least one occasion) a play representing the virtues and vices. These were important events in Rouen's social life: sufficiently so, for instance, to attract the interest of such country visitors as the diarist Gilles de Gouberville. Fifty-nine members were enrolled in the Puy between 1544 and 1554, but only three of them were members of the Par-

---

tions a neighbor: AD S-M, G3442 (Guillaume Tulles, clerc, 1535, and Jean Thorel, clerc, 1559); G3431 (Guillaume Gombault, clerc, 1560); Meubles 2, 31 August 1587 (Charles de La Champagne, 1587); 6 March 1604 (Jean de Cahaignes, 1604); 6 November 1613 (Claude Groulart, 1607); La Riv. Bourdet, 3344 (Charles Maignart, 1622); AD S-M, G6275 (Jacques Voisin, 1633).

[85] Archives Municipales, Rouen, Chartrier, no. 137, "Estat du vin et sildre," 1597 (I owe this reference to Philip Benedict), Registres de Catholicité, no. 266; AD S-M, Registres paroissiaux, St. Laurent de Rouen, 1549-1672.

lement. Three others came from the city's other sovereign courts, but the large majority (59 percent) of the Puy's new members were men described merely as "bourgeois of Rouen."[86]

Though some of them might take part in the amusements and games of the urban crowd, most sixteenth-century magistrates were reluctant to involve themselves with the city in more fundamental ways. The weakness of their social involvements was matched, moreover, by a comparable detachment from the political life of the city. The magistrates insisted vehemently on their ultimate political authority: "When the court commands," the king's attorney told Rouen's city councillors in 1574, "the power of the city council (*ceux de la ville*) and of other judges ceases." In the course of the sixteenth century, the magistrates made use of this power, and did in fact take over functions that had belonged to the city.[87] But such intrusions were exceptional and the normal response of the Parlement to civic affairs was an emphasis on its separation from the city. This position was repeated in a series of decisions, for members of Rouen's city government often turned to the *parlementaires* for advice and assistance. In 1548 the lieutenant general of the bailliage appeared before the court to ask its help in dealing with the crown; the fiscal administration had seized the city's grain reserves to pay off taxes which the city owed the king. After some discussion, the court responded that it "finds reasonable the protests which [the lieutenant general] has made, and . . . if this were a matter of which the court could or ought to take cognizance, it would regulate the matter or give him advice; but the affair [is] *nihil ad curiam*." A comparable situation arose in 1570, when the city's military governor departed without warning and left completely unsettled the question of who would regulate

[86] Blangy, ed., *Journal de Gilles de Gouberville*, p. 128; BM MS Y186.

[87] Reg. sec., 1572-1574, f. 178r. For the city councillors' complaints about such intrusions, Reg. sec., January-May, 1597, f. 107.

the city's fortifications. Keys to the fortifications had been turned over to the court's first president, but he wanted nothing to do with them and passed them to the city council. They asked for a clear resolution of the matter from the Parlement, but were told "that they are to take themselves before the king, who will command them as it pleases His Majesty. . . ."[88]

In this and in numerous similar decisions, the magistrates illustrated the connection which they perceived between detachment from local society and their sense of the crown's domination. It was a perception of their situation which Rouen's city councillors and other local notables sought strenuously to resist, both by arguing directly to the magistrates and (with much greater success) by taking legal actions before the royal council. "This corps is not divided off from the citizenry," they told the Parlement in 1572; *"messieurs sont citoyens."* Only rarely did the magistrates deviate from their carefully maintained detachment; in cases of very clear coincidence between the interests of the court and of the city council, the two bodies might send a joint delegation to the crown to ask for assistance or to present grievances, but this appears to have been the limit of their cooperation.[89]

Relations were similar between the Parlement and the other principal representative of local interests, the provincial Estates. The Norman Estates enjoyed limited rights of approving taxes in the province, and each year presented grievances to the crown. The court might make use of the Estates to voice protests that interested it: for instance, when the crown's use of special commissioners to try cases that normally were the preserve of such established jurisdictions as the Parlement conflicted with the interests of both the Parlement and the provincial Estates. Much more often, however, it was the crown and the Parlement whose inter-

[88] BM MS Y214, III, 427-428; VI, 102-103. For a more general statement of the Parlement's reluctance, Reg. sec., 1546-1547, f. 69.

[89] Reg. sec., 1572-1574, f. 15r. For an instance of cooperation, Reg. sec., 1570-1571, f. 117v.

ests were allied against those of the Estates. Members of the Parlement—usually the first president, king's advocate, and one or two councillors—served as the king's deputies to the Estates; it was they who presented the royal demands for taxes and argued in defense of royal policies.[90] As a result, the magistrates usually saw their role as one of opposing the Estates. In 1579 the king's advocate in the Parlement wrote to Pomponne de Bellievre, who was then in charge of the royal fiscal administration, about the unwillingness the Estates had shown to meet the king's demands. When the Estates had refused to grant the sums which the commissioners had proposed, he reported, he and the other magistrates had simply told them that the amounts requested would be levied with or without their consent; as for a commission from Paris which the Estates wanted stopped, "there is no reason to interrupt the commission, because once the representatives to the Estates have separated the matter will not be spoken of again, and what is more when the Estates' delegates appear at court they can easily be shown the impertinence of their request."[91] The magistrates might manipulate the provincial Estates, and might share certain interests with them, but a more long lasting alliance was not likely. As with the city, they sought to distance themselves from provincial government, and understood their position to be one of representing the crown's interests to the province.[92]

[90] On the history and organization of the Estates, and on their brief moment of political vitality in the later sixteenth century, Henri Prentout, *Les états provinciaux de Normandie*, 3 vols. (Paris, 1925-1927).

[91] BN MS français 15905, f. 406r. The Norman magistrates' attitude to the provincial Estates paralleled the relations between parlements and estates on a national level. See Pasquier, *Les mémoires et recherches*, ff. 118-119, for the view that the Parlement was the institution that ought to link monarchy and society, and that the estates were only a recent and ineffectual addition. But see also Denis Richet, *La France moderne: L'esprit des institutions* (Paris, 1973), pp. 27, 31.

[92] For examples of the Parlement using the Estates to voice its own

At the levels both of daily interaction and of political assumptions, it seems, the *parlementaires* felt little engagement with local society. Detachment in these senses, however, did not prevent the magistrates from perceiving a moral unity of a different kind between themselves and the society around them. For most of the century, the magistrates did not see their role as one of leading local society, certainly not as one of mobilizing local society against an intrusive absolute monarchy, but they were not for that reason less convinced of certain shared values with the rest of their society. Although they did not show signs of closeness with the city's residents, they plainly believed that even the poorest classes in the city and in the province as a whole moved in the same moral universe as they.

This sense of relatedness can be seen most clearly in the magistrates' understanding of political unrest, an issue they often had to deal with in the later sixteenth century; though this issue received much less discussion in the earlier years of the century, it appears that the magistrates' attitudes underwent little change during our period. As has been seen above, the magistrates believed that rebellion was a constant possibility. Members of all social classes, they seem to have believed, were easily roused to violent behavior, and their own function was largely that of keeping these natural inclinations in check. To this extent, the magistrates' view of "the people" as fundamentally dangerous represents yet another aspect of their sense of distance from local society, their sense of their special position within it, symbolized by the robes and demands for special deportment which were attached to the office. But their understanding of the immediate causes which might trigger rebellion went considerably further. They saw the populace as dangerous, but not as merely irrational—that is, as set in motion by purely random causes. On the contrary, the magistrates viewed the

complaints, Reg. sec., 1570-1571, ff. 3-4, 74r, 84r, 217ff; 1575-1576, ff. 21v, 23r, 25v; 1573-1579, ff. 40ff, 607.

people as likely to be aroused by very definite causes, and they usually assumed that these causes had at least a kernel of validity. This was most clearly true of the population of the countryside, because their disorders (in the magistrates' view) were solely responses to oppressions from outside: "the peasants belong to no party," it was confidently affirmed just after the Wars of Religion. They rebelled not out of disloyalty, but because of the demands placed on them, especially the state's demands for taxes. High taxes, the magistrates argued during the reign of Henry IV, were "turning them away from obedience to their prince."[93]

The populace of the large cities posed a more serious problem, for their disobedience was thought to have political dimensions. In contrast to the peasants, the magistrates believed, the urban populace might well form part of larger political units. Their religious feelings were seen as more intense; thus they fell naturally into the warring religious parties. They enormously admired the duc de Guise, and were easily led into acting to support him; and they were the ready victims of manipulation by those whom Claude Groulart described in 1588 as "a few crafty spirits."[94] In addition, they too were likely to be moved by the impulses that fostered peasant unrest: anger at high taxes and high food prices. Grain riots in particular were seen by the magistrates as dangerous but fundamentally predictable and justifiable events, and their punishment of those involved in them tended to be lenient.[95]

[93] Reg. sec., January-May, 1595, f. 130r; January-May, 1597, ff. 98-99.

[94] Claude Groulart's views are to be found in BN MS français 15898, f. 576r (1604); in his *Mémoires*, published in Michaud and Poujolat, eds., *Nouvelle collection des mémoires pour servir à l'histoire de France*, XI (Paris, 1838), 553; and BM MS Y202, f. 78v.

[95] Reg. sec., 1572-1574, ff. 47r, 49-50, for the magistrates' conviction that grain had to be distributed "so that popular tumult not arise." The crowd's *own* interpretation of the situation involved wider ramifications: "it is those *mechantz huguenotz* who are the cause of this," some of them were reported to have shouted. For punishment of

But the most common interpretation that the magistrates offered of urban unrest was different from all of these. Much more common than explanation in terms of manipulation from above or in terms of prices and taxes was explanation in terms of the people's moral sense, in terms of what the magistrates called scandal. Scandal and "to scandalize," as they were used in the sixteenth century, were complicated terms. In some instances they retained the meaning which the Middle Ages attached to *scandalum*, of disturbance or tumult, but more often they referred to moral criticism and indignation. This was one of the meanings Robert Estienne offered for *scandalizer* in his dictionary of 1549: "the commonality," he wrote, "sometimes use this to disapprove of someone's misdeed, and the educated say to condemn the fault." For French equivalents he directed the reader to *"les formules de diffamer et Mesdire."*[96] The magistrates' usage seems to have conformed to Estienne's definition. One source of scandal was the carnival festival of the Conards, the raucous and often satirical procession put on by the *basoche* and others: "abusing the licence which had previously been given them," so ran the complaint of the king's attorney in 1595, "they continue their insolence and marched through the streets yesterday, to the great *scandalle* of everyone." Scandal might equally arise from the magistrates' own misbehavior, for instance, from their fail-

---

grain rioters, *ibid.*, ff. 70-71, and AD S-M, B, Parlement, Tournelle, 4 March 1606. Cf. E. P. Thompson, "The Moral Economy of the English Crowd," *Past and Present*, 50 (February, 1971), 83-88, 94-98.

[96] Robert Estienne, *Dictionnaire Francoislatin, aultrement dict Les Mots Francois, avec les manieres duser diceulx, tournez en Latin* (Paris, 1549), 567: "vulgus vocat interdum, quod Exprobrare culpam alicui, & Culpae damnare periti dicunt." For this and other meanings, and for the world's development, Frédéric Eugène Godefroy, *Dictionnaire de l'ancienne langue française . . .* (Paris, 1880-1902), art. *escandalisation*; Edmond Huguet, *Dictionnaire de la langue française du seizième siècle* (Paris, 1925-1967), art. *scandaliser*; Walther von Wartburg, *Französisches etymologisches Worterbuch* (Basel-Paris, 1928-1969), art. *scandalum*.

ure to wear their robes when in the city. In 1546, when one of the councillors began showing clear signs of madness, the court intervened "so that if *scandalle* came of it no blame was placed on the company." More pointedly, in 1598 a similar situation arose because of the court's delay in dealing with an aristocratic counterfeiter. News of this delay, according to the king's advocate, "has spread all through the populace, and a great *esclaindre* (= *scandalle*) has arisen because the judgment has been so long delayed."[97]

It was in terms of such moral outrage that the magistrates explained many of the popular disturbances which they witnessed. In 1571, for instance, the king's attorney reported to the court on a dangerous situation that had arisen some days earlier. Armed members of the civic militia had entered the Palace of Justice seeking some condemned anti-Protestant rioters, and at this sight "the people was indignant . . . there were people in the hall who were scandalized, . . . the people was greatly moved (*émeu*) and there is danger of upheaval (*émotion*)."[98] This interpretation of popular disturbance was a commonly repeated one: "The people" were seen to be indignant at some event that in one way or another failed to conform to their normal standards, and their outrage was enough to set off their natural inclinations to disorder and rebellion. At one level the populace was seen as dangerous and irrational, "a hard beast to restrain"; at another level, they were seen to have an extremely acute sense of the appropriate, a moral sense which the magistrates viewed as reasonable and correct. It was partly the people's very sensitivity to deviations from what was appropriate that made them so dangerous. Even small incidents might, in the magistrates' formula, be "of perilous consequence."[99]

[97] Reg. sec., January-May, 1595, f. 32r; 1597-1598, f. 225r; BM MS Martainville Y96, p. 228. For further examples, of *scandalle* at the revelation of judicial secrets and at favoritism, Floquet, *Histoire du Parlement*, I, 510-511, 514.

[98] Reg. sec., 1570-1571, f. 248.

[99] For other examples of the danger posed by apparently innocuous

This examination of the terms and concepts which the magistrates used to describe the urban crowd and its actions makes understandable the apparent contradictions in the magistrates' dealings with the people they lived among, between apparent leadership of the local community and apparent isolation from it. In the sixteenth century they appear to have been both involved and detached. They believed in the common moral sensibility which they shared with the urban populace, in the people's rationality. They saw their own role as providing a focus for that moral sense; when they failed to act in the ways appropriate to their position, the people's response was likely to be indignation and rebellion. But community in this sense was not matched by other kinds of involvement, in such areas as residence or daily social intercourse. On the contrary, the magistrates believed that the proper performance of their social role demanded precisely isolation from the society around them. Not to maintain this distance was to invite disrespect and scandal. Nor did their belief in values shared with "the people" entail a sense of security, a belief that the urban population was anything but very dangerous. It was because the urban populace posed so considerable a threat that the magistrates' function was so important. When, in the reign of Henry IV, opposition between the Parlement and the crown began to become acute, it was largely because the magistrates were so afraid that royal policies would encourage rebellion. Certainly there was no sense that the masses could be encouraged to rebel without extreme danger to the society as a whole, and to the magistrates themselves in particular.[100]

events (as the magistrates interpreted them), see Reg. sec., 1593-1594 (Caen), f. 181, 71-72; Reg. sec., January-May, 1595, f. 3.

[100] For important contributions to debate over the causes of popular uprisings in the early seventeenth century, Boris Porchnev, *Les soulèvements populaires en France de 1623 à 1648* (Paris, 1963); Roland Mousnier, *Peasant Uprisings in Seventeenth-Century France, Russia, and China*, trans. Brian Pearce (New York, 1970); J.H.M. Salmon, "Venal Office and Popular Sedition in Seventeenth-Century

Just as the magistrates' ties with the monarchy began to show signs of strain in the later sixteenth and early seventeenth centuries, so also their relations to Rouen itself tended to become somewhat closer in these years. The history of the city's Puy de la Conception provides one example of this development. The Puy had only barely survived the Wars of Religion: in the 1570's members who failed to pay their dues were threatened with election to the once honorable position of prince of the confraternity, and in 1595 the members went to court to force their nominee to accept the position.[101] In 1596, however, the institution was reestablished under the leadership of Claude Groulart, the Parlement's first president. But its social foundations were very different from those of the mid-sixteenth century. Twenty-four new members were enrolled between 1596 and 1610. Exactly one-half were members of the Parlement, and another fifth were members of the city's other courts; only one of the new members described himself as a bourgeois of Rouen.[102] The magistrates were coming to involve themselves more fully in local affairs than had been the case fifty years earlier.

The attempt to understand the magistrates as a professional group has required that we consider a wide range of apparently disparate aspects of their behavior and ideas. We have looked at their education, at both the concrete

---

France: A Review of a Controversy," *Past and Present*, 37 (July, 1967), 21-43; Michael O. Gately, A. Lloyd Moote, John E. Willis, Jr., "Seventeenth-Century Peasant 'Furies': Some Problems of Comparative History," *Past and Present*, 51 (May, 1971), 63-80; William Beik, "Magistrates and Popular Uprisings in France Before the Fronde: The Case of Toulouse," *Journal of Modern History*, XLVI, 4 (December, 1974), 585-608. Sharon Kettering, *Judicial Politics and Urban Revolt in Seventeenth-Century France. The Parlement of Aix, 1629-1659* (Princeton, 1978), is the most recent of several local studies, and summarizes recent findings.

[101] BM MS Y186, f. 26; Reg. sec., June-October, 1595, f. 122v.
[102] BM MS Y186, ff. 31-38.

facts of what their work involved and the intellectual stances that it fostered; and we have considered their relationships with colleagues in other parts of France, with the crown that employed them, and with the population they were expected to govern. Insofar as possible, beliefs and behavior have been set against each other, and an effort has been made to understand the realities of the magistrates' position, rather than only contemporary assumptions about what they ought to have been.

What emerges from this examination, in the first place, is the seriousness of the magistrates' professional commitment and of its effects on them. They were not, as some historians appear to have assumed, merely wealthy members of the third estate who had found an attractive means of attaining a higher social position. One sign of the seriousness of their commitment was simply the time and effort which they devoted to their purely legal tasks. Another was their devotion to the monarchy, and their corresponding reluctance to involve themselves with local society; for most of the century, the magistrates understood their role to be one of representing the crown to the province, not one of representing the province's interests. It has been necessary to insist at some length on these points, for discussions of the *parlementaires* and their place in the society of early modern France have often presented these roles quite differently; and indeed toward the end of our period it is possible to see the magistrates in some degree moving away from this model, their commitment to the crown weakening and their involvement with local society increasing.

Secondly, the effort has been made here to understand more precisely what the magistrates' professional commitment entailed. We have seen that they were above all an intensely conservative group. Partly this seems to have reflected the uncertainties of the legal system within which they worked: by the standards even of contemporary states, French law was incomplete and chaotic, and this tended to make the magistrates as a group extremely anxious about precedent and historical example. Perhaps more fundamental to their conservatism, however, was the fact that their main function was not that of developing legal principles but of maintaining peace. Their function, that is, was at base political. Contemporaries recognized this by stressing the magistrate's need for practical wisdom over abstract learning, and by leaving mainly to the lawyers, rather than to the judges, the elaboration of legal theory—with whom, in French law, it has largely largely remained. Yet further adding to their conservative outlook was the fact that, as the magistrates saw it, their peace-keeping function was an extraordinarily difficult one. They believed all levels of society to be extremely volatile, and that one of the principal ways by which disturbances began was precisely the violation of precedent and normal expectation.

Finally, we have seen here that the magistrates' professional position placed them in a series of relationships with their society: relations of dependence on the crown and on their colleagues in other courts, of detachment from the more immediate society around them. It is the last relationship which appears the most intricate, for with their detachment from the society around them—a detachment that operated at the level of daily realities as well as of ethical principles—came also a surprising belief in the rational and coherent moral outlook of even the urban masses. The emphasis which Roland Mousnier and others have placed on the strength of vertical social bonds within the early modern French city, between such leading groups as the *parlementaires* and those lower on the social scale, in this sense is amply justified by the Rouennais example. But this assumption of shared values and responses to events did not entail attachments of a more concrete kind, nor did it imply a sense of confidence in the face of potential popular disturbances. The magistrates' attitude to the society around them combined paternalism and fear.

We now are in a position more fully to understand Monluc's surprise and distaste "that so many young men could thus amuse themselves in a law court." For magistracy brought with it a whole series of attitudes that were antithetical to the outlook of the military nobleman: a self-inflicted repression of natural and youthful impulses, anxiety, rigid conservatism. These attitudes had little to do with either inferior birth or with an especially bourgeois or urban mentality, qualities which many historians have seen as naturally belonging to the magistrates. However, although we may understand a part of Monluc's views, the question of origins itself remains unexplored. Monluc's statement and the argument of this chapter both imply that birth was relatively unimportant in shaping the magistrates' outlook and that the nobilities of robe and sword were not distinct castes, competing sets of lineages. Was Monluc's perception an accurate one? What were the magistrates' origins, and how did their birth affect their position within the social hierarchy as a whole? These are the questions to which the next chapter is directed.

TWO

SOCIAL ORIGINS AND SOCIAL VALUES

In 1499, on the eve of the Parlement's foundation, only one sovereign court existed at Rouen. This was the Cour des Aides, which included eight members. Only one other judge at Rouen, the lieutenant general of the bailliage, was of comparable importance and status. The Parlement's foundation began a process of growth in the number of high officials that was to continue through 1600, and that was to make of royal officials a dominant group within the city and province. By 1554 the Cour des Aides had grown to fifteen members, and the Parlement itself had expanded from its original thirty-five members to sixty-six. By 1600, as the crown made increasing use of office sales as a source of revenues, the Parlement included eighty-three members, and two new sovereign courts (the Chambre des Comptes and the Bureau des Finances) had been created: the former with sixty-four members, the latter with twelve. In the seventeenth century this expansion nearly ceased. The later seventeenth-century intendant Voysin de La Noiraye listed just two hundred members in Rouen's four sovereign courts.[1]

It is little wonder that those who witnessed this frenetic expansion in the number of high offices believed that a basic social change was taking place. In effect a new social group had been created. The impact which its creation had on contemporaries may be better understood by comparing the two hundred or so high officials at Rouen with the number

[1] AD Eure E2474; BM MS Martainville Y23; AD S-M J57; Jean-Pierre Charmeil, *Les trésoriers de France à l'époque de la Fronde* (Paris, 1964); Edmond Esmonin, ed., *Voysin de la Noiraye. Mémoire sur la généralité de Rouen (1665)* (Paris, 1913), pp. 207-208.

of provincial gentlemen who resided near the city. Although the squires of the region were to be counted in the thousands, there were few families who controlled wealth and influence to match that of the officials. In the later seventeenth century Voysin de La Noiraye listed only thirty-five gentlemen of real wealth and standing in the *généralité* of Rouen. If the high officials remained a minority among the nobility as a whole, their position among the nobility who counted economically and politically was very different. The *parlementaires* by themselves in the mid-seventeenth century outnumbered the influential provincial gentry; numerically if not in terms of prestige, Rouen's high officials had become the predominant group within the provincial nobility.[2]

Its numerical development was the most important fact about the Norman *noblesse de robe* in the sixteenth century. They had evolved from a handful of individuals in 1499 to a large social group by 1600. Contemporaries offered an apparently straightforward description of the recruits in this large process of social change. In the early sixteenth century, for instance, Claude de Seyssel observed that ". . . the offices of justice and legal practice, although the other two estates [the nobility and the poor] are capable of holding them, all the same are commonly and usually in the hands of this middle estate; this is a great thing for both the authority and the incomes [of this estate]."[3] This seems a clear interpretation of the recruitment of the parlements

<hr />

[2] Esmonin, ed., *Voysin de la Noiraye*, pp. 72-78.

[3] Claude de Seyssel, *La monarchie de France*, ed. Jacques Poujol (Paris, 1961), p. 123. See also La Roche Flavin's view that the *parlementaires* represented an Aristotelian middle class, of the sort whom Aristotle described as "the steadiest element, the least eager for change" in the state, and the most likely to produce the best lawgivers (*The Politics*, trans. J. A. Sinclair [London, 1962], pp. 172-173 [IV.2]); Bernard de La Roche Flavin, *Treze livres des Parlemens de France* (Bordeaux, 1617), p. 350. Historians since the seventeenth century, of course, have continued to link middle class recruitment and political moderation in understanding the robe mentality.

and other high magistracies, and it has been widely accepted by historians.[4] Seyssel's comments leave many issues uncertain, however. His concept of the "middle estate," whom he defined simply as the *"Peuple Gras,"* is a very vague category, failing as it does to distinguish between urban and rural, businessman and rentier, *novi homines* and members of long-established families. Nor does Seyssel offer much help in understanding how families from the "middle estate" achieved such dominance of official positions, or in understanding changes in the recruitment of officials. Finally, Seyssel himself points out that dominance by the "middle estate" was habitual rather than absolute; how much recruitment there was from other social groups remains a question very much worth asking.

The principal source for inquiry into the magistrates' origins is the published genealogies of the Parlement's members compiled by Henri de Frondeville.[5] These genealogies are based largely on the materials collected by Alexandre Bigot de Monville, the mid-seventeenth-century president of the court and antiquarian, and even for the sixteenth century they are surprisingly complete. They also have significant shortcomings, however, and these should be noted at the outset. They include a considerable number of outright mistakes, in the first place. Where possible I have corrected these, but many have doubtless escaped my attention. Secondly, Frondeville's collections share with nearly all similar efforts two consistent biases. Much more is known about those families who retained close attachments to Normandy than about those who moved elsewhere after

---

[4] Thus Robert Mandrou, *Introduction à la France moderne, 1500-1640* (Paris, 1961), pp. 157-158; Roland Mousnier, *La vénalité des offices sous Henri IV et Louis XIII* (2nd ed., Paris, 1971), pp. 77-78, 554-555. For doubts about this view, see J. H. Shennan, *The Parlement of Paris* (London, 1968), and, more forcefully though with reference mainly to a later period, Jean Meyer, *La noblesse de Bretagne au XVIII siècle,* 2 vols. (Paris, 1966), II, 929-930.

[5] Henri de Frondeville, *Les présidents, Les conseillers* i, *Les conseillers* ii.

brief service in the Parlement; and much more is known about those families who succeeded, who maintained themselves in high offices or who entered the upper nobility, than about those who in one way or another failed.[6] Little can be done about these biases save to remain aware of them, for they are as apparent in the archival as in the published sources. As will become clear, however, their seriousness tends to diminish as we approach the seventeenth century, and both local and hereditary recruitment become more typical.

Despite these shortcomings, both Frondeville and his source, Bigot de Monville, were seriously interested in the *parlementaires'* origins and critical of families' exaggerated claims of noble birth.[7] They can be used with considerable confidence, in the first place, for establishing the magistrates' geographical origins. These are set out in Table 2:1.

Table 2:1 shows a clear evolution in the magistrates' geographical origins. During the first thirty years of the court's existence, more than a third of its members were from outside Normandy, with the rest divided almost evenly between Rouen itself and the rest of the province. After 1529, the importance of the non-Normans steadily declined;

[6] Frondeville's chief sources are from the mid-seventeenth century. They are BM MS Martainville Y24, the president Bigot de Monville's genealogy of the Parlement, and the genealogical collections of the BN; not surprisingly, these are most detailed for families extant in the mid-seventeenth century. However, Frondeville worked seriously to complete these sources with his own archival research and with use of family histories and other works of local erudition.

[7] Cf. Frondeville's critical treatment of families' claims with the credulity shown by Charles Gaspard Toustain-Richebourg, *Famille de Toustain-Frontebosc* (n.p., 1799). In fact Frondeville has probably underrepresented the number of noble families within the Parlement. Cf. his treatment of the Raoullin de Longpaon and Lefebvre families with Tabel., 2 November 1480 ("Pierre Raoullin escuier seigneur de Longpaon") and AD S-M 6F24 (Fonds Robillard de Beaurepaire) (the *parlementaire* Jean Lefebvre "soy disant noble faisant apparoir d'une lettre de chartre de l'an 1449").

TABLE 2:1

COUNCILLORS' GEOGRAPHICAL ORIGINS

	Rouen	Elsewhere in Normandy	Elsewhere in France or Foreign	Unknown
1499-1528	21 (24%)	27 (31%)	31 (36%)	8 (9%)
1529-1558	34 (43%)	22 (28%)	15 (19%)	8 (10%)
1559-1588	45 (47%)	35 (37%)	4 (4%)	11 (12%)
1589-1618	34 (53%)	23 (36%)	3 (5%)	4 (6%)

SOURCE: Frondeville, *Les présidents, Les conseillers* i, *Les conseillers* ii.

to 19 percent between 1529 and 1558, and to 4 percent between 1559 and 1588. In the second half of the sixteenth century, the court became an essentially provincial institution, with only a slight admixture of outsiders. This evolution was intensified by the fact that in 1565, for the first time, the king named a Norman to the court's first presidency; the experiment was repeated when the first presidency next became vacant, in 1585, and in the early seventeenth century the local recruitment of first presidents had become the norm. Because of this change in the court's leadership, the evolution of the court's geographical orientation was sharper than statistics alone would suggest.[8]

[8] Alexandre Faucon de Ris, named first president in 1607, was from outside the province, but the next two first presidents were both from his family and strongly attached to the province. See the comments of the poet Hercule Grisel, in the mid-seventeenth century (*Les fastes de Rouen*, ed. M. Bouquet, 4 vols. [Rouen, 1866-1868], IV, 395: "As an older Falcon goes off to the heavens from earth, / soon a younger Falcon sits in his place in the citadel. / The province of Normandy does not miss the great departed" ["Maior ut e terris revolavit in aetheram Falco, / Mox Falco ablati sedit in arce Minor. Neustria nec talem sensit Provincia raptum . . ."]). The Parisian orientation of the mid-sixteenth-century presidents was not a matter only of origins. They also spent much of their time in Paris, advising the crown. Thus in 1551 the first president Pierre Rémon was able to visit Rouen only for the opening of the court's sessions; in his speech to his colleagues, "he very eloquently described the causes of his

Change in the magistrates' geographical backgrounds had important implications. Obviously the change implied a closer relationship between the court and provincial society, which was expected to find the magistrates "more agreeable, . . . as we hold dearer the fruits of our own properties,"[9] and which doubtless found more sympathy toward its interests. More local recruitment also meant more complicated attitudes toward the court's legal work. The fact of a magistrate's having extensive connections in the city and province, as the *parlementaires* themselves argued in 1549, "every day would create reasons for objections to his participating in cases, for blocking the court's work, and for breaking up its chambers."[10] Contemporaries at least believed that more local recruitment meant, necessarily, a weakening of professional seriousness.

Equally important, though, were the economic implications of changing geographical recruitment. Contemporaries thought it obvious that officials who were from the province itself were wealthier and more economically independent than those from outside, "who have no revenue there save the salaries and beneficence of the king."[11] What-

---

long absence, the desire he had and the opportunity which he seized for returning here, without letting himself be stopped by anyone or for any reason, although the king and my lord the constable demanded yesterday that he come to court . . ." (Reg. sec., 1549-1556, f. 118r; on Rémon's Parisian background and connections, BN MS français 32318, II, 13). A year later the king's advocate returned from a trip to Paris and reported "that at Paris he had seen my lord the president [*à mortier*] Tournebulle who sends his regards to the company" (Reg. sec., 1549-1556, f. 126r).

[9] Claude Groulart's phrase concerning his own appointment as first president: BM MS Y202, f. 75v. The nomination, Groulart added, was contrary to the king's initial reluctance to appoint someone from the province.

[10] BM MS Y214, IV, 23.

[11] *Ibid.*, III, 59-60. See also *ibid.*, x, 28, for the court's reluctance to accept a candidate "given that the said Ermyle is *estranger sans aucuns biens ny moyens*"; and BM MS Martainville Y96, p. 276, for description of a councillor as "*etranger et pauvre*." For further discus-

ever the magistrate might own elsewhere in the kingdom, his disposable income was limited by the difficulties of transporting money over long distances and by the problems of administering distant properties. He could depend only on properties that were near at hand. The steady narrowing of the Parlement's recruitment thus meant changes in the magistrates' economic position. As a group (at least so ran contemporary assumptions) they tended to become less dependent economically on the crown and better able to establish and expand their private fortunes.

The magistrates' social origins underwent an evolution somewhat different from that of their geographical origins during the sixteenth and early seventeenth centuries.[12] Over the whole of our period, the majority of the councillors were following careers fundamentally similar to their fathers': they were sons of lawyers and officials, and notably of officials in the sovereign courts, the highest level of the French judiciary. The importance of this last group is set out in Table 2:2. Because of the gaps in the data from the early sixteenth century, the table begins with 1539.

As Table 2:2 shows, throughout the sixteenth century about one-fourth of the councillors were the sons of high officials, of men who themselves had been members of the sovereign courts. Small variations in this group's relative importance did take place, but overall the period was one of marked continuity.[13] In the early seventeenth century

---

sion of the problem of distance for *parlementaire* incomes, see below, Chapter 4.

[12] Social origins are here defined in narrow terms, as the profession or status of the councillor's father. So narrow a definition plainly distorts some aspects of the magistrates' social origins, but it is necessary for the statistical approach undertaken here. The long-term study of individual family careers (below, pp. 81 ff) in some measure compensates for these limitations; and it will be shown in Chapter 5 below that the ascents and descents of families were more rapid than historians have sometimes assumed, and that therefore the father's position is in fact the critical indicator of social position.

[13] This in contrast to what Henri Drouot and Roland Mousnier

TABLE 2:2
Sons of High Officials

Date Received	Sons of Parlementaires	Sons of Other Sovereign Court Members	Total
1539-1558	12 (20%)	2 (3%)	14 (23%)
1559-1578	13 (20%)	1 (3%)	14 (22%)
1579-1588	8 (25%)	1 (3%)	9 (28%)
1589-1598	7 (23%)	1 (3%)	8 (26%)
1599-1618	22 (32%)	10 (15%)	32 (47%)
1619-1638	28 (39%)	15 (21%)	43 (60%)

Source: Frondeville, *Les présidents, Les conseillers* i, *Les conseillers* ii.

this situation began to change, and the importance of magistrates who were following exactly the same careers as their fathers increased. Of the councillors received between 1599 and 1618, nearly one-half were the sons of members of the sovereign courts. This was true for 60 percent of the new councillors who entered the court between 1619 and 1638. Less and less room was being left for councillors who were in any sense new to the milieu of the high robe.

The counterpart of this increasing dominance by the sons of high officials was a decline in the importance of councillors whose fathers had been lawyers or lesser officials. Their numbers and relative importance are set out in Table 2:3. Between 1539 and 1588, the sons of lawyers and lesser officials were more numerous among the councillors than the sons of members of the sovereign courts. During these years, they represented just under one-fourth of the councillors received. After 1588 their numbers dropped off sharply. Between 1589 and 1638, the group accounted for just over 10 percent of the new councillors. In the early seventeenth century, it is again clear, the Parlement was becoming steadily less open to new families.

have suggested for other parts of France; see above, Introduction, note 11.

TABLE 2:3
Sons of Lawyers and Lesser Officials

Date Received	Sons of Lawyers	Sons of Lesser Officials	Total
1539-1558	9 (15%)	9 (15%)	18 (30%)
1559-1578	3 (5%)	7 (11%)	10 (15%)
1579-1588	2 (6%)	9 (28%)	11 (34%)
1589-1598	1 (3%)	1 (3%)	2 (6%)
1599-1618	2 (3%)	9 (13%)	11 (16%)
1619-1638	2 (3%)	3 (4%)	5 (7%)

SOURCE: Frondeville, *Les présidents*, *Les conseillers* i, *Les conseillers* ii.

In all, the sons of legal and official families (including families already established in the sovereign courts) accounted for about half of the councillors in the sixteenth century, and for about two-thirds in the early seventeenth century. Origins of the remaining councillors are less easily perceived from the genealogical materials, and for about one-fourth of the councillors no clear identification of the father's position is possible. The remaining councillors, though, can be identified as coming mainly from two groups. They were the sons of bourgeois, defined here as families involved in commerce or in municipal government, or they were the sons of noblemen, defined here as those holding legal title to nobility and not involved in administrative or official positions. Tables 2:4 and 2:5 set out the number of councillors who came from these two social groups.

As Table 2:4 indicates, throughout the sixteenth century sons of bourgeois formed only a small proportion of the Parlement's membership. Only in the decade of the League did their importance rise above 15 percent of the total councillors received,[14] and during the preceding fifty years they

---

[14] Thus following a pattern suggested by La Roche Flavin, who explained some of the seditiousness of the League parlements as the work of magistrates raised "*e fece populi*" (*Treze livres*, p. 348).

TABLE 2:4

SONS OF BOURGEOIS

Date Received	Sons of Bourgeois
1539-1558	9 (15%)
1559-1578	7 (11%)
1579-1588	4 (13%)
1589-1598	6 (19%)
1599-1618	7 (10%)
1619-1638	4 (6%)

SOURCE: Frondeville, *Les présidents, Les conseillers* i, *Les conseillers* ii.

had accounted for just under 13 percent of the total. Relatively few of the councillors were urban notables seeking to escape "the inferior condition of the commoner."

In fact a larger number were from families who had no need of such escape, since they were noble already. The numerical importance of this group is set out in Table 2:5.

TABLE 2:5

SONS OF NOBLEMEN

Date Received	2nd or 3rd Generation Nobility	4th Generation and Older Nobility	Total
1539-1558	2 (3%)	6 (10%)	8 (13%)
1559-1578	3 (4%)	12 (18%)	15 (22%)
1579-1588	3 (9%)	3 (9%)	6 (18%)
1589-1598	1 (3%)	3 (10%)	4 (13%)
1599-1618	5 (7%)	8 (12%)	13 (19%)
1619-1638	5 (7%)	6 (8%)	11 (15%)

SOURCE: Frondeville, *Les présidents, Les conseillers* i, *Les conseillers* ii.

Consistently over the sixteenth century, about 17 percent of the councillors were noblemen whose fathers had held no official positions, members of the "mere gentry."[15] Most

[15] This figure includes only sons of "mere" noblemen, who held no offices; when *all* noblemen within the Parlement are counted they

of these councillors, moreover, were of relatively old noble families. Exactly two-thirds of them represented at least the fourth generation of their families' nobility, and most could trace their ancestry to at least the later fifteenth century. Although they were not of the really ancient nobility, their families were about as old as those of most of the Norman nobility, at least as contemporaries believed. "Under Louis XI," reported a later seventeenth-century magistrate of Parisian origins, "an edict in 1470 provided that all those who owned fiefs would be nobles. . . . It is commonly believed that the majority of the [Norman] nobility comes from this time; at the least, a good two-thirds of them do. . . ." This assessment corresponded to the reality. Already by the 1560's there were few families who could offer proofs of nobility going back before 1400.[16]

Statistical examination of *parlementaire* origins points to several conclusions. Whereas in the early sixteenth century a substantial minority of the magistrates had come from Paris and the rest of France, by the early seventeenth century the court's recruitment had become entirely provincial. This change paralleled some of the changes in

account for 38 percent of the councillors named from 1559 through 1588.

[16] G. A. Prévost, ed., *Notes du premier président Pellot sur la Normandie. Clergé, gentilshommes et terres principales, officiers de justice* (Paris-Rouen, 1915), p. 56. See BN MS français 5351, ff. 85-92, for the nobility of the pays de Caux: of forty-three noble families, only one proved noble status from before 1400. For discussion of the age of the French nobility, see Edouard Perroy, "Social Mobility among the French *Noblesse* in the Later Middle Ages," *Past and Present*, 21 (April, 1962) 25-38; Jean-Marie Constant, "L'enquête de noblesse de 1667 et les seigneurs de Beauce," *Revue d'histoire moderne et contemporaine*, xxi (October-December, 1974), 548-566; and the opposite conclusions of James Wood, "Demographic Pressures and Social Mobility among the Nobility of the Election of Bayeux, 1463-1666," *The Sixteenth Century Journal*, viii, 1 (April, 1977), 3-16. For the issues discussed here, the facts of families' antiquity are less important than contemporary belief that most families were not very old.

the magistrates' professional outlook discussed earlier, in Chapter 1; to contemporaries it was clear that local recruitment meant a magistracy more independent economically of the monarchy and in some ways less able to fill its professional duties. But the process of geographical narrowing at no point limited *parlementaire* origins to Rouen itself. A substantial percentage of the magistrates continued throughout the century to come from the province's smaller towns and villages.

With regard to the magistrates' social origins, we have seen here the relatively small role which the sons of merchants and urban rentiers had in the Parlement, and the more substantial role of the lesser nobility. A process of narrowing took place in this aspect of the court's recruitment also, but it began only at the very end of the sixteenth century. Only toward 1600 did the sons of lawyers, lesser officials, and bourgeois become substantially less numerous, and the sons of *parlementaires* and other members of other sovereign courts substantially more numerous. But once underway, the process of narrowing advanced quickly, and by the 1620's roughly two-thirds of the magistrates were the sons of high officials.

But statistics of the kind presented thus far necessarily give a partial view of the magistrates' social and geographical origins. If we are to explain the patterns which they suggest, statistics must be combined with a narrower analysis, directed to understanding the mechanisms by which families advanced to the Parlement. By looking more closely at the histories of individual families, we can understand the importance of certain groups—especially the lesser officials and gentry—in the magistracy's recruitment.

A first aspect of these histories is their close connection to the political crises which marked French history in the fifteenth and sixteenth centuries: the Hundred Years' War and War of the Public Weal in the fifteenth century, the Wars of Religion in the sixteenth. The devastation created by war and English occupation opened numerous possibilities for entirely new families in the later fifteenth century, and many of the Parlement's leading families traced their histories to that time.[17] An inquest of 1540 concerning the status of Pierre Restault, whose grandson Laurent entered the Parlement in 1581, suggests something of the opportunities which newcomers enjoyed. Two of Restaut's neighbors, aged seventy-six and eighty, swore "that they knew the said Jean Restaut [Pierre's father], in his lifetime nephew of a certain Julien du Gouey, in his lifetime *vicomte* of Pontaudemer under King Louis XI. The said Restaut came to live in this land of Normandy, together with the said du Gouey, about fifty-five years ago. He was du Gouey's heir for the fief of Calligny and for several other lands and houses located at Pontaudemer."[18]

The Bauquemare, who supplied the Parlement with two councillors and a first president during the sixteenth century, claimed a similar history in the course of efforts to secure royal letters of nobility. They too traced their origins to the later fifteenth century, though they also claimed "that they had always lived nobly"; it was around 1500 that they had "betaken themselves to Rouen" and established themselves in judicial and legal positions. Other leading robe families—among them the Maignart, Le Roux, and Jubert—followed much the same history of success.[19]

Political crisis in the sixteenth century was important to a few robe families, but did not open so many positions to

[17] For the possibilities which the late fifteenth century offered for families seeking to establish themselves, see Yvonne Bezard, *La vie rurale dans le sud de la région parisienne de 1450 à 1560* (Paris, 1929), pp. 98-105; Bernard Guenée, *Tribunaux et gens de justice dans le bailliage de Senlis à la fin du moyen âge (vers 1380-vers 1550)* (Paris, 1963), pp. 379-405; René Fédou, *Less hommes de loi lyonnais à la fin du moyen âge* (Paris, 1964), pp. 365-371.

[18] AD S-M, E, Fonds Restaut (unclassed).

[19] AD S-M, 16J8; Oscar de Poli, "Les seigneurs de la Rivière Bourdet," *Revue nobiliaire historique et biographique, nouvelle série*, IV (1868), 97-108, 207-233, 261-275; BN MS français 32318, II, 288; BN Pièces Originales, 1596, 1794.

new families as the Hundred Years' War had done. Although the Parlement went briefly into exile following the Protestant uprising of 1562, only a small minority of its members were seriously affected by the earlier phases of the Wars of Religion. Protestants sacked the properties of one of the most ardently Catholic councillors in 1562, leaving the family in near indigence.[20] In the following decade, several Protestant councillors were expelled from the court; but despite the impressively worded confiscations of all their properties, the families of all five affected by the last expulsion, in 1572, continued to prosper in the late sixteenth century.[21] Only with the Catholic League, in the mid-1580's,

[20] This was the councillor Pierre Dufour. On his ruin, see Frondeville, *Les conseillers* i, 327, and Hérit. 2, 27 October 1570.

[21] Of the five Protestants expelled, two (Civille and Le Roux) were from very important Rouennais families, branches of which remained Catholic and which continued to flourish through the eighteenth century. A third Protestant family, the Quièvremont, apparently turned to careers in the *noblesse d'épée*; a notarial act of 1614 referred to "feu messire François de Quièvremont escuyer seigneur de Heudreville gentilhomme ordinaire de la chambre du Roy," and his widow "dame Claude de Pardieu," from one of the leading Protestant aristocratic families from the area of Rouen (Hérit. 2, 11 March 1614). A fourth councillor, Charles Le Verrier, apparently retired as a country gentleman to his estates: an act of 1580 referred to "noble homme Charles Le Verrier escuyer seigneur et baron de Vassy demourant audit lieu de Vassy," though the family's history after 1580 cannot be followed (Tabel., 22 February 1580). The most complex history, it appears, was that of the councillor Jerome Maynet's family. Maynet, who despite his Protestantism was one of the court's most respected jurists, died in 1574, shortly after having returned to the Parlement by virtue of the peace of 1572; the court took part in his burial in one of Rouen's parish churches. In 1578 his minor children were under the guardianship of "maître Thomas Maynet, advocat du Roy au bailliage et siege presidial de Rouen"; the same act referred to Charles Maynet as former *vicomte* of Rouen and to Moyse Maynet as "receveur des deniers communs de la ville de Dieppe." In 1585, with the revocation of religious toleration, Jerome's son "Danyel Maynet escuyer" was making arrangements for going into exile, but in 1595 he was again in Rouen; in that year he arranged with "Noble homme maitre Charles Maynet aussi con-

did political turmoil again offer substantial chances for new families to advance to eminent positions. In this respect the League conformed to the assumption shared by many contemporaries, that political disruption was chiefly the work of a few ambitious spirits who hoped for economic and social benefits from disorder. A mid-seventeenth-century intendant noted of one family of the leading upper Norman aristocracy that "the father and uncles of the said lord of Fontaine-Martel, to the number of four or five [one of them a councillor in the Parlement] held constantly to the party of the League during the reigns of Henry III and Henry IV, and during those troubles raised the house of Fontaine, which previously had owned very little, to the point where it now stands, as one of the most powerful in the pays de Caux."[22] The Thomas family represented a more dramatic example of success. Gentien Thomas was the son of a petty official in Blois who, "with the aim of advancing himself as far as he could," was drawn "by God's secret leading" (in the view of his Jansenist grandson) first to Paris, then to Rouen, where he settled shortly before 1589. During the League Thomas attached himself to the *ligueur* duc de Villars, and quickly benefited from this position: he was given a position in Rouen's Chambre des Comptes by Mayenne, and shortly after the League bought a large house in Rouen and a substantial country estate. The family remained an important one among Rouen's officials through the eighteenth century.[23]

---

seiller du roy et lieutenant general en Normandye sur le faict des eaues et forestz" concerning some of his father's testamentary dispositions (Reg. sec., 1573-1579, f. 344r; BM MS Y111, f. 283; Meubles 2, 6 September 1585; AD S-M, B, Requêtes du Palais, Contrats, 27 April 1595).

[22] Esmonin, ed., *Voysin de la Noiraye*, p. 73.

[23] For Gentien Thomas' own report on his ascension, AD S-M 10J13; for his grandson's, F. Bouquet, ed., *Mémoires de Pierre Thomas sieur du Fossé* . . . , 4 vols. (Rouen, 1876), I, 7. A sense of the family's newness and tenuous links to its past may be gained from

Robe families who reflected on their origins were aware of how important such moments of political crisis had been, but tended to interpret their advancement in royalist terms: loyalty to the crown during its moments of critical need, during the League, the rebellions of the later fifteenth century, or the Hundred Years' War, was repeatedly offered as an essential reason for success. Writing in the middle years of the seventeenth century, Gentien Thomas' grandson represented this outlook in extreme form. He showed little concern to give his grandfather a more illustrious social background but was intensely concerned to improve his family's political past. His grandfather, he wrote, was chosen "by the good servants of the king, as someone very attached to his service," for several dangerous missions during the League; captured by the *ligueurs*, he managed to escape and bring his crucial messages to the king. "Numerous public acts show," concluded the younger Thomas, "that he demonstrated an incredible zeal for the reduction of Rouen, Le Havre, Pont de l'Arche, Laon, and La Fère to obedience to King Henry IV."[24]

Thomas' royalist past was almost certainly fabricated. Similar doubts may be entertained about the descriptions which other families offered of their ancestors' devotion to the crown. The grandfather of the councillor Laurent Restault, it was claimed, "lived nobly . . . in the service of both the king our lord and the late lord grand seneschal of Normandy, and two of his brothers died beyond the mountains in the king's service." Hugues de Bauquemare, that family's earliest known ancestor and grandfather of

---

Gentien's note in his account book, in about 1612: "Let it be noted that my father was named Denys Thomas, the son of Gentien Thomas, in their lifetimes royal notaries at Blois; from this Gentien Thomas are said to have descended (*seroit yssus*) the said Denys Thomas my father, who died in about 1573 and Gentien Thomas, councillor and secretary of the king, my uncle, still living . . ." (AD S-M 10J13).

[24] Bouquet, ed., *Mémoires de Pierre Thomas*, I, 7.

Jacques, first president in the Parlement from 1565, "during the reign of the late king Louis XI died in battle, in the flower of his age, fighting for the defense of the kings our predecessors, as the Navarrais and Burgundians harassed our land of Normandy." Richard Maignart, grandfather of one of the Parlement's first councillors, was supposed to have aided the king against the English, taking part in their expulsion from the town of Vernon. In 1591 the future president (from 1600) Charles Maignart claimed that he too "had always behaved as a good and loyal (*affectionné*) servant of His Majesty, with all fidelity and obedience"; but he spent the League on his country estates, and seems throughout to have recognized the authority of the *ligueur* Parlement of Rouen.[25]

A history of devotion to the crown was plainly important to families as they viewed their pasts, however erratic these in fact had been, and the crown sought actively to encourage this view.[26] But in fact the real extent of the royalist zeal of families in such critical moments as the League had little to do with their success in establishing or maintaining a position within the high robe. The king's attorney Georges de La Porte, alone of the presidents and *gens du roi*, remained with the *ligueur* Parlement in Rouen, while the royalists went into exile at Caen, but this fact proved no obstacle to his becoming a president shortly after the League had been settled. Nor did Charles Maignart's temporizing prove an obstacle to his becoming a master of requests in 1597 and president in 1600.[27]

[25] AD S-M, E, Fonds Restaut (unclassed); 16J8; La Riv. Bourdet, 2422.

[26] See Reg. sec., June-October, 1597, ff. 8-9, for the arguments of a master of requests urging the magistrates to help the king in the siege of Amiens: "it is certain that if God gives the king the good fortune to recapture Amiens, there will be no one who will regret the service which he has brought . . ." (f. 9).

[27] On La Porte's active role in the League, BN MS français 32318, II, 291. For interpretations stressing the importance of loyalty to the crown in such critical moments as the League for families' success,

What was critical to most robe careers at Rouen was not loyalty to the crown but patronage from members of the great aristocracy. This fact reflected the procedures by which offices in the Parlement were obtained during most of the sixteenth century. At Rouen offices in the Parlement were openly sold by the crown from at least 1543, but they were sold for very low prices, relative both to the income they brought and to the demand for them, a situation which seems to have reflected the monarchy's hesitations in selling offices. The candidate needed more than money to enter the Parlement; usually he needed as well someone to speak in his favor at court. Both Sully and Richelieu justified full venality of office by the implications of this situation. "Because the king and his closest advisers can only be acquainted with someone's merits through the judgment of a third or fourth party," wrote Richelieu, the great noblemen at court would naturally be able to secure their clients' appointment; the only alternative, he argued, was to allow inheritance and the market for offices to determine their recruitment.[28]

Royal letters of appointment to office conformed to Richelieu's arguments, speaking as they did of "the good and praiseworthy report that has been made to us" concerning the candidate's "sense, sufficiency, loyalty, integrity, practical wisdom, learning, experience in judicial matters, and sound diligence."[29] In fact, means other than patronage of the great aristocracy existed for bringing such a "good report" to the king's notice. Family connections and fortunate marriages might certainly help. Claude Groulart, the child of wealthy Dieppois merchants, became first presi-

---

see Roland Mousnier, *Le conseil du roi de Louis XII à la Révolution* (Paris, 1970); Pierre Goubert, *L'ancien régime, 2: les pouvoirs* (Paris, 1973), p. 54.

[28] Louis André, ed., *Cardinal de Richelieu, Testament politique* (Paris, 1947), p. 237; this argument is developed also by Roland Mousnier, *La vénalité*, p. 85.

[29] AD S-M, B, Parlement, Registre d'Audiences, 18 June 1575, 15 July 1575.

dent in 1585 at the age of only thirty-three. He appears to have owed this rapid advancement to his brilliance as a student at the University of Valence, where he came into contact with several children of leading Parisian robe families. Several Parisian lawyers acquired a sufficient reputation for learning and oratory that the magistrates asked the king to nominate them. Claude Groulart's successor as first president, Alexandre Faucon, represented yet another path to high office, that of the "natural *parlementaire*" drawn from the great Parisian official dynasties. Such figures had been especially common at Rouen during the early sixteenth century, when members of such notable families as the Hennequin and Selve served briefly at Rouen before returning to higher positions in the capital.[30]

Yet even connections of family and friendship did not eliminate the need for the patronage of the great. A letter from the president Pierre Rémon to the duc de Guise, in 1550, both illustrates the need which magistrates had for this kind of protection and suggests the obsequious tone which they typically adopted toward their patrons. As the first president at Rouen, Rémon was himself a figure of substance within royal government. He was writing the duc de Guise on behalf of one of his wife's relatives, to whom he had promised a minor office at Falaise. His influence had apparently prevailed with the crown, but (as he reported to the duke) at the last moment the king had changed his decision and given the disposition of the office to a courtier. Despite his outrage, Rémon concluded his letter with a ringing declaration of his loyalty to the duke and willingness to follow the duke's advice: "All the same, I would prefer to lose the office entirely rather than do anything which you would not find good or which in the slightest diminished the good will which you have had for me . . . which if God

[30] On Groulart's educational career, Firmin Didot, *Nouvelle biographie générale*, XXII (Paris, 1858), 230-233; on the magistrates' awareness of Parisian legal reputations, Reg. sec., 1570-1571, f. 25r; on presidents' origins, Frondeville, *Les présidents*.

is willing I will never lose, either because of this matter
or through any other deficiency in performing my duty to
your service, to which I have always devoted myself."[31]
The uncertainties of royal favor made aristocratic protection a constant need, even for someone as well established
as Rémon.

The role of aristocratic patronage in selecting candidates
for the Parlement was rarely explicitly stated, though one
commentator noted of Guillaume Gouel, the court's first
king's attorney, that he had been chosen by the cardinal-
archbishop Georges d'Amboise and that his father had been
a seneschal of the archbishop.[32] More often the relationship
was described in more general terms. The councillor Guillaume Le Roux, who like Gouel entered the Parlement in
1499, was the son of "Guillaume Le Roux, who was suc-
cessively servant, intendant, and secretary of Marie Comtesse de Harcourt, and who became *vicomte* of Elbeuf"—a
property owned by the Guise family.[33] Bigot de Monville
similarly described the position of Denis de Brèvedent, who
became councillor in 1527. "This family," he wrote, "grew
wealthy through the protection of Diane de Poitiers,
duchesse de Valentinois, and in [their] house . . . the arms
of the Brézé (the family of Diane's husband) are to be seen
in several places."[34] Comparable ascensions may be followed
through other sources. The Busquet family, for instance, in
the 1480's were little more than wealthy peasants, but they

[31] BN MS français 20541, f. 70v; on Rémon's extensive and powerful family and close connections with the crown, see BN MS français
32318, II, 13. Cf. Claude Groulart's similar situation. Despite his connections with important Parisian families, aristocratic patronage was
critical for his success: "He was first councillor in the Grand Conseil
and in the Council of the Admiral de Joyeuse, by whose influence
and by his own merits he was named by commission to the office of
first president . . ." (Bigot de Monville, BM, MS Martainville Y24,
f. 25v.).

[32] BN MS français 32318, II, 288.   [33] *Ibid.*, II, 47.

[34] BM MS Martainville Y24, II, 1, f. 152v.

enjoyed the advantage of holding properties from the duchy of Estouteville. This seigneurial connection apparently led to others, for in the 1530's Isambart Busquet, a lawyer, was serving the Estouteville as a seigneurial judge. In 1542 Isambart became a councillor in the Parlement, but his office did not prevent further service to the Estouteville family; in 1553 he served as the duchess' agent in the sale of some properties and borrowed money in her name, while his elder son (who was to enter the Parlement in 1561) had become the duchy's *"bailli et garde des sceaux"* by 1545.[35] We see the earliest phases of this process in the case of the Bretel, who entered the Parlement in the 1570's and quickly became one of its wealthiest families. In about 1524 the councillor Charles Le Roux wrote to the comtesse d'Aumale, asking that a benefice at Aumale be given "in favor of Master Martin Bretel, a lawyer in the Parlement, who has employed himself and continues every day to employ himself in watching over your affairs in this province. For a long time he was a servant of the late lord of Bourgtheroude (Charles Le Roux's father, the councillor Guillaume), under whose direction he worked hard and diligently in pursuing your lawsuits."[36] Patronage networks thus extended beyond the initial bond between the great aristocrat and his client, to include also the latter's own servants and dependents.

Royal legislation sought to restrict the force of these bonds between the king's own officials and the often

---

[35] Robert Busquet de Caumont, *Histoire économique et sociale d'une lignée de huit conseillers au Parlement de Normandie: Les Busquet de Chamdoisel et de Caumont* (Mémoire, D.E.S., Université de Paris, Faculté de Droit et des Sciences Économiques, 1961), pp. 10-16; Archives Busquet de Caumont, liasse "Contrats de mariage," 3 September 1545; Tabel., 13 March 1564. Cf. the very similar progression of the La Vache family, described by M. Charpillon and Abbé Caresme, *Dictionnaire historique de toutes les communes du département de l'Eure* (Les Andelys, 1868-1879), II, 882-884.

[36] BN MS français 20649, f. 167r.

rebellious great aristocracy, by forbidding officials to serve any but the crown, but these efforts had little effect.[37] Throughout the century magistrates continued to express their devotion to the great aristocracy, both in florid letters like Rémon's and in the drier language of legal contracts. In 1550 the councillor Robert Raoullin borrowed money in the name of the duc d'Aumale, on the authority of a previously arranged power of attorney; in 1551 the councillor Jean de Bonshoms did the same for the admiral Claude d'Annebault, the king's lieutenant general in Normandy; in 1575 the president Gilles de Hattes acted in the same capacity for the marquise de Rothelin and the minor duc de Longueville; in 1582 the councillor Guillaume Péricard, whose closest ties were to the Guise family, helped François d'O, the king's lieutenant general in lower Normandy, to borrow money, again acting as his attorney; in the early 1600's, finally, similar functions were performed by the councillor Pierre de Latigeoire for a lesser figure, the courtier Jean de Courseilles, and by Jean Jacques Romé, president in Rouen's Chambre des Comptes, for the duc de Montpensier.[38]

For their loyalty to the great the magistrates received a wide range of benefits. Nomination to office and assistance for relatives and dependents, as Rémon and Le Roux demanded in their letters, were the most important of these, but some magistrates received more dramatic assistance. In

[37] A limited prohibition, against receiving pensions or holding offices from those who might have business in the Parlement, was included in the edict founding the court, in 1499 (AN U754, f. 9r); and the Ordinance of Villers Cotterets forbade magistrates from having any role in others' cases before the Parlement (quoted Pierre Guénois, *La conférence des ordonnances royaux* . . . [nouvelle édition, Paris, 1596], p. 77). But in 1601 the king's attorneys at Rouen were still trying to enforce this principle (BM MS Martainville Y96, p. 314).

[38] Tabel., 17 October 1550, 8 April 1551, 1 February 1575, 19 March 1582; Hérit. 2, 1 August 1601; Meubles 2, 11 October 1601.

1565, for instance, the childless councillor Robert Raoullin arranged the sale of his most important properties to the duc d'Aumale, whose ardent supporter he had been in the Parlement. Raoullin was to receive the money from the sale immediately, but the duc was to take possession of the properties only after both Raoullin and his wife had died; in addition the duc was to pay Raoullin a life rent of 300ł.[39] Forty years later the Guise rewarded another of their robe supporters still more generously. Jean Péricard, son of a king's attorney at Rouen and brother of three clerical councillors, was given by the duc de Guise three seigneuries, "in consideration of the services which the said Péricard had rendered him and the late lord duc de Guise, his father."[40]

In return for what they received, the magistrates performed a variety of tasks for the great aristocracy. They arranged and often guaranteed loans, placing their knowledge and credit at the disposal of the great. In some instances they served as estate agents, checking accounts and offering advice. In the 1520's the councillor Charles Le Roux provided these services for the Aumale, although he was one of the richest men in the city; his grandfather had served as *vicomte* of Elbeuf, and Charles seems to have continued in this capacity several years after his appointment to the Parlement. He served also as a seigneurial judge in the county of Aumale, and reported in 1521 on the execution of "some adventurers and vagabonds who had com-

[39] Tabel., 19 February 1564 (old style).

[40] BN Carrés de d'Hozier, 489. For Protestant magistrates, another service may have been political protection, though this was less clearly stated. In the course of a dispute with a Catholic president, the Protestant councillor Jerome Maynet was threatened with denunciation to the archbishop of Rouen; he replied "that he didn't care, he held a church office (his clerical councillorship) and his brother [was] a judge for my lord the Cardinal [de Bourbon, the archbishop] at Dieppe" (Reg. sec., 1570-1571, f. 49r). At the least, patronage ties might cut across religious differences.

mitted several excesses and pillagings in your county of Aumale; I have exerted myself in this matter for your welfare and honor, so that justice was virtuously done...."[41]

Direct assistance of this kind, however, was probably less important to *les grands* than the legal and political services which the magistrates might provide. As the owners of large estates in the province, such figures as the comtes (elevated later in the century to ducs) d'Aumale had a concrete interest in many of the Parlement's decisions. The greatest of potential patrons, such as the Queen Mother herself, the cardinal de Bourbon, Rouen's archbishop during the Wars of Religion, and Jeanne d'Albret, did not hesitate to write to the Parlement at large to urge the merits of their own or their dependents' cases; the cardinal concluded one such request, in 1575, by stressing "the pleasure you will give me in this matter, as I have every confidence you will, and so that this will serve as an example to others I will take pains to recognize [my gratitude] everywhere where you would wish to employ me, both in general and particular."[42] The Wars of Religion brought further scope for aristocratic interference in the Parlement's decisions, for the Guise made use of such clients as Raoullin and the Péricard to express their extreme Catholic point of view.[43]

Geography both gave added impetus to the forming of patronage relationships and helped shape their character. In the first place, Normandy was easily accessible to Paris and the royal court, and by itself this encouraged close relations between magistrates and *les grands*. More fundamental (though closely related) was the fact that so many of the great owned large properties in upper Normandy,

[41] BN MS français 20649, f. 168r. For similar instances, AD S-M, 1F39 (Abbé Maurice, *Les Romé de Fresquiennes*), p. 56, note 2; BM MS Y214, IV, 407-408.

[42] Reg. sec., 1573-1579, ff. 110-111; for Jeanne d'Albret, *ibid.*, f. 111; for Catherine de' Medicis, Reg. sec., 1570-1571, f. 217r.

[43] A. Floquet, *Histoire du Parlement de Normandie*, 7 vols. (Rouen, 1840-1842), II, 295-296; III, 249, 302-310.

whether because of historical accident or, as the sixteenth-century Rouennais antiquary Noel Taillepied believed, be-cause of "the beauty of the country" and "the serenity of the air."[44] Within upper Normandy were to be found the duchies of Aumale and Elbeuf (both belonging to branches of the Guise family), Longueville, Estouteville, Eu, and Graville. Other great aristocrats owned extensive properties in Normandy, though their principal interests might be elsewhere: thus the duc de Guise himself, Diane de Poitiers, the duc de Bouillon, and the Montmorency. Ecclesiastical holdings were a final element in the concentration of great properties in the province. The archbishopric of Rouen was held by a series of important figures, the Amboise in the first half of the century and the cardinal de Bourbon in the second, while such abbeys as Fécamp and Bec Hellouin were in the hands of the Guise.[45]

Numerous aristocratic families thus had excellent reason to concern themselves with the Parlement's recruitment; this was especially true of the Guise, whose pervasive influence can be seen in the examples presented above. But the concentration of great properties in upper Normandy also affected the qualities of aristocratic patronage. Aristocrats certainly extended their favor to the city as well as to the countryside, but circumstances encouraged their patronage of rural figures, whether squires, wealthy peasants, lawyers, or minor officials. In the nature of things it was from these groups that both servants and seigneurial officials were drawn, and the numerous great aristocratic estates of upper Normandy offered large numbers of such positions: we have seen their importance in the ascensions of the Busquet and Le Roux families, both of whom retained

[44] Quoted by H. Le Charpentier and Alfred Fitan, *La ligue dans le Vexin normand. Journal d'un bourgeois de Gisors* . . . (Paris, 1878), xxiii-xxiv.

[45] See Jean-Pierre Labatut, *Les ducs et pairs de France au XVII*^e *siècle. Étude sociale* (Paris, 1972), pp. 272-273; BN MS français 5351; Tabel., 29 July 1569; AD S-M, 1F39.

their involvement in seigneurial affairs long after having entered the Parlement. Closely related was the encouragement which the feudal structure itself offered to close relations between great aristocrats and lesser figures. Contemporaries at least assumed that relations were close between a great landowner and those who held fiefs from him, and fief holders in turn very often needed the resources which serving a great estate offered.[46] The nature of the aristocratic estate, finally, brought its owner into as much contact with the officials and merchants of the smaller market towns as with those of the provincial capital itself. Much of the estate's legal business would be carried out in these lesser centers, and much of its produce would be sold there.[47]

It is in these terms that the great aristocracy's role in determining the Parlement's recruitment helps to explain some of the more striking results of our statistical inquiry into the magistrates' backgrounds: the relatively small place held by sons of Rouen's commercial bourgeoisie, the relative importance of descendants of the "mere gentry," and the persistent importance of families from outside Rouen, from the province's smaller towns and countryside. This configuration reflected the natural directions in which

[46] For discussion of the force of feudal relations, see below, Chapter 4; and the perceptive discussion of V.-L. Tapié, "Les officiers seigneuriaux dans la société provinciale du XVIIe siècle," *XVIIe Siècle*, 42-43 (1959), 118-140. See also the remark of the jurist Josias Bérault, that "Normally one employs as seneschal (the principal judge of the seigneurie) some local lawyer (*quelque advocat du lieu*)" (Josias Bérault, *La coustume reformée du pays et duché de Normandie* . . . [Rouen, 1614], p. 260); and for the use made by the Guise of their feudal position in upper Normandy, Floquet, *Histoire du Parlement*, III, 251.

[47] See, for instance, a letter from an official in the bailliage de Gisors to the duc de Guise, assuring the duc that "I have consulted about this with . . . my lord Brevet, your secretary, and have drawn up a memorandum which the said Brevet will bring to you . . ." (BN Fonds Clairambault, 348, 7 June 1555).

aristocratic patronage pointed. We may better appreciate the persistent force which these patterns had by considering briefly the court's leadership during the last years of the sixteenth century, for a considerable amount can be clearly established about the paths by which the families of leading magistrates came to the Parlement. Sixteen individuals were named president or king's attorney between 1571 and 1600, representing thirteen families. About the origins of one of these, the Anzeray, we know little. A second, the well-known author Charles Paschal, was an Italian and claimed to be of the nobility.[48] Four others were from the commercial bourgeoisie: the first president Claude Groulart, whose rapid rise from the merchant class of Dieppe was considered above; Emery Bigot, whose family had risen more gradually from Rouen's bourgeoisie before entering the Parlement; Raoul Bretel, whose family had been merchants at Le Havre; and Nicolas Damours, whose grandfather had apparently been a bourgeois of Paris.[49] One family, that of the first president Jacques de Bauquemare, owed its success to a notable lawyer, Jean de Bauquemare, the first of his family to settle in Rouen—despite the family's claim to military glories in the fifteenth century.[50]

[48] On the presidents' origins, Frondeville, *Les présidents, passim*. On the Anzeray at Rouen, Hérit. 2, 23 June 1571 (marriage of François Anzeray and Marie Damours); 17 April 1600 (marriage of Gilles Anzeray). On Charles Paschal, see J. Fr. Michaud, *Biographie universelle ancienne et moderne*, xxxii (Paris, 1854), 214-215.

[49] On the Bigot, see Madeleine Foisil, ed., *Mémoires du Président Alexandre Bigot de Monville: le Parlement de Rouen, 1640-1643* (Paris, 1976); and AD S-M, E, Tabellionage de Rouen, Meubles 1ère série, 6 April 1554 (old style): "honorable homme Estienne Bigot orfebvre"; and Tabel., 8 October 1575: marriage of "damoiselle Marie Bigot fille de deffunct noble homme Jehan Bigot l'un des anciens conseillers et eschevins de ceste ville de Rouen . . . veufve de deffunct honorable homme Jean de Caulmont en son vivant bourgeois de Caudebec." On the Bretel, Baron d'Esneval, "Une famille parlementaire de Normandie. Les Bretel de Grémonville," *Revue Catholique de Normandie*, 1924-1925.

[50] AD S-M 16J8.

In contrast, the remaining six families came to Rouen only as their service in the Parlement began. Their origins were not in the provincial capital but in the smaller market towns, for the most part those along the Seine; only one family, the Vauquelin, came from lower Normandy. All of these families had held minor offices in these towns before being named to the Parlement, and even those who were relatively poor (notably the Le Jumel) owned some feudal properties before they began their ascensions in the official hierarchy; two of the six families (the de La Porte and Maignart) owned only landed property at the time they were named to the Parlement, and had no investments in bonds or urban houses. At least three of the families, finally, had adopted some form of nobility very early in their careers: the Maignart by virtue of royal letters obtained in 1477, the Le Roux (apparently by outright usurpation) at about the same time, and the Vauquelin before 1470.[51] It was principally families of this type, so it appears, who fell into the patronage nets of *les grands*, by virtue of both their nearness and their usefulness to the great aristocratic estates. Such families did not entirely dominate the Parlement's membership, but they constituted its most characteristic group.

Thus far attention has been given mainly to the bare facts of the magistrates' recruitment. We have sought to determine what groups they came from and by what means they

[51] On the Vauquelin, J. Angot des Retours, ed., "Epitaphier des Vauquelin," *Bulletin, Société des Antiquaires de Normandie,* XI (1933), esp. pp. 7-19; on the Le Jumel, AD Eure E3, no. 141, Hérit. 2, 5 May 1598 (Pierre Le Jumel's marriage, 1557), 17 January 1598, 8 April 1601 (marriages of his daughters); on the La Porte, Tabel., 31 January 1582, Hérit. 2, 3 September 1588; on the Le Roux, Archives d'Esneval, Acquigny, BN MS français 32318, II, 47; on the Maignart, BN Pièces Originales, 1794, Poli, "Les seigneurs de la Rivière Bourdet," La Riv. Bourdet, 516, 539, AD Eure E1523, 27 March 1608 (for a collateral branch of the Maignart continuing to reside in Vernon).

reached the Parlement. Equally important, though, were the attitudes and modes of behavior which surrounded those facts. It is important to ask how the magistrates viewed their own social position and their relationship to other social groups.

A first important set of attitudes involves those surrounding the problems of social mobility, particularly with regard to the movement of new men into the Parlement itself. In a purely statistical sense, as we have seen, there was little change during the sixteenth century in the groups from which the magistrates were drawn; until about 1600 "new men" continued to obtain offices in the court in about the same numbers. Further, the creation of new offices in the late sixteenth century offered additional possibilities to satisfy the ambitions of new families: most striking was the foundation in 1580 of Rouen's Chambre des Comptes, with twenty-four members initially and fifty-eight members by 1586. In terms of the actual possibilities which it offered, the later sixteenth century at Rouen was a period of enhanced social mobility.[52]

It is all the more striking, then, that this was also a period of hardening attitudes among the magistrates themselves. During much of the sixteenth century, the movement of individuals to greater positions than their parents had held was, if not seen as a positive goal, as least acceptable. Some magistrates at least believed in encouraging such advance-

[52] This is in contrast to a commonly held interpretation of the League. See above, Introduction, note 11; and J.H.M. Salmon, "The Paris Sixteen, 1584-1594: The Social Analysis of a Revolutionary Movement," *Journal of Modern History*, XLIV, 4 (December, 1972), 540-576. For the expansion of Rouen's Chambre des Comptes, AD S-M, J57. Despite the continuing possibilities for advancement, at Rouen as at Paris, resentment against the *parlementaires* seems to have been an important element in the League. See for Paris Louis-Raymond Lefevre, ed., *Journal de L'Estoile pour le règne de Henri IV*, 3 vols. (Paris, 1948), I, 132; for Rouen, Floquet, *Histoire du Parlement*, III, 299-411, though Philip Benedict's forthcoming study will challenge this view.

ment. Thus the first president in 1545 endorsed the notion of establishing a charitable school in Rouen. The clerk reported him arguing "that the children who would be maintained in the said schools could blossom forth, adducing the example of Bartolus and other great personages, who had advanced to great perfection from humble beginnings; and that some could be instructed in theology and in civil and canon law and in other sciences, from which the Christian Republic might derive great benefit." One concrete manifestation of this outlook has already been seen. In the mid-sixteenth century the magistrates were seriously concerned to honor legal ability, with little regard to candidates' birth.[53]

This relatively liberal attitude underwent considerable weakening in the later sixteenth century, perhaps partly because of the civil wars. By the mid-seventeenth century, Alexandre Bigot believed that the normal procedure had always been to decide questions of precedence in favor of high birth, and noted further that "lowliness of birth . . . has several times been an obstacle to entrance to the sovereign courts"—although other reasons had to be found for such refusals.[54] To magistrates of the later sixteenth and seventeenth centuries, the admission of new men to high

---

[53] BM MS Y214, III, 177-178; above, pp. 28-30.

[54] MS MS Martainville Y23, f. 44r. Increasingly harsh attitudes toward the lower classes are to be seen also in the magistrates' treatment of the city's poor. See Gustave Panel, ed., *Documents concernants les pauvres de Rouen extraits des archives de l'Hôtel-de-ville*, 2 vols. (Rouen-Paris, 1917), I, 50-53 (for the relatively sympathetic attitudes of the 1540's), 120ff. (for the steadily harsher attitudes of the later sixteenth century). See also Natalie Zemon Davis, "Poor Relief, Humanism, and Heresy in Lyon," *Studies in Medieval and Renaissance History*, v (1968), 215-275. For more general treatments of growing concern with noble birth and purity of blood in sixteenth-century France, see Drouot, *Mayenne et la Bourgogne*, I, 32-33; Mandrou, *Introduction*, pp. 149-150, and Ellery Schalk, "The Appearance and Reality of Nobility in France during the Wars of Religion: An Example of How Collective Attitudes Can Change," *Journal of Modern History*, XLVIII, 1 (March, 1976), 19-31.

positions was less likely to be a benefit than a danger to the public welfare. As La Roche Flavin argued in the early seventeenth century, magistrates drawn from the lower classes were more likely to be seditious and indifferent to the general good. Despite his own bourgeois background, Claude Groulart seems to have shared this belief when he stressed (in a letter of 1602 to the chancellor) the benefits which the parlements derived "from the entry of youth of good family, properly brought up, whose ancestry obliges them to acquit themselves with dignity."[55] The lack of such a background, so ran the prevalent belief of the late sixteenth century, posed dangers of political irresponsibility and of judicial dishonesty. The events of the League themselves contributed to the process of hardening attitudes, at least so contemporaries thought. It was on the basis of what he had seen during the League that La Roche Flavin defended his view that magistrates drawn from the lower classes were dangerous to state and society.[56]

A parallel set of changes took place in the magistrates' attitudes to the official hierarchy itself during these years. After about 1550, their sense of different offices and professions as more or less honorable became more acute. The hierarchy of social values became more precisely defined, and the change was apparent in both rhetoric and behavior.

Above all, the prestige attaching to positions in the fiscal administration underwent a catastrophic decline; such positions ceased to be entirely respectable, and became instead mere stepping stones to higher offices. "It used to be," wrote Claude Groulart concerning the operation of the royal salt

[55] La Roche Flavin, *Treze livres*, p. 348; BN MS français 15898, f. 562r. Cf. Richelieu's comment that "venality should not be condemned because it excludes many *gens de basse condition* from offices and high positions; on the contrary, this is one of the things that render it more tolerable" (André, ed., *Testament politique*, p. 238).

[56] La Roche Flavin did concede that some great men had come from the lower classes, but nonetheless believed that the poor man was likely to be seditious and dishonest.

monopoly, "that there were honorable families in each city who lived from this trade"; but, by the time of his memoir, during the League itself, the monopoly had been taken over by tax farmers and had fallen into disrepute.[57] By the time of the League it was very unlikely that an "honorable family," or even one seeking such a reputation, would enter such a position.

Groulart's assessment of the changing prestige of such positions as the administration of the salt monopoly seems to have been accurate, for at least in Normandy in the mid-sixteenth century it had been entirely possible for highly respected families to undertake them. The history of the Becdelièvre, who remained a notable Rouennais family through nearly the whole of the old regime, offers one example. René de Becdelièvre, himself the son of a lesser financial official, entered the Parlement in 1512; by 1545, the year of his death, he was one of four councillors "believed to be the wealthiest of this city." Only one of his sons survived infancy, and he—in a choice that in later years would have been unthinkable—became the manager of the salt monopoly (*grenetier*) at Rouen. This step seems to have reflected the flexibility of social values during this period, for the family's wealth was notorious and its marriage connections excellent: René de Becdelièvre had married within the Parlement itself, and his son's wives were from the Rouennais and Parisian robe. The next generation followed more obviously acceptable careers, one of the *grenetier*'s sons becoming a gentleman of the king's chamber, the other a member of the Chambre des Comptes at Rouen, and in 1604 the family returned to the Parlement, where its members continued to serve through 1740.[58]

Social categories apparently were becoming more sharply defined in the later sixteenth century, and rankings of more

[57] BM MS Y202, f. 104v.
[58] Frondeville, *Les présidents*, 241-258; BM MS Y214, III, 138; BN Carrés de d'Hozier, 77; Tabel., 30 April 1542, 7 May 1558, 9 November 1574; Hérit. 2, 22 September 1574, 13 January 1595.

and less honorable positions were assuming new precision. Positions which in the mid-sixteenth century had been acceptable to the more important Rouennais families were increasingly perceived as the lower steps in a clear hierarchy of prestige.[59] Social advancement itself had lost much of its honorable quality, and was perceived as a danger to be repressed. The realities of social mobility at Rouen, in terms of the high official positions which were open to new men, had changed little by the time of the League; opportunities were in fact greater than they had been in the middle of the century. But the attitudes surrounding social mobility had indeed changed substantially, in the direction of greater harshness and of greater awareness of social distinctions.

Thus far we have been concerned mainly with changes internal to the magistracy. When contemporary theorists discussed the development of the officials as a social group, however, what mainly concerned them was the relationship between these officials and the established nobility, the *noblesse d'épée*. Richelieu was only one of several writers to complain of the expanding number and power of the officials, and to urge the crown to aid the older nobility in withstanding them.[60] His comments suggest that a central issue in understanding the social backgrounds of the magistrates and their social position is that of relations between "robe and sword," between the magistrates and the older nobility. Were offices in the Parlement essentially the mechanism by which new social groups challenged the prestige

[59] For discussion of this hierarchy, see for instance Roland Mousnier, ed., *Lettres et mémoires adressés au chancelier Séguier (1633-1649)*, 2 vols. (Paris, 1964), I, 168-169.

[60] André, ed., *Testament politique*, p. 218. For other noble complaints, Davis Bitton, *The French Nobility in Crisis, 1560-1640* (Stanford, 1969). For classic formulation of the initial opposition and ultimate alliance of magistrates and the older nobility, see Franklin Ford, *Robe and Sword: The Regrouping of the French Aristocracy after Louis XIV* (Cambridge, Mass., 1953); for criticism of it, Meyer, *La noblesse de Bretagne*, II, 929-930.

and power of the older nobility? How sharply felt were the social distinctions between the two groups (as opposed to the intellectual differences discussed in Chapter 1)?

What has been seen thus far of the magistrates' origins suggests already a qualified answer to these questions. The *parlementaires* were often drawn from the nobility itself, and they were closely bound to the great aristocracy, whose patronage had been the critical element in their families' rise to office. Many of the magistrates who were not noble themselves nonetheless came from the smaller towns of the province, thus from a background that was not very distant from the milieu of the lesser nobility. Statistics on the magistrates' origins, in other words, argue against our taking too seriously the opposition between robe and sword.

Other kinds of evidence give the same impression: the division between robe and sword was not the division between antithetical castes, but rather something far more flexible. For members of the Rouennais magistracy moved back and forth between careers in the robe and the sword with surprising ease—both over several generations and within the course of an individual's lifetime. A case of particular relevance here is that of the Le Jumel family, whose small-town origins were discussed above. After filling lower judicial positions at Evreux and serving in the Grand Conseil at Paris, Pierre Le Jumel entered the Parlement in 1571. Shortly before his death, his son (Nicolas) was received as a councillor in the Parlement, and he later became king's attorney. Seen in purely statistical terms, the Le Jumel thus appear to argue for the castelike nature of the Parlement's membership in the seventeenth century. In his speech urging the court to accept his son's candidacy, though, Pierre suggested the complexities which lay behind this apparently straightforward inheritance of career and status: ". . . Of the number of children which he had brought up," he said, "some, according to their inclinations, to fight in the army, others in the navy, for His Majesty's service, he has by now lost three. There remains to him the said Nicolas, who is disposed to continue the said service. He had been trained in the humanities (*nourry aux lettres*) until these most recent wars, when he discontinued his studies to follow and serve his Majesty in arms, both under the king's own command and under that of Monseigneur de Montpensier in Brittany. [His education] has given occasion to the said president to bring him back for the support and comfort of his old age."[61] As Pierre Le Jumel described it, his family's movement between what he called the "profession of arms" and the robe was a straightforward and unsurprising matter. His sons had simply followed careers "according to their inclinations."

Nor were the Le Jumel an isolated instance of such movement. Gilles Charles, younger brother of a councillor in the Parlement, was educated in the law and eventually became a lawyer in the court. Between his education and his career at the bar, however, "he was equipped with arms and horses, and sent to the company of light cavalry of Monsieur de Laigre," in the early 1580's. Jacques II de Bauquemare was the son of the Parlement's first president, and served several years as a councillor in the court. During the League, however, he turned to a military career, and became governor of the military garrison in Rouen. He retained this position (and with it a handsome pension from the crown) for fifteen years. The brothers Jacques and Jean Dyel, councillors respectively in the Parlement and Cour des Aides at Rouen, took a similarly active role in the military engagements of the League. They fortified their country house and briefly held it against a *ligueur* army. Later they joined the king's army, and participated in the Battle of Arques.[62]

---

[61] Reg. sec., 1593-1594 (Caen), f. 26.

[62] Hérit. 2, 21 December 1601; Frondeville, *Les présidents*, 65-66; BN Pièces Originales, 277, no. 10; Robert d'Estaintot, *La ligue en Normandie, 1588-1594* (Paris-Rouen-Caen, 1862), 62-63. See also M. Burel, *La commune de Limésy, souvenirs du passé* . . . (Rouen, 1899), p. 66, for Adrien Toustain's moving from a military career to one in the Parlement, and Frondeville, *Les conseillers* i, 2, for the similar

Such fluidity of careers was encouraged by the fact that in Normandy neither law nor language strengthened social distinctions. In contrast to some other French provinces, Norman provincial law made no distinction between nobleman and commoner. Inheritance procedures were the same for each, and were determined by the kinds of property the individual owned, not by his personal status.[63] Noblemen might demand that their legal cases be tried before special chambers of the Parlement or of other courts, but this was true for royal officials, and for many others as well.[64] Inhabitants of Rouen enjoyed further privileges associated with nobility. They did not pay the *taille*, the principal royal tax, and they were exempt from the *francs fiefs*, the tax which the crown levied on commoners who held fiefs. Freedom from the latter tax must have been especially gratifying, for it represented (in the words of a twentieth-century historian) the "single juridical difference which is essential, incontestable and universal between the nobleman and the commoner"; it was largely on the basis of this freedom that the Rouennais claimed to have "always enjoyed the rights of nobility, 'as if they were nobles, born and descended from noble lineage.'" In fact the Rouennais' privileges may well have exceeded those of the rural nobility, since residents of the city were free from the feudal levy, an event

career of Robert Destain. Families' claims to military backgrounds (as opposed to the individual careers noted here) have been discussed above, p. 61; for other such instances, see also BM MS Y214, III, 24 (Postel), and Angot des Retours, "Epitaphier des Vauquelin."

[63] Thus the late-seventeenth-century lawyer Henri Basnage: ". . . la Coutume n'a point mis de distinction entre les personnes . . ." (*Oeuvres*, 2 vols. [4th ed., Rouen, 1778], I, 396). Cf. the situation in Brittany, in which taking part in a *partage noble* was itself proof of nobility: Meyer, *La noblesse de Bretagne*, I, 108ff.

[64] Criminal cases involving noblemen were to be tried in the Grand' Chambre rather than in the normal criminal chamber, the Tournelle; and some noblemen could bring their civil cases in the first instance to the court's Chambre des Requêtes.

whose meaning had become entirely fiscal by the later six-teenth century.[65]

Thus, in terms of law and privilege there were few real differences between noblemen and commoners who resided in the provincial capital; even for those in the countryside and the smaller towns, the differences were mainly fiscal. The language which sixteenth-century speakers used in speaking of social distinctions corresponded to this state of affairs. As during the later centuries of the old regime, the titles which were in use in sixteenth-century Normandy were abundant and flowery. They seem to offer the possi-bility for distinguishing between the real nobility, who re-served for themselves the title "esquire" (*écuyer*), and the urban notables or rising families, forced to content them-selves with the less honorable "*noble homme.*"[66] But in fact

---

[65] J.-R. Bloch, *L'anoblissement en France au temps de François Ier* (Paris, 1934), p. 214; C. de Robillard de Beaurepaire, *Inventaire som-maire des archives communales antérieures à 1790. Ville de Rouen. Délibérations* (Rouen, 1887), p. 187. For the eagerness with which fief holders might claim the status of "bourgeois de Rouen," in order to avoid serving in the feudal call up, G.-A. Prévost, ed., "Docu-ments sur le ban et l'arrière ban, et les fiefs de la vicomté de Rouen en 1594 et 1560, et sur la noblesse du bailliage de Gisors en 1703," *Mélanges, Société de l'histoire de Normandie*, 3e série (1895), pp. 231-423, pp. 241-332; for complaints about the fiscal functions to which the *ban* and *arrière ban* had been reduced, François de La Noue, *Discours politiques et militaires*, ed. F. E. Sutcliffe (Geneva, 1967), p. 274. For a more general sense of the uncertainties which surrounded noble status in sixteenth-century Normandy, see Josias Bérault's debate with Denis Godefroy, a sixteenth-century commen-tator on the Norman custom: ". . . Godefroy is quite wrong to say . . . that he includes among the nobles those who by common ac-ceptance (*soufrances*) and merit use the quality of nobility, and are born from a father and maternal grandfather who have followed military careers (*ayant profession d'armes*) or served the public in some honorable position . . ." (*La coustume reformée*, p. 120).

[66] For application of this distinction, see Roland Mousnier et al., *Problèmes de stratification sociale: deux cahiers de la noblesse pour les États généraux de 1649-1651* (Paris, 1965), pp. 7-49; Mousnier, *La vénalité des offices*, pp. 542-549; and George Huppert, *Les bour-*

such distinctions did not operate in Normandy. Terms of address were elaborate, but they reflected personal position and function rather than birth. Some examples from Rouennais notarial practice illustrate the character of these distinctions:

". . . *noble homme* Herculles de Vieupont lord of Richeville residing at Neubourg, with power of attorney from *hault et puissant seigneur* Alexandre de Vieupont, lord and baron of Le Neubourg, his older brother." (1587)

". . . *nobles hommes* David and Marin Dumont, brothers, younger children of the late Master Nicolle Dumont, in his lifetime *escuier* lord of La Motte." (1604)

". . . *noble homme* Master Laurens Godefroy councillor in the said court (of Parlement) . . . the late Robert Godefroy *escuier* lord of Ponthion his brother. . . ." (1602)

"Robert Le Cordier *escuyer bourgeoys* merchant residing in the parish of St. Candre the Young of this city of Rouen." (1586)[67]

"Esquire" and "*noble homme*" had complex meanings in the sixteenth century, not all of which we can recover. But it is plain that in Normandy they did not refer to differences of prestige or birth. Brothers might hold different titles, a distinction that was apparently one between older—the heir to the family's chief property—and younger, or between a brother entering royal service and one staying in the countryside. A father might be an *écuyer* and his sons *nobles hommes*; or an individual might combine the title of esquire with the apparently antithetical title of "merchant and bourgeois."

We have seen that in career, legal rights, and titles differences between robe and sword were far less acute than his-

geois Gentilshommes: An Essay on the Definition of Elites in Renaissance France (Chicago, 1977). All of these studies recognize the special forms of address used in sixteenth-century Normandy.

[67] Hérit. 2, 4 February 1586, 28 February 1604, 23 January 1602, 7 November 1586.

torians have often suggested. Robe and sword noblemen came from the same milieux, and might establish their sons in similar careers; they shared social concepts that continually blurred the differences between them. When we have said all this, however, we are left with a residue of tension and conflict between the two groups. At the level of literary culture, tension found expression in innumerable tracts and pieces of social analysis, for instance in Richelieu's *Political Testament*. Officials themselves offered no comments of comparable bitterness, but they responded with the well-worn themes of the superiority of learning over mere force and the importance of virtue for governing the state.[68]

At Rouen such tensions manifested themselves in frequent and sometimes violent conflict. Conflict might take place within a context that testified to the fundamental equality of the two groups, as when duels erupted between *nobles d'épée* and sons of *robins*.[69] More humiliating conflicts also took place. In 1578 a councillor on horseback near the city, who had ridden out "to relax in the countryside and take the air and pass the time," encountered a group of armed noblemen. They forced him to the side of the road, demanded to know who he was, and threatened him when he sought to avoid telling them, despite his protests that they "could see from his clothing that he was a man of peace." When finally he gave them his name, residence, and "his quality of councillor in this court, which is one of the greatest honors which he could have," his assailants' irritation increased. One of them, so the councillor reported to his colleagues, "told him that he was a rogue and a fool and one of those little rogues who, because of their positions, want to strut around and pretend they know everything, repeating these words several times"; it was only his self-restraint, the nobleman said, that prevented him from passing to actions, and beating the councillor with his stick. The two parties

---

[68] André, ed., *Testament politique*, p. 218; Roland Mousnier, *L'assassinat d'Henri IV* (Paris, 1964), pp. 237-266.

[69] Reg. sec., 1593-1594 (Caen), f. 181.

separated before this could happen, but the councillor received the warning that he had spoken with the governor of the city, and that in future he should show more respect.[70]

Such events, it seems, were not extraordinary. Almost exactly a decade later, another councillor had a similar encounter with another of the city's captains, who appeared at his house with twelve soldiers. The soldiers again expressed their unflattering view of the magistracy. "Those beggars the councillors," the captain told the outraged councillor, "have no hesitation about condemning soldiers to hang, even if they don't deserve it, and there wasn't a soldier alive who was not worth more than the best of the councillors."[71] Gentler expression of the same tensions may be seen in Henry IV's amusement at Claude Groulart's fearfulness when, on a visit to the king, he found himself near an actual battle.[72]

Clearly these were real conflicts; on occasion, robe and sword might clash violently. Yet the terms in which this conflict was expressed deserve emphasis. Neither magistrates nor soldiers spoke in terms of caste or even of inaccessible social orders. Rather, they spoke of the opposition between soldier and civilian. The question of nobility was either muted or simply absent: the soldiers at Rouen viewed themselves as a single group, of which the great aristocrats present in the city were only the leaders, and within which a common outlook prevailed.[73]

French glorification of arms represented a deeply rooted theme to those who considered the society, from Castiglione, who reported that "the French recognize only the nobility of arms and reckon all the rest as nought," to Chateau-

[70] Reg. sec., 1573-1579, ff. 575ff (21 April 1578).

[71] Reg. sec., 1589, 1595, 1569, 1570 (bound as one register), f. 48.

[72] D'Estaintot, *La ligue en Normandie.*

[73] Cf. Monluc's comments about the contrast between robe and sword (quoted above, Chapter 1) and Claude Groulart's satisfaction in *"cette vie civile et douce"* (BN MS français 15898, f. 553r).

briand's pained speculations on how his father would have responded to his own literary successes: "A literary renown would have wounded his country gentleman's pride [*sa gentilhommerie*]. He would have seen only a degeneration in his son's talents; even my embassy to Berlin, conquest of the pen, not of the sword, would scarcely have pleased him."[74] Daily experience at Rouen, in the kinds of conflicts that have been described here, directly translated this respect for arms, without, however, giving to the pursuit of arms a hereditary character. Intense conflict between arms and letters, between robe and sword, in no way interfered with a continual movement of individuals back and forth between the two pursuits, nor with an equal amount of familiarity between soldiers and magistrates.

An overview of the social origins and of the evolving social position of the magistrates in the sixteenth and early seventeenth centuries may now be attempted. From a statistical perspective, what has been seen here is first the remarkable growth in the numbers of Rouen's *noblesse de robe* over the sixteenth century, and of the numbers of *parlementaires* especially. In the same years that their numbers grew, the geographical range of recruitment diminished; by the later sixteenth century, only a handful of the magistrates came from outside the province. The combined effect of these changes was to give the magistrates a more powerful position within provincial society. Local recruitment meant more support from family within the region, and a more independent, more secure, economic position. Statistical study of the social origins of the magistrates shows a comparable but somewhat later narrowing in the social range from which they were recruited. After about 1588 the proportion of the magistrates whose fathers had not been members of the sovereign courts fell off sharply, in the early

[74] B. Castiglione, *The Courtier*, trans. Charles Singleton (Garden City, 1959), p. 67; Chateaubriand, *Mémoires d'outre tombe*, 2 vols. (Bibliothèque de la Pléiade, Paris, 1946-1948), I, 121.

seventeenth century to about one-third of the total. Finally, we have seen here the relatively small role of the urban rich in supplying members to the Parlement, and the much larger importance of essentially rural groups: members of the lesser gentry and officials from the lesser centers of both royal and seigneurial government. Families whose roots were in this milieu, rather than in the bourgeoisie of Rouen itself, were the norm among the magistrates. Probably such families were numerically preponderant, although inadequate documentation makes this a somewhat tentative conclusion; such families were certainly preponderant among the most influential and successful members of the Parlement. This pattern of recruitment was largely responsible for the fact that by the later sixteenth century about half of the Parlement's membership were in one sense or another noblemen, and noblemen of relatively long standing.[75]

The second approach used in this chapter—that of considering in more detail the mechanisms of family advancement—provides a means of understanding the importance of rural noblemen and small-town officials within the Parlement. For what such an examination shows is the overwhelming importance of patronage in shaping the rise of families to the high magistracy. Venality of office was practiced from the mid-sixteenth century (at least), but in ways that were suited to the exercise of aristocratic patronage; prices of offices, as we shall see, were sufficiently low that market conditions alone did not suffice to select those who could and could not acquire offices. Money could speak only if it was accompanied by influence at court, and this was exercised by a series of great aristocrats who owned estates in upper Normandy. Not unnaturally, their patronage went first to those who were nearby: to their own officials

[75] This is especially clear-cut if those who were noble by virtue of their families' service in high offices are included: see François Bluche and Pierre Durye, *L'anoblissement par charges avant 1789*, 2 vols. (La Roche sur Yonne, 1962), II, 15-17.

and lawyers, to neighboring esquires and feudal dependents. In comparison with the force of patronage, other plausible keys to family success were of relatively minor importance. Economic and familial dimensions of success must await consideration in later chapters; here we have seen the small importance of loyalty to the crown during its sixteenth-century trials. In Normandy those families who rose to high position during the century's most serious conflict, the League, owed their success to the rebellious *ligueurs*. In cases like these, the superior value of aristocratic patronage over royalist loyalty was publicly and decisively demonstrated.

Finally, this chapter has sought to step outside the immediate context of the *noblesse de robe*, and to inquire into contemporary perceptions of social categories and movement between them. During most of the sixteenth century in Normandy, we have seen, social differences were not so marked as they were to become later. Magistrates did not see positions in the fiscal administration as dishonorable, and they seem to have accepted the advancement of individuals from lower social orders into their own. Relations between the magistrates and the *noblesse d'épée* showed a similar fluidity. Both families and individuals moved easily between robe and sword careers, and the real differences between nobility and commoners were slight: law, social terminology, and common practice conspired to minimize these differences. Such fluidity did not mean an absence of conflicts between robe and sword. At Rouen conflict was a commonplace event, and it might involve the expression of considerable bitterness. But this was not conflict between two hereditary social orders. It was, rather, conflict between two professional models and, by implication, between models of youthfulness and of age. At Rouen conflicts between soldiers and judges seems to have fitted precisely Blaise de Monluc's surprise and scorn that fine young men could submit to the constraints of judicial behavior, rather than giving free rein to their impulses by following a military life: the conflict was between all soldiers, whatever their birth, and *"ces coquins de conseillers."*[76]

From the late sixteenth century onward, the magistrates' acceptance of social fluidity tended to diminish. Their sense of social categories became more clearly fixed, and the value they placed on high birth grew. Changing attitudes seem to have preceded changes in the facts of social mobility, for only in the early seventeenth century did the Parlement become overwhelmingly a hereditary institution.

What has been seen here, then, is a paradoxical process of social change, a process in which major changes were accompanied by important elements of continuity. On the one hand, the *noblesse de robe* at Rouen was essentially a new fact in the sixteenth century. The *parlementaires* and their colleagues in the city's other sovereign courts by 1600 were of far greater numerical importance than the influential provincial gentry. On the other hand, we have seen here the important continuities which lay beneath this apparently cataclysmic social change. The formation of a *noblesse de robe* in sixteenth-century Normandy did not seriously threaten the position of the established nobility, whether of the courtly aristocracy or of the poorer gentry. The former retained firm control over the recruitment and advancement of families within the robe, while the latter supplied a substantial percentage of the membership of at least the Parlement. In this sense, the continued vigor of existing social arrangements through the sixteenth century is more striking than the changes involved in the development of the *noblesse de robe*.

[76] Cf. Mousnier, *Problèmes de stratification sociale*, for the view that early modern France was a "society of orders" midway between a caste society and a modern society of economic classes. Closer to the views offered here are those of Boris Porchnev, Pierre Goubert, and Denis Richet, summarized in Richet, *La France Moderne*, pp. 101-102.

THREE

PARLEMENTAIRE WEALTH

CONTEMPORARIES believed the *noblesse de robe* to be very wealthy, especially in comparison with the military nobility. "The opulence and pride of the officials," wrote Richelieu in the 1630's, "enable them to take gainful advantage of the nobles, rich only in a courage which leads them freely to proffer their lives to the state." As Richelieu and other commentators saw it, the problem was not merely that the magistrates might often have more money than the military noblemen. More serious was the fact that members of the parlements and other high courts were extending their influence into the countryside, buying up estates which once had belonged to the military nobility, and as a result were changing a wide range of established social relationships. Explanations for the officials' success both in accumulating wealth and in invading the countryside were somewhat less clear, but La Noue, Richelieu, and others offered several possibilities: the exorbitant profits of office, economic attitudes that were grasping and careful, the inadequately rational economic attitudes of the military nobility themselves.[1]

Examination of the magistrates' wealth points in two directions. There is, first, what may be called an internal perspective. It is important to understand the economic possi-

---

[1] Louis André, ed., *Cardinal de Richelieu, Testament politique* (Paris, 1947), p. 218. See also the views summarized by Davis Bitton, *The French Nobility in Crisis, 1560-1640* (Stanford, 1969), and the development given these themes by Marc Bloch, *French Rural History. An Essay on its Basic Characteristics*, trans. Janet Sondheimer (Berkeley, 1966), pp. 117-143, and Lucien Febvre, *Philippe II et la Franche Comté. Étude d'histoire politique, religieuse et sociale* (2nd ed., Paris, 1970), pp. 170-198.

bilities and pressures which the magistrates confronted. But it is equally important, as Richelieu's comments suggest, to place the magistrates within the economic structure of the society as a whole, and in particular to understand the economic impact which the growth of the *noblesse de robe* had on rural society, the stronghold of the *noblesse d'épée*. It is necessary to inquire into the size and nature of the magistrates' own wealth, but also to ask how their wealth compared with that of other groups, whether they managed their properties in ways similar to or different from other groups, what kinds of relationships they had with other groups in the countryside.[2] These are the subjects with which the following chapters will be concerned. This chapter will consider the amount and nature of *parlementaire* wealth, and the contribution which office made to it; Chapter 4 will consider landed wealth and the relationships which it created; and Chapter 5 will consider the interrelated problems of expenditures, indebtedness, and the economic successes and failures of families over extended periods.

How wealthy were the *parlementaires*? There are no sources which would permit an answer to this question for the group as a whole. Instead, we need to rely on the information supplied by the probate records and account books of individual magistrates, and at best these offer a limited view.[3] Such documents survive for only thirty-two of the

[2] See the important discussion of these issues by Roland Mousnier: "Problèmes de méthode dans l'étude des structures sociales des XVIe, XVIIe, XVIIIe siècles," repr. in Mousnier, *La plume, la faucille et le marteau. Institutions et société en France du Moyen Age à la Révolution* (Paris, 1970), pp. 12-26.

[3] A few statistical sources exist, especially with regard to the revenues of feudal property, but these must be used with extreme caution, for the values they supply appear often to have been purely conventional. For one example of the disparity between actual income from a property and the value assigned to it in royal tax documents, cf. La Riv. Bourdet, 2698 with G.-A. Prévost, ed., "Documents sur le

more than three hundred magistrates who served in the court in the sixteenth century, and often they fail to provide precise estimates of either income or wealth. In this instance as in so many others, moreover, our sources are consistently biased, in favor of the most successful and solidly established *parlementaire* families.

For all their limitations, however, these sources allow us to establish a range of characteristic *parlementaire* fortunes and to discern certain typical patterns in the ways that this wealth was invested. Precise data on the thirty-two *parlementaire* fortunes that can be clearly analyzed are set out in Appendix B, and do not require detailed recapitulation here. Here we shall be concerned with the broad conclusions that emerge from the data of Appendix B. We shall first consider the magistrates' private fortunes; then, in the second half of this chapter, we shall consider the revenues they received from office.

The first conclusion to be stressed concerns the approximate size of fortunes. The possible range among the fortunes of different magistrates was large: in the late sixteenth century it extended from the meager fortune of the councillor Nicolas Caillot (d. 1588), worth about 8,000ł, to the

---

ban et l'arrière ban, et les fiefs de la vicomté de Rouen en 1594 et 1560, et sur la noblesse du bailliage de Gisors en 1703," *Mélanges, Société de l'Histoire de Normandie*, III (1895), 231-423, 229, showing documents of the *ban* to have underestimated revenues by a factor of fourteen.

For a similar example, compare the *aveux* for the seigneurie of Belbeuf with accounts for the property: AD S-M, 16J204 (*aveu* of 1565, claiming that the property was worth 160ł yearly, and of 1572, claiming its worth as 200ł yearly), 16J178 (accounts showing the property to be worth 1,400ł in 1597). Even with regard to those magistrates about whom adequate documents survive, it is usually impossible to move from the rough estimates that the sources supply of gross income to precise ideas of disposable incomes. In Chapter 5, below, the attempt will be made to assess the fixed charges weighing on most *parlementaire* fortunes, and by that means to estimate disposable incomes.

first president Claude Groulart's huge landed estate, worth about 375,000ł at his death in 1607.[4] Despite these variations, however, the wealth of most magistrates tended to cluster within a narrower range. In the early sixteenth century, among the first generation of magistrates, incomes tended to be around 500ł annually. Thereafter, typical *parlementaire* incomes rose steadily, reflecting changes we shall consider below: the profits of office itself and the advantages enjoyed by large landowners in the mid-sixteenth century. In the 1520's, the incomes of magistrates appear typically to have been about 1,000ł annually; in the 1540's the typical income had risen to 2,000-3,000ł, and at least one magistrate had an income of over 10,000ł. By the 1570's and 1580's, 5,000ł had become the norm, and incomes of over 10,000ł were no longer rare. Precise translation of these figures into estimates of wealth is impossible.[5] For all their imprecision, though, the examples available suggest a fairly clear progression in the size of *parlementaire* fortunes. Those of the first quarter of the sixteenth century seem rarely to have exceeded 10,000-15,000ł, but fortunes steadily increased in value thereafter. By the 1580's fortunes worth about 100,000ł were common, and several magistrates' wealth was much greater, in the range of 250,000ł.

Variation in the sources of this income—in the kinds of investments from which the magistrates lived—was as impressive as differences in the size of their fortunes. Three

[4] On the Caillot, Hérit. 2, 5 January 1591; on Groulart, Meubles 2, 6 November 1613, 19 November 1613; La Riv. Bourdet, 1372; Bibliothèque Municipale, Dieppe, MS 63.

[5] I have followed here contemporary assumptions about the capital value of various kinds of income sources: *rentes hypothèques* were capitalized at ten times their yearly value, *rentes foncières* at twenty times, land at twenty times, and seigneuries at twenty-five times. For an example of these assumptions, see the organization of the first sales of church lands, in 1563: AN G8 1246. Such assumptions oversimplify the workings of the land market in the mid-sixteenth century, as will be seen below, in Chapter 4; they are sufficient for the estimates here, however.

principal forms of investment were available. One was land, in the form both of fiefs and of peasant tenures; a second was urban real estate, especially houses at Rouen; and the third was bonds (*rentes constituées*), both on individuals and on the state.[6] Examples can be found of magistrates whose fortunes were invested exclusively or nearly so in each of these categories. As with the size of the fortunes of magistrates, though, this wide variation conceals a clear central tendency. Of the twenty-five fortunes which we are able to analyze in these terms, thirteen depended for about two-thirds of their value on land or on rights attached to the land; five others depended for about half of their value on land. Moreover, this predominance of landed fortunes held true from the earliest years of the court's existence. Five of the six examples of *parlementaire* fortunes from the first decade of the sixteenth century show magistrates who depended for all or most of their income on landed properties; three of the five owned no property at all in Rouen, not even their own residences.[7]

Clear relations existed between the size and the character of magistrates' estates. The less wealthy the family, the more likely they were to invest their money in private and government bonds and in urban real estate, for these could be expected to bring substantially higher returns than landed property and posed fewer administrative costs and problems as well.[8] There was also a connection between family an-

[6] There are no indications that the magistrates had any investments whatsoever in commerce, banking, and the like, although the idea that such pursuits were incompatible with noble status was relatively new in the sixteenth century. See Philippe Wolff, *Commerces et marchands de Toulouse (vers 1350-vers 1450)* (Paris, 1954), p. 539; and Robert Boutrouche, ed., *Bordeaux de 1453 à 1719* (Bordeaux, 1966), pp. 162-183.

[7] The nature of their properties thus fits closely with what has been seen of the magistrates' geographical and social origins.

[8] On the *rentes* in general, see Bernard Schnapper, *Les rentes au XVIe siècle. Histoire d'un instrument de crédit* (Paris, 1957); on the appeal they might have specifically to new families, Ralph Giesey,

tiquity and the extent of investment in rural properties. At Rouen as throughout France during the old regime, families tended to dispose of urban properties as they advanced in social status, and to turn their attention to more respectable investments in the land. This process has been documented in the case of the Civille, a family of great Rouennais merchants of Spanish origin, who entered the Parlement in 1554: as they moved closer to the Parlement, in the middle years of the century, the family sold most of their urban real estate.[9] A similar transition may be seen in the case of the Puchot family. Vincent Puchot, a successful Rouennais merchant, died in 1566, and most of his fortune was invested in government and personal bonds; these made up 71 percent of the total. During the ten years' minority of Vincent's children, most of the estate's income went to further purchases of *rentes*. Forty-five years later, at the death of the *parlementaire* Pierre Puchot, the family's fortune looked very different. Bonds of all kinds had fallen in importance to 40 percent of Pierre's income and about 28 percent of his total capital; land accounted for 48 percent of his income and 58 percent of his capital. The Civille and Puchot illustrate a characteristic economic history. As their status rose, they shifted their investments from the city to the land.[10]

Such shifts were not unusual among Rouen's magistrates,

"Rules of Inheritance and Strategies of Mobility in Prerevolutionary France," *The American Historical Review*, LXXXII, 2 (April, 1977), 271-289. Some problems surrounding the *rentes* will receive attention below, in Chapter 5.

[9] Christiane Douyère, *Une famille rouennaise d'origine espagnole à la fin du 15ᵉ et au 16ᵉ siècle: les Civille (1484-vers 1600). Schéma d'une assimilation* (Mémoire de maîtrise, Université de Paris, 1973), pp. 114-115.

[10] La Riv. Bourdet, 1967, 3316; Tabel., 21 September 1569, 28 January 1577. For classic discussions of this pattern of social ascent during the old regime, see Febvre, *Philippe II et la Franche Comté*, pp. 189-194; Gaston Roupnel, *La ville et la compagne au XVIIᵉ siècle. Étude sur les populations des pays dijonnais* (2nd ed., Paris, 1955), pp. 199ff.

but (insofar as the sources allow us to judge) they did not represent the predominant pattern. Reflecting the magistrates' rural and small-town origins discussed in Chapter 2, most *parlementaire* fortunes began as predominantly rural and remained so as the family advanced to higher positions. Economic continuity, it seems, was more common than the kind of transition illustrated by the Civille and the Puchot. An especially clear instance of continuity is provided by the Maignart family, who supplied the Parlement with a councillor in 1499 and a succession of presidents from 1600 on (the intervening two generations served in Rouen's Cour des Aides). Between Guillaume Maignart's entry in the Parlement in 1499 and the entry of his great-grandson Charles in 1600, the family's wealth increased enormously. Guillaume begun his career with an income of about 400ł, while Charles' landed income amounted to about 7,500ł (he also received about 5,200ł in *rentes*). All but one of Charles' estates, however, had been in the family's hands since the time of Guillaume—that is, for nearly a century. As we shall see, these estates had undergone important changes during the century the Maignart owned them. The family had continually added small pieces of land to them, making them far more valuable than they had originally been. What is important here, though, is the fact that the core of the family's landed wealth came as an inheritance from the fifteenth century, not as a series of new acquisitions. This was a pattern repeated in the history of several other *parlementaire* fortunes: the early establishment of a nucleus of estates, to which later generations might add substantial amounts of land. Patterns of ownership in this sense reflected what has been seen of the magistrates' origins.[11]

Thus far we have necessarily relied on the indications supplied by a relatively small number of cases—those magistrates whose inheritance records or personal accounts have

[11] La Riv. Bourdet, 516, 539, 2105. For discussion of this pattern, below, Chapter 4, part c.

survived. Fortunately, it is possible to provide some con-
firmation of what has been seen thus far by considering
some broader, more statistical, sources: the evidence on
parlementaire residences considered above in Chapter 1,
and documents concerning ownership of government and
private bonds. These are of particular use in considering
the qualitative aspects of *parlementaire* fortunes, the kinds
of investments in which they were placed. Urban real
estate, from the evidence available, was not an important
source of most magistrates' wealth: as was seen above, a
considerable number of magistrates (more than half in the
1540's) did not own even their own residences in Rouen.[12]

It is possible to say the same of a second important form
of wealth, bonds issued by both the government and private
citizens. These *rentes constituées* were an invention of the
mid-sixteenth century, and they offered the attraction of a
high rate of return: 10 percent at Rouen during most of the
century. But there were also problems with the *rentes*.
The crown was from the beginning ready to delay interest
payments, or even to default on its loans altogether. As
will be discussed in more detail below in Chapter 5, sixteenth-century legal changes tended likewise to improve the
borrower's position, and might make it difficult for lenders
to recover either interest or principal—at least without extensive legal efforts.[13] Perhaps for these reasons, the *parlementaires* as a group invested little in the *rentes*, either
public or private. Table 3:1 summarizes the interest payments made by the regional treasury (*recette générale*) in
Rouen in 1578, and it suggests the small place which the
magistrates held in comparison with other social groups
as investors in these government bonds. Neither in terms of
the Parlement's total membership nor in terms of the magis-

---

[12] Above, p. 55.

[13] For delays in payment and other problems with government
rentes, see Jacques Permezel, *La politique financière de Sully dans la
généralité de Lyon* (Lyon, 1935). The problems surrounding private
rentes are discussed below, Chapter 5.

TABLE 3:1
CROWN BONDS AT ROUEN, 1578

Yearly Interest	Parlementaires	Others	Total
50-99ł	7 (3.6%)	187 (96.4%)	194
100-199ł	11 (8.4%)	120 (91.6%)	131
200-299ł	4 (12.7%)	27 (87.3%)	31
300ł and above	0 (0%)	21 (100%)	21
Total	22 (5.8%)	355 (94.2%)	377

SOURCE: BM MS Y111.

trates' place among Rouennais lenders was *parlementaire* lending to the crown a phenomenon of real importance. Only about one-fourth of the court's members received any income at all from the *rentes* on the general treasury, and none of those received as much as 300ł yearly: in other words, well under 10 percent of most *parlementaire* incomes. Other crown bonds did exist at Rouen, on the salt monopoly and on the indirect taxes, but the example of the general treasury sufficiently suggests the magistrates' reluctance to involve themselves very deeply in this form of investment.[14]

They appear to have been somewhat more willing to invest in *rentes* to private individuals, but here too there was considerable reluctance. We shall consider in greater detail both the institutional context and the magistrates' actual practice with regard to the *rentes* below in Chapter 5, and here we need only point to some of the main results of that inquiry. Members of the Parlement simply took little part in the lending of funds before the late sixteenth century: in 1557, 1567, and 1577 they loaned on average 8.6 percent of the funds loaned at Rouen by means of the *rentes*—well under one-half of the amount loaned, for instance, by members of Rouen's patriciate. As we shall see, moreover, such loans tended to be perceived more as a service than an investment: consistently about half of the

[14] Cf. Schnapper, *Les rentes*, pp. 160-161, 172.

money which the magistrates loaned went to members of the legal and official professions, in other words, to members of their immediate social group.[15]

Statistics of this kind confirm what the example of *parlementaire* fortunes can only suggest. They do not inform us directly about the magistrates' investments in rural property, but they do indicate the relative insignificance to them of the principal alternatives, urban real estate and the various forms of government and private bonds which the sixteenth century offered. There are no comparable statistics which would allow us to test what we have seen about the size of the fortunes of the magistrates. What can be done, though, is to place their wealth in a comparative view. Comparing their wealth with that of other social groups will not necessarily permit greater numerical precision about the value of their patrimonies, but it will permit more firmly based ideas about orders of magnitude—and it should supply a better understanding of the meaning which figures of income and wealth held.

Let us begin by asking where the range of *parlementaire* incomes that have been seen thus far would place the magistrates in relation to other groups. A first comparison is to be made with the Parisian magistracy, especially with the members of the Parlement of Paris. From the vantage point of Paris, the Rouennais magistrates must have seemed relatively impoverished. According to the studies of Denis Richet, the normal fortune for members of the Paris Parlement in 1560 was between 100 and 120,000₶; wealthier magistrates, such as the councillor Pierre Séguier, might have much larger fortunes, in Seguier's case of about 500,-000₶. On the eve of the Wars of Religion, it seems, the Parisian magistrates were about twice as wealthy as their Norman colleagues. Only the wealthiest Rouennais magistrates had fortunes that approached the normal fortunes of the Parisians. The contrast appears to have retained its force

[15] Below, Chapter 5.

through the early seventeenth century; only the very wealthiest Rouennais magistrates, such as the first president Claude Groulart, held fortunes that were comparable to those of the Séguier, Lefèvre d'Ormesson, and other important Parisian families.[16]

Equally striking is the relative modesty of the *parlementaires'* wealth in comparison with that of sixteenth-century merchants, both at Rouen and in the rest of France. One contemporary observer, writing in the 1580's, believed that there were residents of Rouen with incomes of 30,-000ł, and that those with 10,000ł yearly were to be found "in great numbers." Few if any magistrates would have been among this favored group; even in 1600 there probably were only a handful of presidents and other leading members of the court whose incomes reached 10,000ł. Our observer probably exaggerated the wealth of Rouen's merchants, but the example of the Nantais merchant André Ruiz suggests that there was nothing impossible about the figures. Ruiz left a fortune evaluated at 200,000ł at his death in 1577, and there were undoubtedly Rouennais merchants as wealthy as he.[17]

Comparison with the upper nobility suggests much the same picture. Robe fortunes seem especially small, of course, when set against the fortunes of the highest level of the French aristocracy, the "dukes and peers." For the period 1589-1624, according to J.-P. Labatut, the mean fortune of the dukes who were unconnected to the royal house was

[16] The results of Richet's research have thus far been presented only in Roland Mousnier, ed., *Lettres et mémoires addressés au chancelier Séguier (1633-1649)*, 2 vols. (Paris, 1964), I, 26-38; see also I, 112-183, for the economic position of the masters of requests; M. Chéruel, ed., *Le journal d'Olivier Lefèvre d'Ormesson . . .*, 2 vols. (Paris, 1860), I, xix.

[17] Charles de Bourgueville, *Les recherches et antiquitez de la province de Neustrie, à présent de Normandie* (2nd ed., Caen, 1833), p. 43; Henri Lapeyre, *Une famille de marchands: Les Ruiz* (Paris, 1955), p. 63.

on the order of 800,000ł; average wealth of the princely families was about twice this amount.[18] Again, however, the two ranges of wealth did overlap. The wealthiest Rouennais magistrates—Claude Groulart, Charles Maignart—had fortunes that equalled those of the poorest "dukes and peers."

In the later sixteenth century some of the magistrates stood on a position of near equality with a second group within the aristocracy, the solidly established provincial aristocracy, those families who dominated provincial society and who had the resources needed for occasional forays into the world of courtly life and politics. Such a figure, for instance, was Blaise de Monluc, the Catholic military leader who described his fortune in the 1570's, after his long career of military success, as worth about 10,000ł yearly. In upper Normandy itself there was the Roncherolles family, whose lands brought an income of about 10,000ł in 1570—though to this sum must be added the pensions which the family received from the crown. That such an income may be taken as characteristic for the well-to-do provincial gentry is suggested by the remarks of a later seventeenth-century intendant about "the principal noble houses of the region" of upper Normandy. Most of these families were described as having incomes in the range of 15-25,000ł in the 1660's—in view of rising prices during the seventeenth century, roughly the equivalent of the incomes we have described as characterizing the solid provincial nobility.[19]

[18] Jean-Pierre Labatut, *Les ducs et pairs de France au XVIIe siècle. Étude sociale* (Paris, 1972), pp. 248-249.

[19] Blaise de Monluc, *Commentaires, 1521-1576* (Bibliothèque de la Pléiade, Paris, 1964), p. 16; Monluc's claim is of particular interest not because it was necessarily accurate (he was defending himself against charges of profiting from his official positions) but precisely because he was seeking to show his position to be that of an honest country gentleman—an income of 10-12,000ł was at least what he thought such a figure ought to have. Hérit. 2, 20 July 1570, 16 February 1571; AD S-M, E, Fonds Baronnie du Pont St. Pierre, Accounts,

Contemporary complaints about aristocratic impoverishment vis à vis the *parlementaires* and other officials were hardly justified insofar as this group was concerned. Though some magistrates in the later sixteenth century reached or surpassed this level of wealth, these were a minority. Most *parlementaires* were substantially less wealthy, with incomes that were closer to 5,000 than to 10,000ł. Contemporary complaints take on greater force, however, when we consider the vast majority of the nobility, the mere "esquires." Again, we must rely on literary assessments rather than solid statistics in attempting to determine the incomes of this group. François de La Noue, in the 1580's, believed that "it is notorious that there is a great number of gentlemen worth 700 or 800ł of revenue," and this indeed is a generous estimate in comparison to some of the statistics which historians have offered.[20] Here we have a group that was far less wealthy than such magistrates as the *parlementaires*, whose incomes might easily be ten times as large. These lesser noble families might legitimately feel impoverished in comparison to the *parlementaires*.

Table 3:2 attempts to summarize the comparisons which have been made thus far, by placing the *parlementaires* within a rough hierarchy of incomes and wealth as they existed in the late sixteenth and early seventeenth centuries.

1572-1573; Edmond Esmonin, ed., *Voysin de la Noiraye. Mémoire sur la généralité de Rouen (1665)* (Paris, 1913), pp. 72-78.

[20] François de la Noue, *Discours politiques et militaires*, ed. F. E. Sutcliffe (Geneva, 1967), p. 150; see also Pierre Deyon, "À propos des rapports entre la noblesse française et la monarchie absolue pendant la première moitié du XVIIᵉ siècle," *Revue historique*, ccxxxi (April-June, 1964), 341-356, developed in Deyon, *Amiens. Capitale provinciale. Étude sur la société urbaine au 17ᵉ siècle* (Paris, 1967), pp. 265-270; and Giuliano Procacci, *Classi sociali e monarchia assoluta nella Francia della prima metà del secolo XVI* (n.p., 1955), pp. 105-107. Cf. the arguments against noble poverty of Jean Meyer, "Un problème mal posé: la noblesse pauvre. L'exemple breton au XVIIIᵉ siècle," *Revue d'histoire moderne et contemporaine*, xviii (April-June, 1971), 161-188.

TABLE 3:2

A Hierarchy of Incomes and Wealth, ca. 1580

Group	Income	Wealth
Dukes and Peers	—	800,000ł (1589-1624)
Provincial Aristocracy	10-15,000ł (1570-1600)	—
Parisian Magistrates	—	100-120,000ł (ca. 1560)
Leading Merchants	10,000ł (ca. 1580)	200,000ł (1577)
Parlementaires	5,000ł (ca. 1580)	100,000ł (1580)
Lesser Gentry	700-800ł (ca. 1585)	—

Table 3.2 tries to describe the *parlementaires'* place within a broadly defined elite of French society, the collection of groups who, whether at the provincial or national level, dominated the society. What the table suggests, first, is the magistrates' position as a provincial group. Their wealth was substantially less than that of the important Parisian robe families, and of course much less than that of the great aristocracy. Even within provincial society they were by no means a dominant group. Both the important Rouennais merchants and the leading gentry of the province were wealthier, sometimes substantially so. On the other hand, the magistrates might legitimately feel themselves to be securely a part of leading provincial society, considered in purely economic terms. Their wealth towered over that of the lesser gentry in the province; many of them could compete on terms of full equality with the wealthier gentry, and even a normal *parlementaire* fortune was not too distant from those of the leading gentry.

Such is the pattern which our examples of *parlementaire* wealth suggest prevailed in Normandy in the later sixteenth century. But we have seen that both *parlementaire* incomes and *parlementaire* wealth underwent important changes during the sixteenth century; did their position relative to other social groups—that is, within the hierarchy of wealth sketched here—change also? For this purpose a different kind of source is needed, one which offers greater possibilities for quantification and for comparison over long periods of time. The only Norman sources which fit these needs are marriage contracts, and I want now to consider the problems sketched here, of the evolution of *parlementaire* wealth and of its place in comparison to the wealth of other social groups, from the vantage point of these sources.

Marriage and the contracts which surrounded it will occupy us at some length at later points in this study, and more attention will then be given to the exact nature and development of Norman marriage contracts.[21] Only a few words need be said about them here. In contrast to marriage contracts used in the region of Paris and in many other parts of France, Norman contracts are very simple documents. They say nothing at all about the husband's fortune, and confine themselves to setting forth the donation which the bride's parents or brothers have made to her; unless the bride had no brothers, and thus took a share in her parents' estate, these donations were limited to one-third of the family's wealth, and might be considerably less. There was, in other words, no necessary relationship between the size of dowries and the actual wealth of either family, save under carefully specified circumstances. Nonetheless, the Norman marriage contract can be used to supply an approximate idea of the wealth of different groups; they do not permit precise evaluations, but they do allow us to compare orders of magnitude, to base these on substantial numbers of cases, and to follow their evolution over the sixteenth and early seventeenth centuries. These are the ways that the marriage contracts will be considered here.

We may begin with the static picture which marriage contracts offer of wealth in the later sixteenth and early

[21] Below, Chapter 6. For the limited character of the Norman marriage contract, see J.-C. Perrot, "Note sur les contrats de mariage normands," in A. Daumard and F. Furet, *Structures et relations sociales à Paris au milieu du XVIIIe siècle*, *Cahier des Annales*, XVIII (1961), 95-97.

seventeenth centuries. The dowries received by the *parlementaires* and other groups within the province fall into a pattern which closely approximates that suggested by Table 3:2. Seen through this less direct but statistically bet-

TABLE 3:3

MEDIAN DOWRIES, 1568-1614

	Median Value of Dowries	Number
Écuyers	2,625ł	10
Avocats	5,368ł	12
Parlementaires	27,000ł	33
High provincial gentry	55,000ł	8

SOURCE: *Écuyers*: Hérit. 2, 19 December 1572, 2 January 1574, 12 June 1574, 28 April 1603, 11 July 1606, 6 April 1606, 22 November 1609, 6 June 1610; AD Eure E 1249, 12 August 1568; E 1246, 26 July 1569.

Avocats: Tabel., 15 February 1575, 29 May 1575, 19 June 1580; Hérit. 2, 29 May 1579, 28 December 1597, 22 June 1602, 24 January 1604, 17 August 1607, 22 August 1608, 29 November 1608, 21 August 1609, 19 November 1609, 20 July 1610, 18 September 1610; Meubles 2, 23 March 1600.

Parlementaires: Below, Appendix F.

High provincial gentry: Hérit. 2, 16 February 1571, 13 October 1601, 5 June 1603, 20 April 1605, 14 June 1608, 12 May 1610, 12 August 1610; AD S-M 7J2 (Chartrier de Clères).

NOTE: *Écuyers*' marriages include only those within the "mere gentry," between *écuyers* and *écuyers*' daughters; not included here, for instance, are marriages between *écuyers* and *parlementaires*' daughters.

ter founded set of documents, the magistrates again appear about half as wealthy as the higher provincial gentry and about ten times as wealthy as the lesser gentry, the mere "esquires." Table 3:3 sets out median values of dowries from the 1568-1614 period for these and for one further group of interest, Rouennais lawyers (*avocats*).[22] The typical

[22] The dowries of merchants are not included here because of the wide variations in wealth and social status concealed by the notarial term "*marchand*" or "*bourgeois marchand*."

parlementaire, as Table 3:3 indicates, was not so wealthy as the leading groups within the provincial nobility, though examination of the dowries indicates that a substantial minority of magistrates were indeed of comparable wealth, or at least received comparable marriage portions. On the other hand, the magistrates' wealth decisively separated them from the lesser gentry and the lawyers. However inadequate dowries may be to measure more subtle distinctions of wealth, the difference they indicate between the magistrates and the lawyers and gentry was plainly a real one.

When we turn from this static picture and attempt to understand the evolution of *parlementaire* wealth over the sixteenth century, it is the change in this relationship between *parlementaire* and gentry wealth that is most striking. Even in the early sixteenth century, differences existed between *parlementaire* dowries and those of lesser esquires and lawyers, but the differences were considerably less great than they later became. Table 3:4 presents the median dowries for the groups we have been considering for the period 1500-1550; it is not possible to include the higher provincial gentry in this comparison, for there are too few cases to be statistically meaningful. In the first half of the sixteenth century, *parlementaire* dowries were about three times as large as those of lawyers and lesser gentry; in

TABLE 3:4

MEDIAN DOWRIES, 1500-1550

	Median Value of Dowries	Number
Écuyers	1,320ł	6
Avocats	1,375ł	6
Parlementaires	4,500ł	12

SOURCE: *Écuyers*: Tabel., 28 September 1530; 16 August 1537; 8 May 1538; 27 October 1538; Hérit. 2, 20 February 1549 (old style), 17 February 1549 (old style).

Avocats: Tabel., 25 July 1530; 12 July 1538; 13 January 1538 (old style), 17 May 1547; 12 September 1547; 16 August 1548.

Parlementaires: Appendix F.

the later years of the century, they were five times as great as the lawyers' and ten times as great as the lesser gentry's.[23]

Marriage contracts thus confirm what has been seen earlier of the *parlementaires'* rising level of wealth. From a position not too distant from that of the esquires and lawyers in the first half of the century, they had risen to wealth of an entirely different scale. Their rise was especially clear with regard to the esquires: to this group, all those involved in the law and public office must have appeared steadily wealthier, while their own position remained static or (given the pace of sixteenth-century inflation) declined. The comparisons drawn here suggest a further point, however. They suggest again the relative closeness of the magistrates during the earlier part of the sixteenth century to the milieu of the poorer nobility. The evidence of dowries shows clearly that, from the start, the magistrates were the wealthier group, but it also shows that their wealth did not separate them too sharply from this milieu. Their position was analogous to that of the wealthier statum within the "mere gentry." Only in the later part of the century did this relationship change, and the magistrates come to form a group that was much wealthier than the ordinary gentlemen.

Despite the inadequacies of our sources, then, a fairly clear picture of *parlementaire* wealth emerges. We have seen, first, its predominantly rural character. From the start of the sixteenth century, so far as can be seen, the magistrates depended on rural properties for most of their private incomes, to the relative neglect of both urban houses and government bonds. Secondly, we have seen a steady rise in *parlementaire* wealth over the century, both absolutely and in comparison to the wealth of such other groups as the lawyers and the lesser gentry. In the early years of the

[23] On the lawyers' situation in the sixteenth and seventeenth centuries, see Roland Mousnier, *La vénalité des offices sous Henri IV et Louis XIII* (2nd ed., Paris, 1971), pp. 548-549.

century, the magistrates appear not to have been much wealthier than these last groups; by the end of the century their position was quite different: they were closer to the wealthiest provincial nobility than to the mere gentlemen. Finally, we have tried to view the magistrates' wealth in comparative terms. We have seen that their wealth was considerably less than that of Parisian colleagues; even within Normandy they were less wealthy than the leading nobility, and within Rouen they were less wealthy than leading merchants. In these quantitative terms, it appears, only the poorer gentry and lawyers could legitimately feel threatened by the development of the robe nobility.

Thus far, however, we have considered only the magistrates' private fortunes. Now we must consider the economics of office itself: what their investment in office amounted to, and the economic returns which they derived from office. As with so many other issues concerning the *parlementaires*, contemporaries gave a great deal of attention to the economics of office holding, but, again characteristically, the descriptions they provide are in many respects contradictory. Resentful members of the *noblesse d'épée* stressed both the immense profits which (they believed) were to be made from holding positions in the parlements and other courts, and the high costs of attaining these offices: sufficiently high to prevent most noble families from aspiring to the magistracy. "They sell retail what they have bought wholesale," ran a common proverb concerning the judges; and irritated noblemen sought to do something about the problem by insisting at several meetings of the Estates General that special provisions be made to allow poor noblemen to enter the parlements and other magistracies.[24]

[24] La Noue, *Discours*, pp. 126-127. For similar comments, see Samuel Kinser and Isabelle Cazeaux, eds., *The Memoirs of Philippe de Commynes*, 2 vols. (Columbia, South Carolina, 1969), I, 121; François Hotman, *Francogallia*, ed. Ralph Giesey and J.H.M. Salmon (Cambridge, 1972), p. 497; André, ed., *Cardinal de Richelieu. Testament*

Members of the parlements themselves, of course, presented a different view of the economics of office. "This company. . . ," the Parlement's first president told the king in 1557, "is poor, as indeed it is an honor for a judge to be poor, and we earn nothing from the exercise of justice with which to maintain ourselves; none of us has any possessions save those acquired by our ancestors. . . ." When he spoke the costs of office were not yet of great concern, but sixty years later, when Bernard de La Roche Flavin composed his description of the parlements, the costs of buying their offices added a further element to *parlementaire* complaints of impoverishment. "With incredible effort and assiduity," wrote La Roche Flavin, "they [the magistrates] still are unable to earn half of the income which they could receive by investing the price of their positions in *rentes* at 6.25 or even 5 percent—with no effort at all. So one may say that our positions for *gens de bien* are honorable servitudes and a source of honest poverty." The rapacious, La Roche Flavin implied, might draw a profit from offices in the parlements, but they were a small minority. For most magistrates, the rising costs of office meant only growing difficulty in recovering the initial investment.[25]

politique, p. 234; and the opinions quoted by Mousnier, *La vénalité des offices*, pp. 74-77, 462-469. For the eagerness with which noblemen sought to acquire offices, see Mousnier, *L'assassinat d'Henri IV* (Paris, 1964), pp. 183-192, and Pierre Guénois, *La conférence des ordonnances royaux* . . . (nouvelle édition, Paris, 1596), p. 735.

[25] BM MS Y214, v, 227; Bernard de La Roche Flavin, *Treze livres des Parlemens de France* . . . (Bordeaux, 1617), p. 350. For another expression of this view, Reg. sec., 1546-1547, f. 99v. Most historians dealing with the question appear to have accepted this view, although with various reservations. Thus Edouard Maugis, *Histoire du Parlement de Paris de l'avènement des rois Valois à la mort d'Henri IV*, 3 vols. (Paris, 1914; repr. New York, 1967), I, 494; Mousnier, *La vénalité*, pp. 468-469 and, more strongly, in "Trevor-Roper's 'General Crisis:' Symposium," in Trevor Aston, ed., *Crisis in Europe, 1560-1660* (Garden City, 1967), pp. 106-107; and Raymond Kierstead, *Pomponne de Bellièvre: A Study of the King's Men in the Age of Henry IV* (Evanston, 1968). On the other hand, Denis Richet, in his

If we are to understand the economics of office holding, contemporary discussions must plainly be set against more concrete forms of evidence. We must try to calculate the costs and returns of office, and the ways in which these evolved over the sixteenth and early seventeenth centuries. This means, first, establishing the cost of the legal education which was prerequisite to entering the Parlement. Most magistrates, as was seen in Chapter 1, underwent elaborate educations, with travel to several universities in France and in Italy and Germany. The cost of such a program of study might be considerable. Nicholas Romé, who entered the Parlement in 1568, spent the first eight years of his education at Paris, from 1548 through 1557; each year cost his father 140ł. He then spent ten years in a succession of law schools throughout France (Poitiers, Orléans, Toulouse, Bourges), at a cost of 230ł annually. The total expense thus amounted to 3,420ł. Romé's younger brother, who became a *secrétaire du roi* and city councillor, traveled more widely and spent more: eight years at Poitiers, for 300ł yearly, a year in Rome for 600ł, and so on.[26]

Costs of education were increasing quickly in the later sixteenth century, and in the years around 1600 robe families were spending several times as much as the Romé had spent in the 1550's and 1560's. Pierre Charles entered the Parlement in 1596. Over the previous twenty years, his family estimated, 12,000ł had been spent on his "schooling and normal expenses," in other words an average of 600ł

---

as yet unpublished study of the Séguier family, stresses the very high profits of judicial offices. Closest to the views presented here are those of Pierre Deyon, *Amiens*, p. 278. Superior documentation from the middle and later seventeenth century has allowed historians to calculate with some assurance the economics of office for that period. See Jean Meyer, *La noblesse de Bretagne au XVIIIᵉ siècle*, 2 vols. (Paris, 1966), II, 937-943; and John Hurt, "Les offices au Parlement de Bretagne sous le règne de Louis XIV: Aspects financiers," *Revue d'histoire moderne et contemporaine*, XXIII (January-March, 1976), 3-31.

[26] AD S-M, 1F39, p. 30.

yearly. In the first decade of the seventeenth century, the Godart family was paying about 2,400ł annually to maintain three of its sons in Parisian colleges; one entered the Chambre des Comptes at Rouen in 1608, another the Parlement in the same year, and the third the Parlement in 1609. These expenditures came without the three students having indulged in the luxury of foreign travel.[27]

Although greater costs were clearly possible, families such as the Romé, Charles, and Godart seem to have represented what the well-to-do normally spent on education. Less wealthy families could educate their children for much less—but the minimum costs of education were also rising sharply in the sixteenth century. Charles de Bourgueville, a judge at Caen in the later sixteenth century, recalled fondly his own education in the 1520's and 1530's. His costs even at the more prestigious law schools which he attended amounted to only about 50ł yearly, and private account books from the period confirm his recollections.[28] Bourgueville himself stressed the contrast between these costs and the much greater expense of education in the 1570's and 1580's, and, again, his complaints are amply justified by other sources. We are able to follow with particular clarity the education of a poor lawyer's son between 1571 and 1580. The family's total income in these years was about 300ł, in other words about one-half of what the Charles family spent yearly to educate only one son, so that the family had little margin for extravagant educational expenses. Yet the son's expenses for a year of elementary schooling in a rural parish near Rouen came to 40ł; a year in a college in the University of Caen cost 80ł, a year at Paris 150ł, and another year at Caen 140ł. The education of a single son thus consumed nearly half of the family's income. In the early

[27] Hérit. 2, 21 December 1601; AD S-M, 16J178.

[28] Bourgueville, *Les recherches*, p. 346; Abbé Aubert, "Notes extraites de trois livres de raison de 1473 à 1550. Comptes d'une famille de gentilshommes campagnards normands," *Bulletin historique et philosophique du Comité des travaux historiques*, 1898.

seventeenth century such costs had risen still further. A year's pension in the Collège des Bons Enfants in Rouen, an institution that normally educated the poor but to which a few leading families sent their children, cost 135ł in the first decade of the seventeenth century, and by 1607 elementary schooling with a private teacher in Rouen cost 150ł yearly.[29] The one improvement in the situation was the establishment in 1592 of a Jesuit college at Rouen, which took over some of the functions of university education at lower cost, but some attendance at the university remained necessary.[30]

Very quickly in the course of the sixteenth century, thus, the cost of education reached levels that effectively limited access to the Parlement and to other legal offices. By the later sixteenth century this was true for even such relatively favored groups as the country gentlemen described above, with their revenues of 700-800ł. It must have considerably strained their resources to supply their sons with any university education, and the kinds of expenditures that were typical among the wealthier *parlementaire* families were impossible for them. The strain would have been considerably less in the early sixteenth century, Bourgueville's golden age of low expenses even in the great university centers. But already by 1546 one candidate for judicial office explained that he had no law degree, "although he had studied at Poitiers, where, *propter eius penuriam*, he did not receive the degree."[31]

Education was the first and for a long time the most prominent economic barrier to office in the Parlement. From the mid-sixteenth century on, though, the cost of acquiring the office itself came to be a second element

---

[29] AD S-M, B, Parlement, Affaires Civiles, tutelles: tutelle Bazire, 1583; 16J178; 10J13.

[30] For stress on the costs of Jesuit education, Georges Snyders, *La pédagogie en France aux XVIIe et XVIIIe siècles* (Paris, 1965), pp. 36-37.

[31] Reg. sec., 1546-1547, f. 2v.

in the economics of office holding. Like the cost of education, the costs of office underwent large changes in the sixteenth and early seventeenth centuries, changes whose effect was to transform completely the character of office holding. There had probably always been some corruption involved in appointments to such judicial offices as the *parlementaires'*, and it was commonly believed that as early as 1519 payments were made to the king by new appointees to the court. But it was only in 1543 that venality was systematically extended to offices in the Norman Parlement. In that year fifteen new councillors entered the court, each with letters from the king explaining that he, "considering the urgent necessity of our affairs . . . following what we have demanded and required in providing him with this office of councillor," had loaned the king 4,500l. From this time on, venality of office was definitively and publicly established for every office in the court save the first presidency; in 1585, when Claude Groulart became first president, he too paid for his office. The Parlement belatedly recognized this changed state of affairs in 1553, by changing the oath which it demanded of all new candidates: rather than swearing that they had paid nothing for their offices, candidates now swore that they had paid nothing save to the king.[32]

Venality was entrenched, but in an uncertain and limited fashion. In the first place, this form of venality implied little about the inheritability of offices. Numerous mid-sixteenth-century councillors were simply taking over their fathers' positions, but the crown usually exacted from them

[32] Frondeville, *Les conseillers* i, 183; AD S-M, B, Parlement, Registres d'Audiences, 2 May 1543; BM MS Y23, f. 25v (Groulart paid 18,000l for his position, but was later reimbursed by the crown); BN MS français 32318, 1, 22. Because the first president held such important political responsibilities, throughout the old regime the position was treated differently from others in the Parlement. The candidate paid for his position, but held it only as a commission from the king; he was subject to removal, and had no right to hand the position on to his children.

the same amount of money that it took from those who were buying offices for the first time.[33] Membership in a powerful robe dynasty had probably always been advantageous to those seeking office, but as yet it conferred no economic advantages. Secondly, the payments which candidates made to the crown were described as loans, and the crown usually treated them this way. "There is no one," as one Rouennais councillor argued in 1570, "who in paying money to the king to have himself provided with the office of president [à mortier, as opposed to the first presidency] or councillor does not hope for reimbursement." Reimbursement might come only "avecques le temps," as a Parisian president told Henry II, but at least at Rouen the hope was not a chimerical one.[34]

Most important was a third facet of mid-sixteenth-century venality. What the crown charged candidates to office in the Parlement was in fact a very low price, in terms both of the candidates' resources and of the profits which the investment offered. Graph 3:1 sets out the price which twelve councillors paid for their positions between 1543 and 1573. The range of prices remained essentially unchanged during this thirty-year period, from 2,500 to 6,750₺, with the most frequent value being 4,500₺. Given the pace of sixteenth-century inflation, this stability of nominal values meant a considerable drop in the real cost. As we shall see in greater detail below, the returns which office offered made this an extremely profitable investment: even the ordinary salaries of councillors in the Grand' Chambre amounted to about 10 percent of what the office cost, a return equal to that of government bonds at Rouen. Offices were equally cheap in terms of the private fortunes of most parlementaires. Above we saw that in the middle years of

[33] Thus BM MS Y214, II, 435.

[34] BM MS Y214, VI, 92; Maugis, Histoire du Parlement de Paris, I, 228. For instances in which repayment actually took place, Meubles 2, 7 May 1568 (payment in the form of a rente to the councillor's heirs); Frondeville, Les conseillers i, 303, 315, 360.

the sixteenth century, the personal incomes of magistrates typically amounted to about 2,500ł, representing a capital of about 50,000 ł. In terms of fortunes of this size, office represented a serious but hardly overwhelming investment. In the case of most councillors, office would have represented 10 percent or less of total wealth.[35]

In the mid-sixteenth century, then, there was no real market economy of offices in the Parlement. Offices were sold, but in ways that showed the importance of non-economic considerations. In 1571, for instance, the crown sold a councillorship to Nicolas Caillot for 5,000ł, but in the same year sold the same office to Marin Benoist for 2,500ł; presumably the difference reflected previous services to the crown, since Benoist was ennobled "for services" some years later. Equally striking was a third transaction from 1571. In the same year that Caillot and Benoist bought their offices, the crown sold the much less important and prestigious office of *lieutenant particulier* in the bailliage of Rouen for 3,500ł.[36] Venality of this kind plainly did little to interfere with what we have earlier seen to be the essential mechanisms by which families entered the Parlement, the system of patronage and dependence on the great aristocracy.

After 1575 the costs of entering the Parlement began to change dramatically. Having remained about constant during the middle thirty years of the sixteenth century, the price of councillorships more than doubled between 1575 and 1588, and doubled again by 1604. A councillorship in that year, as graph 3:1 shows, cost 20,000ł. The cost of presidencies in the court rose with equal speed. They had cost between 6,000 and 10,000ł in the mid-sixteenth century; by 1600 they cost about 40,000ł. In 1604 came the establishment of the Paulette, the annual tax on officials which served to make the ownership of offices more secure

[35] Office prices are set out in Appendix C, below.

[36] Reg. sec., 1570-1571, ff. 201v-209r; Frondeville, *Les conseillers* i, 510.

GRAPH 3:1.
THE PRICE OF OFFICES IN THE PARLEMENT

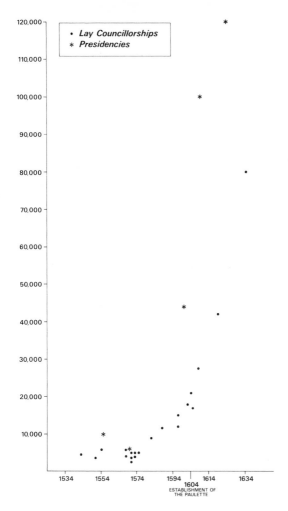

and more easily sold or inherited, and thereafter prices continued to climb. The price of councillorships doubled again by 1615, and again by 1634. By the 1670's—the high point for office prices in the parlements—councillorships were evaluated at 88,000₶. Presidencies too increased in cost after the Paulette's establishment. By 1610 they were being sold for 100,000₶, and by the 1670's 180,000₶.[37]

Contemporaries were understandably impressed with the rise in office prices that came after 1604, and they (followed by many historians) tended to explain rising office prices in terms of the increased security which the Paulette offered purchasers.[38] For offices in the Parlement, however, this explanation is plainly inadequate. The cost of both councillorships and presidencies increased by as great a percentage in the thirty years before the Paulette was introduced as they did in the next thirty years, and more quickly than in the forty years thereafter. Doubtless the Paulette encouraged officials to spend more for their positions, but even in the late sixteenth century provisions had been established which facilitated the sale or inheritance of positions. Under Henry III the heir needed only pay a percentage of the office's value to secure his right to inherit it; usually the percentage was set at one-fourth or one-third of the office's value, but the crown used artificially low estimates of these values as the basis for what it demanded. There was the additional requirement that the owner of the office survive the transaction by forty days, a requirement that made deathbed resignations difficult, but legal devices established in the later sixteenth century effectively dealt with this problem also. In 1553, for the first time, a councillor

[37] See Appendix C.

[38] Mousnier, *La vénalité*, pp. 359-360, argues for the central importance of the Paulette in producing higher prices, but also argues that rapidly rising prices before the Paulette were already closing access to offices (thus p. 83); see also pp. 365-368 for discussion of contemporary opinion about the Paulette's importance. Mark Cummings of the University of Colorado has recently undertaken reexamination of the Paulette's impact, in an as yet unpublished study.

was allowed to resign his position but retain the right to
attend the Parlement regularly; this right was only grudg-
ingly allowed at first, but was steadily extended during the
course of the century, thus permitting concerned parents
to resign offices to their children without giving up their
own rights.[39]

Changes in the laws surrounding inheritance of offices
may thus have contributed to raising prices, but they clearly
were not the essential cause. The same was true of speculative impulses, which plainly surfaced as the cost of offices
continued to rise. Speculative buying may help to explain
the continued vigor with which prices rose, but it does
not explain the initial rise.

The principal explanation for the rising cost of entering
the Parlement appears to lie in a combination of changes in
the crown's position toward venality and changing attitudes
among the buyers of office. The former of these changes
was the more straightforward. During the reign of Henry
III, the crown gave up its reluctance to treat offices in
the highest courts in purely economic terms, and began
selling them for whatever price it could get. The same effect was achieved indirectly as well, as the crown made use
of gifts of offices to reward courtiers and officials, who in
turn sold them as dearly as possible.[40] In these same years,
the crown gave up any pretense that magistrates were loan-
ing money to obtain their offices, and the transaction came

---

[39] On such provisions as the *quart* and *tiers denier*, Mousnier,
La vénalité, pp. 51-54, 223-226. For an example of the low evaluations
made of offices for this purpose, compare AD S-M, 16J3 and Hérit.
2, 6 December 1602: the Godart family paid 19 percent of the real
value of their position as master in the Chambre des Comptes and
10 percent of the value of their position as Secretary of the King.
For 1553 as the first introduction of honorary service in the court,
BN MS français 32318, 1, 22. For the court's initial view of this as
"chose nouvelle et qui ne leur semble bonne," BM MS Y214, v, 56
(5 August 1554).

[40] For a Rouennais example, see the king's gift of four councillorships to Claude Groulart, as recompense for having loaned money
to the crown (Frondeville, *Les conseillers* i, 640).

to be treated as a straightforward sale. The financial exigencies of the Wars of Religion pushed the crown toward an ever more businesslike use of even the highest judicial positions.

Changing attitudes on the part of those who bought offices in the Parlement may be seen most clearly if we compare the changing cost of office in the Parlement with the changing cost of the position of other officials. For, despite the belief of contemporaries (and of some historians) that all office prices were advancing at the same rate,[41] the economics of public offices were complex, reflecting the mingled influences of quite different impulses. The cost of a councillorship in the Parlement, we have seen, slightly more than quadrupled between 1575 and 1604, from 4,500ł to 20,000ł. But during these same years the office of treasurer general in Rouen, involving control over the fiscal administration of upper Normandy, increased in price by only about 20 percent. The office had cost 25,000ł in the period 1557-1577, 24,000ł in the period 1581-1586, and 30,600ł in 1602. Only with the institution of the Paulette did its cost begin to rise with the dynamism that offices in the Parlement had shown for the previous thirty years: by 1606 a treasurer generalship cost 45,600ł, and, by 1626, 72,000ł. The example of the treasurers general should alert us to several of the complexities which the early years of venal office holding displayed. Obviously different offices were subject to different economic processes, and responded to quite different market conditions. Equally clear is the fact that the structure of office prices might reflect a variety of concerns on the part of buyers. The treasurer general was a much less important and less prestigious figure than even the least important *parlementaire*, yet in the mid-sixteenth century the *parlementaire*'s office cost only one-fifth as much.[42]

[41] Thus Martin Göhring, *Die Amterkauflichkeit im Ancien Regime* (Berlin, 1938), 266ff.

[42] For this and other office prices, Appendix C. On the low status

This difference in prices reflected the fact that until about 1570 offices were sold for prices corresponding to the economic returns they offered, rather than in terms of the prestige or political importance they conferred. The normal price for both councillorships in the Parlement and treasurer generalships in the mid-sixteenth century was about ten times the office's yearly salary (*gages*): money rather than status was the basis on which buyers made their calculations.[43] The rising cost of offices in the Parlement during the last quarter of the sixteenth century, both absolutely and in relationship to such positions as the treasurer generals', suggests that different kinds of calculation were now coming to the fore. The change suggests that greater importance was coming to be attached to the social status and political influence that office conferred, and that merely economic considerations were coming to seem less important. We saw above, in Chapter 2, that status concerns were indeed coming to be more frequently expressed in the magistrates' deliberations; the economics of office holding also gave expression to this hardening of social values.

For our concerns here, though, it is the effects of rising office prices which are of greatest importance. The cost of office in 1600 was a much more serious barrier to families entering the Parlement than it had been earlier. Understood simply in terms of the amount of money needed to secure positions, venality had now become a regulator of the flow of new men into the court. This was especially true with regard to presidencies, whose cost had reached 100,000₶ by 1610, excluding all but the very wealthiest; this had not been the case in the middle years of the sixteenth century,

<hr />

of the treasurers general, see Claude Groulart's comment that "for money one easily can reach their position, but ours require long studies" (BM MS Y202, f. 129r); more generally, see above, Chapter 2.

[43] For the earnings of treasurers general, Jean-Pierre Charmeil, *Les trésoriers de France à l'époque de la Fronde* (Paris, 1964), p. 84. For the *parlementaires'* earnings, below, pp. 146-156 ff.

when a succession of relatively poor but distinguished figures occupied the presidencies (Jean Lallement, Pierre Le Jumel).

Equally important, the rising cost of offices in the later sixteenth century for the first time gave decisive economic advantages to those who inherited their positions, rather than acquiring them by purchase. We saw that such an advantage had not existed in the mid-sixteenth century. Then the right to inherit had cost as much as a new purchase. As prices rose and the crown made increasing use of the "quarter penny" or "third penny," in which the magistrate's heirs paid one-fourth or one-third of the office's assessed value, the advantages of inheritance grew. The Paulette, which made inheritance cheaper yet, only completed this evolution. The effect of these changes was not only to give established robe families an important economic advantage over newcomers. Just as important was the effect on the choices of established families. Robe families in most of the sixteenth century, we saw in Chapter 2, moved with surprising ease among a range of positions: from robe to sword and back again, from one kind of office to another. As the cost of offices and the advantages of inheriting them grew, this kind of movement became more difficult. A family which gave up its position in the Parlement now risked losing any chance of returning to it. Families had now to organize themselves in more strictly dynastic terms, preserving their official position from one generation to the next, for the cost of any break in continuity was steadily rising.

Changes in the cost of offices thus formed the counterpart to what we saw earlier of changes in the *parlementaires'* social origins and their sense of themselves as a group. Both of these became narrower in the late sixteenth and early seventeenth centuries, as a steadily higher proportion of the magistrates was recruited from families already in the high robe, and as attitudes toward the entry of those from lower social groups became harsher. The rising price of offices in the Parlement was both a cause and a reflection of these changes: cause, in that higher costs of office cut off social mobility and forced families to think in heavily dynastic terms; reflection, in that rising office prices were apparently caused in part by a growing concern with status and a sharper sense of social differences.[44]

One last consequence of the rise in office prices needs to be emphasized. By 1610, office had become a much larger part of most *parlementaire* fortunes than had been the case forty years earlier. In the middle years of the century, we have seen, a magistrate's office was usually worth about 10 percent of his private fortune. By the death of Henry IV, office normally was worth about one-third of the magistrate's personal fortune, and might be of much greater importance. Office by this point represented an immense investment; it was not the most important element in *parlementaire* fortunes—that place was still held by land—but it was now sufficiently important to give a distinctive coloring to them.

[44] For efforts to explain the rising cost of offices, Meyer, *La noblesse de Bretagne*, II, 937-943 (emphasizing the relation between the parlements' chances for political power and the cost of offices in them); Mousnier, *La vénalité*, pp. 83, 364-369 (stressing hopes of rising in social position and also more purely economic considerations: the difficulties that the Wars of Religion had created for other sources of wealth, the dangers of oversupply, and so forth). These views are not inherently contradictory, but Mousnier has suggested that rising office prices in fact tended to make officials more dependent on the crown, because they were increasingly concerned for the security of their increasingly large investments—and hence more reluctant to jeopardize monarchical authority. What has been seen in this study of the magistrates' reluctance to assume political power argues strongly against Meyer's view; on the other hand, it is equally clear that the magistrates' objections to royal policies increased with the increasing price of their offices. I have argued elsewhere for a direct relationship between the anxieties which rising office prices produced and the magistrates' defensive attitude toward the crown in the early seventeenth century: "Magistracy and Political Opposition at Rouen: A Social Context," *Sixteenth Century Journal*, V, 2 (October, 1974), 66-78.

Nothing has yet been said about the return which the magistrates derived from this investment, and it is to this problem that we must now turn. Were the profits of office as great as numerous critics from the *noblesse d'épée* argued? Or should we believe La Roche Flavin's contention that, even with enormous effort, magistrates could barely achieve a return of 2 percent on the money they invested in office?

The profits of office fell into several different categories, some of which are largely invisible to the historian, while others varied widely from one magistrate to another—or even during the course of a single magistrate's career. It is because of these variations that both contemporaries and historians have had so much difficulty in establishing clearly the returns of office. Here (as in most treatments of the problem) it will not be possible to say much about a first category of profits from office: those which were in varying degrees illegal. Outright bribery certainly flourished during some periods of the Parlement's existence, and in 1540 its prevalence caused Francis I to disband the court altogether. In 1532 the first president told the court that he had been informed that some councillors accepted money, game, and the like from litigants, "and that there is a rumor that women's beauty had a great deal to do with winning cases, and that wives ought to be the ones to solicit the family's cases. . . ."[45] Probably of much greater importance than these casual forms of bribery—both in their effect on the court's decisions and as a source of the magistrates' incomes—were the services which magistrates continued to provide the great aristocracy even after their entry in the Parlement. From the beginning, royal legislation sought repeatedly to eliminate this kind of service by royal officials, but (as was seen in Chapter 2) with little success. *Parlementaires* continued to manage the financial affairs of the great, reported to them on the state of cases that might affect them, and sought to ensure that the Parlement gave approval to measures (especially royal favors which needed registration from the court) in their interest. Failure of royal measures to eliminate such practices was made inevitable by the fact that the princes and the Queen Mother herself made full use of the system whenever their own interests were at issue. Profits of this kind were clearly important, and were probably enjoyed by a majority of the magistrates, but they are largely invisible to us. Income from services to the great must have been substantial, though, and the indirect rewards must have been still greater: in terms of further assistance in the magistrate's own career and in those of his relatives and connections.

A second category of rewards from office, almost as difficult to measure but probably much less significant, included the legal and fiscal privileges that came with high royal offices. The magistrates were free from nearly all royal and municipal taxes, they received their salt tax-free, in contrast to the rest of the population, who were forced to pay exorbitant prices to the royal salt monopoly, and even their tenant farmers were allowed to pass, without paying, through the customs barriers that surrounded the city. All citizens of Rouen were free from many of the most onerous royal taxes, but the purchase of a position in the Parlement conferred additional privileges.[46]

[46] BM MS français Y214, I, 154-177; for the extension of these freedoms to tenant farmers and servants, see AD S-M, B, Requêtes du Palais, "1570-1580" (in fact 1560-1570), 5 October 1570. All bourgeois of Rouen were free of the *taille*, the *francs fiefs*, and for their own produce from the tolls around the city. The main advantage which the magistrates enjoyed was freedom from the salt taxes (*gabelles*) and at most times from taxes and forced loans which the city had to pay. The magistrates' freedom from the salt tax was worth about 50₤ yearly in the early seventeenth century, though its value increased thereafter. Compare La Riv. Bourdet, 2781 (for the *maître des comptes* Alexandre Du Moucel's expenses for tax-free salt) and AD S-M, 32H, unclassed, Accounts of Rouen's Carmelites

Only when we turn to a third category of profit from office is it possible to measure in clear monetary terms what the magistrates derived from their positions. This is the category of official salaries (*gages*) which the magistrates received from the royal revenues, and which we encountered earlier, in discussing mid-sixteenth-century office values. Complaints abounded about both the inadequate size and erratic payment of these salaries, and for most magistrates they were indeed unimpressive. A clerical councillor in the Chambre des Enquêtes received only 275ł annually in salary, and the highest paid councillors—lay councillors serving in the Grand' Chambre—received only 475ł. Various forms of special service enabled the more diligent councillors to add to this sum: for service in the court's criminal chamber (14ł yearly in 1571, increased to 25ł in 1593), and for service during the autumn recess (70ł). And, despite complaints and occasional failures, at Rouen magistrates received their salaries on a regular basis. Delayed payments were eventually made good, at least through the 1570's.

These figures acquire real meaning only when seen in comparative perspective. Most clearly they need to be set against the prices which councillors paid for their offices, and seen from that vantage point the *gages* appear more impressive: until the mid-1570's they represented by themselves a 10 percent return on the capital invested in office, and in this sense they were very high. The councillors' *gages* must also, though, be set against what has already been seen of the size of magistrates' personal fortunes. Councillors

---

(for their expenses for taxed salt). For the workings of the salt monopoly in general, Martin Wolfe, *The Fiscal System of Renaissance France* (New Haven, 1972), pp. 330-342. The question of the *parlementaires'* exemption from municipal taxes and obligations was a vexed one in the mid-sixteenth century, and the magistrates were not always able to escape taxation. For examples, BM MS Y214, III, 59-60, 138-140, 146-149; Reg. sec., 1572-1574, f. 14v; Gustave Panel, *Documents concernants les pauvres de Rouen extraits des archives de l'Hôtel de ville*, 2 vols. (Paris, 1917), I, 66-70.

in the first quarter of the sixteenth century rarely had private incomes of more than 500ł, so that in these years the returns of office were of considerable importance. In the middle and later years of the century, of course, the situation was quite different. To councillors with incomes of 3,000-5,000ł, the *gages* obviously were of little significance, representing an addition of only about 10 percent to the family's income.[47]

By 1600, then, the *gages* had ceased to have much significance for most councillors, either as a return on the capital they had invested in office (since they had remained stationary, while office prices quadrupled) or as an element in personal incomes (which had increased perhaps tenfold during the century). The situation was considerably more favorable for the four presidents, however. Normally the first president was the best treated of these—not surprisingly, in view of his importance to the crown in guiding and controlling the Parlement. In the 1570's the first president received 3,000ł yearly from the crown, and most holders of the office could count on adding to this the returns from other offices (for instance councillor of state) and royal pensions. The three presidents à *mortier* had salaries of 1,200ł, but they also often received additional revenues from the crown. The president Raoul Bretel, for instance, in the 1590's was councillor of state as well as president in the Parlement, and for this largely honorific position he received an addition of 2,000ł yearly to his *gages*.[48] The

---

[47] *Gages* are set out in Floquet, *Histoire du Parlement*, II, 214-215; see also BN, Pièces Originales, 2537, 7-8, and 503, 32. For complaints about irregular payment, Maugis, *Histoire du Parlement de Paris*, II, 494. Despite some delays, *gages* were paid with reasonable regularity at Rouen: see the receipts in BN Pièces Originales, 227, 115-116; 503, 32. Parisian councillors received substantially higher salaries than the Rouennais, and this probably was a source of some resentment among the Rouennais (see Maugis, *Histoire du Parlement de Paris, loc.cit.*).

[48] For the *gages* and pensions enjoyed by the presidents, AD S-M, J 57, pp. 17-18, 37-42; all presidents named after 1581 received 2,000ł in yearly salary. See, however, La Riv. Bourdet, 2105, for the presi-

presidents' salaries thus retained a real economic importance much longer than the councillors', and it is not surprising that this disparity was one cause of tension within the court. The issue burst out in 1571, for instance, in the course of an argument between a Protestant councillor and a Catholic president. The president, so the councillor told his colleagues, "wants to rule the councillors by tyranny and fear: he gets the honors and the big salary, while the councillor receives nothing and in addition is thus mistreated."[49]

Fortunately for the councillors, the *gages* represented only part of their earnings from office. As important as what they received in salary from the crown was what they extracted in fees from litigants whose cases they decided, the *épices*. Because of the *épices*, most mid-sixteenth-century councillors enjoyed much more than a 10 percent return from their investments in office, and some councillors enjoyed very high incomes from office. The establishment of a royal tax on *épices* in 1583 permits some estimate of these revenues, though a precise accounting is impossible.[50] In the early 1580's it appears, the average councillor earned about 340ł annually from *épices*: about 215ł from civil cases and about 125ł from cases tried in the criminal chamber. A councillor in the Chambre des Requêtes would have earned somewhat less, about 312ł yearly. These fees apparently increased in value over the early seventeenth century, and in 1665 Voysin de la Noiraye estimated that the typical magistrate earned about 600ł from them.[51]

---

dent Charles Maignart's note that 800ł of his salary was less certain of being paid (because constituted on a separate revenue source) than the rest. For the example of Raoul Bretel, Reg. sec., 1595, f. 87r.

[49] Reg. sec., 1570-1571, f. 50r. For discussion of the implications of tensions of this kind for the Parlement's political position, see Dewald, "Magistracy and Political Opposition."

[50] On the difficulty of calculating the value of the *épices*, Mousnier, *La vénalité*, pp. 462-463.

[51] Calculated from AD S-M 10J180 ("Comptes . . . de la recepte et despence que i'ay faicte du revenu du parisis des espices des proces en Normandie") and, for the law surrounding this surtax, Anthoine

Such averages are misleading, however, for the distribution of fees among the councillors was uneven. This was true in particular of the most important fees, those paid for reporting cases: that is, summarizing the legal issues and evidence in a case and guiding the court through them. The presidents decided which councillors were to be given the responsibility of reporting specific cases and, once the court had reached its decision, how much the reporter's efforts had been worth. Fees usually were charged to the losing party, and were then distributed among the councillors who had taken part in the decision: through the sixteenth century, half went to the reporter himself and half was divided among the councillors in the chamber, with the reporter himself receiving one of the latter shares.[52] Both the value of individual cases and the number of cases which councillors might report varied widely. Between July 21 and August 16, 1610, for instance, there were cases for which the report cost 3l, 12l, and 15l, but also cases worth 150l, 156l, and 210l. Variation in how much councillors earned reflected differences in seniority, talent, and learning, and might also depend on more personal considerations: in 1610, for instance, the Protestant councillor Jacques Moynet, having

Fontanon, *Les édicts et ordonnances des rois de France*, 4 vols. (2nd ed., Paris, 1611), iv, 706-707. The tax, established in 1583, added 20 percent to the fees which litigants paid, and this went to the crown. The measure created widespread irritation in Normandy (see C. de Robillard de Baurepaire, ed., *Cahiers des États de Normandie sous le règne de Henri III*, 2 vols. [Rouen, 1888], ii, 24, 62), and was withdrawn after two years; on the use of the *parisis* as a tax, see R. Doucet, *Les institutions de la France au seizième siècle*, 2 vols. (Paris, 1948), ii, 574. For Voysin de la Noiraye's estimate, see Mousnier, *La vénalité*, pp. 462-463; though this may have been a reasonable estimate of the earnings of the less active majority of the court, it is certainly far below the arithmetic mean of earnings from *épices*.

[52] For these procedures, La Roche Flavin, *Treze livres*, p. 520; BM MS Y214, ii, 441; iii, 4; and BM MS Martainville Y96, pp. 266, 307. At certain points in the early seventeenth century, it appears, *épices* were shared equally among the councillors: Mousnier, *La vénalité*, p. 462.

managed to enter the court only with the king's strong support, ranked forty-fourth in the value of the cases he reported but fourteenth in the length of his service, a disparity reflecting his colleagues' resentment at both his Protestantism and the conditions of his reception. But, in general, more important cases and higher fees came with greater seniority in the court. Not only were senior councillors more likely to have the confidence of the presidents, but the court's organization also gave them substantial advantages. The twenty-three senior councillors shared all the fees in the Grand' Chambre, whereas in the early seventeenth century there were forty-five councillors to divide fees in the Chambre des Enquêtes; and any cases involving more than 10,000ł went automatically to the Grand' Chambre.[53]

Because of the complex way in which these fees were distributed, it is impossible to establish the exact difference between the more favored councillors' earnings and that of their colleagues. It appears, however, that the most successful councillors might earn several times what the less successful majority earned. In 1610 the eleven most successful councillors from the Grand' Chambre would have earned about 2,000ł yearly from reporting cases, while the fifty-seven remaining councillors from the Grand' Chambre and the Enquêtes averaged roughly 350ł.[54]

[53] AD S-M, B, Parlement, Registre d'Arrêts, June-July 1610, July-August, 1610. In 1610 the precise correlation between order of reception and order of the importance of cases reported, using Spearman's Rank Order Correlation Coefficient (defined as $R = 1 - \dfrac{6\Sigma d^2}{n^3 - n}$: see M. J. Moroney, *Facts from Figures* [London, 1951], pp. 334ff.), was .53. On the distribution of cases between the chambers, BN Fonds Dupuy 498, ff. 153ff. As with the disparity between the salaries of presidents and councillors, this difference in official incomes was a cause of substantial tensions within the Parlement. See above, Chapter 1, and my article, "Magistracy and Political Opposition."

[54] AD S-M, B, Parlement, Registre d'Arrêts, June-July, July-August, 1610. In contrast to salaries paid by the king, during the sixteenth century the value of *épices* rose at least as quickly as other prices, and probably more quickly; real profits from this source, in

For the most active and respected councillors, then, fees from reporting cases might be the source of a very substantial income. Such fees were much less important for the majority. Other *épices* were more evenly divided, however. Litigants were charged special fees each time the court met in "extraordinary session"; in fact these were regular late morning and late afternoon sessions, reserved for hearing cases which the presidents had decided were particularly complex. Even so ardent a defender of the parlements as La Roche Flavin viewed these as merely devices for extracting fees, and in 1580 each councillor received about 70₶ for participating in them.[55] Additional fees were charged for questioning witnesses, a task that was distributed by a system of rotation. Finally, though the practice was repeatedly condemned, councillors charged small fees for reporting litigants' requests to the court.[56]

---

other words, probably increased. Thus, in 1520 the value of the cases which the median councillor reported over a three-month period was 11 *écus*; in 1610 the median councillor reported cases worth 58 *écus* over a similar three-month period (*ibid.*, June-August, 1520). This is in contrast to both my own conclusions in "Magistracy and Political Opposition," where I failed to take into account the rising number of cases that the Parlement dealt with, and Mousnier, *La vénalité*, pp. 462-463.

[55] On the putative functions of the extraordinary sessions, BM MS Martainville Y96, p. 287; La Roche Flavin, *Treze livres*, p. 444; fees charged for meeting in extraordinary session are calculated from AD S-M, B, Parlement, Registre d'Arrêts, June-July, July-August, 1580.

[56] BM MS Martainville Y96, p. 307 (for the distribution of *instructions* by rotation), pp. 266, 316 (for attempts in 1532 and 1607 to do away with the charging of fees for reporting requests); and AD S-M, B, Parlement, Registre d'Arrêts, June-July, July-August, 1610, for the continued payment of such fees. A further practice that persisted despite efforts to halt it was the magistrates' right to name a *procureur* in the court, a right claimed by all presidents and by those councillors who had served for twenty years. Since in the late sixteenth century the *procureurs* had been transformed into venal officials, the right of nomination might be worth a great deal: in 1586 a *procureur* in the Parlement paid 2,000₶ for his position (Hérit. 2,

As far as most councillors were concerned, the economic returns of office were made up entirely of the elements that have been considered thus far: fees, salaries, fiscal privileges, and illicit but universally enjoyed pensions from aristocratic patrons. For a minority within the court, however, these revenues were supplemented by a final set of revenues, those which came from performing particular services for the crown or the court itself. These commissions, as they were known, might go to any member of the Parlement, but it was only the court's more influential members, those who had a well-established position with the crown, who could count on more than an occasional windfall from them. Those who *were* regularly given such commissions could expect a very considerable addition to their income. Thus, for his yearly service as the king's commissioner before the provincial estates the first president received 500ł; from 1566 on he was also given the *"charge et intendance"* of the Queen Mother's affairs in Normandy, for an unspecified but doubtless impressive salary. In 1556 two councillors and the *avocat général* were given 200ł each for a month spent investigating and punishing heretics in the area of Le Havre, and in the early seventeenth century three magistrates were given 300ł each for the expenses of a trip to Paris on the Parlement's business. When issues of taxation were involved in such commissions, the chances for profit were greater still—but again generally for the presidents, king's attorneys, and the most influential councillors.[57]

---

12 March 1587). More often, however, the right of nomination was used to reward servants and other dependents (thus La Riv. Bourdet, 2105, and Reg. sec., 1573-1579, f. 467ff.). For the crown's effort to stop this practice, Reg. sec., 1572-1574, f. 35r.

[57] BN Pièces Originales, 227, #88 (in addition, one of Bauquemare's brothers held the office of chief clerk of the estates, for 600ł yearly); for Bauquemare's other commissions, *ibid.*, #75, 76, BN MS français 15551, f. 176r; Reg. sec., 1549-1556, f. 179r. For other commissions, Reg. sec., 1570-1571, ff. 214-215; *ibid.*, June-October, 1597, ff. 131v, 160v; *ibid.*, 1572-1574, ff. 104-105.

Finally, the crown offered the court's most important figures, notably the first presidents, chances for special profits. Claude Groulart (first president from 1585 to 1607), having loaned money to the crown during the League, in recompense was given several councillorships to sell as he chose. His successor, Alexandre Faucon, was given the chance for profits on a really large scale from a real-estate venture characteristic of early seventeenth-century urbanism. Following the League, the crown had dismantled the fortress which dominated the city's northern walls, near the present-day Place St. Godard. In 1610 the crown made over this area to Faucon and an associate, in exchange for a modest ground rent (of 12 d the *toise*); Faucon was "to construct there buildings and houses for the public welfare and the embellishment of the said city," the only limitation being that the crown (in the person of the duc de Sully) approve any building plans. Four years later there was a newly built rue de Faucon (there is today still a rue Morant, named for Faucon's associate in this speculation) and a few buildings, and Faucon was able to sell vacant lots for two hundred times the ground rent that he had been paying. This was the kind of operation from which real wealth might be created.[58]

Plainly it is inadequate to speak, as contemporaries tended to do, of the returns of office fitting a single pattern. While figures such as Groulart and Faucon might reap enormous profits from their positions, junior councillors with neither commissions nor significant cases to report were in an entirely different situation. Nearly the whole range of magistrates (there were individual exceptions, such as the Protestant Moynet), however, derived substantial incomes from their offices. For the councillor at the start of his career in

[58] Frondeville, *Les conseillers* i, 640; AD S-M, B, Parlement, Registre d'Arrêts, 29 July 1610, Hérit. 2, 17 February 1614. On Sully's encouragement of this kind of project, see David Buisseret, *Sully and the Growth of Centralized Government in France* (London, 1968), pp. 132-139.

about 1580, we may evaluate this income at about 725ł yearly: 375ł salary, 250ł from reporting cases, and 100ł as a share in the court's other fees and commissions. A better established councillor in the same years might earn three or four times as much: in the course of three and one-half months in 1580, for instance, there were five councillors who each earned 300ł just from reporting civil cases. Presidents à *mortier* and the king's attorneys probably earned about the same amount as the most successful councillors, since they had no share in the court's fees but a much larger share in profitable commissions. The first president, profiting as he did from high salary, pensions, numerous commissions, and chances for such ventures as Faucon's real estate dealings, made more money still: 7,500ł yearly seems a conservative estimate.

Office was thus economically important to nearly everyone in the Parlement. For even the least important councillors, income from office might easily represent one-fourth of personal income, and for the most active and respected councillors office represented much more. And such calculations take no account at all of the indirect benefits of office: the chances which it offered to serve the great, fiscal exemptions, and so on. Families who chose in the mid-sixteenth century to invest in legal education and office were obviously making a sound decision.

Rising costs of both education and office in the later sixteenth and early seventeenth centuries somewhat changed this situation, however. Partly, this was simply because costs were rising more quickly than returns, and thus reducing the rate of return from office. Between 1580 and 1610, the most profitable aspect of office holding—fees received for reporting cases—roughly tripled, while salaries remained unchanged. But in the same period the cost of a councillorship in the court increased approximately sixfold, and the cost of education roughly tripled. The councillors' return on their investment had been substantially cut. This was only part of the problem, however. As serious was the fact that all those purchasing office in the Parlement had now to do so with borrowed money, for the sums required were now beyond the cash reserves of even the wealthiest families. Interest rates fell in the late sixteenth and early seventeenth centuries, but they remained above 7 percent even at the end of our period. Not only had the rate of return which offices provided fallen substantially, but interest payments cut into the profit that remained.[59]

For the less affluent among the magistrates, this might mean outright disaster. The councillor Charles Le Doulcet, for instance, entered the Parlement in 1592, but a decade later was forced to sell his office to meet his family's debts. He and his brothers had inherited some of these debts from their father, but some of them had arisen "because of the said position of councillor." For Le Doulcet, more than a decade of service in the court was insufficient even to meet the initial costs of entry, let alone to turn a profit.[60] The greatest rewards of office holding had always come relatively late in the careers of magistrates, as they were given more commissions and more significant cases, but in the late sixteenth century this fact assumed greater importance. The issue was no longer merely one of not being able to amass large amounts of money at the start of a career, but included an outright loss, since earnings of less than 7 percent from office meant that interest payments would outweigh earnings.

This shift did not mean that office ceased to be profitable, even for younger councillors. But it did mean that chances for profit were limited to a much smaller group than had been the case earlier in the century. The advantages of inheriting office, and thus avoiding the whole range of prob-

---

[59] AD S-M, B, Parlement, Registre d'Arrêts, June-July, July-August, 1580; June-July, July-August, 1610. *Parlementaire* borrowing is discussed in detail below, in Chapter 5; for a particularly clear example, La Riv. Bourdet, 2105 (the accounts of the wealthy president Charles Maignart).

[60] Meubles 2, 28 May 1602; BM MS Y214, IX, 60-61.

lems associated with borrowing money and holding out until profits were possible, were now overwhelming. The changing economics of office also favored certain groups even among families new to office. Very simply, the situation of the early seventeenth century favored the very wealthy. For those who could meet the requirements of entry, office still offered large profits; families of only moderate wealth found themselves sacrificing future profits to the effort of acquiring office.

This chapter began with the anxieties that Richelieu and other noblemen expressed concerning the wealth and arrogance of the *noblesse de robe*; now we are in a position to compare these assessments of the situation with the experiences of sixteenth-century upper Normandy. Some of the issues which most disturbed Richelieu and his fellows must await attention in the next two chapters. In particular, this is the case with regard to *parlementaire* purchases of rural estates, and to the more general problem of economic attitudes. What has been seen in this chapter, however, is already enough to suggest the complex ways in which Richelieu's comments are at once accurate and misleading.

On the one hand, members of the Parlement were becoming wealthier over the course of the sixteenth century—just as the military noblemen gloomily reported. This was apparently true in both absolute and relative terms. In absolute figures what the *parlementaires* derived from their private fortunes in land, bonds, and urbal real estate, increased at least tenfold over the century, and probably more. Personal incomes of 500ł had been typical in the early years of the century; by the 1580's the normal range was around 5,000ł. Yearly income from office also increased at a rapid pace: although salaries remained fixed, fees appear to have increased eightfold between 1520 and 1610. This rise in absolute income produced a change in the magistrates' position relative to other social groups. At the start of the sixteenth century, their position was that of wealthy members of the petty gentry. Both what we know of income levels and the evidence of marriage contracts suggest that differences existed between the magistrates and the mass of poorer noblemen, but that these differences were not too great. At the start of the seventeenth century, the *parlementaires* stood in a quite different position within the provincial nobility. Now they were to be ranked as poorer members of the high provincial nobility, standing far above the level of the ordinary gentlemen. To understand the full impact of this process, we need to recall that this growth in wealth was accompanied by a still more dramatic growth in the number of magistrates: as far as the Parlement was concerned, from thirty-five in 1499, to eighty-six in 1610. There were ample grounds for complaint by the poor nobility.

Noble complaints were accurate in another sense as well. Office in the Parlement was not for most magistrates a source of fabulous wealth, but for nearly all it provided a considerable income, and for some it did offer chances of real wealth. We may estimate the official income of a moderately assiduous councillor in the early 1580's at about 725ł, in other words roughly the total income of François de La Noue's typical noble family. The most diligent councillors might earn three or four times as much. And to these profits we must add tax exemptions and chances to earn both money and favors from the high aristocracy. Office was not the only factor in the growth of *parlementaire* wealth during the sixteenth century, but it was an important one—as many noblemen suggested.

But aristocratic complaints prove to be only a partial guide to an understanding of *parlementaire* wealth. While noblemen were correct to stress the profits of office, in the first place, their comments fail to suggest the complexities that costs and profits involved. The range of such profits from one magistrate to the next was very large, and the economics of office changed considerably over the sixteenth century. Most dramatic was the increasing cost of entering the Parlement, the result of rising costs of education as well as the booming market in official positions. This meant first a narrowing of the Parlement's recruitment, as fewer families were able to meet these costs, and above all a growing economic advantage to inheritance of office. By 1610 the chances of creating a new fortune from the profits of office had become very small. Office might still be profitable, but mainly to those who had inherited their positions or to those who could afford to wait for profits, while they paid off the debts that obtaining office had required. The changing economics of office reinforced the changing social values that were examined in Chapter 2: dynasticism was becoming economically as well as psychologically necessary.

Aristocratic comments about the wealth of the *noblesse de robe* are misleading in another sense. From the start of the sixteenth century, the Rouennais *parlementaires* were mainly a class of landowners, and in this sense their economic triumphs in the sixteenth century may be thought of as the triumphs of a part of the landed gentry, rather than as the triumphs of an alien, essentially urban, group over the noblemen. Reasons for this predominance of landed fortunes among the *parlementaires* should be clear from what has been seen of the group's social origins. Magistrates were drawn from the lesser nobility itself or from the very large group of seigneurial officials, far more often than from among urban merchants, and their fortunes reflected these origins. Only the conditions of the later sixteenth century forced some change in these circumstances. In these years office itself came to occupy a much larger place in most *parlementaire* fortunes than had hitherto been the case; for reasons and to a degree that will be considered below, the share of magistrates in private *rentes* at Rouen also increased. In the late sixteenth century, *parlementaire* fortunes thus tended to become somewhat more urban in orientation than they had earlier been, but they still did not lose their basically rural character. Aristocratic complaints about the wealth of the *noblesse de robe* suggest a sense of basic opposition between the two groups, and this may indeed have been the case in some areas of France. But in Normandy the character of the fortunes of the two groups was fundamentally similar during the sixteenth century. Both were representatives of the landed elite that dominated French life. It remains now to ask whether more subtle differences existed between the two groups—differences not in the kind of fortunes they possessed, but in the ways they managed them and the profits they derived from them. These are the questions to which the next chapter is addressed.

FOUR

THE MEANINGS OF LANDOWNERSHIP

LAND held the central place in most *parlementaire* fortunes. Now it is necessary to consider this economic configuration more closely. The present chapter seeks to analyze the social as well as the more purely economic dimensions of *parlementaire* landowning. We shall be concerned, first, with the relationships that their country properties created between the magistrates and their rural neighbors, whether of the peasantry or of the nobility; then we shall consider the attitudes and techniques they brought to landowning, and some of the problems they encountered; the last part of this chapter, finally, will analyze the changing economics of the magistrates' landowning, in particular the changing revenues which the magistrates received from their rural properties.

In approaching these issues, we need to consider questions that go beyond the *parlementaires* themselves, particularly with regard to the legal structure and actual workings of the seigneurie, the most important form of large landed property. Historians of early modern France have given relatively little attention to the structure of the seigneurie, or to such related issues as the land market and the problems of administering large estates.[1] In order to understand *parle-*

[1] Exceptions include Robert Forster, *The Nobility of Toulouse in the Eighteenth Century* (Baltimore, 1960), and *The House of Saulx-Tavanes. Versailles and Burgundy, 1700-1830* (Baltimore, 1971); Pierre Goubert, "Le paysan et la terre: seigneurie, tenure, exploitation," in Ernest Labrousse et al., eds., *Histoire économique et sociale de la France* (Paris, 1970); André Plaisse, *La baronnie de Neubourg. Essai d'histoire agraire, économique et sociale* (Paris, 1961); E. Le Roy Ladurie, "La verdeur du bocage," introduction to Abbé Tollemer, *Un sire de Gouberville, gentilhomme campagnard au Cotentin*

mentaire landowning, thus, it will be necessary at several points to consider the Norman large estate more generally.

A. THE SEIGNEURIE

Writers in the late sixteenth and early seventeenth centuries agreed that landowning involved much more than purely economic relations, and that the large landowner, especially the owner of a seigneurie, enjoyed a special authority within the countryside. It was in these terms that Charles Loyseau, the first French jurist to concern himself with venal office holding, introduced his treatise on the seigneurie. Having written "on Offices and on [social] orders, which are the other two forms of Dignity, there is no reason that I should fail to explicate the third form." To Loyseau, as to other writers in the sixteenth and seventeenth centuries, the seigneurie was a form of authority that paralleled public office and social status.[2]

Yet Loyseau also recognized the problems inherent in such a view, for the seigneurie was a difficult institution to define and understand. "I say it having tried," wrote Loyseau about the difficulty of defining most seigneuries. "Read all the customary laws that treat of [seigneurial] justices, and you will find nothing but diversity and confusion; study all the ancient and modern authors who have written about

---

de 1553 à 1562 (Paris-The Hague, 1972); and Guy Bois, *Crise du féodalisme. Économie rurale et démographie en Normandie orientale du début du 14e siècle au milieu du 16e siècle* (Paris, 1976), pp. 195-234.

[2] Charles Loyseau, *Traité des seigneuries*, in *Oeuvres* (Paris, 1701; first published 1613), p. 1. See also Loyseau's arguments that fief and office initially had been the same thing; *ibid.*, p. 6. For discussion of Loyseau's preconceptions, especially his belief in the superiority of public to feudal authority, see Roland Mousnier, *L'assassinat d'Henri IV* (Paris, 1964), pp. 237-266; for more general discussion of sixteenth-century critiques of feudal authority, William Farr Church, *Constitutional Thought in Sixteenth-Century France. A Study in the Evolution of Ideas* (Cambridge, Mass., 1941), pp. 180-194, 295-302.

them, and you will find nothing but absurdity and re-
pugnance."[3] Sources of confusion were numerous. Seigneuries varied widely in size and organization, and might
change in both respects within short periods of time. The
institution's origins were unclear, and so also were its relations to the monarchy, the embodiment of public authority.
The uncertainties which surrounded it limited the seigneurie's effectiveness as a center of authority within the
countryside.

Norman law defined the seigneurie, first, as a fief: that is,
as a property which required homage when it changed
hands and which gave rise to wardship (*garde noble*) when
it was inherited by a minor.[4] A further defining element of
the seigneurie was equally straightforward. All seigneuries
enjoyed some rights of justice, as "an integral part of the
fief," in the words of an eighteenth-century jurist.[5] The
seigneurie's owner was thus necessarily involved in social
relations that extended upward, to the feudal superiors who
received his homage and might have the wardship of his
children, and downward, to those who were subject to his
judicial powers. It was in the definition of these judicial
rights, however, that the seigneurie's limited character became apparent. A handful of Norman seigneuries enjoyed
the right of high justice, which allowed them to judge and
to execute criminals and to maintain the gallows which symbolized these rights. But these were more unusual than in
most parts of France, a fact that impressed a Parisian official
sent to the province in the mid-seventeenth century. "High

[3] Loyseau, *Traité*, p. 53.

[4] See Maître de La Tournerie, *Traité des fiefs à l'usage de la province de Normandie* (Paris, 1763), p. 73.

[5] Maître Houard, *Dictionnaire analytique, historique, étymologique,
critique et interprétatif de la coûtume de Normandie*, 4 vols. (Rouen,
1780), II, 451. Cf. Loyseau, *Traité*, p. 54: "in truth all seigneuries, and
above all the lesser ones, consist principally and formally in their
rights of justice"; and the similar view of the sixteenth-century lawyer René Choppin, quoted by Pierre Le Mercier, *Les justices seigneuriales de la région parisienne de 1580 à 1789* (Paris, 1933), p. 48.

justices (he wrote) are not common in Normandy as they are in the Île de France, where there are nearly as many as there are parishes . . . nearly all [of the Norman high justices] cover very wide areas"; and thus, he noted, there were none at all in the viscounty of Vernon and only ten in the viscounty of Andely. Norman law presented these rights as independent of the seigneurie itself, and required that they be justified by explicit grant from the sovereign.[6]

The vast majority of Norman seigneuries enjoyed only the more modest rights of low justice. These included some degree of public authority—for instance the right to punish assaults on seigneurial officials—but the main functions of low justice were not judicial at all. Its main concerns were clerical, for the chief task of the low justice was to record transactions between the seigneurie's owner and those who held their properties from the seigneurie, as manorial tenants. For this reason, noted an eighteenth-century jurist, "the jurisdiction of the seneschal (the chief official of a low justice) ought to be described less as a jurisdiction than as an office, whose goal is, first, to oversee the enforcement of regulations of superior judges within the seigneurie, and, secondly, to give the seigneur and his vassals copies of the declarations which they pass with each other relative to their tenures . . . his functions [are] limited to the conservation of the rights of the lord and his vassals." A low justice might levy small fines (of 18 sols 1 denier, according to the custom's article xxxiii) against tenants who failed to pay the rents owed by their tenures, but any more serious action had to be taken in the higher courts.[7]

[6] Edmond Esmonin, ed., *Voysin de la Noiraye. Mémoire sur la généralité de Rouen (1665)* (Paris, 1913), p. 93, n. 2. See also Robert d'Estaintot, *Recherches sur les hautes justices féodales existant dans les limites du département de la Seine-Inférieure* (Rouen, 1892); though outmoded with regard to the actual workings of the high justices, this study at least summarizes the most important legal texts.

[7] Houard, *Dictionnaire*, II, 458. See also Josias Bérault, *La coustume reformée du pays et duché de Normandie* (Rouen, 1614), pp. 252, 258-259; for detailed discussion of specific rights, pp. 50-60. Low

Norman law thus limited the judicial rights of most seigneuries in the province. The law tended also to restrict the
other rights associated with lordship: the milling and baking
monopolies, pigeon houses, tolls, rents, and the like which
made the seigneurie so onerous an institution for peasants
in such provinces as Burgundy. All of these existed in Normandy, but, as in the case of high justice, the custom tended
to restrict their incidence. This was the case with the right
to construct a pigeon house, one of the most visible signs of
seigneurial authority. The custom allowed fiefs to be divided
into as many as eight parts, and few were actually full *fiefs
de haubert*; but only one pigeon house was allowed within
each full fief. All fief holders enjoyed a monopoly on constructing water mills within their seigneuries, and it was
generally agreed that the same monopoly applied to wind-
mills; but very few lords enjoyed the much more profitable
right to compel their tenants to use only their mill (the right
of *moulin à ban* or *banalité*) and those who claimed it were
required to show clear title. His own lord's mill was only
one of several to which most seigneurial tenants could turn,
and it was hoped that this limited the system's abuses. Likewise, labor services (*corvées*) and feudal dues that involved
a share in the crop (*champarts*) were to be found on some
Norman seigneuries, but apparently on very few—and the
cens, the most common form of feudal due in most of
France, was rarely to be found in sixteenth-century upper
Normandy.[8]

---

justice in Normandy corresponded more closely to the *justice foncière* of the Parisian custom than to Parisian low justice, to which
there was no real equivalent in Normandy. Middle justice seems to
have been completely unheard of in sixteenth-century Normandy.
See Le Mercier, *Les justices seigneuriales*, p. 39, and Bernard Guenée,
*Tribunaux et gens de justice dans le bailliage de Senlis à la fin du
moyen âge (vers 1380-vers 1550)* (Paris, 1963), pp. 311-343.

[8] For the extent to which upper Norman fiefs had been divided, see
G.-A. Prévost, ed., "Documents sur le ban et l'arrière ban, et les fiefs
de la vicomté de Rouen en 1594 et 1560 et sur la noblesse du bailliage

These circumstances did not mean that seigneurial dues lacked economic importance, to either lord or tenants. As we shall see, they were usually of great importance to both. The thrust of Norman law, though, was to reduce whatever personal content seigneurial obligations may have had, and to throw into greater relief the tenants' purely monetary obligations. In most Norman seigneuries, and especially in the smaller ones, the principal form of feudal income was simply a form of fixed rent (the *rente foncière*) owed by most of the seigneurie's tenants. There was nothing specifically seigneurial about this form of permanent tenancy (known as the *fieffe*), and it was widely employed in urban as well as rural areas. But on most Norman estates it was the principal link between seigneurie and peasants.

One last aspect of Norman law further reinforced these tendencies toward limiting the seigneurie's impact. In contrast to the law in some other parts of France, the Norman custom encouraged a good deal of fluidity and change in the seigneurie's structure—to a degree that discourages thinking of the Norman seigneurie as a tradition-bound institution of immemorial antiquity. New seigneuries might be created with some ease, through an act of the crown followed by judicial inquest in the area concerned. Seigneuries might also disappear; a seigneurie that had been divided into more than eight parts simply fell back into the realm of or-

---

de Gisors en 1703," *Mélanges, Société de l'Histoire de Normandie,* series 3 (1895), 241-332; of fifty-three fiefs in the sergeantry of Pont St. Pierre, for instance, twelve were full fiefs or baronies; fourteen were of unknown size; and twenty-seven were part fiefs. On specific seigneurial rights, Bérault, *La coustume,* pp. 192-193, 276-278. The only example I have encountered of the *champart, tierce gerbe,* and *corvées* is Hérit. 2, 13 January 1597. On the substitution of *rentes* for *cens,* see Leopold Delisle, *Études sur la condition de la classe agricole et l'état de l'agriculture en Normandie au moyen âge* (Évreux, 1851; repr. New York, n.d.), pp. 45-46. Cf. descriptions of the seigneurie in other parts of France, e.g., Pierre de Saint Jacob, *Les paysans de la Bourgogne du Nord au dernier siècle de l'ancien régime* (Paris, 1960), pp. 51-72.

dinary properties. But such excessively divided seigneuries might also be resuscitated, in the event that enough of their parts came into the hands of a single owner.[9] Most important, Norman law allowed much greater changes in the seigneurie's internal structure than was possible in most provinces. Until the reform of the custom in 1583, heirs were allowed to divide fiefs as they wished. When the custom was revised and an official version produced, this possibility was restricted to daughters. For male heirs, the maxim that "every fief is indivisible" was now to prevail. But this change reduced the fluidity of the seigneurial structure only slightly. An eighteenth-century lawyer suggested the limited importance of the "indivisibility" of fiefs:

"Does this mean that every fief ought always to remain in its primitive state, having always the same extension, and that its essence is to remain through all time exactly as it was created? No. Such is not at all the intention of the custom; such is not at all its true meaning in the eyes of reason enlightened by principles. A lord sells part of his domain, and it becomes a tenure held from his seigneurie; he gives it to the church, and it becomes a free donation; he sells it to the lord from whom he holds his fief, and loses any right over it as a tenure. It is thus that a lord can change, modify as he wishes, the original state of his fief . . . that a fief loses or acquires a piece of land—does this lead to any increase in the number of fiefs?"[10]

To Norman legal theorists, the feudal structure was a flexible one that permitted wide changes in actual property relations without affecting the fief's legal character. More-

---

[9] Bérault, *La coustume*, p. 190; Houard, *Dictionnaire*, II, 476.

[10] Houard, *Dictionnaire*, II, 487-488; see also Bérault, *La coustume*, p. 190: " . . . ce n'est pas diviser le fief que de mettre en un lot le fief, la court et usage [i.e., the seigneurial justice], reliefs, treizièmes, & telles autres choses qui sont *de substantialibus feudi*, & en l'autre part héritages, rentes, droitures de moullin . . . colombier, & autres dépendances de la terre. . . ." For an instance of a fief's complete division prior to the reformed custom's prohibition of such divisions, La Riv. Bourdet, 1843.

over, seigneuries could expand as easily as they could contract. It was an easy matter to incorporate newly acquired
lands in the seigneurie though they had not originally been
held from it. Larger changes, such as uniting several fiefs
into one, were also possible, but required letters from the
king and judicial approval. Norman law gave encouragement to one last form of change, within the seigneurie's
boundaries. It allowed lords to intervene in any sales of
property that depended on the seigneurie. By meeting the
sale price, the lord could substitute himself for the buyer
and thus convert the property in question from tenure, held
of the seigneurie, to part of the demesne, under the lord's
direct control.[11]

Legally, then, the Norman seigneurie was a relatively
weak institution. Jurists were perplexed about the institution's origins, justification, and essential nature; few seigneuries had any but the most modest public authority, and
few demanded much more than monetary payments from
those who resided in them.[12] The law permitted—in some
ways even encouraged—a large degree of fluidity in the
seigneurie's character and organization. But to what extent
did the legal conditions surrounding the seigneurie cor-
respond to the institution's actual character and workings?
It is important that we establish some idea of the realities of
seigneurial organization.

This cannot be done in any statistical sense, for there were

[11] For these rights, Bérault, *La coustume*, p. 268. Cf. the more
inflexible custom of Burgundy: Saint Jacob, *Les paysans*, p. 57. For
the absence of *retrait féodal* in the custom of Paris, Jean Meuvret,
"Domaines ou ensembles territoriaux? Quelques exemples de l'implication du régime de la propriété et de la structure sociale dans la
France du XVIIᵉ et du XVIIIᵉ siècles," repr. in Meuvret, *Études d'histoire économique. Recueil d'articles* (*Cahiers des Annales*, XXXII,
Paris, 1971), p. 189.

[12] For stronger statements of the seigneurie's impact, Goubert, "Le
paysan et la terre," pp. 122-130, and Yves-Marie Bercé, *Histoire des
Croquants. Étude des soulèvements populaires au XVIIᵉ siècle dans
le sud-ouest de la France*, 2 vols. (Geneva, 1975), I, 127-129.

enormous differences in size among Norman seigneuries, even among those which lacked the distinction of high justice: between, for instance, the fief of Esquetot l'Auber, whose revenues in 1569 were 4ł 7s, and the fief of St. Aubin, sold in 1581 for 72,000ł.[13] But certain characteristics were shared by many Norman seigneuries, if not by most, and gave broad shape to seigneurial organization. Contemporaries had a sense, in the first place, of how much space a "normal" seigneurie ought to occupy. The demesne and peasant tenures of an undivided fief ought in all to be about 180 hectares, according to one lawyer; a barony represented merely a collection of at least four fiefs, and thus ought to cover about 720 hectares. On the other hand, the smallest form of fief, the vavassorie, in the early seventeenth century might represent about 55 hectares.[14] However approximate, these figures indicate the small scale on which even full seigneuries were organized. Villages in upper Normandy covered several hundred hectares of land, some of them more than a thousand hectares, and few normal fiefs would have occupied more than a small part of their area. Wealthy peasants might easily match the holdings of the smaller seigneuries, even those which had not been so reduced as Esquetot l'Auber.[15]

[13] AN G8 1246; La Riv. Bourdet, 1372, ff. 4-6.

[14] Bérault, *La coustume*, p. 226. Bérault did not take these dimensions very seriously, and presented them merely as common opinion about the medieval seigneurie. For the size of a noble vavassorie, AD S-M, E, Fonds Poerier d'Amfreville, terrier de La Neuville Chantdoissel. Cf. the larger estimates offered by Paul-Edouard Robinne, *Les magistrats du Parlement de Normandie à la fin du XVIIIe siècle (1774-1790). Essai d'étude économique et sociale*, 2 vols. (unpublished thesis, École des Chartes, 1967), I, 211.

[15] The village of La Neuville Chantdoissel covered about 660 hectares (AD S-M, E, fonds Poerier d'Amfreville, terrier, La Neuville Chantdoissel). See also M. Charpillon and Abbé Caresme, *Dictionnaire historique de toutes les communes du département de l'Eure*, 2 vols. (Les Andelys, 1868), II, 252-255, 882-884, for villages of similar size. On the size of substantial peasant holdings, see Pierre Goubert,

A second characteristic shared by many Norman seigneuries (and probably by most) was dependence on seigneurial revenues, for the most part on permanently fixed
rents. Most Norman estates, it appears, derived between
one-fourth and one-third of their revenue from permanently
fixed rents, paid by those who held tenures from the seigneurie; a further substantial share, usually between one-
tenth and one-fifth but in some cases much more, came from
milling rights. Together, these revenues accounted for about
half of the seigneurie's income. The remaining half came
from the seigneurie's demesne, that part of the seigneurie
which was under the lord's direct control and which he
could either farm directly or (the far more typical case)
lease for short periods of time for variable rents. Despite
the weaknesses and uncertainties of the seigneurie's legal existence, the institution's economic vitality was considerable.[16]

A final trait which seems to have characterized most seigneuries in upper Normandy was fluidity, of both internal
structure and ownership. In this the realities of seigneurial
organization corresponded to the stress of the legal theorists
on the institution's flexible nature. A characteristic example is the seigneurie of Thibermesnil, in the pays de Caux.
Through the sixteenth century Thibermesnil belonged to
the Bigot, who supplied the Parlement with two successive king's advocates; in the seventeenth century it passed
to the Guéribout family, another *parlementaire* dynasty.
Thibermesnil illustrates the ease with which a seigneurie's
demesne (the land within it under the lord's direct control)
might grow at the expense of its "enfeoffed domain," land

"The French Peasantry in the Seventeenth Century: A Regional Example," *Past and Present*, 10 (November, 1956), 66-67.
[16] See Appendix D. Cf. the similar conclusions of Guy Bois, *Crise
du féodalisme*, pp. 233-235; however, Bois presents the seigneurie's
mid-sixteenth-century prospects as more limited than those suggested
here.

which had been granted out as permanent tenures. In 1512 Thibermesnil's demesne represented only 7 percent of the seigneurie's 250 hectares. A century later, in 1603, the demesne had tripled, and now represented 20 percent of the total. By 1641 a further large farm had been incorporated, and the demesne now included half of the seigneurie's original area, although this acquisition may have come from outside the seigneurie itself.[17]

Changes of comparable magnitude may be seen in the seigneuries of La Court and St. Aubin, which the first president Claude Groulart bought in 1581. In 1505 these properties had been sold together for just under 3,800£. By the time Groulart bought them, in 1581, their value had increased nineteen-fold, to 73,000£, and under his remarkable management they expanded still further. In the twenty-five years before his death Groulart made at least sixty-five purchases of land around St. Aubin, worth in all about 54,000£. By his death, in 1607, the value of the property had thus reached at least 127,000£, thirty-four times its value a century earlier and the sign of a complete transformation in the seigneurie's character.[18]

Such expansion of the demesne was only the most spectacular of the changes which the seigneurie might experience. Other changes in the balance of the seigneurie's revenues, hence its character, might occur with equal rapidity. In the barony of Pont St. Pierre, for instance, forest revenues accounted for one-fourth of the total revenue in 1506-1507, but nearly three-fourths of the total in 1572. Careless administration might quickly lead to uncertainties about whether specific properties were held from the seigneurie or not. "All of these rents," noted the receiver's accounts for Pont St. Pierre in 1561, "are marked 'nothing' because the receiver does not know where these properties are situated." Forty years later, in arranging the sale of two plots of land in a nearby village, the seller noted that he

17 AD Eure, E 3207, 3208.
18 Bibliothèque Municipale, Dieppe, MS 63, pp. 794-868.

"does not know from which seigneurie they might be held, since they have not been claimed (*recherché*) by any seigneurie."[19]

Fluidity of the seigneurie's internal structure was matched by changes in the feudal structure as a whole. Fiefs in six-teenth-century Normandy passed rapidly from family to family, and this also tended to weaken the non-economic aspects of seigneurial land ownership. Several examples suggest the speed at which properties might change hands. Thus, the Bigot's Thibermesnil belonged to four families in just over a century; when he bought St. Aubin, in 1581, Claude Groulart became the third owner in seventy-five years; Nicolas Romé represented the fifth family in 130 years to own the barony of Bec Crespin, when he purchased it in 1579. These fiefs changed hands roughly once each generation, and this during a period of apparent consolida-tion and stabilization of land ownership, following the economic and political disasters of the fifteenth century.[20]

A somewhat different view of the same phenomenon is provided by study of the homages which feudal suzerains required each time ownership of a fief changed, whether "naturally," through inheritance, or through some transac-tion such as sale, marriage, or exchange. Acts of homage

[19] AD S-M, E, Fonds Baronnie du Pont St. Pierre, Accounts, 1560-1561, AD Eure, E 1261, 27 December 1601.

[20] AD Eure, E 3208; Bibliothèque Municipale, Dieppe, MS 63, pp. 794-868; A. Le Chevalier, *Notice historique sur les barons et la baronnie du Bec* . . . (Paris, 1898), pp. 10-12. Historians have gen-erally viewed the sixteenth century as a period of diminishing turn-over in the feudal structure, after the exceptional problems created by the Hundred Years' War. See Yvonne Bezard, *La vie rurale dans le sud de la région parisienne de 1450 à 1560* (Paris, 1929), pp. 98-105; for a somewhat less cataclysmic view of the period, Guy Fourquin, *Les campagnes de la région parisienne à la fin du moyen âge, du milieu du XIIIᵉ siècle au début du XVIᵉ siècle* (Paris, 1964), pp. 465-474. However, see Lucien Febvre's stress on the frequency with which fiefs changed hands in the sixteenth century: *Philippe II et la Franche Comté. Étude d'histoire politique, religieuse et sociale* (2nd ed., Paris, 1970), pp. 188-189.

to the crown, for fiefs held directly from it, usually specify the reasons for change in ownership, and it is thus possible to measure the strength of the ties of families to feudal properties and the likelihood that a fief would have new owners, unconnected to it by family tradition. Table 4:1 summarizes such a study of homages; it concerns 254 acts, for the period 1530-1580. At any one moment, these fig-

TABLE 4:1

TURNOVER OF FEUDAL PROPERTY, 1530-1580, BAILLIAGE OF ROUEN

Fiefs changing owners by—		
Direct succession:	106	(41.7 percent)
Collateral succession:	6	(2.4 percent)
Total succession:	112	(44.1 percent)
Purchase:	39	(15.4 percent)
Marriage:	19	(7.5 percent)
Exchange:	4	(1.6 percent)
Total acquisition:	62	(24.4 percent)
Fiefs—		
Belonging to the Church:	29	(11.4 percent)
Unknown:	51	(20.1 percent)
Total:	80	(31.5 percent)
Total:	254	(100.0 percent)

SOURCE: AN P265¹ (*Registre d'hommages du bailliage de Rouen*).

ures suggest, fewer than one-half of the fiefs in upper Normandy were held by "natural" heirs, either immediate or distant. About one-sixth had been purchased or acquired through exchange by their current owners, and about one-twelfth had been acquired through marriage arrangements. Almost one-fourth of these properties had in one way or another just been acquired by the families who held them, and thus did not have traditional ties to particular families. This is particularly striking in view of common assumptions that at least three generations were needed before a family could secure full acceptance as feudal landowners.[21]

[21] Thus Roland Mousnier, *Peasant Uprisings in Seventeenth-Century France, Russia and China*, trans. Brian Pearce (New York, 1970), p. 20.

For reasons that will be considered below, this fluidity of landownership probably diminished in the late sixteenth and early seventeenth centuries. Even in the mid-sixteenth century, of course, many families were able to keep estates for long periods of time; indeed, it is only these estates whose internal workings we can follow in detail, since stability of ownership was usually a prerequisite for the orderly conservation of estate documents. Nonetheless, for a large number of Norman estates frequent changes of ownership served still further to weaken bonds between lord and tenant.

Only a few *parlementaire* estates allow us to observe together, in some detail, the varied elements of seigneurial organization. One estate for which sufficient documents do survive is that of Les Maisons, about 20 km to the south of Rouen, which the councillor Guillaume Maignart bought in 1503 and which his descendants retained—along with an important place in the Parlement—until 1670. Examination of Les Maisons can provide a sense both of the seigneurie's inner workings and of the qualities of *parlementaire* involvement with the seigneurie.

During the sixteenth century Les Maisons was one of the family's principal residences. An early seventeenth-century traveller described the house as small but elegant, with galleries in the Italian style along the front and Latin inscriptions celebrating the family's past. The house was set within a courtyard of farm buildings, and was approached by a formal, tree-lined drive through the communal pasture, the result of an agreement between the Maignart and the parish, in 1561.[22] Inside there were eight rooms, along with an attic, kitchen, and four large closets. There were five bedrooms, a servants' room, and two salons. The house was apparently comfortable rather than palatial, and it ap-

[22] Chanoine Porée, ed., *DuBuisson-Aubenay, Itinéraire de Norman-die* (Paris-Rouen, 1911), pp. 59, 61; La Riv. Bourdet, 774; AD Eure, E 1242, 1 January 1560 (old style); E 1247, 25 August 1566.

pears to have been typical of sixteenth-century robe country dwellings. The Maignart's decision, apparently made in the early 1600's, to construct a far more grandiose house at another of their estates, La Rivière Bourdet, was apparently likewise typical of the Rouennais robe; elaboration in rural architecture was an element in the magistrates' increasingly dynastic outlook.[23]

Like the examples cited above, Les Maisons was a property undergoing a process of dramatic growth in the sixteenth century. The estate which Guillaume Maignart bought in 1503 included only the house itself, 8 hectares of land, and the right to construct a pigeon house. This last right was purchased from the monks of Bec Hellouin, and gave Les Maisons a quasi-seigneurial character; but the monastery retained seigneurial authority over most of Les Maisons. The property steadily expanded in the sixteenth century, as the Maignart bought up small pieces of land in the area: to 33 hectares in 1522, 42 hectares in 1529, 54 hectares in 1583. A considerable part of this land consisted of a few large enclosed fields near the manor itself, but much lay scattered in holdings of an acre or two each; despite the relatively small amount of land it included, Les Maisons extended into four parishes.[24]

[23] For the house and its contents in 1583, La Riv. Bourdet, 2123. The Maignart's chateau of La Rivière Bourdet, completed in about 1650, was estimated to have cost 150,000ł—by sixteenth-century standards a large fortune in itself: Pierre Hurtebise, "Charles-Etienne Maignart de Bernières, Maître des requêtes et intendant (1667-1717)," in Roland Mousnier, *Le conseil du roi de Louis XII à la Révolution* (Paris, 1970), pp. 300-301. For mid-seventeenth-century appreciation of La Rivière Bourdet's splendor, Hercule Grisel, *Les fastes de Rouen*, ed. W. Bouquet (Rouen, 1866-1868), winter trimester, 11. 320ff. Other sixteenth-century descriptions of *parlementaire* country houses suggest that Les Maisons was quite typical: thus Meubles 2, 15 November 1602 (Latigeoire); AD S-M, E, Fonds Caillot de Coquéraumont, liasse no. 6 (Villy); and AD S-M, E, Fonds Restault, unclassed (Restault).

[24] The property's history may be traced through a large number of sources, the most important of which are La Riv. Bourdet, 611, 774, 1592; Hérit. 2, 25 November 1627; AD S-M, E, Fonds Caillot de

Equally important were the peculiarities of Les Maisons' feudal position. Les Maisons was subject to the high justice of the barony of Pont St. Pierre, the principal property in the area, and some of its land was also held from the barony. Most of Les Maisons, though, formed part of the seigneurie of Bec, belonging to the monastery of Bec Hellouin. The seigneurie typified the disordered nature of seigneurial institutions in the area. Not only had its most visible right— that of constructing the pigeon house—been sold to the Maignart, but both its demesne and its dependent tenures had shrunk to miserable proportions. In 1569 its demesne amounted to about 6 hectares, in 4 parcels; its "enfeoffed domain"—land which had been granted out as permanent, hereditary tenures—included about 33 hectares, divided among 19 tenants and spread over 4 parishes. In 1610 the whole seigneurie was leased for 80ł yearly, less than one-tenth of the revenue of its supposed dependency Les Maisons.[25]

The seigneurial structure in which Les Maisons was situated, thus, was far from being a clearly organized hierarchy. Seigneurial authority itself was fragmented, and in the case of Bec had been largely detached from large landownership. It was characteristic of this fragmentation that Charles Maignart's account book for the 1590's and early 1600's described Les Maisons as a *"fief terre et seigneurie,"* though legally the property was only a tenure held from the seigneurie of Bec.[26] But the Maignart were intent on ending this confusion of feudal authority, and their efforts to do so continued over three generations. In 1563 they bought the seigneurie of Bec in the course of the church land sales, sponsored by the crown to pay off some of its debts. Within a year, however, the monks exercised their right to repurchase the property. In 1610 the Maignart

---

Coquéraumont; Charpillon and Caresme, *Dictionnaire historique*, II, 674-677.
[25] La Riv. Bourdet, 1731, 2932.   [26] *Ibid.*, 2105.

again acquired a form of indirect control over the seigneurie: a servant of the president Charles Maignart leased the seigneurie, in the company of two other representatives of Maignart. Three years later, negotiations began for the seigneurie's outright sale, a process complicated by the theoretical inalienability of church land. Only in 1627 was the sale completed. Though Bec Hellouin retained its patronage of the church of Pont St. Pierre, the other elements of seigneurial authority were finally united with most of the property that was held of the seigneurie. A substantial strengthening of seigneurial authority had taken place.[27]

In the course of the sixteenth and seventeenth centuries, it appears, seigneurial organization at Les Maisons became less fragmented and more hierarchical; and this appears to have been typical of *parlementaire* estates (we will return to this question below). Despite this evolution toward greater clarity, however, examination of both the seigneurie's legal structure and its actual workings suggests the seigneurie's limited capacity for serving other than economic ends. The legal confusions surrounding the seigneurie, its fragmented and changing character, and the frequent changes of ownership to which it was often subject—all these placed severe limits on its function as a framework for bonds between lord and peasant. Institutional obstacles did not entirely eliminate such ties, however. The magistrates appear to have enjoyed especially close relationships with their own superiors in the feudal hierarchy, those from whom they held their seigneuries. Several families owed their advancement to the Parlement to such ties: thus the Busquet, who

[27] AN G8 1246; La Riv. Bourdet, 1592, 2932, 3018, 3114; Hérit. 2, 25 November 1627. Possibly the abbot's willingness to sell reflected the important lawsuits which Bec had pending before the Parlement in the early seventeenth century, concerning especially the reform of St. Maur: see Chanoine Porée, *Histoire de l'abbaye du Bec*, 2 vols. (Évreux, 1901), II, 365ff.

were first the vassals, then (in the 1530's) the officials and clients of the ducs of Estouteville.[28] Something of the tone of contemporary assumptions about these ties is suggested by a dispute of 1598. At the start of a lawsuit, the councillor Robert LaVache was asked to withdraw "because he is the owner of a fief at Saussay, held directly from the said sieur [André] de Vieupont [baron of Le Neubourg and one of the litigants], and because of this the said sieurs have developed a great friendship; further, because the said sieur de Vieupont has boasted that the said sieur de LaVache would use all his friends in order to please him."[29] The relationship between fief holder and feudal suzerain plainly retained a great deal of force, as the role of patronage in the Parlement's recruitment would suggest.

The magistrates might also have close relations with the wealthier peasantry, despite the institutional obstacles that have been considered here, and they often spoke of their patriarchal role within the seigneurie. In 1559 the councillor Robert LeRoux settled a lawsuit with one of his tenants, he said, "considering that the said Guillaume is his vassal and man."[30] In 1589, when marauding soldiers seemed to threaten one of his estates, the future president Charles Maignart sought and was granted permission by the Parlement to sound the tocsin and call out "his subjects and other inhabitants of the surrounding parishes" for defense.[31] Feudal language of this kind was typical, and social realities in certain ways actually reinforced it. The strength of the ties which bound the *parlementaires* to the countryside has already been seen: substantial numbers of them owned no property at all in Rouen, and spent no more time there than professional commitment demanded, returning to their estates whenever possible. It was characteristic of this situation that in the later sixteenth century the Maignart house

[28] Above, Chapter 2.   [29] Reg. sec., 1597-1598, f. 280v.
[30] Meubles 2, 24 February 1558 (old style).
[31] AD S-M, B, Parlement, Arrêts, 11 March 1589. I owe this reference to Philip Benedict.

at Les Maisons was more elaborately furnished than their house at Rouen.[32] Burials, especially, provided conspicuous expression of this kind of attachment. When Madeleine Bigot (mother of one councillor and daughter of a king's attorney in the Parlement) died, in 1616, her body was ceremoniously conveyed from Rouen to her son's estate near Pontaudemer, much of the way by boat, and with distribution of alms along the way. When Jean Godart, master in the Chambre des Comptes and father of two councillors, died in 1601, he too was buried at the family's seigneurie, and among other expenses involved in the burial was 12₶ spent in painting "a black band around the church of Belbeuf." Especially during the first half of the sixteenth century, the custom of burying the dead man's heart at the country estate and the rest of the body in the urban parish retained much popularity among the magistrates.[33]

Yet, despite such ceremony and symbolism, the *parlementaires* were surprisingly ready to employ economic terms when speaking of the relations between seigneur and "vassal and man." These, for instance, were the terms which Jacques de Bauquemare, the court's first president and the king's commissioner to the Estates of Normandy, used in an address of 1566 to the Estates, in defending the first and second estates' right to vote on taxes which they did not pay. The three estates, according to Bauquemare, were "tied and united like the members of a single body," but the essential point was economic: "How many tenant farmers are there (he asked) who lease the properties of ecclesiastics and gentlemen and pay 60 and 80₶ in taxes (*tailles*) and who, without the said farms, would not pay 100s? Does not this charge come from a reduction of their rents? Here then is the special interest [of ecclesiastics and gentlemen] in attending the Estates." The central bond between lord

[32] La Riv. Bourdet, 2123.

[33] AD S-M, E, Fonds Restault, unclassed; 16J178, ff. 45-46; BM MS Martainville Y2, pp. 29, 138, 165; Louis de Souillet, *Histoire de la ville de Rouen* (3rd ed., Rouen, 1731), epitaphs, parish of St. Nicolas.

and peasant, as Bauquemare presented it, was their economic partnership; it was this partnership that really "tied and united" them.[34] A similar consciousness of common interests colors Charles Maignart's description in his account book of his relations with one of his principal tenants: "Wednesday of the Easter holiday, 2 April 1603, having gone to dine at Saussey, at the home of Theroude, my tenant, as we were leaving I made an agreement with him to sell him 100 *mines* of wheat which he was to deliver to me at Andely, for the price of 530 *livres*, for which we have only the word the one of the other."[35]

As seigneurs, the *parlementaires* were on terms of some closeness with such members of the village elite, but they saw the relationship for what it was: one of mutual economic convenience. There was apparently a similar relationship with other leading residents of the village. Thus, the magistrates were likely to be on close terms with the *curé*; when the seigneurie included the patronage of the church, this was likely to be either a relative (thus the Toustain appointed successive younger brothers to be *curé* of Limésy) or a dependent, named in part (it seems) because of the help he might offer in administering the estate (thus the *curé* of Thibermesnil served as an agent for the Bigot, passing rental contracts in their absence).[36] But there is much less evidence of mutual interest or involvement with lower elements of rural society. As will be seen in the following section, discrimination in economic matters was clear and consistent: small tenants were charged substantially higher rentals than the prosperous farmers described above. Nor (as will be seen) did the magistrates hesitate

[34] Charles de Robillard de Baurepaire, ed., "Les harangues prononcés par le président de Bauquemare aux États de la province de Normandie, de 1556 à 1583," ext. *Précis des Travaux de l'Académie des Sciences, Belles Lettres et Arts de Rouen*, 1871-1872, pp. 14, 13.

[35] La Riv. Bourdet, 2105.

[36] M. Bourel, *La commune de Limésy, souvenirs du passé* . . . (Rouen, 1899), p. 152; AD Eure, E3212.

to employ the mechanisms of debt and foreclosure in order to extend their property. When the *parlementaires* dealt with residents of their seigneuries on other issues, there was a similar sense of detachment. Thus, when money was needed for parish improvements, *parlementaire* seigneurs appear as purchasers of parish property, but not as donors or patrons.[37] Most strikingly absent is evidence that the magistrates or their families served with any frequency as godparents to children born in parishes where they were seigneurs. At least in those parishes where sixteenth-century registers exist, the magistrates and their families participated in only a small fraction of the baptisms that took place.[38] Although their participation was more frequent in the country than in their urban parishes, their participation in most parish life, it appears, was negligible.

It is this combination of apparent detachment from the mass of the village community, with an explicitly economic alliance with the more important farmers, that seems to have characterized most *parlementaires'* relations with their seigneuries. Such attitudes did not exclude common action or sentiment altogether, as when bands of soldiers threatened the seigneurie. Common action of this kind, however, appears to have been at best an exceptional response to crisis situations. Were these attitudes particular to *parlementaire*

[37] AD Eure, E, 1435, 19 November 1596; E 3208.

[38] See Registres paroissiaux, Berville-sur-Seine and La Neuville Chantdoissel, on deposit at AD S-M; both were sites of *parlementaire* seigneuries, and in both magistrates or their families took part in about 5 percent of baptisms in the later sixteenth century. For a further example of the ambiguous relations between *parlementaire* seigneurs and the peasantry, see Hérit. 2, 29 May 1600: the president Louis Bretel, "pour le desir et affection qu'il a de subvenyr et ayder de ses biens a Catherine Baujot petitte fille de deffunct Pasques Baujot . . . et afin qu'elle puisse trouver parti honneste en mariage et s'entretenyr commodement a l'advenyr en consideration que Nicolas Baujot son pere filz aisné dudit Pasques seroit a present dyminue de moyens pour la decretation qui a este cy devant faicte de ses heritages a ledit [sic] seigneur de Lanquetot [Bretel]," gives Catherine three acres of land.

seigneurs, or did they characterize the older nobility as well? Until much more is known about the sixteenth-century *noblesse d'épée*, answers to such questions must remain speculative. Evidence for similarity of economic practice during the sixteenth century will be presented below; members of the older aristocracy responded as aggressively as the *parlementaires* to the economic pressures of the age.[39] Here it is sufficient to point to what has been seen about the broad structures of seigneurial landownership in sixteenth-century upper Normandy, structures that must have affected robe and sword about equally. Seigneurial justice there was limited, and gave the seigneur little that really partook of public power. There was a continuous turnover in seigneurial property during the sixteenth century, and this must have weakened traditional associations of family with property. In any event, most seigneuries were small and were fragmented among several peasant communities.

This is quite distant from Loyseau's stress on the political authority that the seigneurie included, and from the stress that some historians have placed on the still-"feudal" character of sixteenth-century society.[40] The seigneurie in sixteenth-century upper Normandy was in fact a vital institution, but its vitality was economic. Seigneurial revenues were an important source of income, and the seigneurie offered large possibilities for acquiring new properties.

B. Administering the Estate

"In the matters which so closely concern me, I do not want to neglect my duties, but rather to try to accumulate as much money as I am able."[41] These were the terms that the president Charles Maignart used, writing in his account

---

[39] In Part C of this chapter.

[40] Thus Roland Mousnier, "Les survivances médiévales dans la France du XVII⁰ siècle," *XVII⁰ siècle*, no. 106-107 (1975), 73-78.

[41] La Riv. Bourdet, 2105.

book around 1600, to describe his approach to estate administration. This section attempts to assess the ways in which such attitudes found expression in the daily realities of estate administration, and to understand at least some of the problems that estate administration met with.[42] This will lead to an effort, in the third part of this chapter, to evaluate the profits and losses which the magistrates derived from their concentration on landed investments, and to describe changes which took place in this regard over the sixteenth century.

Evidence for the workings of the attitudes that Maignart expressed is easily found. His accounts for the late sixteenth and early seventeenth centuries show a great deal of attentiveness to possibilities for profit and considerable tenacity in pursuing them. Through his leasing arrangements, Maignart disposed of substantial quantities of grain and wine, and he had a businessman's attitude toward both. Grain sales invariably were made in May and June, when reserves from the previous harvest were lowest and prices likely to be highest. He took considerable care to be well informed about prices in the markets nearest his estates; one whole page of his account book consists of listings of such prices. To be sure, Maignart was not always successful at this trade, but even in failure his attitudes were calculating and grasping. In May, 1604, he sold 100 *mines* of grain to a Rouennais merchant, but found that he had sold too early. Prices rose, and he noted in his account book that "for not having taken my time, I lost 100ł on my property this year." Maignart's dealings in the wine trade involved an equal element of calculation. He kept a large store of wine in the cellar of his house in Rouen, and was able to await the best prices; thus, in early 1606 he refused to sell early in

[42] The analysis presented here owes much to Lawrence Stone, *The Crisis of the Aristocracy, 1558-1641* (Oxford, 1965), pp. 273-334, and Georges Duby, *La société au XIᵉ et XIIᵉ siècles dans la région maconnaise* (2nd ed., Paris, 1971), esp. pp. 73-88.

the year "in order to await, with God's help, the chances after Easter."[43]

It is impossible to follow so closely the calculations of other magistrates, but that they made similar calculations is certain. When the Rouennais city councillors in 1597 drew up an "*estat du vin et sildre*" found in the city, they detailed the impressive stocks of both which most *parlementaires* held, some of it intended for home consumption, but much of it plainly awaiting "*le hasart du vin*" on the market.[44] Involvement in the grain trade appears to have been less important (as indeed it was for Maignart). Some *parlementaires*, though, were accused of hoarding during a period of high prices,[45] and many received large amounts of grain from both the payments of tenant farmers and seigneurial dues: thus the councillor Guillaume Jubert, who in the early 1540's received from tenants a total of about 1,280 *mines* of wheat each year, worth at current prices about 6,400l.[46] From the limited evidence that we have,[47] the *parlementaires* approaches the administration of their landed properties with attitudes that were rational, calculating, and acquisitive. More precisely, there seem to have been few inhibitions of honor or concern for patronage on their economic drives. Like Maignart, they sought "to accumulate as much money" as they were able.[48] But their success in

[43] La Riv. Bourdet, 2105.

[44] Archives Communales, Rouen, Chartrier, 137; I owe this reference to Philip Benedict.

[45] AD S-M, 16J3: 20 (Chambre de Police, Rouen).

[46] AD Eure, E 2474, 2 February 1553 (old style).

[47] This evidence, as will be discussed below, is biased; as in other issues, more is known about families who were wealthier, better established, and longer-lasting than the majority.

[48] For more general statement of this kind of attitude, see Bernard de La Roche Flavin, *Treze livres des Parlements de France* (Bordeaux, 1617), pp. 436-437: "Aristides by his poverty prohibited his children from taking important public positions, and buried the memory of his posterity. The wise magistrate will avoid this problem by prudent management (*oeconomie*). And when honorable oppor-

doing so depended on more than simply their economic attitudes. They had to apply their attitudes within certain fundamental limits and possibilities, and it is these which need now to be considered.

The most basic problems and possibilities for *parlementaire* estate administration were those imposed by geography. The map on page 189 attempts to illustrate some of these, by situating the estates of sixteen *parlementaires* from the period after 1550;[49] these are the families for whom reliable and complete evidence on rural properties is available, and together they include about one-tenth of the magistrates who held office between 1550 and 1610 and (because of the biased nature of the surviving records) a much larger proportion of the most important *parlementaire* dynasties. Several conclusions about the estate management practiced by at least the wealthier magistrates are suggested by this map. Perhaps clearest is the wide dispersion of the magistrates' properties. Their estates did not fall into a tidy circle around Rouen itself. Rather, they were to be found all through upper Normandy, from Dieppe and Le Havre in the pays de Caux to Gisors and Les Andelys in the Vexin normand. Such properties might be a day's journey from Rouen, and in some cases probably more.[50]

---

tunities present themselves for acquiring properties, he will take advantage of them without harming others or injustice. . . ." Anthropologists, although continuing to debate the nature of pre-modern economic attitudes, supply a number of helpful ways of defining and clarifying these. See especially Maurice Godelier, *Rationalité et irrationalité en économie* (Paris, 1968), and *Horizons, trajets marxistes en anthropologie* (Paris, 1973). For sophisticated application of ideas about fundamental differences in economic systems and rationalities, see M. I. Finley, *The Ancient Economy* (Berkeley and Los Angeles, 1973).

[49] Because a requirement for this map was the complete enumeration of properties, only those magistrates for whom there are full listings of properties are included. These are essentially the fortunes analyzed above, in Chapter 3.

[50] On rates of travel along the Seine valley (in this case to Paris),

That such distance from the city was in fact typical of *parlementaire* estates is suggested by other documents as well. A list of fief holders in the viscounty of Rouen, for instance, drawn up in 1594 to serve as the basis for the feudal levy, shows only seventeen *parlementaires* among the 137 fief holders in the region immediately surrounding the city —these represented only about one-fifth of the Parlement's membership.[51]

Distance from Rouen had important implications. The peculiar nature of the magistrates' ties to the city are again evident. They were plainly not an urban class whose interests had spread into the neighboring countryside,[52] but a group whose economic bases lay at a considerable distance from the city. Distance also had implications for the quality of estate administration. The *parlementaires* were almost by definition absentee landowners, but the map on page 189 should make clear what an acute problem this might be. Estates separated by at least a day's journey from the magistrates' residence posed difficult problems of overseeing and accounting. Distance also made more difficult the problem of disposing of an estate's produce. These were not suburban farms whose produce could easily be transported to residences in the city, but estates sufficiently removed that

---

see, for instance, Reg. sec., 1572-1574, f. 152v. On the still tenuous connections between the Vexin and Rouen, despite the small distances involved, see J.-P. Fruit, *Vexin normand ou Vexin parisienne? Contribution à l'étude géographique de l'espace rural* (Paris, 1974).

[51] Prévost, ed., "Documents sur le ban et l'arrière ban," pp. 241-332. Conversely, the relative unimportance of *parlementaire* landownership outside the Seine valley is supported by AD Eure, E 3 (role of the *arrière ban*, bailliage of Évreux, 1562): only two *parlementaire* families were listed in this region, which stretched west of Évreux to Conches, Breteuil, and Orbec.

[52] The pattern demonstrated by Pierre Goubert for Beauvais and its surrounding countryside: *Beauvais et le Beauvaisis de 1600 à 1730. Contribution à l'histoire sociale de la France du XVIIe siècle*, 2 vols. (Paris, 1960), I, 17-20.

transport might be expensive and difficult to arrange and control.[53]

Distance from Rouen was not the only problem that geography posed. The map of *parlementaire* estates makes clear also that the fragmentation of property seen within the individual seigneurie existed also on the scale of the province itself. Families of any importance owned properties throughout a wide area, partly because of the interplay of marriage alliances and inheritances. Thus the Jubert, a family with members in the Parlement from the 1520's through the eighteenth century, in the later sixteenth century had their principal seigneuries in the Vexin, between Les Andelys and Gisors. But they also owned important properties at Bourg Achard, on the Seine downstream from Rouen, and in several villages still further downstream—at Caudebec, Marais-Vernier, and near Dieppe.[54] In effect their interests were spread over the length of the province, and this was an altogether typical situation for at least the wealthier *parlementaire* families: thus the Maignart, Groulart, Romé, Croismare. This fact compounded the obstacles which geography placed in the way of effective administration, by making it still more difficult to survey carefully any one property and by limiting still further the degree to which the *parlementaire* landowner could be effectively present to his agents, tenants, and to the peasantry in general.[55]

Fragmentation and distance appear to have been the major difficulties which the geography of *parlementaire*

[53] The magistrates' own awareness of what distance might mean was acute, and shaped their actions. Thus in 1526 the lawyer Louis Roussel and his bride Florence Bordel, daughter of a president in the Parlement, renounced her inheritances in the area of Orléans, "considerans qu'ilz sont demourans et residens en ceste ville de Rouen et qu'il y a longue distance jusques a Orleans," which would render her properties nearly worthless (Tabel., 28 May 1526).

[54] AD Eure, E 2474, 2 February 1553 (os); Hérit. 2, 28 June 1580.

[55] For discussion of the effects that distance had on seigneurial administration, Duby, *La société aux XIe et XIIe siècles dans la région maconnaise*, pp. 84-86.

landownership created for effective estate administration. But geography offered advantages also. The principal of these came from the clustering of *parlementaire* estates (as seen on this page) along the valley of the Seine, the main

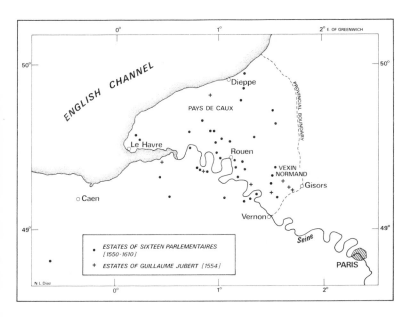

line of transport and communication to both Rouen and Paris. Few of the magistrates seem to have had important estates outside this area. This probably worked against the formation and maintenance of provincial solidarities and loyalties. The wealthiest and most respected *parlementaire* families, at least, had little attachment or economic interest in lower Normandy, and their interests easily drew them outside Normandy altogether, into the orbit of Paris. A family such as the Jubert, whose principal estates lay in the Vexin, was indeed nearly outside the province already; it was nearly as great a distance from their estates to Rouen as it was to Paris. Although this geographical position sub-stantially weakened their attachments to the province, it

189

meant easy access to important urban markets: Rouen, of course, but also such smaller markets as Vernon and Les Andelys, which in turn were linked to the vast Parisian market. The magistrates thus had the opportunity to profit from urban demand for grain, wine, cider, and other commodities. They were in a position very different from the autarchic seigneurial regime represented by the lower Norman Gilles de Gouberville.[56] The situation of their estates allowed, and in some degree even forced, them to think in terms of a commercial, market-oriented administration.

Geography placed especially heavy demands on the magistrates' accounting procedures. Only thus could they overcome the related problems of distance and fragmentation. Here, however, a second set of constraints on *parlementaire* estate management becomes apparent. To secure effective bookkeeping was difficult and, above all, expensive. Magistrates who wished for a really accurate idea of their economic situation might have to spend large amounts of money to acquire it. Just how much money this might involve is illustrated by surviving inventories after death, which represent an exact evaluation of income, debts, and assets: in other words, a complete picture of the individual's economic situation at his death. These were time-consuming and expensive documents to compile. It took the clerks just over a month to list all the papers connected with Claude Groulart's succession, in 1607, and the document which they produced came to well over 1,000 pages.[57] In this case the cost was not noted, but other, less impressive, successions fill this gap. To compile an account of the Godart estate during the minority of its heirs (between 1601 and 1606) cost the family 150£; inventories drawn up in 1616 after the death of Madeleine Bigot, mother of the councillor Laurent Restault, cost 108£.[58]

[56] See especially Le Roy Ladurie, "La verdeur du bocage."
[57] BM, Dieppe, MS 63, pp. 1, 1306-1307.
[58] AD S-M, 16J178; E, Fonds Restault, unclassified.

These were substantial sums of money, but compiling such statements represented only the start of the expenses that effective administration might involve. In addition to the need for careful accounting, there was a constant need for legal expenditures. It was necessary that continuous legal representation be retained, if the estate was to be adequately guarded against encroachments and if advantage was to be taken of opportunities which the law created for extending the estate. This was not a very heavy burden in itself. The Godart spent only 20ł yearly on the pension of a *procureur* who would represent their legal interests. But this was only a preliminary expenditure. The Godart accounts include 127ł 15s paid to "Master Nicollas Richard *praticien* . . . for three trips taken by him to Falaise and to Caen to deal with the judicial seizures that were being undertaken," and this was without even the expenses of a serious lawsuit. Some idea of the legal expenses that any extraordinary problem might entail is given by the costs which the Godart had to bear in 1601, when Jean Godart died. Simply to assure the transmission of the fiefs which he held cost the family 450ł, in addition to the costs of drawing up inventories and accounts, noted above.[59]

Several factors contributed to making administration so expensive. Most obvious was the structure of the seigneurie itself, and in particular the relationship of the tenures that made up its *domaine fieffé* to the seigneurie. Constant attention was neded to assure that tenures did not slip away from the seigneurie, through their owners' failure to acknowledge their dependence and pay the required dues.[60] Still greater care was required if the seigneur was to take full advantage of the possibilities for acquisition that the seigneurie offered: to make use, for instance, of the *retrait féodal* and of the possibilities for seizing properties because of debt. The frag-

[59] AD S-M, 16J178. For more general discussion of the costs of litigation, Guenée, *Tribunaux et gens de justice*, pp. 251ff.

[60] On the uncertainty of ostensibly immemorial custom, see Guenée, *Tribunaux et gens de justice*, pp. 90-92.

mentation of peasant holdings added still further difficulties. Seigneurial dues, we have seen, were an important component of the revenues of at least many upper Norman estates, but they were not established in a form that made collection easy. Thus the Romé's barony of Bec Crespin: in 1572 its *domaine fieffé* was divided among 269 tenants spread through 19 villages. Each tenant paid relatively small amounts for his property, a few *livres* in cash, some poultry or grain, but collectively they were extremely important to the value of the seigneurie. In 1572 their dues accounted for about 44 percent of its total revenues.[61] Failure to keep careful track of each tenant's obligations might thus be dangerous to the barony's overall economic position, but failure could be avoided only by tedious record-keeping and equally tedious procedures of collection. And, although Bec Crespin posed these difficulties in an acute form, they were in fact common to all seigneuries that derived important income from tenants' dues.

Seigneurial dues posed a conspicuous problem for estate administration because of the quaint forms which inheritance might give to tenants' obligations. As tenures were divided, their obligations were divided too, leading to payments expressed in quarters of fowl and the like.[62] But the problems and expenses posed by the seigneurie's demesne were as difficult and ultimately more serious. For it was as necessary and as difficult to oversee carefully the tenants who leased parts of the demesne for short terms as those who held hereditary tenures. In the first place, short-term lease holders might be very numerous, even within a single seigneurie. Thus the Maignart's property of

[61] AD S-M, E, Fonds Romé du Bec, unclassified.

[62] Thus in the barony of Bec Crespin in 1572-1573, in the parish of Notre Dame du Bec, Geoffroy LeMarchant owed dues of one-third of a capon at Christmas and 4₶ 12s 15d during Lent; Guillaume LeMarchant (presumably a relative, although this is not specified) owed two-thirds of a capon at Christmas and 16s 8d during Lent (*ibid.*, accounts 1572-1573). Cf. Meuvret, "Domaines ou ensembles territoriaux?" p. 189.

Les Maisons, although exceptionally compact, included a large number of plots of land that, in the mid-sixteenth century, the Maignart leased separately; in the autumn of 1543, there were twenty such separate leases, in addition to the main fields of the property.[63] Each of these lease holders had to be overseen, and the problem was multiplied by the fact that Les Maisons was only one of several Maignart properties.

A second problem was that of assuring the flow of payments from tenants. Rental contracts specified the terms and forms in which rents were to be paid, but these rarely were followed with great precision. The accounts of the president Charles Maignart for the years around 1600 allow us to see the realities which lay behind the apparent simplicity of the contracts. Payments from his tenants reached Maignart in the most haphazard ways: in small sums spent for repairs, in direct payments to Maignart's creditors, in sums of cash or provisions in kind paid when he happened to visit a particular property. Even to determine how much of the rental had been paid in effect required visiting the property, verifying receipts, and examining the repairs.[64]

Compounding these difficulties was the problem of the tenants' tardiness in payment. Holding back payments formed one of the few means of economic negotiation available to the tenant, and its prevalence in part resulted from its effectiveness for this purpose.[65] But tenants fell behind in payments for simpler reasons also. The military crises of the later sixteenth century and the destruction they caused made it simply impossible to pay. Maignart's accounts indicate the magnitude which the problem might assume. Between 1595 and 1606, for example, his farm of Calletot was leased for 300l yearly, but by 1606 the farmer there was

[63] AD Eure, E 1224. [64] La Riv. Bourdet, 2105.
[65] See Jean Jacquart, *La crise rurale en Île de France 1550-1670* (Paris, 1974), pp. 236-238, and for a comparable English example, B. J. Harris, "Landlords and Tenants in England in the Later Middle Ages," *Past and Present*, 43 (1969), 146-150.

in arrears for more than 1,300*l*. For another parish, Hauville, Maignart himself drew up around 1600 a "memoir of what is owed me." The total debt was 2,614*l*, an average of 238*l* for each of the eleven tenants involved.[66] The need to deal continually with tenant arrears was thus yet another element making really effective and continuous estate administration an expensive and demanding affair.

It is not surprising that many magistrates settled for much less. Indeed, given the costs of really good administration, to settle for less may have been a more rational economic choice. Such compromise was to be seen first in the accounting procedures that they employed. Most magistrates seem to have reserved full accountings, with complete statements of expenditures and revenues, for moments when it was absolutely necessary, for closing up the administration of the properties of minors and as a basis for dividing inheritances.[67] Most of the time their accounts were done in a much simpler form. Little more was done than to note receipts from rentals as they came, in whatever form, with each property receiving its particular page in the account book and with receipts noted consecutively until space ran out and a new book had to be begun. Expenditures were not noted at all, except in special circumstances. Accounting of expenditures amounted to no more than keeping receipts, in sacks in the large chests which always figure in inventories after death.[68]

[66] La Riv. Bourdet, 2105.

[67] Yet again, our sources are limited, and it is impossible to generalize with full confidence. Because of their bias toward the wealthiest and most successful families, though, it seems likely that the extant sources reflect the most sophisticated accounting techniques.

[68] Thus BM Dieppe, MS 63, pp. 2-3, etc. There seems to have been nothing in France comparable to the sophisticated accounting literature that had already developed in thirteenth-century England; see Dorothea Oschinsky, *Walter of Henley and Other Treatises on Estate Management and Accounting* (Oxford, 1971). On the reluctance of French noblemen to acquire practical mathematics, Natalie Zemon Davis, "Sixteenth-Century French Arithmetics on the Business Life,"

Accounting procedures of this kind favored neither the careful adjustment of expenditures to revenues, nor even a clear evaluation of income. At best the magistrate's account books placed before him a clear statement of the rental contracts he had passed with his tenants. They gave him no very clear idea of what his actual income was. To obtain such an idea, separate accountings—with receipts on both sides collected and verified—had to be held with each tenant. Expenditures since the previous accounting were deducted, cash and produce changed hands, and a total of arrears was arrived at and carried forward until the next meeting. These accountings took place, it appears, infrequently and irregularly—in the case of Charles Maignart, about once every two years, when he happened to visit the farm in question.[69] Procedures of this kind were above all unresponsive. Debts and arrears rarely seem to have escaped ultimate detection, but it was likely to be some time before the magistrate became aware of specific problems and could begin to respond to them.

An alternative choice was simply to avoid as many as possible of the expenses and difficulties of administration by leasing land to only a few major tenants. All through the sixteenth century magistrates had leased substantial farms to the well-to-do *laboureurs* who could afford to rent them. But, in the later sixteenth century, for reasons we shall consider below, there was a tendency to dispense with the village *laboureurs* and to lease still larger blocs of property to still wealthier tenants, often merchants from Rouen itself. To them could be left many of the costs and risks of administering and maintaining the property. An extreme example may illustrate the tendencies that were involved. In 1603 Alfonce Jubert, councillor in the Parlement and Charles Maignart's son-in-law, leased to one Robert Halley

Journal of the History of Ideas, XXI, 1 (January-March, 1960), 18-48, esp. 27, 44-46.
[69] La Riv. Bourdet, 2105.

of Rouen about 350 hectares of his land, lying in several villages between Les Andelys and Gisors. This represented a huge concentration of property, and, in fact, until 1603 the property had been rented in much smaller parcels. Halley was replacing thirteen separate tenants, several of whom themselves held farms of considerable importance. His contract left Halley with the major responsibilities of administering these large and dispersed properties. He was to arrange subleases as he saw fit, thus taking over the problems of arrears that have been seen above. He also was left with all responsibility for maintaining and repairing all buildings. Finally, there was provision that Halley "maintain the ownership of the said seigneur over the things here leased." In other words, the contract freed Jubert from all the problems of legally defending his property. The time, energy, and expense that were needed to watch out for encroachments and to combat them in the courts were to be expended by his tenant. Jubert was leasing more than land alone. One of these properties included the seigneurie of Arquency. Its lease involved the manor house itself, and also left the tenant with full enjoyment of all seigneurial rights whatsoever. The tenant was effectively left with the whole seigneurial administration as well as the lands attaching to the seigneurie.[70]

Jubert's leasing of virtually the whole of his landed property was exceptional for the thoroughness with which he renounced control over his estates. Most magistrates, it appears, retained parcels of land, certain seigneurial powers (notably the dues required when tenures changed hands), and use of the seigneurial manor when they leased their properties; and in the sixteenth century leases of such a scale as Jubert passed were unusual. Leases of a single seigneurie and 100 acres of land appear to have been much more common. Nonetheless, the rental arrangements of

[70] Meubles 2, 17 July 1603. Four years later Alfonce Jubert sold Halley a fief worth 9000l, suggesting the resources Halley controlled (Hérit. 2, 18 January 1607).

THE MEANINGS OF LANDOWNERSHIP

other magistrates tended to follow essentially the lines of Jubert's, and with the same purposes.[71] By concentrating his leases and creating such huge tenancies as Halley's, the magistrate avoided nearly all the costs of operating the estate, maintaining its buildings and land, defending it against enroachment, watching over the obligations of the small tenants. In addition to these advantages was the benefit of at least relative assurance against the problem of the tenant's impoverishment. To deal with a large-scale entrepreneur such as Halley involved many fewer risks of nonpayment than was the case with small farmers, who lacked the reserves necessary to take on more than a few acres of land, and who were continually vulnerable to poor harvests. Large-scale tenant farming offered a streamlined, untroublesome administration of the estate.[72]

Contemporaries were aware of these benefits, and also of the price that had to be paid for them. A letter to Charles Maignart in the early 1580's, apparently from an estate agent, described the advantages that would come from taking a small property away from the tenant who had leased it, and confiding it instead to one of Maignart's principal tenants: ". . . I have found a man who will take [the farm] (wrote this correspondent) if we allow him some reduction in its price. It seems to me that you will be better off leasing it to him at a lower price than Faurel paid, and being sure of being well paid. If it pleases you I will draw up a lease for him. He wants to pay no more than 70 *livres* yearly, but I have told him that 80 *livres* is as low a price as we will accept. If it is your pleasure to lease it to him, you will tell me, and there will be no need for guarantees against nonpayment (*pleges*) in his case."[73] The advantages of dealing

---

[71] See below, pp. 212-213.

[72] On the spread of such farming in the Hurepoix, south of Paris, see Jacquart, *La crise rurale*, pp. 156, 340-342; Jacquart speaks of "la simplification apportée, un peu partout, à partir de 1550, à l'administration des seigneuries . . ." (p. 156).

[73] La Riv. Bourdet, 2105.

with large tenants, in other words, came at the cost of lower rents. The large tenant farmer was thus recompensed for the services that he supplied; and, as the letter to Maignart suggests, his bargaining position was likely to be far stronger than that of the poor peasant who could lease only a few acres.

Precisely how much these advantages cost the *parlementaires* is not easily determined, but the cost was plainly substantial. In 1554 the Jubert leased the seigneurie of Arquency for 800ł yearly.[74] Fifty years later, when Alfonce Jubert leased the larger portion of his lands to a single farmer, Arquency was included in the lease; it accounted for about 62 percent of the land leased in terms of area, though not necessarily in terms of value. Since the total rental charged in 1603 was 1,550ł,[75] the revenue which Jubert received from Arquency in that year may be very roughly estimated at 960ł (62 percent of 1,550ł), one-fifth more than what the property was worth in 1554. But between 1554 and 1603 the real value of the *livre tournois* had declined, by at least 50 percent when measured in terms of grain prices, and thus the real value of Arquency to the Jubert had fallen by about 40 percent. This it seems was the cost of confiding their property to a single large tenant. No such speculation is required to determine the cost of large-scale tenant farming on the Maignart estates. There the difference between rent charged the principal tenants and that charged the lesser tenants was on the order of 40 percent. Thus, in the seigneurie of Thibouville, in the late sixteenth and early seventeenth century: plots of 5.5 hectares and less were rented for 14.5ł the hectare; a farm of 20 hectares rented for slightly more than 10.5ł the hectare; and the main farm of the seigneurie, amounting to 47.6 hectares, was rented for 8.8ł the hectare. At the Maignart's seigneurie of Les Maisons the differences were still greater: in 1594 a farm of 7.6 hectares was leased for 8ł per hectare,

---

[74] AD Eure, E 2474.   [75] Meubles 2, 17 July 1603.

whereas farms of 2 hectares and less were leased for 18₤ per hectare, well over twice as much.[76]

Major tenants enjoyed other advantages. Because farmers with the necessary capital were not easily found or replaced, they readily formed dynasties, maintaining their hold on certain properties over several generations. The Maignart's farm of Thibouville was leased in 1570 to Pierre Auber, in the 1590's to Jean Auber; their farm of Calletot was held by Jean Rivière in 1570, by Anthoine Rivière in 1594, and by Guillaume Rivière in 1604; Saussey was held by Cardin and Jean LeTellier in 1522, by Jean LeTellier and two others in 1566 and 1575.[77] It is not surprising that, as seen above, the relationship between such men and the magistrates was a close one.[78]

One further point about the large blocs in which the magistrates leased their landed properties deserves emphasis: the artificial character of most such large farms. Few large farms had the unified, compact quality that—elsewhere in France—would qualify them as *métairies*.[79] Rather, these were collections of large numbers of small pieces of land, often dispersed over a considerable area and joined only by the accident of ownership. A particularly clear example of this fragmentation is provided by two leases which Pierre Jubert (Alfonce's first cousin) passed in the 1590's and early 1600's, concerning his seigneurie of Bonnemare. Each lease involved a major farm, one of 82 acres, the other of 67 acres. But between them the farms included eighty-seven separate pieces of land, none of them larger than 8 acres.[80] This remained the typical character of the upper Norman large farm through the early twentieth century, especially in the

[76] La Riv. Bourdet, 2105.

[77] *Ibid.*, 769, 1653, 2105; AD Eure, E 1246, 1247.

[78] See above, pp. 179-181.

[79] Thus Louis Merle, *La métairie et l'évolution de la Gâtine poitevine de la fin du Moyen Age à la Révolution* (Paris, 1958).

[80] AD Eure, E 1428, ff. 288-293; E 1465; see also Archives d'Esneval, Acquigny.

Vexin.[81] These farms, in other words, were more the product of administrative needs than of technical progress, such as expansion in the size of fields. Perhaps partly for this reason, the spread of large-scale tenant farming seems not to have been associated with a serious improvement in agricultural productivity.[82]

As will be seen below, in the course of the sixteenth century a steadily larger part of the *parlementaires'* land was leased in such large farms. The basic reasons, although not explicitly stated, seem clear. They derived from the increasing economic exhaustion of the lesser peasantry during the later sixteenth century, under the impact of warfare and population growth, and their consequent difficulty in meeting the demands which landlords placed upon them. Especially from 1570 on, peasant arrears became more serious, and peasant bankruptcies more frequent. In short, precisely those administrative problems which large-scale tenant farming was intended to meet became more acute.[83] For the moment, however, such changes are less important than a basic continuity. Throughout the sixteenth century, the structural conditions within which the *parlementaires* administered their estates imposed narrow limits to the profits

[81] Jules Sion, *Les paysans de la Normandie orientale: Pays de Caux, Bray, Vexin Normand, Vallée de la Seine. Étude géographique* (Paris, 1909), pp. 417-418.

[82] French historians have only begun to examine relationships between such large-scale *fermage* and agricultural improvement: see Bois, *Crise du féodalisme*, pp. 220-230. Cf. the progressive role which British historians have assigned to large tenant farmers; see Eric Kerridge, *The Agricultural Revolution* (London, 1967), and Robert Brenner, "Agrarian Class Structure and Economic Development in Pre-Industrial Europe," *Past and Present*, 70 (February, 1976), 30-75, 61. On evidence for the stagnation of French agriculture, see E. Le Roy Ladurie and Joseph Goy, eds., *Les fluctuations du produit de la dîme; conjoncture décimale et domaniale de la fin du Moyen Âge au XVIIIe siècle* (Paris-The Hague, 1972), esp. pp. 334-374; Michel Morineau, *Les faux-semblants d'un démarrage économique: agriculture et démographie en France au XVIIIe siècle* (*Cahiers des Annales*, xxx, Paris, 1970), pp. 97-162.

[83] Pp. 212-214.

which they could draw from landowning. Geography, the costs of accounting procedures, the resistances and impoverishment of peasant tenants—all restricted the extent to which the magistrate, no matter how calculating and acquisitive, could exploit fully his properties.

c. The Evolution of Property and Revenue

Thus far we have been concerned with the essentially unchanging aspects of *parlementaire* landowning, with tracing the broad contours of institutions, attitudes, and technological conditions. Now it is necessary to adopt a different viewpoint, and to consider changes in landowning over the sixteenth and early seventeenth centuries. Three broad themes will be considered. The first concerns changes in the property structure of the region, especially in the organization of seigneurial property; the second, the evolution of revenues from both land and seigneurial rights; the third, the nature of economic difficulties in the countryside. Finally, attention will be given to a further dimension of the problem, that of comparing the magistrates' experience of landowning with that of the *noblesse d'épée*. The lack of studies of the sixteenth-century nobility means that comparisons can be only fragmentary, but comparison will allow some understanding of the magistrates' special impact on the sixteenth-century countryside.

Change in rural property relations during the sixteenth and early seventeenth centuries involved several elements, but most of these pointed in the same direction. The seigneurie was becoming more monolithic, more dominant, and more inaccessible to all but the very wealthiest groups. The most visible of these changes was the increasing difficulty in acquiring seigneurial properties, for their cost was rising at a speed far greater than that of inflation. It is possible in only a few instances to separate the effects of rising prices from those of changes in the property's size, but one exception is the seigneurie of Belbeuf, bought in 1559 by the fiscal official Nicolas Puchot, in 1597 by the master of accounts Jean Godart, and in 1619 by Godart's widow Marie Ygou from her son. While the property's size remained constant, its price increased about fivefold over these sixty years: its price nearly tripled in the first thirty years, and increased more slowly thereafter.[84] In other cases we see only the increasing price of seigneurial property, and cannot be certain how much of the increase was due to growth in its size rather than to changes in its market value. The nineteenfold increase in the value of Claude Groulart's estate of St. Aubin between 1505 and 1581 has already been cited; almost as impressive was the changing value of the Bauquemare's seigneurie of Bourdeny, purchased in 1507 for 4,224l, sold in 1682 for 58,000l.[85] These were increases much greater than the pace of inflation in these years.

These examples testify only to the fact that seigneurial property had been relatively accessible in the early sixteenth century and became steadily more difficult to acquire thereafter. We see the change in somewhat greater clarity by comparing the prices for which seigneuries were sold with the net returns they offered their buyers. Such analysis, yet again, is possible for only a few cases, but these suggest a straightforward pattern.

Even if we assume the Bauquemare's purchase of Bourdeny in 1507, for only ten times its estimated yearly value, to have reflected the special conditions of enforced sale for debt, we are nonetheless left with an impressive decline in the rate of return which buyers were willing to accept: from 4 or 4.5 percent in the sixteenth century, to only 2.2 percent in the 1620's. This decline roughly paralleled the rising cost of office in these years, and probably reflected some of the same causes: a growing concern for social status, which seigneuries and offices alike conferred, uncer-

[84] Hérit. 2, 23 July 1559, 27 Januray 1571, 5 August 1577, 13 January 1597; AD S-M, 16J204.
[85] AD S-M, 16J8, 16J14.

TABLE 4:2

COSTS AND RETURNS OF THE SEIGNEURIE

Date	Seigneurie	Cost	Net Revenue	Rate of Return
1507	Bourdeny (Bauquemare)	4,224ł	424ł	10 percent
1563	Bec (Maignart)	1,250ł	50ł	4 percent
1597	Belbeuf, Cabot, Normare (Godart)	45,000ł	2,026ł	4.5 percent
1601	La Rivière Bourdet (Maignart)	33,000ł	1,000ł	3.3 percent
1627	Bec (Maignart)	3,600ł	80ł	2.2 percent

SOURCE: AD S-M, 16J8:9; La Riv. Bourdet, 1173, 1174, 2658, 2666, 2932; Hérit. 2, 13 January 1597, 25 November 1627; 16J178.

tainty about other forms of investment, a slowing down of the economy at large.

A similar degree of activity characterized the market in smaller pieces of rural property, those which lacked the prestige of seigneurial authority. In the space of a single year, thus, a property bought by the Maignart family increased in value by 11 percent.[86] But the profits which these smaller plots of land offered were quite unlike those of seigneurial property. In 1548 a quarter acre of land at Romilly, near the Maignart's estate of Les Maisons, was purchased for 11ł and immediately leased to the seller for 22s 6d, for an immediate return of 10.2 percent.[87] In the same years, the Maignart were leasing small plots of land at Les Maisons for between 9 and 16ł per hectare, but in the 1550's

[86] AD S-M, E, Fonds Caillot de Coquéraumont, 255. This piece of land was purchased by the Maignart in 1566, then purchased from them by virtue of *retrait lignager*, and finally repurchased by the Maignart in 1567. Cf. the very different view of changing land costs proposed by H. J. Habakuk, "The Price of Land in England 1500-1700," in W. Abel *et al.*, eds., *Wirtschaft, Geschichte, und Wirtschaftsgeschichte: Festschrift zum 65. Geburtstag von Friedrich Lütge* (Stuttgart, 1966), pp. 119-128. Habakuk argues that only in the seventeenth century did a genuine land market develop in England.

[87] AD Eure, E 1229, 26 January 1547 (old style).

they bought several pieces of arable land for between 37 and 53½ per hectare; returns of at least 10 percent were plainly the norm in this area. At another of the Maignart's properties, the nearby seigneurie of Saussey, the family bought a little over one hectare of land in 1575, for the price of 200½; this was immediately leased (again to the seller) for 4⅙ *mines* of wheat, worth between 4 and 6½ per *mine*; the purchase, in other words, brought the Maignart at least an 8.3 percent return.[88] Other forms of rural property might be still more profitable. In the 1580's and 1590's, it was possible in the vicinity of Les Maisons to buy cattle and other livestock for only three or four times its yearly rental, and to rent out these animals on terms that made the renter partly responsible for any harm that came to them.[89]

In making these purchases, buyers were usually taking advantage of the indebtedness of peasant sellers. It was this indebtedness which allowed such handsome profits. The Maignart purchases at Saussey, thus, were the means by which two of their tenant farmers acquitted themselves of rents which they had owed for several years, and this was a common pattern. Peasants were especially vulnerable to their lords, to whom they were continually in debt for seigneurial dues and who also enjoyed the right of replacing any purchasers of land within the seigneurie, by meeting the price which they had offered.[90]

[88] La Riv. Bourdet, 1173, 1174, 1592, 2932; AD S-M, E, Fonds Caillot de Coquéraumont, unclassed; AD Eure, E 1224, E 1242; E 1246, 18 April 1575, ff. 42-44. Estimates of wheat prices can be only approximate, in view of both the paucity of sources and the wide fluctuations which characterized late-sixteenth-century prices. The estimate used here is based on AD S-M, 32H, Accounts of the Carmelites of Rouen, and La Riv. Bourdet, 1653; the latter source supplies an estimate of wheat prices at Les Andelys in 1574, and on the basis of it the Maignart would have enjoyed a 9.4 percent return on their purchase.

[89] For instance AD Eure, E 1259, 5 October 1584; E 1260, 29 September 1585; E 1261, 10 June 1591; AD S-M, E, Tabellionage royal, Pont St. Pierre, 17 November 1601.

[90] AD Eure, E 1246, ff. 41-44; E 1295, f. 11; La Riv. Bourdet, 1891;

Under these circumstances, it was natural that *parlementaire* fortunes in the countryside tended to expand around a few seigneurial centers, rather than through the accumulation of numerous seigneuries. Owning a seigneurie conferred both prestige and practical advantages, but the economics of the situation favored adding to the seigneurie's demesne over acquiring new ones; and the disparity between the two forms of property increased considerably in the late sixteenth and early seventeenth centuries, when the sharpest increases in the seigneurie's cost took place. The effects of this imbalance were to be seen in the fortunes of even the wealthiest robe families. Of the half dozen estates which the president Charles Maignart owned in 1600, all but one had been acquired between 1474 and 1509. The exception—the seigneurie of La Rivière Bourdet—had come to the family through marriage rather than purchase, though in 1601 Charles Maignart was able to buy out the second half of La Rivière Bourdet, which had gone by marriage to another family.[91] Like the Maignart, the Jubert were among the wealthiest and longest established of Rouennais robe families, and the centers of their landed wealth had been established almost as early in the century. Of the seven fiefs which the councillor Guillaume Jubert left at his death in 1543, only two had not belonged to the family in one form or another at his father's death, in 1510; Guillaume's oldest son, the councillor Claude Jubert, appears not to have added any fiefs to the family's wealth by his death in 1578.[92] Not all robe families fitted this pattern of land buying, but the

---

AD S-M, E, Fonds Caillot de Coquéraumont, 255. Use of seigneurial rights as a means of acquiring peasant properties has long been seen as a central element in the seigneurial reaction of the eighteenth century. See Marc Bloch, *French Rural History. An Essay on its Basic Characteristics*, trans. Janet Sondheimer (Berkeley, 1966), pp. 135-136, and Robert Forster, *The Nobility of Toulouse in the Eighteenth Century*, pp. 50-52.

[91] La Riv. Bourdet, 516, 539, 2105, 2658.

[92] BN Carrés de d'Hozier, 358; AD Eure, E 2474; Hérit. 2, 28 June 1580.

exceptions tended to be significant ones: they involved families who benefited directly from royal patronage. During his twenty-two years as the Parlement's first president, thus, Claude Groulart bought three major fiefs and at least ten smaller ones. Adrien de Croismare was first president in Rouen's Cour des Aides and councillor of state, after serving five years in the Parlement. In his twenty-five years of royal service, from 1563 to 1589, he bought seven large fiefs, extending over 500 hectares of land. Groulart and Croismare illustrate the landed wealth which those who were the king's immediate councillors might accumulate.[93] Even very wealthy families, such as the Maignart and Jubert, in contrast, limited their efforts mainly to adding small pieces of land to estates which their families had owned for some time.

Changing conditions in the land market, especially the growing difference between the costs of large and small properties, thus encouraged changes in the nature of large property itself. Seigneuries tended to become larger and more dominant within the countryside. As in the case of the Maignart's estate of Les Maisons, seigneurial authority was coming to be more closely attached to the ownership of large pieces of land; the seigneurie was becoming a more imposing institution. Probably the speed with which feudal properties changed hands was also reduced, and the seigneurial structure made more imposing in that respect also. But estate owners may also have been encouraged to sell off their smaller estates and focus their efforts on their principal properties—and in any event changing prices did not affect the frequency with which families failed to produce male heirs and estates changed hands for that reason.

Numerous studies have stressed the difficulties that all sixteenth-century landowners faced in trying to maintain

[93] Bibliothèque Municipale, Dieppe, MS 63; Hérit. 2, 15 March 1595. See also below, Appendix E, for discussion of the presidents' prominence in the church land sales of the sixteenth century.

real incomes. Between the 1520's and the 1590's, prices increased fourfold or fivefold; a comparable though less visible inflation had prevailed in the late fifteenth and early sixteenth centuries.[94] Simply to maintain their incomes required of landowners an awareness of economic change and a willingness to respond to change by disrupting established relations with tenants. The problem was sufficiently acute with regard to demesne properties, those over which the landowner had full control and which he could rent out on short-term, variable leases. More serious, however, were the problems posed by the "enfeoffed domain," that part of the seigneurie which was divided among hereditary tenants and for which rents were permanently fixed. For this part of the estate, response to economic change was inhibited by law as well as by habit and lack of calculation.[95]

Few *parlementaire* estates can be followed in detail over the sixteenth century. Those whose revenues can be fol-

[94] M. Baulant and J. Meuvret, *Prix des céréales extraits de la Mercuriale de Paris, 1520-1698*, 2 vols. (Paris, 1960); Guy Bois, "Le prix de froment à Rouen au XVe siècle," *Annales. Économies, Sociétés, Civilisations*, XXIII, 6 (December, 1968), 1262-1282; and, for stress on the severity of early sixteenth-century inflation, Georges Frêche, *Toulouse et la région Midi-Pyrénées au siècle des lumières (vers 1670-1789)* (Paris, 1974), pp. 689-690.

[95] For classic statements of this view, see Bloch, *French Rural History*, pp. 122-130; Lucien Febvre, *Philippe II et la Franche Comté*, pp. 112-145. A more recent statement, stressing economic rather than psychological causes and suggesting stagnation rather than decline in the large landowners' position, is offered by E. Le Roy Ladurie, *Les paysans de Languedoc*, 2 vols. (2nd ed., Paris-The Hague, n.d.), I, 280-296. Cf. the similar terms in which Lawrence Stone describes the situation of English large landowners: *Crisis*, pp. 138-144. For arguments stressing seigneurial successes during the sixteenth century, see Fernand Braudel, *The Mediterranean and the Mediterranean World in the Age of Philip II*, 2 vols., trans. Sian Reynolds (New York, 1972-1973), I, 527; Merle, *La métairie et l'évolution agraire de la Gâtine poitevine de la fin du Moyen Âge à la Révolution*, pp. 63-74; and Jacquart, *La crise rurale en Ile-de-France*, pp. 47-48, though Jacquart also emphasizes the difficulties which the events of the civil wars created for large landowners (pp. 235-239).

lowed, however, suggest that inflation was not the landowner's most serious problem, and that, for most, responding to rising prices was a relatively straightforward matter. Losses to inflation were indeed serious on some robe estates, especially on those whose "enfeoffed domains" were leased for money rents. In 1507, when the Bauquemare bought the estate of Bourdeny, fixed revenues were estimated to be worth 150ł annually, more than one-third of the estate's value. Fifty years later even the nominal value of these revenues had fallen: in 1553 Bourdeny's "enfeoffed domain" was leased for a rent of 100ł yearly.[96]

More typical, however, was the Romé's estate of Bec Crespin. In the years 1517-1529, the whole of Bec Crespin's revenues—demesne as well as enfeoffed domain—was leased for 666⅔ł annually. In 1604 the estate's enfeoffed domain alone was rented for three times as much (2,075ł yearly), and its value continued to rise in the following years, to 3,150ł yearly by 1638. Fixed rents at Bec Crespin retained their value over the sixteenth century because they were set largely in kind rather than in money.[97] Doubtless many Norman estates were not so fortunate, but those which can be followed were in much the same situation as Bec Crespin. The estates which the master of accounts Jean Godart bought in 1597 derived well over one-fourth of their total revenue from fixed rents, but only 15 percent of these rents was set in money. Both the Maignart and the Jubert received large quantities of wine and grain from the fixed rents on their estates, and both received considerable income from marketing these commodities in Rouen and in other markets along the Seine. For them the enfeoffed domain was the source of large-scale commercial profits.[98]

[96] AD S-M, 16J8: 9, 14.

[97] AD S-M, E, Fonds Romé du Bec, unclassed. On the basis of the barony's accounts for 1572, it appears that 30 percent of the value of the property's fixed rents was set in money, 46 percent in grain, and 24 percent in poultry.

[98] Hérit. 2, 13 January 1597; La Riv. Bourdet, 2105, 3895; AD Eure, E 2474, 2 February 1554.

Examination of the magistrates' demesne properties, those over which they had full control to arrange short-term leases, likewise suggests the ease with which most estates' revenues kept up with inflation. At the Maignart's estate of Les Maisons, for instance, the nominal rent charged for small plots of land, of between one-fourth and one-half hectare, increased about fivefold between 1511 and 1594, a pace about equal to rising grain prices. Here rents rose in accordance with market pressures, for the Maignart arranged leases at public auction, like many other large landowners.[99] At the Maignart's large farm of Saussey, amounting to about 50 hectares of land, rents were set in kind rather than in money, and underwent a 50 percent real increase between 1522 and 1572, from 8 to 12 *boisseaux* of wheat per acre.[100]

Other robe families showed a comparable willingness and ability to raise rents on their demesne properties over the sixteenth century. Rent from the "domain of the château" of the Romé's barony of Bec Crespin increased by 140 percent between 1565 and 1585. On the Bauquemare's estate of Bourdeny, the rent received for arable land increased fourfold between 1507 and 1585. The Jubert rented the fief of Le Val for 160₶ in 1554 and for 400₶ thirty years later, an increase of 150 percent.[101]

Yet the evolution of landed revenues involved more than the landowner's willingness to raise rents or the existence of

---

[99] AD S-M, E, Fonds Caillot de Coquéraumont, 255; AD Eure, E 1224; La Riv. Bourdet, 1173, 1174, 2105. For examples of the Norman *noblesse d'épée* similarly arranging leases by public auction, see AD S-M, E, Fonds Caillot de Coquéraumont, 252 (for the Roncherolles family, barons of Pont St. Pierre), and A. de Blangy, ed., "Tutelle de René du Parc, baron d'Ingrande, 1579-1585," *Bulletin de la Société des Antiquaires de Normandie*, xxv (1906), 155. At Ingrande, fifty proclamations of the coming auction of leases were placed at markets, parish churches, and other likely meeting places in the villages near the barony.

[100] La Riv. Bourdet, 769, 1653; AD Eure, E 1246, 24 January 1575.

[101] AD S-M, E, Romé du Bec, Accounts; AD S-M, 16J8: 9, 14; Meubles 2, 24 October 1585; AD Eure, E 2474, E 1419.

procedures, such as competitive bidding, which assured him of receiving full market value for his properties. Much depended also on the bargaining position and solvency of those who leased his properties; this at least is suggested by the contrasting terms on which landowners might lease different kinds of property. One example is provided by the Bauquemare's estate of Bourdeny. The Bauquemare received a steadily rising income from Bourdeny's arable land, as noted above, but much of the estate's value (about one-fifth in 1507) derived from its mills—and the income from these followed a distinct pattern. Even nominal increases in rent were small during the sixteenth century, and measured in real terms they produced a steadily smaller income. Table 4:3 sets out the rents charged for Bourdeny's mills.

The changing conditions under which these mills were leased in the sixteenth century make precise comparison of the revenue they produced impossible. But it is clear that throughout the century conditions favored the tenant. On the one hand, steadily more property was included in these leases. On the other hand, even in nominal terms rents increased very little: in one case by 25 percent between 1535 and 1581, in the other by 80 percent between 1535 and 1597. In terms of real income, there had been a substantial decline. The situation changed in the seventeenth century. Rents increased sharply, doubling in one case, tripling in the other, while the amount of property remained unchanged or actually decreased. Why Bourdeny's millers should have been less vulnerable to seigneurial pressures than those who rented the estate's arable land is unclear. Presumably the reasons lay in the capital and expertise that milling demanded, and that may have given the miller an advantageous position in dealing with seigneurial landowners.[102] Whatever the reasons, the example suggests the complex determinants of seigneurial incomes.

[102] For a listing of the equipment which leasing a seigneurial mill demanded see AD Eure, E 1499, ff. 214-217 (2 August 1605).

TABLE 4:3
RENTS FROM MILLS, BOURDENY

Date	Rent
	"LE MOULIN A DRAPS"
1507	42ł (estimate for one mill, "*une place de moulin en vide place*")
1535	80ł (for "*les deux moulins à draps avec une pièce de pré*")
1553	80ł (for the two mills, with "*une pièce de pré*")
1575	100ł (for the two mills, "*une pièce de prey . . . une pièce de terre labourable*")
1581	100ł (for the two mills, "*une pièce de prey et une pièce de terre labourable*")
1607	110ł (for one mill, "*une pièce de prey . . . une pièce de terre labourable*")
1613	110ł (same conditions)
1622	120ł (same conditions)
1628	130ł (same conditions)
1634	150ł (same conditions)
1640	180ł (same conditions)
1646	200ł (same conditions)
1652	300ł (same conditions)
1679	300ł (same conditions)
	"UNG MOULIN A BLE"
1507	50ł (estimate)
1535	100ł (with 7 *acres* of arable, 5 *acres* of meadow)
1568	152ł (with 7 *acres* of arable, 5 *acres* of meadow, "*ung petit jardin . . . et oultre . . . un moulin a draps assis en la parroisse Sainct Aulbin*")
1597	180ł, twelve hens, one barrel of cider (for one mill, two plots of meadow, an unspecified amount of arable, and "*deux petitz jardins*")
1606	190ł (same conditions)
1624	250ł (same conditions)
1633	300ł, twelve hens (same conditions)
1669	400ł, twelve hens (same conditions)

SOURCE: AD S-M, 16J8: 9, 16J8: 14.

The most important element shaping seigneurial incomes was the economic condition of the peasantry at large, those to whom the magistrates rented their demesne properties. The relationship between tenants' prosperity and the magistrates' incomes may be seen with particular clarity in the Maignart's estate of Saussey. Table 4:4 sets out the total rent which the family received from Saussey between the late

TABLE 4:4

TOTAL RENT, SAUSSEY

Date	Rent
1483	46₶ (= about 92 *mines* wheat)
1522	99 *mines* wheat
1566	174 *mines* wheat
1575	181 *mines* wheat
1583	168 *mines* wheat
1589	150 *mines* wheat
1594	100 *écus* and 72 *mines* wheat
	(= about 115 *mines* wheat)

SOURCE: La Riv. Bourdet, 516 (1483); 769 (1522); 1653 (1566); 2147 (1583); 2105 (1589, 1594); AD Eure, E 1246, 24 January 1575 (1575).

fifteenth and the late sixteenth centuries. Table 4:4 shows both the Maignart's economic success at Saussey during the first three-fourths of the sixteenth century and the limits of that success. Because of the increasing rent charged per acre of land and because of some acquisitions at Saussey, the Maignart received in 1575 almost twice what they had received in 1483; and since grain prices increased more rapidly during these years than most other prices, their real income from Saussey more than doubled. But after 1575 revenue from Saussey began to fall. The decline amounted to about one-sixth by 1589 and about one-third by 1594, and it came despite further increases in the property's size. The decline resulted directly from the economic troubles of the tenants who had held Saussey during most of the sixteenth century. In November, 1574, these tenants were in arrears for more than 1,500ł, and could extricate themselves only by selling property to the Maignart. In 1580 they were again in arrears, and the debt was settled by Maignart's receiving the harvest of 38 acres of one tenant's land. The agreement specified that this was to be "in addition to and not including the monetary debts (*les obligations liquides*) which he owes me," which suggests that the tenants' troubles went considerably further. By 1594 Maignart was unable to find tenant farmers for Saussey, and was forced to turn to a different kind of tenant. Whereas the previous occupants of Saussey had been described simply as *laboureurs*, in upper Normandy a term shared by all but the poorest peasants, the new tenant was "Master Guillaume Theroulde, *receveur fermier*." The Theroulde were a family of notables, including notaries at Rouen and several clergymen. Guillaume Theroulde was already the tenant of the Maignart's much larger estate at La Rivière Bourdet.[103] He seems thus to have been a figure with sufficient financial resources to meet the economic crises of the late sixteenth century. But, for the same reason, he was far less susceptible to pressure from the Maignart; they needed the resources he offered.

Economic crisis appears to have been general in the upper Norman countryside during the later sixteenth century. A sense of its gravity may be gained from the large parish of La Neuville Chantdoissel, which adjoined the Maignart's estate of Les Maisons. Despite occasional gaps in the records of the village's parish registers, it is possible to follow the course of baptisms there during the later part of the century. Averages of baptisms per month are set out in Table 4:5. Between the middle years of the century and the decade before the League, the average number of baptisms each month at La Neuville dropped by nearly one-third. In the later sixteenth century, thus, the Maignart confronted a broader problem than just the economic exhaustion of their wealthier tenant farmers. The rural population as a whole

[103] La Riv. Bourdet, 1891, 2070, 2105; on the Theroulde, see *ibid.*, 853, 1518, 1899, 2446, 2971.

TABLE 4:5

BAPTISMS PER MONTH, LA NEUVILLE

1547-1557:	4.17
1560-1567:*	3.69
1567-1576:	3.53
1577-1589:	2.87

* Through month of April, 1567.
SOURCE: AD S-M, 4E 1900.

was diminishing, and this meant fewer bidders for short-term leases of small farms and fewer buyers of agricultural products.[104]

Decline of rural population, so the example of La Neuville suggests, was a continuous and accelerating process in the later sixteenth century. Political events and short-term economic crises further intensified the process of peasant impoverishment and thus further limited the revenues which magistrates could draw from their properties. Most severe were the damages caused by the League, whose impact was felt from 1589 through the early seventeenth century, well after the end of hostilities. Both royalists and *ligueurs* suffered the seizure of their properties and the loss of estate papers. The royalist councillor Laurent Restault described how, "because of the hatred which the *ligueurs* have for him and because of the closeness of his lands to the [*ligueur*] cities of Pontaudemer and Honfleur, he has received nothing from them; in fact everything has been pillaged and ravaged, and even now not a day passes but they are further pillaged. Nothing remains on his farms, because some of his

[104] On the impact of the Wars of Religion, Jacquart, *La crise rurale*, pp. 168ff, and Philip Benedict, "Catholics and Huguenots in Sixteenth-Century Rouen: The Demographic Effects of the Religious Wars," *French Historical Studies*, IX, 2 (Fall, 1975), 209-234; these are in contrast to the relatively optimistic view taken by Pierre Goubert, "Recent Theories and Research in French Population between 1500 and 1700," in D. V. Glass and D.E.C. Eversley, eds., *Population in History. Essays in Historical Demography* (Chicago, 1965), pp. 457-473.

tenants are currently prisoners in the hands of the *ligueurs* and the rest . . . are in flight."[105] Such events left a long train of complex litigation (Restault was being sued by his mother) and rent reductions. The councillor Anthoine de Boislevesque in 1597 was still deep in litigation with a former tenant. Since 1590, when he had leased the Boislevesque's property, the tenant "having been found liable for a large sum of money . . . the said lord (de Boislevesque) had allowed a reduction of half of the said rent, and in addition to this acquitted and discharged him of all the submissions and charges (demands for labor services and minor payments in kind) included in the contract, likewise of all the interest which he might properly demand for the nonfulfillment of the lease." The parties ended the contract in 1594, by mutual consent, but three years later the tenant's debt remained large. He claimed that he had been unable to sell his own land for a price that would permit repayment of what he owed, and the matter was only settled with his ceding his land to Boislevesque.[106] Nearly all magistrates experienced similar troubles,[107] and problems did not end with the arrival of peace. The reign of Henry IV marked a precipitous decline in the price of grain and other agricultural products. Declining prices for his grain, complained Charles Maignart beside his accounts for 1602, meant "a great diminution in the rent from my land." Only in the reign of Louis XIII did prices again begin a moderate rise.[108]

[105] AD S-M, E, Fonds Restault, unclassed.

[106] Hérit. 2, 30 June 1597.

[107] For other examples of magistrates' losses during the League: Bibliothèque Municipale, Dieppe, MS 63, pp. 385-386 (Groulart); BM MS Y214, VII, 78 (Bretel); AD S-M, B, Parlement, Arrêts, 29 April 1593 (Rassent); 22 June 1594 (Le Roux de Tilly); 5 August 1590 (Toustain); 30 July 1590 (La Roque); 11 May 1590 (Boisivon); 3 August 1591 (du Perron); 4 May 1591 (Péricard); 26 October 1589 (Duquesne); Archives d'Esneval, Acquigny (Le Roux de Bourgtheroude).

[108] La Riv. Bourdet, 2105; Baulant and Meuvret, *Prix des céréales*, I, 243; for the Europe-wide character of this decline, see also Wil-

The combined effect of long-term impoverishment of the peasant community and short-term political and economic crises was to set clear limits to the incomes which most landowners could draw from the countryside. Many robe families, it appears, responded to these circumstances by turning over the administration of their estates to more sub-stantial tenants, often urban businessmen. Thus they avoided the delayed payments and litigation which might arise with the less wealthy *laboureurs*, when peasant tenants could be found at all. But (as seen above) the security which such businessmen offered came at a substantial cost, of as much as 40 percent of the revenue to be had from dealing with smaller tenants. Other magistrates continued to lease their properties to small tenants, but accepted stagnant or actually declining revenues after about 1585.

Whichever policy the family adopted, its real revenues from the land reached a limit in about 1585, thus following the pattern of the Maignart's estate of Saussey. Tables 4:6 and 4:7 set out the evolution of rents in two *parlementaire* estates, the Romé's Bec Crespin and the Bauquemare's Bour-deny. Throughout most of the sixteenth century, revenues from both Bec Crespin and Bourdeny had at least kept pace with inflation. After 1585, however, rents increased little in nominal terms, and in real terms actually declined. In the seventy years from 1585 to 1653, rent from Bec Crespin's "*domaine du château*" increased by a little more than one-fourth; in the forty-five years after 1585, revenue from Bourdeny's arable land increased by only 17.5 percent. These increases were insufficient even to compensate for the diminishing monetary value of the *livre tournois*, let alone to match increases in prices.[109]

---

helm Abel, *Geschichte des deutschen Landwirtschaft von frühen Mittelalter bis zum 19. Jahrhundert* (2nd ed., Stuttgart, 1967), pp. 261ff.

[109] Moreover, it was precisely in the late sixteenth and early seven-teenth centuries that wages at Rouen began to increase in real terms; although the *parlementaires'* patterns of consumption cannot be ana-

TABLE 4:6

RENT OF THE *Domaine du Château*, BEC CRESPIN

Date	Rent
1565	200ł
1572	240ł, two fatted pigs, fifty pounds of butter, half the product of the fruit trees and pigeon house
1580	400ł, one fatted pig, one-third of the product of the fruit trees, half the product of the pigeon house
1585	480ł
1653	600ł, two pigs of six months, "*et douze boyseaux de dragée*"
1660	Same
1666	Same

SOURCE: AD S-M, E, Fonds Romé du Bec, unclassified.

TABLE 4:7

RENTS OF ARABLE LAND, BOURDNEY

Date	Rent
1507	100ł (contemporary estimate)
1585	400ł
1611	450ł
1617	450ł
1623	460ł
1629	470ł

SOURCE: AD S-M, 16J 8:9; Meubles 2, 24 October 1585; 16J 8:14.

Studies are lacking which would permit extensive comparison of *parlementaire* landed revenues with those of the military nobility. Comparison is possible, however, with the evolution of four estates belonging to the upper Norman nobility. For at least the first three-fourths of the sixteenth century, all of these estates followed the pattern which characterized the robe estates studied here: rents increased

---

lyzed with precision, higher wages must have affected their position much more than other forms of inflation. See Raymond Quenedey, *L'habitation rouennaise: étude d'histoire, de géographie et d'archéologie urbaines* (Rouen, 1926), pp. 390-391.

at a pace at least equal to that of inflation. The barony of Pont St. Pierre adjoined the Maignart estate of Les Maisons and belonged to one of the leading families of the Norman nobility. Its gross revenue rose from 1,100₺ in 1506-1507 to more than 5,000₺ in 1572. The lordship of Beuzemouchel, also held by an eminent military family, brought a gross yearly revenue of 642₺ in 1537 and a net revenue of 2,200₺ in 1586. Yet another estate belonging to the substantial nobility of the province, the barony of Le Neubourg, underwent a comparable evolution. Rents charged for arable land near the château of Le Neubourg increased sixfold between 1514 and 1591; on a nearby farm there was a ninefold increase in rents between 1455 and 1542 and an almost fourfold increase between 1542 and 1616. As an example of the lesser nobility, finally, there is the Dubosc family, who owned several lordships also in the vicinity of Les Maisons. Between the 1550's and the 1570's they roughly doubled rents on many of their properties.[110]

Families of the military nobility, it appears, shared in the rising landed incomes of the first three-fourths of the sixteenth century; in this respect there was little difference between robe and sword. But in the late sixteenth century at least three of these four estates also encountered economic difficulties much like those seen in *parlementaire* estates, difficulties which reflected peasant impoverishment and the need to turn to urban businessmen for tenant farmers. The barons of Pont St. Pierre had employed a salaried receiver to collect rents and arrange short-term leases within the barony, but in 1574 this policy was changed: in that year "all the revenue and dependencies of the said property and barony"—in fact with important exceptions—were leased to one "Pierre Le Maistre, merchant, residing at Heugueville," described a decade later as "*honorable homme* Pierre

[110] AD S-M, E, Fonds Baronnie du Pont St. Pierre, Accounts; AD Eure, E1261; La Riv. Bourdet, 3316; Plaisse, *La baronnie du Neubourg*, pp. 372-373; BM MS m254, ff. 7r, 9v, 13v, 18r, 23 r-v, 45r.

Le Maistre, bourgeois of Rouen."[111] Like the *parlementaire* landowners described above, the barons of Pont St. Pierre were sacrificing some chances to profit from direct estate administration for the sake of more regular and assured revenue. With regard to the lordship of Beuzemouchel, we are able to see only the overall evolution of revenues, but these tell a similar story. Revenue from the estate had nearly quadrupled between 1537 and 1586, but in the next forty years yearly revenue increased by only 50l, a total increase of just over 2 percent.[112] The Dubosc present the clearest case of economic difficulties. Despite the rising rents of the mid-sixteenth century, by 1601 the family's property was "so heavily encumbered and mortgaged, with debts far heavier than its annual revenue could support," that a substantial amount of property had to be sold. The family's account book suggests that at least one cause of indebtedness was the financial exhaustion of their tenant farmers. Starting in about 1575, the Dubosc tenants began to fall behind in their rent payments, in some cases spectacularly so. The tenant Guillaume Isobel, for instance, belonged to a dynasty of farmers who had held lands from the Dubosc since the early sixteenth century. Isobel had paid his rents through 1572, but by 1583 owed Dubosc 233l and 123 *boisseaux* of wheat. He managed to repay part of this debt in the following years, but by 1587 his position was still worse. He owed now 310l and 120 *boisseaux* of wheat, and had signed a note for this amount to the Dubosc.[113]

What emerges most clearly from our investigation of *parlementaire* landowning is the force of the economic and technological limits on landed revenues. Land was the most important part of most *parlementaire* fortunes, and the mag-

[111] AD S-M, E, Fonds Caillot de Coquéraumont, Baux du revenu général, Pont St. Pierre; AD Eure, E1260, 29 December 1585.
[112] La Riv. Bourdet, 3316.
[113] Hérit. 2, 12 March 1601; BM MS m254, ff. 15-21.

istrates—like the members of the military nobility—sought to draw as much money as they could from these properties. Seigneurial institutions and ideals, moreover, posed few obstacles to this effort; neither the magistrates nor other large landowners appear to have been deterred by tradition or bonds with the peasant community from raising rents, buying land cheaply, and otherwise profiting from peasant indebtedness. During much of the sixteenth century this concern with profit led to steadily rising incomes. Although there were difficulties on some estates, in general landed incomes matched or exceeded the rate of inflation. After 1575, however, the limitations on what could be extracted from the countryside began to become apparent. The impoverishment of ordinary tenant farmers led to delays in paying rents and limited the extent to which rents could be further raised. Both magistrates and military noblemen found themselves forced to turn to urban businessmen as tenants. Such figures controlled sufficient capital that they could continue paying their rents even in difficult years, and they saved the landowner the administrative costs that came from dealing with numerous small tenants. But these advantages came at the cost of substantially lower rents, and as large-scale tenant farming became more prevalent rents ceased to rise or (in real terms) declined.

Aggressive and profit-oriented administration could do little against these fundamental economic conditions, for the magistrates (like other large landowners) were bound in close economic alliance to those who worked their land. As the president Bauquemare had recognized, it was this economic alliance—far more than any relationship of political deference or communal feeling—which united rich and poor in the countryside.

FIVE

THE ECONOMICS OF SUCCESS
AND FAILURE

PREVIOUS chapters have considered the size and sources of *parlementaire* incomes. The present chapter asks how the magistrates spent this money, how expenditures balanced against incomes, and what this balance meant for the growth or decay of *parlementaire* fortunes over time. Ultimately, then, the chapter is directed to understanding some of the processes by which families built up fortunes, or failed to do so, and to understanding some of the economic dangers which confronted even the successful.[1]

The magistrates' robes symbolized restraint in expenditure as in other aspects of life, but the robe milieu was not immune to the wild dispendiousness which often characterized the courtly aristocracy. In 1575, for instance, several relatives of Madeleine de Montfault, the daughter of a former president in the court, appeared before the court to attempt an arrangement for the settlement of her debts. "In so short a time that he is ashamed to say it," reported one of her relatives, "she [has] sold a great amount of her father's property, . . . boasting every day that she would consume his whole patrimony." Despite previous sales of her property, she was now 15,000l in debt and new property sales seemed neces-

---

[1] Historians have long stressed the relationship among the *noblesse de robe*'s consumption patterns, its resistance to debt, and its economic successes. Thus Lucien Febvre, *Philippe II et la Franche Comté. Étude d'histoire politique, religieuse et sociale* (2nd ed., Paris, 1970), pp. 191-192, 223-228; and Gaston Roupnel, *La ville et la campagne au XVIIᵉ siècle. Étude sur les populations du pays dijonnais* (2nd ed., Paris, 1955), pp. 237-238.

sary.[2] Even without this kind of headlong rush into debt, it was possible for magistrates and their families to spend a great deal. In 1546 the councillor Baptiste Le Chandelier, one of the three *parlementaires* in the 1540's who belonged to Rouen's Puy de la Conception, sponsored a banquet for his fellow poets, and he recorded its details in a Latin poem. Le Chandelier's banquet included twenty-six different kinds of roasts, and the diners were entertained throughout: by flutes during the first course, wind instruments in the second, violins in the third, and at the meal's conclusion by a mechanical boar, which moved around the room by a hidden mechanism and sent forth fire from its nostrils.[3] Both marriage and death provided further occasions for ceremonial ostentation. When the first president Jacques de Bauquemare arranged his elder daughter's marriage in 1575, she received just under 4,000₶ worth of jewelry (including a belt of gold and pearls worth 1,100₶ and a necklace of diamonds, rubies, and pearls worth 1,207₶) and clothing worth over 1,600₶.[4] By the later sixteenth century, *parlementaire* funerals had reached a considerable degree of elaboration and cost: the funeral procession of the first president Claude Groulart, in 1607, included about 1,000 marchers,

<hr />

[2] AD S-M, B, Parlement, Registre d'Audiences, 16 February 1575.

[3] F. Bouquet, ed., *La Parthénie, ou Banquet des Palinods de Rouen en 1546. Poème latin du XVIe siècle par Baptiste Le Chandelier* (Rouen, 1883), introduction. Complaints about excessive expenditures on banquets were general in the late sixteenth and early seventeenth centuries. Thus, in 1602, Claude Groulart complained about "the luxuries and superfluous and too ungoverned expenditures which for the last few years, because of some individuals' competitions or whims [*curiosité*]," had come to characterize the annual banquet of the court's Grand' Chambre; this was now to be paid for from fines which the court levied, and was to cost no more than 300₶—a suggestion of how serious a drain they might be on *parlementaire* incomes (BM MS Y214, IX, 182). See also the chancellor's complaint in 1540 that "several of the company are people ordinarily giving and attending banquets, frequenting dissolute and improper games . . ." (*ibid.*, II, 204).

[4] Hérit. 2, 2 September 1575.

and even the funeral of a councillor's mother, in 1616, cost over 1,400ł.[5] At least the wealthiest magistrates spent lavishly on their houses also. Shortly after the League, Groulart claimed that the *ligueurs* had stolen or destroyed 30,000ł worth of possessions from his house in Rouen. His future colleague Nicolas Le Roux claimed comparable losses at his country house; just the clothing in his daughter's room, he claimed, had been worth 3,000ł, his books had been worth 3,600ł. Both might have exaggerated their losses in the hope of compensation, but such figures suggest the luxury that the wealthiest families might enjoy.[6]

Despite such examples, however, the normal level of *parlementaire* expense seems to have been lower, and few fortunes appear to have been destroyed by either outright folly or by the luxuries in which Bauquemare, Groulart, and Le Roux might indulge. Marriage contracts provide one indication of normal expenditures, for many of them included estimations of personal possessions—especially clothing, jewelry, and furniture—which the bride would receive at her husband's death; though the conditions of this provision varied considerably, these estimates provide a view of the norms of conspicuous consumption, of what was expected in most robe families. Eighteen marriage contracts of *parlementaire* daughters included such provisions between 1580

[5] Groulart's funeral is described below, Chapter 6. For Madeleine Bigot's, AD S-M, E, Fonds Restault, unclassed. Others, equally elaborate and expensive, are described in AD S-M, 16J178 and La Riv. Bourdet, 2139.

[6] Bibliothèque Municipale, Dieppe, MS 63; Archives d'Esneval, Acquigny. Another form of conspicuous expenditure apparently also reserved for the presidents was literary patronage. See Jean Auvray, "avocat au Parlement," *Le banquet des Muses, ou Les diverses satires du sieur Auvray* . . . (Rouen, 1628), "Stances funèbres sacrées à la mémoire de feu messire Claude Groulart . . . :" "Poets, your Maecenas . . . is dead; what will you do?" (402), and his dedication to Charles Maignart: "the reputation which you have of naturally cherishing the Muses" (dedication, no pagination). Among other beneficiaries of Groulart's patronage was the poet Malherbe.

and 1610, and the median estimate of their personal belongings was 1,950ł, about one-third of what Jacques de Bauquemare gave his daughter at marriage.[7] In much the same way, normal expenditures on furnishings were much lower than the example of the court's wealthiest members would suggest. The house in Rouen which the future president Charles Maignart inherited in 1582 held furnishings and personal effects worth about 3,800ł: about one-eighth the value of what Claude Groulart claimed to have lost during the League, and only slightly more than the value which Nicolas Le Roux set on his daughter's clothing or his own library.[8] A few *parlementaire* families (notably the Le Roux and Romé) built impressive stone houses in Rouen, but most of those who owned houses were content with the half-timber construction typical of the city—and only with the reign of Louis XIII did enthusiasm for large-scale building projects become at all common.[9]

[7] The contracts of eighteen first marriages of *parlementaire* daughters (including the daughters of presidents and *gens du roi* as well as of councillors) between 1580 and 1610 include provision for the furnishings and other moveables which the bride would receive after her husband's death. Of these provisions, five were set at less than 1,500ł; four at 1,500ł; one at 2,400ł; five at 3,000ł; and three at between 3,600ł and 4,500ł. Eight of the nine contracts providing for 1,500ł or less in *meubles* concerned councillors' daughters; in contrast, all three of those providing for 3,600ł or more concerned the daughters of presidents and *gens du roi*. For the councillors' daughters, the median value was 1,500ł; for the presidents' daughters, the median value was 3,600ł. These figures again suggest the superior wealth and higher level of expenditure of the presidents and *gens du roi*.

[8] La Riv. Bourdet, 2123.

[9] The Le Roux and Romé houses still stand, though most of the latter was destroyed in 1944; for description and evaluation, see AD S-M, 1F39, Abbé Maurice, *Les Romé de Fresquiennes*. The houses of the Bigot family, also still standing, suggest the older style of construction and its continuing use by even relatively wealthy families: see A. Cerné, "Les hôtels des Bigot," *Bulletin, Société libre d'émulation du commerce et de l'industrie de la Seine Inférieure*, 1935. More generally, see Raymond Quenedey, *L'habitation rouennaise: étude d'histoire, de géographie et d'archéologie urbaines* (Rouen, 1926),

In the sixteenth century few robe fortunes appear to have been endangered by wild extravagance. But restraint by itself did not assure economic stability, for even the ordinary costs of daily life were surprisingly high and inflexible. We see this first in the prosaic expenditures described by inventories after death. The two coach horses which Charles Maignart inherited in 1582, for instance, were evaluated at 240₶; his bed at 75₶; a single scarlet robe at 50₶. Even so moderate a family as the Maignart expected to live surrounded by colorful furnishings: hence the high cost of beds, which were surrounded by brightly colored curtains, and the frequency of tapestries in *robin* houses (those in the main room of the Maignart's house were evaluated at about 400₶).[10] Such unpredictable but inevitable calamities as lawsuits and illness demanded further expenditures: during the illness which preceded his death in 1601, Jean Godart (master in the Chambre des Comptes) spent 533₶, most of this going to two doctors, with smaller amounts for apothecaries, a surgeon, and servants. Magistrates enjoyed obvious advantages in litigation, but for them as for others even the most mundane legal actions could require large fees.[11]

But such expenditures, which even the more frugal magistrates might normally incur, were less important in determining the magistrates' economic positions than expenses of a different kind, those associated with household, estate management, and office. Some of these have received atten-

---

and Jean-Pierre Bardet, "La maison rouennaise aux XVIIe et XVIIIe siècles, économie et comportement," in Bardet et al., eds., *Le bâtiment. Enquête d'histoire économique, XIVe-XIXe siècles* (Paris-The Hague, 1971), pp. 313-518, 316-319.

[10] La Riv. Bourdet, 2123.

[11] AD S-M, 16J178. The attentions of the medical profession were much sought after in sixteenth-century Normandy. See La Riv. Bourdet, 2139, and Abbé Tollemer, *Un sire de Gouberville* (2nd ed., Paris-The Hague, 1972), pp. 228-269. On the costs of litigation, see Bernard Guenée, *Tribunaux et gens de justice dans le bailliage de Senlis à la fin du moyen âge (vers 1380-vers 1550)* (Paris, 1963), pp. 251-260.

tion in previous chapters. We have seen that the magistrate with a son to raise and educate faced a yearly expense of about 600ł in the 1580's and perhaps twice as much twenty years later. The cost of his own office might be a still larger expense, for by the 1580's most magistrates needed to pay for their offices with borrowed money: interest payments for this purpose would have amounted to about 700ł in 1580, and steadily more thereafter. Likewise, some attention has been given above to the costs of estate management. Although these varied widely, 200ł—spent in paying for laborers, repairs on property, and legal representation—is a reasonable estimate.

Other ordinary expenditures were equally impressive. Daughters were less costly to support than sons, by a considerable margin, but their maintenance was still expensive. Madeleine Voisin, who in 1583 married the future president Charles Maignart, and her sister Catherine, later the wife of a councillor in the Parlement, together cost their parents' estate 400ł yearly for their "*entretenement,*" along with lesser expenditures for education, medical care, and the like. This was not an unduly expensive upbringing: even the orphaned daughter of a middling Rouennais lawyer was estimated in 1585 to cost her tutors 100ł yearly simply for "*nourriture et pention.*"[12] Servants were another large expense, although the *parlementaires* did not support the crowds of servants that were expected to surround a great aristocrat. But every magistrate needed several servants: a legal clerk, usually someone of obscure origins, without formal legal training, who expected ultimately to be recompensed with a position as *procureur* in the Parlement;[13]

[12] La Riv. Bourdet, no. 2139, ff. 133-134; Meubles 2, 23 November 1585.

[13] On these figures, Reg. sec., 1593-1594 (Caen), ff. 1, 40, 43-44; Meubles 2, 6 March 1604; La Riv. Bourdet, 2105. See also Meubles 2, 11 September 1601, for an act by which a councillor made over to his *procureur* a group of houses in Rouen, in recompense for twenty-four years of service collecting rents "en quelques lieux pays et de quelques personnes et pour quelque cause que ce soit."

seven or eight personal servants; and varying numbers of farm servants. Personal servants, at least, were very expensive. Well-paid servants in early seventeenth-century Rouen might receive 100ł yearly, presumably in addition to their maintenance in the household.[14] Not all servants received such high wages, but by the early seventeenth century the overall cost of servants' wages must have been at least 400ł yearly. In the 1580's the cost would have been less, perhaps 250ł or 300ł. Although there is no direct evidence concerning normal adult expenditures, what we have seen of the costs of having children suggests that the normal expenditures of the head of the household and his wife must have been about 600ł yearly.

Two final categories of expenditures are of a somewhat different character, and will receive greater attention below. First, most *parlementaires* by the late sixteenth century were in debt, in addition to the money they owed for their offices, and thus a part of their incomes went for interest payments. Secondly (and more seriously), almost every family had to deal with one form or another of major family obligation. In the early years of his career, the magistrate was likely to owe his mother a jointure on his estate, amounting roughly to one-third of its total value. Later in his career, this would be replaced by obligations to his own daughters, for their dowries. Exceptionally unfortunate families (the Maignart were one) might be confronted with both obligations at the same time. Detailed examination of debt, jointure, and dowry will occupy us at later points. Here it is sufficient to note that they too formed part of the normal expenditures of most *parlementaire* families by the late sixteenth century.

Table 5:1 attempts to summarize what has been seen thus

[14] Their numbers and cost can best be seen from testamentary bequests. See AD S-M, G3442 (Tulles, 1535, and Thorel, 1559); G6275 (Voisin, 1633); Meubles 2, 6 March 1604 (Cahaignes, 1604); AD Eure, E 1504, ff. 18-19 (Jubert, 1603). Servants' wages, like others at Rouen, underwent very rapid increase in the later sixteenth century: in the 1530's, the clerical councillor Guillaume Tulles had paid his servants only 8ł yearly.

TABLE 5:1
ORDINARY ANNUAL EXPENDITURES

i.	Family Support		
	Two daughters	400ł	
	Two sons, including education	1,200ł	
	Husband and wife	600ł	
	Total	2,200ł	
ii.	Administrative Costs		
	Estate costs	200ł	
	Servants	250ł	
	Total	450ł	
iii.	Major Obligations		
	Payment for office	700ł	
	Other debts	200ł	
	Jointure or dowries	2,000ł	
	Total	2,900ł	
TOTAL		5,550ł	

far about these normal expenditures. It assumes a family of two sons and two daughters, in the 1580's, when the sources first permit such estimates. Table 5:1 represents only an approximation of magistrates' expenses, for these must have varied widely from one family to another. The magistrate who inherited his office had fewer expenses in acquiring it (though he did have some), while the magistrate with several daughters to marry had higher expenses for dowries. But Table 5:1 appears accurately to represent the most important facts about this set of expenditures. First, they were relatively inflexible. Only small savings were possible in most of the categories set out in Table 5:1, and the largest single expenditure, the jointure owed the magistrate's mother, was completely rigid. Secondly, the expenses set out in Table 5:1 would have absorbed nearly the whole of the incomes of most magistrates. Few magistrates in the

1580's and 1590's had incomes much greater than 6,000ł, yet such an income barely served to meet the demands set out in Table 5:1. The surplus which remained after these demands had been met would have amounted to about 500ł, roughly the cost of a single lawsuit or extended illness, of two sets of horses, of furnishing a room or of a large banquet. Even this margin of saving could rarely be counted on, for it could easily be absorbed by the delays of tenant farmers or of the royal treasury. In the late sixteenth century especially, rural rents, official salaries, and interest from government bonds were all subject to delay. For most magistrates in the later sixteenth century the delicate balance between expenses and incomes meant that deficit years were a predictable fact of life. The possibility of deficits had existed even in the early sixteenth century, but the likelihood increased as the century progressed; not only were incomes subject to the pressures seen in Chapters 3 and 4, but costs of education, office, and the like were also increasing.

The very problems that created deficits meant that the magistrates' cash reserves to meet them were usually small. In an accounting of 1605, Charles Maignart estimated his cash reserves to be worth 610ł; the father of the councillor Laurent Restault left at his death in 1583 about 1,400ł, "in cash and *obligations*" (non-interest bearing loans); the master of accounts Jean Godart in 1601 left a larger cash reserve, of about 2,500ł. None of these, however, could compare with the sums commonly held by members of the merchant community, such as Jean Voisin, who at his death in 1583 held cash reserves amounting to 9,400ł.[15] This relatively low level of savings meant that borrowing might be necessary to meet immediate needs and that any larger project—the acquisition of an office or estate, a politically useful marriage—would require extensive borrowing.

Thus, in the late sixteenth century even the wealthiest

[15] La Riv. Bourdet, 2105 (Maignart), 2139, ff. 2-3 (Voisin); AD S-M, 16J178, ff. 1-6 (Godart); AD S-M, E, Fonds Restault, unclassed.

parlementaires had debts. The first president Claude Groulart provides, in this respect as in much else, an extreme
example. Groulart's successes have been considered at some
length above. During his years in the Parlement, from 1585
to 1607, he managed to acquire three major fiefs and at least
ten smaller ones. Yet Groulart was not able to do without
borrowing money. In 1601, for instance, he owed annual
interest payments of about 1,600£, corresponding to a total
debt of about 22,400£. These debts were not a sign of serious
trouble, and Groulart was able to acquit them very quickly,
usually within three or four years.[16] Nonetheless, they
testify to the prevalence of borrowing. Probably the president Charles Maignart's position was closer to that of most
parlementaires. Maignart's personal income (exclusive of his
office and his wife's dowry) in the early seventeenth century was about 12,700£, making him also one of the court's
wealthiest members. Yet in 1603 nearly one-fourth of this
income (2,961£) was spent in interest payments. This represented an impressive amount of borrowing, about 42,000£ at
current interest rates. Maignart's borrowing, like Groulart's,
was not a sign of serious trouble. Most of his debts had been
contracted to finance important stages in the family's advancement: his daughters' marriages (both of them to important robe families, and thus involving very high dowries); the acquisition of his presidency in the court; and the
purchase of land. Also like Groulart, Maignart was able to
repay his debts very rapidly, both with profits from his
landed estates—in particular the profits from cutting forest
property—and with the profits from his two very astute
marriages. Yet occasionally Maignart had also to borrow to
meet immediate needs. "The necessity of my affairs," he
noted of one debt contracted in the 1590's, ". . . at that time
was very pressing."[17] Less wealthy magistrates probably
faced this situation more often than Maignart.

Two principal mechanisms of credit were available to

[16] Bibliothèque Municipale, Dieppe, MS 63, pp. 333-355.
[17] La Riv. Bourdet, 2105.

meet these needs. The less important was the outright loan (the *obligation*), legally interest-free and therefore, despite the possibilities that existed for disguised interest payments, mainly used within families to meet exceptional circumstances.[18] The second alternative was the *rente constituée*, a device developed during the first half of the sixteenth century to meet ecclesiastical prohibitions of usury. In the constitution of a *rente*, the buyer (lender) made over to the seller (borrower) a sum of money. In return, the seller committed himself to paying the buyer an annual rent, the *arrérages*; this rent was guaranteed by the whole of the seller's property. At any time the borrower could reimburse the capital of the *rente*, but the lender could never demand that he do so. For the lender, the *rentes* offered the advantages of high, legally sanctioned interest rates and of effective security. For the borrower, there was the advantage that no fixed date was set for repaying the loan. Notarial terminology in fact preserved the notion that the *rente constitutée* was not a loan but a sale of property rights.[19]

Both the legal regulation of interest rates and the liberty enjoyed by the borrower made the *rentes* too cumbersome a device for the needs of merchants, and they tended to employ instead the more flexible letter of exchange. This too avoided condemnation as usury, but (unlike the *rentes*) did not engage the creditor's funds for indefinite periods of time at a legally fixed interest rate.[20] Precisely these qualities made the *rentes* attractive to the landed classes, among them the *parlementaires*, both as borrowers and as lenders in search of secure investments. Even for landowners in need of funds, however, the *rentes* had important limitations. Interest rates were high, at Rouen 10

[18] On evasions of laws surrounding lending at interest, E. Le Roy Ladurie, *Les paysans de Languedoc*, 2 vols. (2nd ed., Paris-The Hague, n.d.), I, 303-305.

[19] On the development of the *rentes*, see Bernard Schnapper, *Les rentes au XVI⁰ siècle. Histoire d'un instrument de crédit* (Paris, 1957), *passim*, and especially pp. 117-136.

[20] *Ibid.*, p. 65.

percent until the 1590's, when, at Rouen as throughout Europe, rates began to decline: to 8.5 percent by 1597, to 7.14 percent by 1601.[21] Even in the early seventeenth century the cost of borrowing was higher than the rate of return on most other investments. The magistrate seeking to buy an estate or office could not expect to repay his loans with current income.

A more fundamental defect of the *rentes* was the ease with which crippling debts might be accumulated. By the mid-sixteenth century, jurists had done away with the medieval practice of securing specific loans on specific pieces of property, which then automatically passed to the creditor in case of default. Instead, the *rente* was assimilated to the Roman *hypotheca* and set on the whole of the debtor's property. One aim underlying this evolution was to supply greater protection to the borrower, by making the seizure of his property in cases of default more difficult. His creditors now had to undertake formal and expensive judicial proceedings in order to get control of the property. But until the very last years of the old regime the public registration of debts was a haphazard matter, and thus it was relatively easy for those already deep in financial difficulties to borrow still more money from unsuspecting creditors. The only restraints on a borrower's running into debt beyond hope of recovery were the personal knowledge which lenders might have of his situation and the threat of judicial seizure and auction of the borrower's properties. If the former was too weak a defense, the latter was too strong, and in any event so expensive that creditors were unlikely to use it until the situation appeared desperate. An edict of Henry II noted in 1553 that

[21] Interest rates are taken from the Tabellionage de Rouen. For most of the century, interest rates were lower at Paris than at Rouen; see Schnapper, *Les rentes*, pp. 102, 111, 293. Cf. Lawrence Stone, *The Crisis of the Aristocracy, 1558-1641* (Oxford, 1965), pp. 530-538, for the forces behind changing interest rates in sixteenth- and seventeenth-century England.

the length of the procedure "has often been the ruin and destruction of both creditors and debtors," and legal treatises continued to repeat the warning into the seventeenth century.[22] Contemporaries recognized the problems that resulted from the lack of a central registry of debts, and periodically the crown sought to create one: in 1581, 1606 (for Normandy alone), and 1673. Despite royal success in establishing registration of other kinds of contracts, however, registration of debts met with steadfast resistance from the aristocracy and was established only in the late eighteenth century.[23]

Aristocratic resistance to the publicity of debts was based on the advantages which secrecy was thought to offer the borrower. In France, argued an early-eighteenth-century opponent of registration, "one survives only on opinion; credit and confidence are founded on nothing but public opinion, and it would mean taking men's last form of wealth, to take from them that reputation which serves them in place of possessions, even when in fact they have lost everything. With it (public opinion), an infinite number of fortunes are daily seen to reestablish themselves, which,

[22] Anthoine Fontanon, *Les édicts et ordonnances des rois de France* . . . , 4 vols. (2nd ed., Paris, 1611), I, 636. See also Henri Basnage, *Traité des hypothèques*, in *Oeuvres* . . . , 2 vols. (4th ed., Rouen, 1778), II, 85, for nearly the same words, and Charles Loyseau, *Traicté du déguerpissement et délaissement par hypothèque* . . . (Geneva, 1636), p. 136. For the need to know well one's debtors, Basnage, *Oeuvres*, II, 1: ". . . whatever contracts [lenders] draw up, and whatever precautions they include, it is often impossible for them to penetrate to the bottom of the affairs of those with whom they are contracting and uncover their insolvency." For the procedures of *decret, Ordonnances des rois de France. Règne de François Ier*, v (Paris, 1936), 121-123 (registered 27 March 1527, old style).

[23] For these efforts and the resistance they met, *ibid.*, II, 2; François Isambert et al., *Recueil général des anciennes lois françaises* . . . (Paris, n.d.), IX, 73ff; V.A.D. Dalloz, *Répertoire de droit civil* (2nd ed., Paris, 1973), article "Hypothèque." In Normandy the Contrôle Normand functioned from 1606, but contracts apparently continued to be passed privately, without even notarial registration.

without this advantage, would have been lost without return."[24] Yet the dangers of virtually unrestricted borrowing for the ultimate survival of families were nearly as great. Because of both this danger and the high interest rates that prevailed, sixteenth- and early-seventeenth-century noblemen were severe in their condemnations of borrowing. "Above all be sure to live without debts," wrote an early-seventeenth-century Breton country gentleman to his son, "for when you have them you will be in perpetual anxiety."[25] Louis de Lorraine, a nephew of the duc de Guise and the abbot of Fécamp, dealt more analytically with the evils of borrowing in a letter to the Rouennais magistrate Nicolas Romé, in 1577. "And as to what you write me about the tax on my abbey of Fécamp, I will always find it better and more expedient to sell out than to borrow money (prendre argent à rente), since the interest, even if the loan were repaid within six months, given the scarcity of money and the interest rates which are current today, would amount to much more than the loss of what will be put up for sale possibly could."[26] Fécamp was the wealthiest monastery in upper Normandy,[27] and Louis de Lorraine's position was quite unlike that of an ordinary landowner seeking to defend his family's patrimony. But for all sixteenth-century landowners, borrowing was clearly a step to be taken only in serious circumstances.

For this reason, there is considerable interest in a statistical evaluation of *parlementaire* borrowing, in terms both

[24] D'Aguesseau, quoted by Baron Grenier, *Traité des hypothèques* . . . , 2 vols. (2nd ed., Clermont-Ferrand, 1829), I, xiii.

[25] Jean Meyer, ed., "Un témoignage exceptionel sur la noblesse de province à l'orée du XVIIᵉ siècle: les 'advis moraux' de René Fleuriot," *Annales de Bretagne*, LXXIX (1972), 328.

[26] AD S-M, 1F39, p. 56, note 2.

[27] In the church land sales of the later sixteenth century, Fécamp was invariably the most heavily taxed institution in the bishopric of Rouen: in 1575, for instance, its tax was nearly twice that set on Bec Hellouin, three times that on Jumièges, nearly four times that on St. Ouen, and five times that on the archbishop of Rouen (AN G8 1247).

of its chronology and its quantity. Because most sales of *rentes* at Rouen were registered with a single set of notaries, such analysis is a relatively straightforward matter, and it is possible also to compare *parlementaire* borrowing with that of other social groups at Rouen. What follows is based on notarial registers for seven years, from 1557 through 1614.[28] These include a total of 1,251 sales of *rentes*, 912 of them newly created *rentes*, a number sufficient for viewing at least upper class borrowing at Rouen. Tables 5:2 and 5:3 present the results of this investigation.

Table 5:2 is limited to newly created *rentes*, because these involved a mortgage on the seller-borrower's properties, and thus the risk of judicial seizure and forced sale. However, statistics for the sale of all *rentes*—that is, the transfer of existing *rentes* as well as new creations—give almost exactly the same results as those presented in Table 5:2. Table 5:3 presents these statistics. The tables demonstrate a striking shift in the magistrates' financial position. During the middle years of the sixteenth century, between 1557 and 1577, both the *parlementaires* themselves and other members of the high robe had been essentially independent of Rouen's money market. Borrowing was an unusual step and

[28] Notarial contracts at Rouen continued to be registered with a single tabellionage through the mid-seventeenth century, when series of private notaries' registers begin. There is thus no bias in the figures below to certain neighborhoods, as in the case of other French cities. However, the series Héritages 2 employed here seems to have included only contracts of some importance, involving sums of roughly 100 *livres* and more. Peasants, artisans, and other members of the lower classes are thus substantially under-represented in statistics drawn from this series (cf. the example of Paris: W. R. Newton and J. M. Ultee, "The Minutier Central: A Research Note," *French Historical Studies*, VIII, 3 [Spring, 1974], 489-493). Not all sales of *rentes* were registered with the tabellionage (see, for instance, Hérit. 2, 6 March 1597); however, there is little reason to suppose that among Rouen's upper classes one group was more likely than another to register its contracts. The analysis here begins with 1557 because it was only in the 1550's that the *rentes* became a fully developed "instrument of credit" (Schnapper, *Les rentes*, pp. 135-136).

TABLE 5:2
CREATIONS OF *Rentes* AT ROUEN, 1557-1614

I. PERCENTAGE OF THE VALUE OF ALL *rentes* CREATED (BORROWING)

	1557	1567	1577	1587	1597	1604	1614
Parlementaire	2.4%	.4%	1.9%	2.5%	7.3%	28.1%	7.5%
Other High Robe[a]	0	0	.9%	7.5%	11.0%	20.8%	13.1%
total	2.4%	.4%	2.9%	10.0%	18.3%	48.9%	20.6%
Country Gentry[b]	8.9%	31.2%	7.4%	13.7%	9.4%	12.7%	12.5%
High Aristocracy[c]	13.8%	8.4%	22.8%	13.7%	14.7%	9.9%	12.5%
total	22.8%	39.6%	30.3%	27.5%	24.1%	22.7%	25.0%
Urban Elite[d]	22.5%	35.5%[e]	13.4%	5.5%	22.5%	5.4%	6.3%
Total Value (in *livres*)	61,468	48,122	110,395	175,274	285,899	189,034	259,48
Total Number	75	62	146	190	227	82	130

II. PERCENTAGE OF THE VALUE OF ALL NEW *rentes* PURCHASED (LENDING)

	1557	1567	1577	1587	1597	1604	1614
Parlementaire	6.5%	14.0%	4.0%	13.8%	9.1%	11.9%	19.4%
Other High Robe[a]	0	2.1%	5.2%	14.7%	12.1%	35.9%	5.0%
total	6.5%	16.1%	9.2%	28.5%	21.2%	47.8%	24.4%
Country Gentry[b]	0	0	0	0	1.0%	1.5%	.8%
High Aristocracy[c]	0	0	0	8.8%	6.1%	0	1.9%
total	0	0	0	8.8%	7.1%	1.5%	2.7%
Urban Elite[d]	16.8%	34.6%	25.2%	18.1%	10.9%	10.5%	17.7%
Total Value (in *livres*)	61,468	48,122	110,395	175,274	285,899	189,034	259,48
Total Number	75	62	146	190	227	82	130

NOTES: a. Includes members of the Cour des Aides, Bureau des Finances, and Chambre des Comptes (established in 1580) of Rouen, Masters of Requests, and members of Parisian sovereign courts.

b. Defined as "*nobles hommes*" and "*écuyers*" not residing in Rouen or other large cities. For discussion of honorific titles in Normandy, and especially for the use of the title "*noble homme*" by the old nobility, see above, pp. 105-106.

c. Defined as those using the titles "*haut et puissant seigneur*," "*messire*," "*messire, chevalier*," etc.

d. Defined as "*nobles hommes*" and "*écuyers*" residing in Rouen, exercising honorable professions (not, for instance, those of merchant or *changeur*), and not forming part of the legal or official hierarchies. These were Rouen's equivalent of an urban patriciate.

e. This figure is inflated by the extensive borrowing of a single Rouennais family, the Grouchet de Soquence. They accounted for three-fourths of the money borrowed by the "urban elite" in 1567. Their financial troubles probably resulted from their conspicuous leadership of Rouen's Protestants during the first civil war.

SOURCE: Hérit. 2, May-July, 1557; June, 1557; April-June, 1567; January-March 1577; April-June, 1577; January-February, 1587; March, 1587; January-February, 1597; March-May, 1597; June-August, 1597; November-December, 1597; January-March, 1604; April-June, 1604; January-March, 1614.

TABLE 5:3

CREATIONS AND TRANSFERS OF *Rentes* AT ROUEN, 1557-1614

I. PERCENTAGE OF THE VALUE OF ALL *rentes* SOLD (BORROWING)

	1557	*1567*	*1577*	*1587*	*1597*	*1604*	*1614*
Parlementaire	2.4%	.4%	1.6%	2.4%	8.4%	28.3%	7.0%
Other High Robe	0	0	.7%	10.9%	11.7%	16.2%	11.7%
total	2.4%	.4%	2.3%	13.3%	20.1%	44.5%	18.7%
Country Gentry	9.5%	28.5%	11.2%	15.3%	11.2%	14.0%	12.6%
High Aristocracy	12.4%	7.5%	18.9%	12.1%	11.9%	7.6%	12.6%
total	21.9%	36.0%	30.1%	27.4%	23.1%	21.6%	25.2%
Urban Elite	21.4%	34.5%	14.6%	5.4%	22.9%	6.1%	8.6%
Total Value (in *livres*)	68,654	53,976	133,607	199,014	375,367	272,170	291,946
Total Number	102	77	193	211	330	173	165

II. PERCENTAGE OF THE VALUE OF ALL *rentes* PURCHASED (LENDING)

	1557	*1567*	*1577*	*1587*	*1597*	*1604*	*1614*
Parlementaire	6.1%	13.6%	6.2%	15.6%	8.3%	13.4%	18.3%
Other High Robe	1.5%	1.9%	6.5%	12.9%	13.3%	35.1%	4.4%
total	7.6%	15.4%	12.7%	28.5%	21.6%	48.5%	22.7%
Country Gentry	0	0	0	.5%	1.5%	4.9%	1.1%
High Aristocracy	0	0	0	1.0%	5.1%	.2%	1.7%
total	0	0	0	1.5%	6.6%	5.1%	2.8%
Urban Elite	15.8%	34.0%	23.7%	17.5%	13.6%	13.1%	15.4%
Total Value (in *livres*)	68,654	53,976	133,607	199,014	375,367	272,170	291,946
Total Number	102	77	193	211	330	173	165

SOURCE: See Table 5:2.

involved only small sums. During the last years of the sixteenth century and the early years of the seventeenth, however, this situation changed. Borrowing increased rapidly in
importance through 1604, when the high robe was by far
the most important single group of borrowers in the city.
By 1614 the situation had improved somewhat, but borrowing remained about as important as during the 1590's: in
1614, as in 1597, the *robins'* demand for funds was nearly

237

as large as that of the country gentry and high aristocracy combined. The history of *parlementaire* debt, then, closely followed the economic changes that have been seen in earlier chapters: rising sharply with the difficulties of the League, and remaining at high levels through the reign of Henry IV.

Even during the first decades of the seventeenth century, the magistracy remained on balance a creditor group. As borrowing increased after 1577, so also did lending by members of Rouen's sovereign courts. Between 1557 and 1577 lending by these groups had been relatively unimportant, about 10 percent of the total funds loaned by means of the *rentes*. From 1587 on, the lending of the robe classes roughly doubled in relative importance, ranging from one-fifth to nearly one-half of the total. For the *parlementaires* themselves the increase in lending was less dramatic but still clear-cut. In 1557, 1567, and 1577, they loaned an average of 6.9 percent of the total; in 1587, 1597, 1604, and 1614, they loaned an average of 13.5 percent of the total.

Parallelism between borrowing and lending resulted from the character of borrowing itself in sixteenth-century Rouen. The lack of public documentation meant that lenders wanted as much personal knowledge as possible about those to whom they loaned money, and thus magistrates in need of funds could expect a more favorable response from relatives and colleagues than from businessmen outside their own milieu. The debts contracted by the president Charles Maignart in the early seventeenth century suggest the range of connections from whom the magistrate might borrow. Among his creditors were his paternal grandmother (to whom he owed 6,000ł), a clerk in the Parlement (1,500ł), his tenant farmer at the estate of La Rivière Bourdet (1,000ł), and two members of the Asselin family, future magistrates to whom Maignart was linked by marriage (6,000ł). Together these debts accounted for about half of Maignart's total indebtedness. A similar tendency prevailed within the magistracy as a whole.[29] Of the money which the magistrates borrowed, 54 percent came from members of the sovereign courts and 25 percent from other officials and lawyers. Conversely, of the money which the magistrates loaned during the seven years studied here, 16 percent went to members of the sovereign courts and 30 percent to other officials and lawyers. Borrowing was the sign, in other words, of the ambiguous ties that bound together the city's robe classes. Assistance was given, but on terms that made no concession to the fact of common group membership. Even with family members, lenders made use of the *rente*, with its high interest rates and dramatic provisions against default, rather than the interest-free *obligation*.

This pattern of borrowing meant that even *parlementaire* families who were not in debt were likely to be drawn into the problems that debt created. Creditors had numerous reasons for anxiety, as we have seen. Colbert's short-lived attempt at reform in 1673 was introduced with the declaration that "by this means one will be able to lend with security . . . creditors will be certain of the wealth of their debtors, and will have neither the fear of seeing it disintegrate nor the anxiety of watching over it."[30] Moral anxieties existed as well (and may help to account for the lender's unfavorable legal position). Jean Maignart, the son of a king's attorney in Rouen's Cour des Aides, expressed one of these anxieties in his testament of 1537: he asked that the interest on the *rentes* which he had bought be reduced from 10 to 9 percent.[31] Both royal legislation and legal

[29] La Riv. Bourdet, 2105. Cf. the tendency among French rural historians to treat debt as an aspect of economic warfare between competing classes: thus Marc Bloch, *French Rural History. An Essay on its Basic Characteristics*, trans. Janet Sondheimer (Berkeley, 1966), pp. 123-124; Febvre, *Philippe II et la Franche Comté*, pp. 186-187; Pierre Goubert, *Beauvais et le Beauvaisis de 1600 à 1730*, 2 vols. (Paris, 1960), I, 214-218. Cf. Stone's discussion of relations between creditors and debtors, *The Crisis of the Aristocracy*, pp. 532-538.

[30] Isambert *et al.*, *Recueil général*, IX, 74.

[31] BN MS français 5346 (Register of Testaments, St. André of Rouen), f. 45r.

commentaries expressed the view that, although the *rentes* were a necessity, their profusion was an evil, which had led merchants to give up their businesses and peasants their farms, "for the profits which they find with neither costs nor the danger of loss."[32]

The magistracy as a whole, then, was being drawn into a new and uncomfortable condition of economic interdependence in the late sixteenth century. As the examples of Groulart and Maignart indicate, even the wealthiest *parlementaires* had at some points to borrow funds. When they were not forced to borrow money, magistrates were drawn into a much more intense round of credit relations after the 1570's, and this in itself brought a greater element of risk, uncertainty, and dependence on others. Rouen's high robe families were certainly not becoming impoverished in the later sixteenth century. Incomes remained very high, and were apparently spent with considerable lavishness in these years. But there had taken place, it seems, a fundamental change in the nature of their economic position. In place of the security from debt of the middle years of the century, there had developed a situation in which dependence and instability were normal conditions.

The full force of this shift becomes apparent when the problems of the magistrates' economic security is examined in somewhat different terms: in terms, that is, of families' changing positions over several generations. Two points about such changes are of particular importance. First, the high level and relatively inflexible character of the normal expenses required of nearly all *parlementaire* families severely limited chances in the later sixteenth century of building a fortune from current income. The savings which most families could accumulate would barely have supplied some security against extraordinary needs. Far less could they have been the basis for acquiring new estates or offices. Apparently conditions had been more favorable in

[32] Fontanon, *Les édicts et ordonnances*, I, 770-771 (March, 1567); see also Basnage, *Oeuvres*, I, 3.

the middle years of the century, when relatively higher revenues from offices and rising landed revenues offered greater possibilities of accumulation. Secondly, the rising level of *parlementaire* indebtedness meant that many families confronted the real possibility of outright ruin, should short-term difficulties make it impossible for them to meet their debts. The combination of these two circumstances seems to have dominated the course of the histories of families in the later sixteenth and early seventeenth centuries. Over the long term, the wealth of *parlementaire* families tended to move in a series of violent shifts, rather than as steady progression or decline.[33]

Once again, the example of Claude Groulart offers an extreme manifestation of general phenomena. Groulart's parents, from wealthy Protestant business families in Dieppe, left him with a substantial fortune at the start of his career. The successes which that career brought have already been considered: as the Parlement's first president between 1585 and 1607, Groulart increased the family's wealth several times over. Royal favor was partly responsible, but Alexandre Bigot in the 1640's thought that marriage was the main reason for Groulart's wealth. "He acquired the estate of Saint Aubin . . . with the money that his first wife brought him," wrote Bigot; "from her as from his second wife he received a great deal of property."[34] At Groulart's death in 1607, the family was apparently well established. Groulart's sons and daughters were connected by marriage with some of the Parlement's most important families, one son was a councillor in the Parlement, and the family was one of the wealthiest in the city. But within sixty

[33] Cf. the stress which Roland Mousnier and his students have placed on families' slow, patient establishment of their positions: thus Mousnier, ed., *Le conseil du roi de Louis XII à la Révolution* (Paris, 1970), pp. 100-101, 319, and *passim*. For helpful discussion of the processes of advancement in contemporary society, Lester C. Thurow, *Generating Inequality. Mechanisms of Distribution in the U.S. Economy* (New York, 1975), pp. 129-154.

[34] BM MS Martainville Y23, f. 25v.

years this apparently secure position had been lost. Claude Groulart's grandson, according to a seventeenth-century description of the "gentlemen and principal properties" of the region, was *"un misérable, ruiné, nulle considération."* The same observer thought that an improvident marriage was at least partly responsible.[35] Only three generations had been necessary for the Groulart to establish and lose an imposing position within provincial society.

The rapidity of the Groulart's rise and fall was unusual but not unique. The family of Jean Godart, whose seigneurie of Belbeuf was described above, underwent a comparable evolution. During the 1580's and 1590's, Jean Godart had emerged from the middling ranks of Rouen's merchants and had acquired several estates and a position within the high robe. At his death in 1601, Jean Godart was secretary of the king and master in the newly created Chambre des Comptes. His eldest son inherited these offices, while his two younger sons were established in the Parlement itself. Given the price that such offices reached in the first decade of the seventeenth century (about 20,-000ł), this was testimony to an impressive fortune. Jean Godart's daughter was married to a councillor in the Parlement. Like the Groulart, the Godart in the early seventeenth century appeared to have acquired an unshakeable place within Rouen's *noblesse de robe.* By 1620, however, at least part of the family was on the verge of ruin. By that year, the wife of Jacques Godart (Jean's eldest son) had secured the legal separation of her property from that of her husband, the normal legal step when there was fear that the husband's difficulties would compromise the financial position of his wife. In 1621, proceedings for the seizure and auction of Jacques' property were begun by one of his creditors. Apparently in an effort to limit the damage to the rest of the family, Jacques' mother had purchased his estates

[35] G. A. Prévost, ed., *Notes du premier président Pellot sur la Normandie. Clergé, gentilshommes et terres principales, officiers de justice* (Paris-Rouen, 1915), p. 183.

two years earlier. The Godart managed to survive as an important Rouennais family, but their position had been seriously threatened.[36]

Few *parlementaire* families displayed this combination of meteoric rise and rapid decline so clearly as the Groulart and Godart, but numerous families underwent comparable difficulties after more gradual advancements. In 1558, the guardian of the minor children of Pierre Rémon, first president between 1543 and 1553, "having found the great debts owed by the said deceased lord president, and that the succession would thus be onerous to the said minors," renounced the succession in their name. In the same year, the heirs of the councillor Anthoine Postel accepted his estate "*par bénéfice d'inventaire*": only with specific provision, that is, against having to pay the estate's debts from their own funds.[37] Seizure and sale of properties belonging to the Lefebvre, a family which had supplied two councillors to the Parlement during the middle years of the century, were begun in 1570; and the same procedures were begun against the minor children of the councillor Louis Raoullin in 1577.[38] In 1599, similar procedures were begun against the Boislevesque, councillors and chief clerks in the Parlement since 1499, and in 1600 against Robert de Villy, grandson of a first president and son of a councillor.[39] In 1602, there was the near collapse of the Le Doulcet, which the family averted by selling its councillorship.[40]

Two last examples concern the mid-seventeenth-century fates of two of the wealthiest and best established *parlementaire* dynasties, the Jubert and Bauquemare. Previous chapters have described the great wealth of both families. The Jubert, in particular, were among the four or five wealthiest

[36] Frondeville, *Les conseillers* ii, 149-153; AD S-M, 16J204.

[37] Meubles 2, 17 November 1558.

[38] La Riv. Bourdet, 1870; AD S-M, B, Parlement, Registre d'Audiences, 19 November 1577.

[39] Meubles 2, 6 April 1601; AD S-M, E, Fonds Caillot de Coquéraumont, liasse 6.

[40] Meubles 2, 28 May 1602.

families in the sixteenth-century Parlement, and benefited also from an impressive circle of marriage alliances; by the mid-seventeenth century their income was reported to be between 40,000₶ and 50,000₶ annually, as large as the annual revenue of the duchy of Aumale. Yet in about 1660 it was reported that the family was ruined and its property seized. The same report noted of a second branch of the family, the Jubert of Bonnemare, that they held "large properties, but numerous debts discommode them"—and a later note added "ruiné."[41]

The Bauquemare were not so wealthy but had held higher positions: Jacques de Bauquemare had been first president between 1565 and 1584, and the family continued to serve in the Parlements of Rouen and Paris over the following century. Their final ruin came in 1682. In that year a lengthy list of creditors, headed by the master of requests Olivier Lefèvre d'Ormesson, completed the auction of the Bauquemare's estates. But this outcome had apparently been expected since the early 1660's, when the two daughters of "Messire Charles de Bauquemare, conseiller du Roy en sa cour de Parlement [de Paris] et président aux requêtes du palais" abandoned his inheritance.[42]

Our sources are more eloquent about success than failure, and thus the examples presented here probably include only a minority of the *parlementaire* families who came to spectacular economic collapse during the sixteenth and seventeenth centuries.[43] Even the examples given here, though, should demonstrate how serious was the possibility of ruin in these years, among even the best-established

[41] Prévost, ed., *Notes du premier président Pellot*, pp. 227, 68.

[42] AD S-M, 16J8: 14.

[43] The more successful the family, the more likely that its papers would be preserved in a reasonably coherent state; the more likely also that its fate would attract the notice of contemporaries. Characteristic of this bias is the fact that the list of bankruptcies here includes the families of four of the Parlement's first presidents. Cf. Roupnel's stress on the small number of *parlementaire* bankruptcies at Dijon: *La ville et la campagne*, p. 237.

robe families. These instances of collapse are the most striking manifestations of the insecure economic conditions of
the late sixteenth century. Bankruptcy was by no means a
new phenomenon in these years (as the examples above indicate), but it was becoming a more common one. As such,
it was the most extreme manifestation of the more general
problem of *parlementaire* indebtedness.

Study of *parlementaire* debt, then, is important partly because it shows the reality of the economic difficulties that
the group experienced after about 1575. But the spread of
large-scale *parlementaire* borrowing in these years was not
simply an economic phenomenon. Debt was a manifestation of economic pressures, but it was also a creator of new
social patterns. One of these was a pattern of interdependence. Both as debtors and as creditors, robe families had
increasingly to rely on a network of credit relations if they
were to survive. Their financial position was not quantita-
tively the worse for this fact. If anything, modes of living
were becoming more luxurious in these years. But reliance
on credit did mean a position that was more complex, more
vulnerable, less predictable.

The second pattern created by the rising level of indebtedness concerns the family's position over time. During
the middle years of the sixteenth century, it appears, conditions favored the steady expansion of families' wealth and
control over official positions. Magistrates enjoyed a margin
of income over expenditures that allowed them, for instance, to place more than one son in high office, or to
expand their landed property. After about 1575 the situation
was different. Continuity rather than steady progress became the normal state of affairs, but dramatic changes in
the family's position also became far more likely: in the
form of bankruptcy, or in the form of new wealth coming
to the family from outside, above all through astute use
of the marriage market. The issues of economic change, in
other words, lead necessarily to questions about the family's
structure and workings. These are the subject of the following chapter.

SIX

THE *PARLEMENTAIRE* FAMILY

"HE WAS very wealthy, both in his own right, through his mother and paternal grandmother, and by right of his two wives, and he enjoyed great credit at Rouen in the minds of the populace." These were the terms that a mid-seventeenth-century magistrate used to describe his predecessor in office, Charles Maignart (president *à mortier* from 1600 to 1621).[1] Bigot's comments point to an obvious fact: the centrality of family relationships in determining the *robin*'s economic and social position. Contemporaries understood family arrangements to be crucial sources of wealth, equal in importance to office and land—and over the long term perhaps more important. Previous chapters have touched on the influence of family organization, for instance with regard to the magistrates' greater concern in the late sixteenth century with inherited status and families' troubles in maintaining their wealth over several generations. The present chapter examines the *parlementaire* family more directly and more broadly.

Its concerns are twofold. Family organization both reflected and, in its turn, helped to shape the social and economic patterns discussed in previous chapters. On the one hand, then, this chapter seeks to describe the impact of social patterns on personal experience, in such areas as marriage, household organization, inheritance. On the other hand, as Bigot's comments suggest, marriage and inheritance had an independent causal force of their own, which needs to be analyzed if the magistrates' evolution as a social group is to be understood.[2]

[1] Frondeville, *Les présidents*, p. 280.
[2] The analysis which follows owes much to studies of family or-

The arguments to be presented here concern first the economics of *parlementaire* marriage. These changed considerably over the sixteenth and early seventeenth centuries. In the middle years of the sixteenth century, monetary concerns were of relatively limited importance in shaping the magistrates' marriage choices, and this fact left a large role to considerations of social status and political alliance. After 1570, on the contrary, money came to be the critical issue in most *parlementaire* marriage choices, and for most families it reduced concern for social and political advantage to a secondary position. The economics of marriage are thus closely related to a second central theme of this chapter, that of the *parlementaire* family's limited ability to fill many of the roles that contemporaries assigned to it: binding together the social group, allowing families (for instance, by marrying their daughters to members of the aristocracy) to rise

---

ganization in other aristocratic groups, notably to Lawrence Stone, *The Crisis of the Aristocracy, 1558-1641* (Oxford, 1965), pp. 589-669; Philippe Ariès, *Centuries of Childhood. A Social History of Family Life*, trans. Robert Baldick (New York, 1962); Natalie Zemon Davis, "Ghosts, Kin, and Progeny: Some Features of Family Life in Early Modern France," *Daedalus*, CVI, 2 (Spring, 1977), 87-114; Georges Duby, "Lignage, noblesse et chevalerie au XIIᵉ siècle dans la région maconnaise," *Annales. Économies, Sociétés, Civilisations.* XXVII. 4-5 (July-October, 1972), 802-823; Robert Forster, *The Nobility of Toulouse in the Eighteenth Century: A Social and Economic Study* (Baltimore, 1960), pp. 120-151, and *The House of Saulx-Tavanes. Versailles and Burgundy, 1700-1830* (Baltimore, 1971); Richard Goldthwaite, *Private Wealth in Renaissance Florence. A Study of Four Families* (Princeton, 1968), pp. 251-275. As with studies of the impact of landowning by the *noblesse de robe*, some historians have assigned a special place to the robe family in the sixteenth and seventeenth centuries as a precursor of the nuclear and bourgeois family of the nineteenth century: thus Roland Mousnier, *Les institutions de la France sous la monarchie absolue, I, Société et état* (Paris, 1974), p. 74. For a very different analysis, which nonetheless gives the development of the *noblesse de robe* an important role in shaping attitudes toward the family, see Carolyn Lougee, *Le Paradis des Femmes. Women, Salons, and Social Stratification in Seventeenth-Century France* (Princeton, 1976).

in social status, providing assistance to an extended network of kin, securing property and power from one generation to the next. All of these were important aims to many robe families, and in some periods circumstances favored their realization: for the *parlementaires* the mid-sixteenth century was one such period. At all times, however, these aims met with serious obstacles, and in the later sixteenth century such obstacles became more difficult to overcome. Money was the most important problem, but there were others. In arranging marriages, for instance, there was a need to reconcile the divergent interests of the numerous family members who had a part in its decisions, as well as to fore-stall runaway marriage and royal interference. The family's dynastic functions were subject to similar complications. For most robe families, the moment of inheritance involved both psychological and economic disruptions, and these made even the maintenance of its position from one generation to the next a difficult task.

Broadly put, then, this chapter examines the interplay between the goals of the *parlementaire* family—to assure dynastic continuity, to provide a wide network of kinship, to improve its members' social status—and the various restrictions on its actions. Examining this interplay, it is hoped, will serve a further purpose, of allowing some insight into the magistrates' personal attitudes and sensibilities —attitudes which can be set against the professional, social, and economic values which have concerned us thus far.

Marriage provides a good starting point for our examination of the *parlementaire* family. Like all other facets of family life, marriage was governed by the customary law of the province, which received its final form only in 1583. In the preceding years a commission from the Parlement (following the example of nearly all other French provinces) had toured the province, collected the varying usages that were in force, and had tried to settle ambiguities. The "reformed custom" that they produced, like the tradition on which their work was based, gave special qualities to Norman family organization. "No law," commented a seventeenth-century jurist, "has ever been so mistrustful of the indivdual's wisdom and good behavior as that of Normandy," and one of the custom's chief concerns was to restrict the individual's rights over his property.[3] This tendency was most clearly expressed with regard to the individual's rights of testation: for nobility and commoners alike, the custom required equal division of property among all the sons of a marriage. What a parent could settle on a daughter was severely limited. If there were sons of a marriage, all the daughters together could receive no more than one-third of the total inheritance, with the further restriction that no daughter could be given any more than any of the sons—for instance, in a family with only one daughter and several sons. Only when there were no sons could a daughter receive more than a third of the estate. Then she became an heir to her parents' estate, which was divided equally among the daughters.[4]

These formed one set of restrictions on what a parent

[3] Henri Basnage, *Oeuvres*, 2 vols. (4th ed., Rouen, 1778), I, 337. For general discussion of the character of customary laws and their impact, see E. Le Roy Ladurie, "Système de la coutume. Structures familiales et coutume d'héritage en France au XVIe siècle," *Annales. Économies, Sociétés, Civilisations*, xxvii, 4-5 (July-October, 1972), 825-846; and Ralph Giesey, "Rules of Inheritance and Strategies of Mobility in Prerevolutionary France," *The American Historical Review*, LXXXII, 2 (April, 1977), 271-289.

[4] On Norman marriage law, see the commentaries of Basnage, in *Oeuvres*, I; Josias Bérault, *La Coustume réformée du pays et duché de Normandie* (4th ed., Rouen, 1632); Denis Godefroy, *La coutume réformée du pays et duché de Normandie* (BM MS Y94, also from the early seventeenth century); and Maître Houard, *Dictionnaire analytique, historique, étymologique, critique et interprétatif de la coutume de Normandie*, 4 vols. (Rouen, 1780); among modern studies, Roger Bataille, *Du droit des filles dans la succession de leurs parents en Normandie* (Paris, 1927), and J. C. Perrot, "Note sur les contrats de mariage normands," in A. Daumard and F. Furet, *Structures et relations sociales à Paris au milieu du XVIIIe siècle* (*Cahiers des Annales*, xviii, 1961), 95-97, are especially helpful.

could do for his daughters at their marriages, and on the uses he could make of marriage alliance. A second important group of restrictions had to do with the absence in Normandy of community of property between husband and wife. Under the custom of Paris, husband and wife were given equal shares in their total liquid wealth (*meubles*) and in all real wealth acquired during their marriage; the bride also had a large share in her husband's estate if he died before her, amounting to a usufruct of half of her husband's properties. Norman law was in every way less protective of the bride. Her jointure was smaller, amounting to one-third of her husband's revenue, and usually she received only one-third of his *meubles* also. Most important, she had only a limited share in the acquisitions made during the marriage. Until the reformed custom of 1583 she had no share at all in acquisitions of land or fiefs. Even thereafter her share was smaller than that of a Parisian wife (one-third rather than one-half), and the acquisitions to which she had rights were more narrowly defined. The wife had a share only in properties that had been purchased during the marriage, since purchases were presumed to reflect her thrift and good management, and (in contrast to Parisian law) she received no share in gifts received during the marriage. Finally, her share in these properties was lost if she separated from her husband or died before him; in these cases nothing went to her heirs.[5]

To the lawyers of the old regime, the importance of these differences was, again, the restriction they placed on personal impulses. "If one compares the two customs," wrote one lawyer in 1705, "that of Normandy is throughout founded on the wisdom and foresight that one ought to have to prevent the disorders which amorous passion creates in families' fortunes: it is no honest liberty which the custom of Paris allows, it gives full rein to passion." His point

[5] See Paul Viollet, *Histoire du droit civil français* (Paris, 1905; repr. Darmstadt, 1966), pp. 829-833, for brief summary of the evolution of French customs on this point.

was that in Normandy, though the possibility of a wealthy young man marrying a poor bride remained real, its effects on his patrimony were less serious; the bride could expect only a small part of her husband's fortune.[6]

Together, the restrictive provisions of the Norman custom made the marriage contract in Normandy a very limited document. In contrast to Parisian marriage contracts, which might go on for tens of pages listing the properties which husband and wife brought to the marriage, Norman marriage arrangements rarely amounted to more than two or three pages. Since there was no community of property, there was no need to say anything about the husband's properties; and since most brides had no rights of inheritance over their parents' properties, extensive discussion of the bride's portion was unnecessary as well. The main function the contract had to fill was to specify a gift (normally one of cash, though in the earlier sixteenth century gifts of property were also common) from the bride's parents to the couple; conditions surrounding the gift were spelled out, and in particular a distinction was made between the dowry proper (the *dot*), which was the bride's own property and could pass only to her direct heirs, and a donation (the *don mobil*), an outright gift to the husband, to do with as he wished. Additional provisions might be included in the contract—for the couple's residence, for the bride's rights over her husband's estate if she survived him, and so on—but these were not essential and were to be found in only a minority of cases.[7]

But such limitations on what could be done in the Norman marriage contract did not prevent notable Norman families from devoting a great deal of time and calcula-

[6] Olivier Estienne, *Nouveau traité des hypothèques* . . . (Rouen, 1705), p. 131.

[7] For examples of Norman marriage contracts, see below, Appendix F. See Perrot, "Note sur les contrats de mariage normands," for a strong statement of the differences between Norman and Parisian contracts.

tion to the arrangement of marriage alliances. The correspondence between Margueritte Thomas, the wife of an official at Troyes, and her brother, a member of the Chambre des Comptes at Rouen, illustrates the efforts that were required. Early in the seventeenth century (probably in 1614), Margueritte wrote that:

". . . an *honeste homme* named Croule, who was secretary to the late chancellor (Pomponne de Bellièvre) and who, until the recent death of the chancellor's widow, resided in their household, seeks marriage with my daughter, through his contact with one of my nieces . . . who is married . . . to one of the companions and friends of the said sieur Croule. . . . I will have the honor of discussing this further with you and of having your opinions, without which I would not think of taking any sort of action. I only beg that, if there is someone in your city among your friends who would have some acquaintance with [Croule], that you inform yourself about him, if it is something you may properly do, and you will still further oblige me to offer you my humble services. . . ."

A short time later there was another letter from Margueritte, asking that Thomas make use of a connection in the Parlement, a magistrate who was married to one of Bellièvre's daughters; Margueritte apologized for her importunity, but begged "that you excuse me, as the subject is of great importance. I pray you: is there a means of learning something, as secretly as you can?" Barely a month later there was yet another letter on the subject from Margueritte, this time concerning the marriage of one of Thomas' own daughters:

"I have rejoiced at the news of the marriage which you have begun arranging for my niece, recalling the desire which my late mother had that this be arranged soon. May God give you the good fortune to manage it. I pray with all my affection that He console you in this. It is a great burden and thus I am sorry for you, and about the expense, but

God will comfort you and will give you the means to emerge from this to your satisfaction."[8]

Despite the custom's limitations on dowries, as Margueritte's comments suggest, marrying off a daughter was a difficult matter. There was the expense of dowry and of the wedding celebrations; there was also the need to learn as much as possible about the prospective groom, and this effort required parents to call on a wide range of relatives and friends.

Parental calculations of this kind were especially needed because a constant danger existed of more spontaneous marriages. In a lengthy Latin poem describing the varied events of Rouen's year, Hercule Grisel described late night balls as one of the city's principal winter attractions. Groups of young ladies together could arrange such events for neighbors of their own rank. As Grisel described them, they were a principal source of romantic intrigues. "If anyone is seen there with a beautiful face, / if she is charming, and gives hope of her love— / then more than one rich friend will watch over her comfort; / some will bring lutes, others refreshments. / If her coloring and her nose arouse no passion, / a girl can overcome everything by her expenditures."[9] And romance might have serious consequences: in 1608 the son of an auditor in Rouen's Chambre des Comptes married against his parent's wishes, and both he and the bride were severely punished, with floggings, exile, and imprisonment.[10] Despite the dangers of personal involvement, it was at least acceptable for personal attachments to have developed before a marriage was negotiated.

[8] AD S-M, 10J10.

[9] *Hercule Grisel, Les fastes de Rouen* . . . , ed. F. Bouquet, 4 vols. (Rouen, 1866-1868; first published Paris, 1643), Winter Trimester, p. 16 ("Si qua tamen pulchro fuerit spectabilis ore, / Si lepida est, veneris spem dederitque suae; / Non unus locuples ipsam relevabit amicus; / Hi citharas, illi quae comedenda ferent. / Si color et nullam nasus commovit orexim, / Impensis solvet cuncta puella suis.").

[10] The case is discussed by Bérault, *La coustume reformée*, p. 390.

This was one argument that the tutors of Catherine Martel in the 1570's used to defend their arrangement for her of a marriage with Pierre de Becdelièvre, a member of a distinguished *parlementaire* family who entered the Chambre des Comptes in 1587. Catherine, they argued, had held for her husband "for a long time a good and honest affection," and this had continued into their marriage; whether or not the couple's affections were in fact thus engaged before the marriage, the girl's guardians at least believed this an appropriate argument to make to the judicial authorities.[11]

So long as her father lived, a girl's marriage was largely his decision, though some jurists believed that once she had reached twenty-five she might legitimately arrange her own marriage if her father refused to arrange one for her.[12] Most daughters of *parlementaire* families had their marriages arranged by their fathers; this was the more likely in that, as we shall see, most girls from this milieu married at about twenty. A considerable minority, however, married after their fathers' deaths. This was the case for 45 percent of the *parlementaires*' daughters who married between 1570 and 1610.[13] In this instance, marriage arrangement became a

---

[11] BN Carrés de d'Hozier, 77, ff. 112-113. See the more general discussion by Jean-Louis Flandrin, *Les amours paysannes. Amour et sexualité dans les campagnes de l'ancienne France (XVIe-XIXe siècle)* (Paris, 1975), pp. 43ff.

[12] Bérault, *La coustume reformée*, pp. 275-276; Godefroy, *La coutume*, f. 319v. This view followed a law of Henry II, but Bérault presented it as by no means fully assured in judicial practice.

[13] The likelihood of a father's arranging his daughter's marriage himself declined over the sixteenth century; of *parlementaires*' daughters marrying before 1570, 27 percent married after their fathers' deaths, while of those marrying between 1570 and 1610, 45 percent married after their father's death. This decline was closely related to a second pattern: when fathers arranged their daughters' marriages, there was a greater likelihood that marriage would be within the Parlement than if the marriage arrangement was in the hands of brothers or tutors. Of eighteen daughters who married within the Parlement, four (22 percent) married after their father's death; of sixty-one daughters who married outside the Parlement,

more complicated affair, and the tensions surrounding marriage received sharper expression: for the girl's fate was now to be determined not simply by her father's decision, but by the colliding intentions of a wide range of parties. This meant, first, the crown. If, as was normal among *parlementaire* families, the family held fiefs from the crown, the minor children came under the monarch's wardship; and he might hand both responsibility and profits over to interested courtiers, who then became responsible for arranging marriages, normally in their own interests. Relatively few *parlementaire* fortunes were sufficient to tempt important courtly families, but the problem did arise. In 1544 Francis I gave the guardianship over the daughter and heiress of Jacques de Cormeilles, king's attorney in the Parlement, to the Montgomery family, along with a straightforward statement of his motives: "you are aware," he told the girl's unwilling mother, ". . . of how much concern I have for the affairs of my said cousin (Montgomery), because of the greatness of his merits, and how much I desire the advancement of his house—and he has a son, an honest gentleman, who seems to me to promise so much virtue that he could not be other than an appropriate and suitable match for your daughter." The family's resistance to this arrangement lasted some years, but in 1554 a compromise was at last arranged. The marriage would indeed take place when the couple reached an appropriate age; until then the girl (and her revenues) would remain with her mother. These provisions were settled in a marriage contract signed when the bride-to-be was eleven years old and the groom fourteen.[14] Claude Groulart was involved in a similar dispute during the League, when the wardship of his stepson, the

---

twenty-five (41 percent) married after their father's death. However, the number of marriage contracts available is too small for this difference to be statistically significant.

[14] Tabel., 9 August 1569. For the laws surrounding wardship, see Houard, *Dictionnaire*, II, 363-364.

future councillor Robert Le Roux, was given to the maréchal de Bassompierre. The profits which the maréchal drew from the Le Roux estate were the subject of litigation after the League, but Groulart was able to defend his family's interests with some success.[15] More general complaints about the ways wardship was handled abounded. "You know what the merchandising of *gardes nobles* is like," wrote the councillor Baptiste Le Chandelier to Thomas Maignart, with particular reference to the deprivations children might suffer at the hands of greedy guardians. Wardships were indeed a source of income to many noblemen, and in 1584 the nobility of the province complained that wardships, "with which the nobility has been accustomed to be assisted (*gratifiée*)," were now instead being given to tax farmers. In either case, the danger to families' estates might be considerable.[16]

Even when the king preserved the family's guardianship of a youthful heiress, moreover, his interference was not necessarily at an end. In 1548 the relatives of Catherine Maignart assembled before Rouen's chief local magistrate, the lieutenant general of the *bailliage*, to discuss her marriage arrangement. Catherine was the daughter of a lawyer in the Parlement, the granddaughter of a king's attorney in the Cour des Aides, and the niece of one of the Parlement's original members, and she also was the heir to a considerable fortune. Her relatives had been summoned at the king's command to resolve a conflict over whom she should marry. The majority favored an alliance with yet another member of Rouen's *noblesse de robe*, the *parlementaire* Guillaume Le Roux. Without their knowledge (so they claimed), two other relatives had given their approval to

[15] Reg. sec., 1595, f. 125r.

[16] La Riv. Bourdet, 1381 (1555); C. Robillard de Beaurepaire, ed., *Cahiers des États de Normandie sous le règne de Henri III*, 2 vols. (Rouen, 1888), II, 96. See also Bérault's discussion of a case in which, "in order to succeed in marrying a ward, the man who was pursuing her had obliged himself to her tutor" (*La coustume reformée*, p. 242).

an entirely different kind of match, with "an Italian gentleman, from the Queen's household, named Marc Anthoine, *escuier trenchant* of the Queen and nephew of Baptiste, the Queen's first butler." Numbers were on the side of a local marriage, within the robe itself, but the engagement of royal interests on the side of a courtly marriage carried the day, and Catherine was duly married to Marc Anthoine de Seguzzo.[17]

But the family's defeat was only temporary. Fifty years after the Maignart had lost their heiress to the courtly nobility, they managed another marriage that reversed the process. In 1597 Catherine Maignart herself arranged the marriage of her granddaughter and partial heiress to Catherine's great-nephew Charles Maignart, at the time master of requests and from 1600 on president in the Parlement of Rouen. The marriage enabled the thirty-five year old Maignart (this was his second marriage) to recover many of the properties which Catherine had carried out of the family.[18]

The Maignart's persistence in their efforts to keep intact their inheritance, or at least to keep it within the circle of notable Rouennais families, suggests a principal tension between the goals a family might strive for in arranging its daughters' marriages. There was something in favor of marriages with the courtly aristocracy; connections with the court were obviously useful. At least when substantial amounts of money were involved, however, robe families apparently were more intent on preserving their patrimonies than with extending their alliances. Seemingly glamorous connections with the courtly aristocracy had to be forced on them by an interested crown.[19]

Concern for preserving the family's wealth, of course,

[17] La Riv. Bourdet, 1133.

[18] Hérit. 2, 19 April 1597; see also *ibid.*, 13 November 1601 ("dame Catherine de Gouel seulle heritiere de la maison de Paville").

[19] For discussion of the complexity of families' aims in marriage arrangements, see Davis, "Ghosts, Kin, and Progeny."

was still more evident when marriage arrangements were in the hands of a brother, for then financial interests were in direct conflict. Whatever dowry the girl received went to diminish her brother's inheritance, and for this reason the custom afforded girls protection against their brothers' greed. In contrast to their lack of rights in dealing with a father who refused to arrange a marriage, girls could compel their brothers to arrange marriages for them by legal action; and, whereas a father could give his daughter as small a dowry as he wished, a brother was compelled to give his sisters dowries appropriate to the family's wealth, what the custom called a *mariage avenant*: that is, one-third of the total estate was to be divided among the sisters, provided that the sisters' shares did not amount to more than any one of the brothers'. Further, as an early-seventeenth-century Norman lawyer stated, a brother could arrange his sisters' marriages only on the "condition that they not be married beneath their station and that [their brother] not marry them so cheaply that he gives them to men of lesser quality and unworthy of the alliance."[20] The claims of money and status were in direct conflict, and it was assumed that only careful regulation could assure some balance between them. Such danger existed even among in-laws. In the late 1570's, the tutors of Catherine Martel, a wealthy Rouennais heiress, accused her sister's husband of trying to prevent her marriage, "in order to get into his hands the whole succession." The unsucrupulous brother-in-law, so the tutors claimed, was seeking to use all available legal delays, in the hope that the girl would die before a marriage could be arranged. When the tutors had gone ahead with an appropriate marriage, he had gone to the

---

[20] Godefroy, *La coustume reformée*, f. 321v. See also Bataille, *Du droit des filles*, pp. 100-108, for discussion of the sister's difficulty in securing her rights from her brother, and pp. 109ff. for the legal development of the *mariage avenant*. In the course of the seventeenth and eighteenth centuries the Parlement's decisions appear to have steadily reduced the rights of sisters.

Parlement with an accusation of rape, as unauthorized marriages were legally defined.[21]

For the bride's family, finally, there were considerations created by the publicity in which even the financial aspects of marriage were arranged. A suggestion of the anxieties which this situation raised is given by an agreement of 1550 between a nobleman from the countryside near Rouen and his father-in-law. The dowry of 3,500ł specified in the nobleman's marriage contract, they agreed before the notaries, was fictitious, designed "only to give contentment to my relatives and friends," and the real dowry was only 2,500ł.[22]

Families with daughters to marry thus found themselves in a complicated situation, with interests that pulled them in several directions. This was true even with regard to the apparently absolute control enjoyed by the bride's father, and the complexity of choice grew if the marriage came after the father's death. Families' interests pulled them toward both local and courtly marriages, toward earlier and later marriages, and toward more and less generous dowries. Marriage arrangements reflected the collison of these interests, and, when brides married after their fathers' deaths, the diverse collection of relatives and public authorities who might be involved in the decision.

Men from the *parlementaires'* milieu were in a much simpler situation. In the first place, the negotiations leading to marriage were normally (though not invariably) initiated by the man's family; in that sense the man usually had somewhat greater liberty of action.[23] Secondly, the magistrates

[21] BN Carrés de d'Hozier, 77, ff. 111-113.

[22] Hérit. 2, 20 February 1549 (old style).

[23] This was not always the case, however. In arranging the marriage of the future councillor Robert Le Roux in 1557, his tutors noted that "the said lord . . . has been solicited for several *beaulx et bons* marriages, with fine and important families (*maisons*):" Archives d' Esneval, Acquigny. For the man's normal role, see the correspondence of Margueritte Thomas, above, and AD S-M, B, Parlement, Registre d' Audiences, 5 July 1575.

themselves were normally older than their brides, and in a position to have a considerable role in determining their marriage choices. For most magistrates, marriage came as they were entering the court: well over half of the magistrates for whom marriage contracts survive married within two years before or after entering the Parlement. By the time he married, the magistrate was likely to be in his middle twenties, and the holder of an independent position and income. He was independent at the time of his marriage in a deeper sense as well. Between 1500 and 1610, about three-fourths of the magistrates whose marriage contracts survive married after their fathers' deaths: in other words, as adults who were largely free of parental control.[24]

Men awaited their father's death to marry for both psychological and economic reasons. As we shall see below, at least some *parlementaires* shared the distaste with which sixteenth-century Frenchmen commonly regarded the prospect of marriage, and this in itself discouraged early marriage.[25] Economic reasons for delay lay both in a generalized reluctance to have the generations crowd too closely together, thus requiring the family's property to support too many people at once, and in the more specific problems created by widowhood.[26] For, although marriage offered the obvious benefits of the bride's dowry, it posed also the risk that, at the husband's death, she would receive a substantial part of his estate. The widow's share involved a

[24] This is based on the sample of marriage contracts discussed below, Appendix F.

[25] Robert Mandrou, *Introduction à la France moderne (1500-1640). Essai de psychologie historique* (2nd ed., Paris, 1974), pp. 118-122; David Hunt, *Parents and Children in History. The Psychology of Family Life in Early Modern France* (New York, 1970), pp. 69-74; Lougee, *Le paradis des femmes*, pp. 59-62; and the suggestive examples discussed by Flandrin, *Les amours paysannes*, p. 209.

[26] For discussion and examples of the dangers of "clustering" of the generations, see Robert Forster, *The House of Saulx-Tavanes*, pp. 50, 132, 204.

jointure of one-third of her husband's patrimonial income and a substantial share (usually one-third) of both her husband's liquid wealth and any acquisitions made during the marriage. Her part in her husband's liquid wealth and acquisitions became her absolute property, to do with as she wished; her jointure was a life interest only, but she kept it even in the case of remarriage. Finally, the widow regained control over the larger part of her dowry, the *dot*, and this too she might take with her to a new husband. Given the considerable properties which she often controlled, moreover, her chances of finding a new husband were excellent; to suitors in need of funds, a widow was nearly as attractive as an heiress.[27]

Supporting a widow might thus lead to a substantial disorganization of the family's finances, and this risk was to be put off as long as possible. The father's death, however, immediately changed this situation. There was now an immediate need to repair the losses which obligations to his widow were creating. Other obligations were equally acute. There were funeral expenses and the costs involved in inheriting property (to be considered below), and there might be the cost of acquiring office itself. Marriage was the obvious source for funds to meet these needs, and magistrates tended to turn to it shortly after their father's death. The Maignart family typified this pattern. Guillaume Maignart, one of the Parlement's founding members, died in December, 1525; his son, Thomas, soon to be a member of the city's Cour des Aides, married five weeks later. Thomas died in 1559, two years *after* his son Jean had married—but also two years after his own wife's death had removed the problem of widowhood. Jean Maignart became president in the Cour des

---

[27] See the comparative discussion of Pierre Guénoys, *La conférence des coustumes tant générales, que locales et particulières du Royaume de France*, 2 vols. (Paris, 1596), II, 548v, 551r, 604r. Cf. Lawrence Stone's discussion of widowhood in England: *The Crisis of the Aristocracy*, pp. 621-623.

Aides, and died in October, 1582; and in May, 1583, his son, the future master of requests and *parlementaire* Charles, married for the first time, following a contract arranged the month before his father's death.[28]

Marriage for most *parlementaires* thus came at a critical moment, the moment at which the family's inheritance changed hands and at which they began their careers in high office. As a result, the economic role which marriage might have was enormous. We obtain a clearer idea of its potential importance from the example of individual *parlementaires*. Only a few magistrates have left documents on both their marriages and their private fortunes. The earliest and most striking of these is provided by the Maignart family. Over four generations, from 1525 through 1614, the Maignart married a succession of heiresses, most of them from families still closely associated with commerce and tax farming. The first of these marriages, made in 1525, approximately doubled the family's patrimony; the second, in 1557, brought an increase of about one-third to the family fortune; and the third marriage, that of the future president Charles Maignart himself, in 1583, increased his fortune by about two-thirds.[29]

The Maignart were exceptional among robe families in the consistency with which they made use of marriage to build up their patrimony. But they certainly were not unique in the importance of their brides' contribution to their total wealth. Jean Cavelier, a councillor who married in 1582, received from his bride properties worth about 3,250ł in yearly income; when his mother-in-law died, twenty years later, the couple received further properties worth nearly 3,000ł in yearly income. All of this was prob-

[28] Frondeville, *Les présidents*, pp. 282-283; Hérit. 2, 22 May 1583.

[29] Frondeville, *Les présidents*, pp. 282ff.; Oscar de Poli, "Les seigneurs de la Rivière Bourdet," *Revue nobiliaire historique et biographique, nouvelle série*, IV (1868), 97-108, 207-233, 261-275; Tabel., 19 November 1572; Hérit. 2, 22 June 1583, 19 April 1597; La Riv. Bourdet, 1031, 1460, 1512, 1559 *bis*, 1574, 1772, 2105, 2916.

ably worth more than Cavelier's own fortune.[30] The councillor Nicolas Caillot married in 1572 for a relatively meagre dowry, of 5,000l; but this was roughly two-thirds as large as Caillot's own fortune at his death in 1588.[31] Artus Godart, who entered the Parlement in 1608, was much wealthier than Caillot but relied still more heavily on his marriage portion: Godart inherited a fortune worth about 2,300l in annual revenue, but this was only half the income which his bride's dowry produced.[32]

Examples like these indicate that for some magistrates the calculation of marital economics was a matter of intense concern. The Maignart show how such concern might extend over the generations, both in the consistency of their pursuit of heiresses and in their patient efforts to recover a collateral inheritance that had apparently been lost to the high aristocracy. But examples of this kind need to be set against statistical evidence concerning the magistracy as a whole. For this purpose we may turn to *parlementaire* marriage contracts and the indications they supply about the financial aims of marriage. Marriage contracts survive for about one-fourth of those who served in the Parlement through 1610.[33] They suggest that the Maignart were exceptional in the consistency with which they pursued economically advantageous marriages, but that this kind of economic calculation became more important as the sixteenth century progressed. By the turn of the seventeenth century, money had become the crucial element in most *parlementaire* marriage arrangements. This shift is to be seen, first, in the growing numbers of *parlementaire* brides who were heiresses: that is, who had no brothers and were thus eligible to inherit part of their parents' estates. Table 6:1 sets out these numbers for three periods over the sixteenth and early

[30] Hérit. 2, 8 January 1587, 19 April 1602, 18 May 1604, 24 April 1620.

[31] Tabel., 28 September 1572; Hérit. 2, 5 January 1591.

[32] AD S-M, 16J178; Hérit. 2, 18 July 1609.

[33] For discussion of these, Appendix F.

TABLE 6:1

MARRIAGE WITH HEIRESSES[34]

Date	Total Brides	Heiresses
1500-1569	27	5 (19 percent)
1570-1589	25	8 (32 percent)
1590-1610	23	9 (39 percent)

SOURCE: See Appendix F.

seventeenth centuries. Magistrates in search of a bride in the early and middle years of the sixteenth century had not neglected the possibility of marrying heiresses, but such marriages remained unusual. After 1570 their importance grew, and by the early 1600's heiresses represented about one-third of *parlementaire* brides.

This was not the only sign of the increasing importance of money in *parlementaire* marriage arrangements during these years. Magistrates who were not so fortunate as to find heiresses were marrying for steadily larger dowries during the years after 1570. The evolution of the dowries which magistrates received from their brides is set out in Graph 6:1. As it shows, parlementaire dowries remained roughly constant between 1500 and 1573; in nominal values the typical dowry increased by about 50 percent in these seventy-three years, an increase substantially below the rate of inflation. Between 1576 and 1610, on the other hand, the nominal

[34] If the surviving contracts of *parlementaire* marriage are assumed to be a random sample of all *parlementaire* marriages, it is possible to test the statistical significance of the change shown in Table 6:2: that is, the likelihood that the contrast reflects only a fluke in the available evidence. A chi-square test of the significance of the differing frequency of marriage with heiresses before 1570 and after 1589, calculated as $x^2 = \Sigma \dfrac{(O-E)^2}{E}$, gives the result $x^2 = 1.76$, indicating that there is about one chance in five that the difference results from chance. See M. J. Moroney, *Facts from Figures* (3rd ed., London, 1956), pp. 249-269; A. L. Edwards, *Statistical Methods* (2nd ed., New York, 1967), 424.

GRAPH 6:1
Parlementaire Dowries

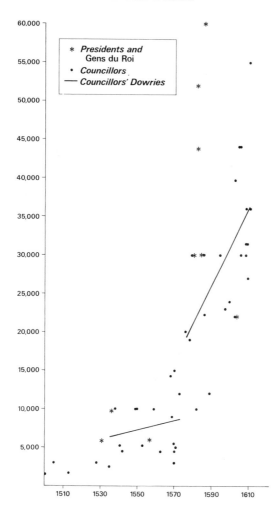

value of a typical dowry more than doubled, and the typical dowry of 1610 represented four times that of 1573—in all an increase about twice the rate of inflation.[35] Plainly the economic importance of marriage was growing. It is equally striking that variation among the dowries which the magistrates received from their brides was diminishing. Thus, of four dowries from the year 1570, the largest was seven times the value of the smallest—whereas of five examples from the years 1608-1609 the largest was just over twice the value of the smallest. Table 6:2 offers better measurement of this

TABLE 6:2
VARIATION IN COUNCILLORS' DOWRIES

Date	Coefficient of Variability	Number
1530-1573	50 percent	18
1574-1589	35 percent	7
1590-1610	26 percent	15

SOURCE: See Appendix F.

phenomenon. It presents the coefficient of variability of our sample of *parlementaire* dowries for three periods in the sixteenth and early seventeenth centuries: that is, the sample's standard deviation as a percentage of its mean. The changes

[35] Some of this increase, of course, is to be accounted for by the inflation of the sixteenth century. Several facts, however, point to the greater importance of other causes of change. First, substantial inflation had characterized the middle years of the century, when *parlementaire* dowries were roughly constant; second, as will be seen, no comparable rise took place in the dowries with which *parlementaire* daughters were married—and thus the rise in dowries was accompanied by changes in the social status of *parlementaire* brides; third, at least in the period after 1590, the size of dowries increased more rapidly than most magistrates' chief source of income, rentals of land, and therefore had real economic meaning for them, whatever other changes were taking place in their costs of living. For all of these reasons, there has seemed little reason to convert the nominal value of dowries into some arbitrary unit of "real" value, such as gold or grain.

of the later sixteenth century, Table 6:2 suggests, involved more than simply an increase in the size of dowries. The economic choices which the magistrates made in arranging their marriages were falling within narrower limits. Even the poorest magistrates, it seems, needed a basic level of wealth from their brides.

Change in the economics of marriage was accompanied by change in its social functions. Very simply, the magistrates' pursuit of wealthy brides during the later sixteenth century was accompanied by a decline in the social status of their brides, and thus by a weakening of the functions of the marriage alliance of binding together the social group.[36] The same needs that encouraged the *parlementaires* themselves to seek out rich brides discouraged most of them from giving their own daughters high dowries, and the dowries which magistrates' daughters offered thus lagged farther and farther behind the magistrates' own. Graph 6:2 sets out this process. Through the early 1570's, as it shows, the dowries with which *parlementaires'* daughters married were about equal to the magistrates'. Between 1570 and 1610, however, while the magistrates' own dowries roughly quadrupled, dowries of *parlementaire* daughters perhaps doubled. By 1610, the normal *parlementaire* dowry was nearly twice the value of the normal *parlementaire* daughter's dowry.

As a result, marriage alliances within the Parlement itself and within the robe classes more generally became increasingly rare during the later sixteenth century. Table 6:3 sets out the social status of *parlementaire* brides during three periods of the sixteenth century; the categories used are very

[36] For stress on this function of marriage in early modern France, see Roland Mousnier, "Problèmes de méthode dans l'étude des structures sociales des XVIe, XVIIe, XVIIIe siècles," repr. in *La plume, la faucille et le marteau. Institutions et société en France du Moyen Âge à la Révolution* (Paris, 1970), p. 14; and Marcel Couturier, *Recherches sur les structures sociales de Châteaudun, 1525-1789* (Paris, 1969), pp. 129-142.

GRAPH 6:2

DOWRIES OF PARLEMENTAIRES' DAUGHTERS

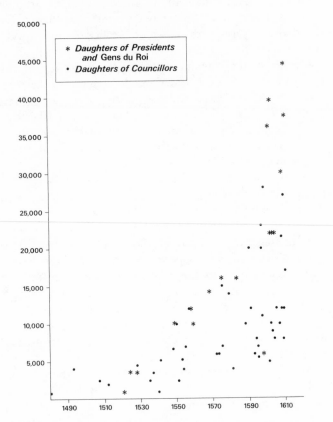

broad ones, as befits the vagueness of the documents themselves, but the pattern which Table 6:3 shows is nonetheless very clear. In the mid-sixteenth century, as Table 6:3 shows, marriage within the Parlement had been common, and marriage within the legal and official classes had been overwhelmingly predominant. Fewer than one-fourth of the magistrates married outside these groups altogether. After 1570 this situation was reversed. Only about a third of the magis-

TABLE 6:3
BRIDES' SOCIAL STATUS[37]

| | BRIDE'S FATHER IS | | | |
Date	Parlementaire	Other Robe	Notable	Total
1530-1569	8 (44%)	6 (33%)	4 (22%)	18
1570-1589	3 (12%)	2 (8%)	20 (80%)	25
1590-1610	6 (26%)	7 (30%)	10 (43%)	23

SOURCE: See Appendix F.

trates married within the robe classes, while two-thirds married outside.[38]

Who were the "notables" whose daughters the *parlementaires* married after 1570? Marriage contracts are laconic in their descriptions of the social origins of brides, and great precision is often impossible in this matter. Nevertheless, it is clear that a majority of these brides (probably a substantial majority) came from the Rouennais bourgeoisie—from families still involved in commerce and tax farming. Of the thirty notables' daughters between 1570 and 1610, the origins of one are entirely unknown. Two others, both of them the brides of presidents, were from the upper nobility. On the other hand, sixteen brides (just over half) clearly were from the Rouennais bourgeoisie: four of them were the daughters of *honorables hommes*, a term reserved for the city's merchants, and twelve were the daughters of *nobles hommes* who owned no seigneurial property—normally the

[37] Again, it is possible to test the likelihood that the pattern seen in Table 6:3 resulted from flukes in the sample of marriage contracts that have survived by means of a chi-square test. Calculated as above, note 34, $x^2 = 14.73$, indicating that there is less than one chance in 100 that this distribution resulted from chance. The fundamental contrast suggested by Table 6:3, between frequent marriages within the robe classes before 1570 and frequent marriages outside the robe between 1570 and 1610, is of equal statistical significance.

[38] Moreover, the exceptions are significant ones. Of the nine brides from within the Parlement during the period 1570-1610, only three were the daughters of councillors; four were presidents' daughters, and two were daughters of the king's attorneys.

first step by which families advanced to greater social esteem. The remaining eleven brides were of more ambiguous status. They were the daughters of *nobles hommes* who owned seigneurial properties, and thus might have been either noblemen or commoners. Most of these families, though, were still very close to the world of commerce and tax farming. In 1583, for instance, the future president Charles Maignart married "lady Madalaine Voisin, daughter and partial heir of the late *noble homme* Thomas Voisin, in his lifetime lord of Freville"; but Thomas Voisin's father in 1562 had been a mere "*honorable homme . . . bourgeois marchand*," and in 1563 Thomas Voisin himself had been described as a "bourgeois of Rouen."[39] The development of more purely economic approaches to marriage was requiring magistrates to ally with groups lower on the social scale. Table 6:4 shows the corresponding change in the alliances

TABLE 6:4

HUSBANDS' SOCIAL STATUS[40]

| | HUSBAND IS | | | |
Date	Parlementaire	*Other Robe*	*Notable*	*Total*
1500-1569	9 (35%)	8 (31%)	9 (35%)	26
1570-1589	3 (19%)	3 (19%)	10 (63%)	16
1590-1610	6 (17%)	9 (26%)	20 (57%)	35

SOURCE: See Appendix F.

which magistrates arranged for their own daughters. Like the magistrates themselves, the magistrates' daughters were increasingly forced to marry outside the Parlement, and in

[39] La Riv. Bourdet, 1559 *bis*, 1574. It should be emphasized that, although ambiguities existed in the use of titles at Rouen (as argued above, Chapter 2), *honorable homme* almost always was associated with bourgeois status.

[40] The statistical significance of the contrast between councillors' and daughters' marriages before and after 1570 is about 10 percent; there is less than one chance in ten that the difference in the frequency of marriage outside the robe classes is accidental, a result of a fluke in the sample.

the early seventeenth century a majority married outside the robe classes altogether. The character of these marriages, however, was different from the magistrates' own. Whereas the magistrates who married outside the Parlement tended to ally with urban and commercial families, *parlementaire* daughters tended to marry in the countryside, with members of the Norman gentry. Of the thirty notables in Table 6:4 from the years 1570 through 1610, one was a medical doctor and fourteen were of ambiguous status; though all of them owned seigneurial property, they were described as *nobles hommes*. The remaining fifteen (just half) were described as "esquire" (*écuyer*), *noble seigneur*, or *baron*, all of them terms used mainly by the rural nobility. Several of the marriage contracts further specified that the husband resided at his rural property.[41] In contrast to the magistrates themselves, *parlementaire* daughters were able to marry with families whose status was about equal to their own.

But these marriages were nonetheless the result of economic necessity rather than of the magistrates' choice. For one thing, the dowries with which *parlementaire* daughters married were usually too low to tempt members of the higher nobility, even those who resided within the province itself. In the later sixteenth century, the typical dowries received by members of the more important Norman gentry (to say nothing of the courtly aristocracy) were eight or nine times those with which *parlementaire* daughters married.[42] Under these circumstances, magistrates could expect

[41] Again, the ambiguities surrounding forms of address in Normandy caution against classifying these husbands too firmly in the old nobility. What is clear is that they, in contrast to the fathers of the magistrates' brides, were an essentially rural group, in their property and often in their residence.

[42] The median dowry for which eight sons of leading provincial aristocratic houses in upper Normandy married between 1568 and 1614 was 55,000ł, while even in the early seventeenth century the vast majority of *parlementaires*' daughters received dowries of less than 12,500ł; see above, Table 3:3 (p. 128). Thus, although these

to marry their daughters only to the lowlier members of the local nobility, to those poor squires whose plight evoked so much concern from sixteenth-century commentators.

That these were in fact marriages of necessity, rather than of a successful pursuit of higher social status, is shown also by the example of the Parlement's wealthiest members. Those magistrates who could afford the higher dowries now required continued during the late sixteenth century to marry their daughters within the high robe itself. This group included a few of the ordinary councillors, but it was dominated by the court's leadership, the presidents and king's attorneys. Graph 6:3 presents the evolution of the dowries which presidents and king's attorneys gave their daughters. It shows that, despite occasional exceptions, the presidents did not face the economic constraints that other *parlementaires* confronted in arranging their daughters' marriages. The typical dowries received by presidents' daughters approximately tripled between 1573 and 1610, while the dowries given councillors' daughters increased by perhaps 50 percent. As a result of this more favorable economic situation, the presidents were able to marry a considerable number of their daughters within the high robe—and they chose to do so. Table 6:5 gives the social status of the presidents' and king's attorneys' sons-in-law over the sixteenth century, and contrasts this with the status of the ordinary council-

---

marriages have certain resemblances to the *"hypergamie des femmes"* stressed by Roland Mousnier and his students, they were at best marriages of equals, and more probably represented for the bride some drop in status. For Mousnier's views on misalliance, see for instance *Peasant Uprisings in Seventeenth-Century France, Russia, and China*, trans. Brian Pearce (New York, 1970), p. 7; insofar as *parlementaire* daughters are concerned, the situation presented here is closer to Mousnier's original (and opposite) view, expressed in "Problèmes de méthode," according to which "the difficulty of placing daughters sometimes leads to marrying them in an inferior social group, just as the desire of social ascension pushes men to marry in a higher category" (p. 23). Cf. the broader discussion of contemporary views on misalliance by Lougee, *Le paradis des femmes*, pp. 49ff.

GRAPH 6:3

Dowries of Presidents' and King's Attorneys' Daughters
Compared with Those of Councillors' Daughters

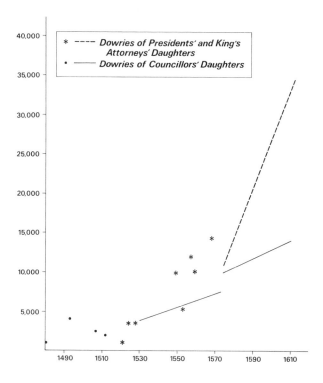

lors' sons-in-law. Between 1570 and 1610, fewer than one-
tenth of the councillors' daughters married within the Parlement, and just one-fourth married other members of
the legal and official professions. In the same years, 40 percent of the presidents' and king's attorneys' daughters married within the Parlement, and in all 60 percent married
within the robe classes. Those who could afford an alliance
within a tightly defined milieu of equals continued to find
such marriages attractive.

TABLE 6:5

STATUS OF DAUGHTERS' HUSBANDS[43]

	I. PRESIDENTS' AND KING'S ATTORNEYS' DAUGHTERS			
		HUSBAND IS		
Date	Parlementaire	Other Robe	Notable	Total
1500-1569	5 (56%)	3 (33%)	1 (11%)	9
1570-1610	6 (40%)	3 (20%)	6 (40%)	15
	II. COUNCILLORS' DAUGHTERS			
		HUSBAND IS		
Date	Parlementaire	Other Robe	Notable	Total
1500-1569	4 (24%)	6 (35%)	7 (41%)	17
1570-1610	3 (8%)	9 (25%)	24 (67%)	36

SOURCE: See Appendix F.

Marriage arrangement, as we have seen, was highly sensitive to economic aims and conditions. This did not mean that money was the *parlementaires'* only concern in arranging their own marriages or those of their daughters, and in the middle years of the sixteenth century the monetary aspects of marriage arrangement appear to have been less important than other aims. Marriage in these years served to bind the magistracy together as a social group. In the years around 1570, however, the economic ends of marriage began to assume a greater importance. Magistrates began seeking out wealthy brides with greater assiduity, and typically found them among the daughters of Rouen's commercial and financial families. Most magistrates provided their own

[43] The difference over the sixteenth century between the frequency of daughters of presidents and *gens du roi* marrying within the Parlement and that of the councillors' daughters is highly significant statistically; there is less than one chance in 100 that it arose by chance. The same is true with regard to the differing frequency with which the two groups married within the robe classes as a whole; there is about one chance in twenty that this difference arose by chance. For the period 1570-1610 the difference is less clearly significant; there is about one chance in five that the differing frequency of marriage within the robe classes arose by chance.

daughters with dowries that were insufficient for marriage within the Parlement, and, in contrast to the situation of the mid-sixteenth century, most councillors' daughters married with the middling gentry of the region; only the leading members of the Parlement, the presidents, were able to afford the close marriage alliances within the Parlement that had earlier been typical of all *parlementaire* families.[44]

Such a change in the primary function of marriage—from binding together the group to supplying the young magistrate with funds at the start of his career—paralleled the broader changes that were taking place in the *parlementaires'* economic position. The same needs that led members of the Parlement to borrow increasing sums of money in the late sixteenth and early seventeenth centuries also led to an increased stress on the economic aims of marriage. Both the troubled economic conditions of the period after 1570 and rising expenditures for education, office, and the like lent greater importance to the economics of marriage. But, like the rise of borrowing in the years after 1570, this change in the economics of marriage was not simply a matter of increased financial difficulties. It was also part of a broader change in the magistrates' organization of their finances. In the mid-sixteenth century the robe milieu at Rouen had been above all self-sufficient and secure, with little need either to borrow money or to marry outside the immediate social group. From the 1570's on, the magistrates' economic lives tended increasingly to involve moments of dramatic transition, at which assistance from outside, in the form of borrowing or of wealthy marriage, became necessary. They were not necessarily poorer than they had been in the middle years of the century, but they were much more likely to encounter crippling debts or even ruin.

[44] The case of the *parlementaires* suggests the possibility that for some social groups misalliance was normal rather than exceptional; at the least, it suggests how substantially patterns of intermarriage might change within relatively short periods of time.

The varied aims and influences which determined marriage choices shaped much of the character of marriage as well. Characteristic of the tight marriage alliances within the Parlement during the middle years of the sixteenth century was the frequency with which marriage involved the establishment of a common household. About one-third of the marriage contracts of both *parlementaires* and *parlementaires*' daughters included provision for the couple's residence with one or another of their parents. Such arrangements did not always work well, and many marriage contracts dealt with the possibility that the two generations would be unable to live harmoniously together. The frequency of such common households nonetheless testifies to the solid self-sufficiency of the robe milieu at Rouen during the mid-sixteenth century.

Predictably, such joint households became less frequent during the later years of the century, as the purposes of *parlementaire* marriage changed. Table 6:6 traces this

TABLE 6:6

JOINT HOUSEHOLDS

Magistrates' Daughters	Co-Residence	Independent Household	Unknown
Before 1570	11 (41% of known)	16 (59%)	1
1570-1610	6 (13%)	40 (87%)	5
Magistrates			
Before 1570	7 (32%)	15 (68%)	5
1570-1610	7 (16%)	37 (84%)	4

SOURCE: See Appendix F.

change. Between 1570 and 1610, only 16 percent of *parlementaire* marriage contracts included provision for even temporary residence with parents or in-laws, and, for *parlementaire* daughters, the percentage fell to 13 percent. As marriage within the immediate social group became less frequent, the close alliances that common residence implied tended also to become more unusual. Those common residences that were established during the late sixteenth and early seventeenth centuries tended to conform to this basic pattern. More than half of them involved the families of presidents in the Parlement, precisely that group of magistrates who continued after 1570 to marry chiefly within the high robe.[45]

A similarly close relationship between the economics of marriage and its emotional qualities existed in regard to the couple's ages. Variation in this respect, we have seen, was a normal result of the familial economy, for age at marriage was determined more by events than by an absolute chronological scale: such events as a parent's death, the start of an official career, the complex pressures of suitors and relatives, the acquisition of sufficient funds to pay for a dowry.[46] These events appear to have followed a somewhat more regular course for men than for women. At the least, the future magistrate was unlikely to marry before his return from the universities and the beginnings of his finding an office, in other words before his mid-twenties. No such clear determinants operated for women, but they tended to

[45] The decline in co-residence among *parlementaires'* daughters is statistically significant; that of the magistrates themselves is not significant. This change was not the result only of changing social functions of marriage. It appears also to have reflected the more luxurious mode of life adopted by many robe families in the later sixteenth century, which probably encouraged young families to set up their own households. For discussion of the frequency of joint households in pre-industrial Europe, see Peter Laslett, *The World We Have Lost* (New York, 1965), pp. 89-92; Lutz K. Berkner, "The Stem Family and the Developmental Cycle of the Peasant Family: An Eighteenth-Century Austrian Example," *The American Historical Review*, LXXVII, 2 (April, 1972), 398-418; and the extremely perceptive review by Robert Wheaton, "Family and Kinship in Western Europe: The Problem of the Joint Family Household," *Journal of Interdisciplinary History*, V, 4 (Spring, 1975), 601-628.

[46] Characteristic of these complex considerations is the fact that two of Claude Groulart's daughters and one of his sons signed marriage contracts on the same day (Hérit. 2, 16 December 1602, 17 January 1603).

marry much younger. Among sixteen *parlementaire* daughters from the late sixteenth century (nine councillors' daughters and seven presidents') whose ages at marriage can be firmly established, one married at fifteen, three at sixteen, one at seventeen, and four at twenty; the oldest married at twenty-five, and the mean age was 19.9.[47]

Such examples are hardly sufficient for serious demographic inquiry, but they do suggest the frequency with which *parlementaire* brides might be a full decade younger than their husbands. They can rarely have been within five years of their husbands' ages. To this imbalance of age were added the effects of the imbalance in the education which husbands and wives had received. In 1583, for instance, the future president Charles Maignart married a notable Rouennais heiress, Madeleine Voisin, apparently only fourteen at the time. Madeleine's education was described in the accounts for her minority: 18½ had been spent on her behalf "for having been with the *filles dieu* to learn her hours and service, for the space of an entire year," and 3½ had been given "to Master Anthoine d'Arques for having taught her to write."[48] Madeleine was literate and had received some religious training, but that was the extent of her education. A generation later, when the maître des comptes Gentien Thomas set forth what he had spent on his children's educations, the situation was only slightly improved. A writing master had instructed Anne Thomas together with her younger brothers, at a substantially higher wage than

[47] Sources for age at marriage are noted in Appendix F. Although using Frondeville's genealogies would provide a larger number of brides' ages, his data on daughters' and brides' ages are not sufficiently trustworthy for this purpose. It seems likely that daughters who married within the Parlement married earlier than those who married outside, though this cannot be demonstrated; the inference is suggested by the greater likelihood that girls who married within the Parlement would marry before their fathers' deaths, as seen above, note 13.

[48] Frondeville, *Les présidents*, p. 283; La Riv. Bourdet, 2139, ff. 133-134.

Madeleine Voisin's, and for several years she received lessons from a dancing master, at a cost of 2₺ monthly.[49] In the mid-sixteenth century at least some *parlementaire* brides had been illiterate. This was no longer the case at the end of the century, but women's education in the *parlementaire* milieu remained rudimentary.[50]

Differences in age and education seem to have encouraged a rather sharp separation of the spheres of husbands and wives within the household. Some *parlementaire* brides at least had their own servants or poorer relatives who served as paid companions.[51] With some notorious exceptions, the magistrates apparently spent little time in socializing outside the household, but husbands and wives nonetheless normally spent large parts of the year apart; those magistrates with estates of any size often left their wives and families in the countryside, while they stayed in Rouen for the Parlement's sessions.[52]

This degree of separation was not incompatible with notions of the affection that àt least ought to exist between husbands and wives. When the tutors of Catherine Martel defended her marriage with the future maître des comptes Pierre de Becdelièvre (as seen above), they stressed the "honest affection" that the couple shared even before their marriage.[53] Stronger sentiments received expression in the epitaph of Marie Maignart, daughter and wife of *parlementaires*, who died in 1610 at the age of twenty-three:

[49] AD S-M 10J13.

[50] For examples of *parlementaire* brides signing their marriage contracts with marks rather than full signatures, Hérit. 2, 9 January 1554 (old style); Tabel., 20 May 1570.

[51] Thus BN MS français 5346, ff. 25-26 (testament of Marguerite Le Gras, widow of Guillaume Maignart, councillor); AD S-M, G6275 (testament of Jacques Voisin, councillor). See also Hérit. 2, 26 January 1613, for the marriage contract of the councillor Nicolas Romé, in which the bride was to bring to the marriage "the ornaments and furnishings of a chapel," worth 80 *écus* and over which she was to have full control.

[52] Above, p. 55.   [53] Above, p. 254.

The flame of conjugal love
Their hearts and wills makes equal
And makes of two bodies one soul. . . .

The basis for the couple's love, as Marie's epitaph idealized it, was piety. Marie was portrayed on her tomb kneeling in prayer, and her epitaph stressed the point:

But above all piety
And works of charity
Were her daily concerns.[54]

Much the same linkage of conjugal love and active piety recurs in the lamentations of the first president Claude Groulart for his wife Barbe Guiffart, who died in 1599, both in the sentiments which Groulart himself expressed in his memoirs, and in the words which the poet Anthoine de Montchrestien attributed to the couple in a versified rendering of "The last words of the late noble lady Barbe Guiffart, wife of my lord the first president."

"This year (wrote Groulart in his memoirs) was from the beginning very painful for me, because of the loss of my wife, on the fourth of January, *quae maximum sui deside-rium mihi reliquit.* I had lived with her since the eighth of October, 1584, in great affection. She followed me with great constancy during my exile because of the League. She feared God and honored Him greatly, was charitable to the poor, and served as an example to her family of all things good. She died [in childbirth] after having successfully delivered Barbe. Before dying she had asked me to name the child Hélène, in memory of my late mother, but since she died and I had no daughter with her name, I preferred that she have it."[55]

Groulart remembered, with considerable emotional force, his wife's strength, virtue, charity, and piety. Montchrestien amplified these themes in his description of the deathbed

[54] The statue and inscription are in the Église Collégiale, Vernon.
[55] BM MS Y202, f. 23v.

scene. The scene he depicted was a public one, with an initially happy crowd gathered to watch Barbe give birth. As the imminence of Barbe's death becomes clear, Groulart and the visitors are overcome with emotion, and are comforted only by Barbe's patient religious teaching; these she renews in a vision before the sleepless Groulart, the night after her death. Further to comfort him, she emphasizes that

> If in dying I must leave you
> My daughters will remind you of me.
> This gage I give you, this fine mirror,
> In which you will see all the lines of my face.

"They said farewell until the Last Judgment," Montchrestien continues, "when they will renew their first love."[56]

Idealized portrayals of *parlementaire* marriage thus presented the wife's sphere as that of morality and religion. She served as an example to her husband and children, and to the rest of the community as well in the case of Barbe Guiffart. Conjugal love grew out of this function, and retained pious overtones: both Marie Maignart and Barbe Guiffart were to be fully united with their husbands only at the Last Judgment. But the roles of wives were not so limited as these idealizations suggest. The dispersal of magistrates' landed properties and other business interests necessarily left a considerable part of estate administration to the wives' supervision. When the councillor Louis Le Masson in 1600 made over the management of his properties to his sons, he cited as one reason "the recent death of his wife, to

---

[56] These are included in *Les tragédies d'Anthoine de Montchrestien, sieur de Vasteville* (Rouen, 1627), pp. 361-369. See also the epitaph of Marie Droullin, wife of the *avocat général* Guillaume Vauquelin: "Féconde en biens et féconde en enfans, / Vivante j'eus des gens de bien la grace, / Comme une vigne en sions triomfans, / J'ai provigné de mon époux la race. / Les biens n'ont pu mon trepas retarder / Mais piété dévotement suivie / En mes enfans sa flamme peut garder / Et me donner apres mort double vie" (J. Angot des Retours, "Epitaphier des Vauquelin," *Bulletin de la Société des Antiquaires de Normandie*, XI [1933], 11).

whom he had formerly left the larger part of the administration of his affairs."[57] In a series of notarized acts, magistrates entrusted their wives with arranging leases, borrowing
large sums of money, examining accounts from tenants, ne-
gotiating the administration of minorities. The scale of these
transactions might be very large. In 1604, for instance, the
president Nicolas Le Roux authorized his wife to borrow
as much as 24,000ł in his name, the equivalent of at least
three years' income from most *parlementaire* fortunes.[58]

Parlementaire marriage in these respects seems to have
been a successful institution. It was expected that real affection would bind husband and wife, and the couple's feelings
were ideally an element in marriage negotiations. Separation of roles within the family was an element of ideal
family organization, but economic circumstances nonetheless required of wives an active role in running the family's
affairs—in at least some *parlementaire* families the predominant role. Alongside these positive aspects of marriage, however, were currents of anxiety about marriage. Probably
least serious were the strains imposed by the magistrates'
considerable number of illegitimate children. These appear
often to have grown up in the magistrates' households, and to
have been on close terms with their legitimate half-siblings.
Illegitimate daughters were given dowries that were small
for the milieu, about one-tenth those of the magistrates'
legitimate daughters, but these were enough to secure them
respectable marriages with Rouennais lawyers and merchants.[59]

[57] Hérit. 2, 10 February 1600.

[58] Meubles 2, 29 March 1604, 18 April 1601; AD Eure E1252, 7
October 1577, 11 June 1581; La Riv. Bourdet, 2105. For the role of
wives in defending family properties during the League, AD S-M, B,
Requêtes du Palais, 5 February 1597.

[59] See, for examples, Tabel., 5 June 1577; Meubles 2, 15 November
1605; Hérit. 2, 13 September 1602; AD S-M, B, Requêtes du Palais,
Contrats, 27 April 1595; Frondeville, *Les présidents*, p. 284. The arrangements made for the marriage of Fleurie Romé, in 1602, are suggestive of the kind of relationships that might be involved: Fleurie

Illegitimacy presumably reflected the inevitable short-comings of marriage arrangements whose principal aims were economic.[60] More disturbing to contemporaries, it appears, were persistent fears about the domineering impulses that women brought to marriage, against which men had to be continually on guard. An extended satirical piece by Pierre Brinon, who entered the Parlement in 1602, presented the comical side of these anxieties. In the book, Brinon adopted the role of a woman defending her own sex from men's slanderous criticism, a well-worn genre but one appropriate to Brinon's theme of disordered conditions within the household: ". . . everyone will agree with me that there are few happy households to be seen. . . . This is general throughout the world; we are born thus, we live thus, and we die thus. The men wish us evil, and we do not love them too well ourselves." The problem, as Brinon presented it, was that husbands had lost the habit of governing their homes. "The man not knowing how to command, the wife cannot obey; and since the wife does not know how to govern, the husband cannot endure her rule."[61]

Similar complaints received more serious expression in the writings of Brinon's contemporary, the Norman lawyer Denis Godefroy. Godefroy's influential commentary on the

---

could sign her marriage contract, unlike her future mother-in-law, and her husband was described as a "bourgeois of Rouen"; on the other hand, her husband's family appear to have been the Romé's dependents, and in 1581 they were engaged in selling grain with two of the Romé's tenant farmers (Hérit. 2, 13 September 1602; AD S-M, 16J3: 20, 4 August 1581).

[60] It should be noted that infidelity was not limited to men. At least one councillor, Étienne Lhuillier, "repudiated" his wife because of adultery: BM MS Martainville Y55 ("Recueil sur les livres et lieux communs de monsieur maître Jean Lefebvre . . ."); this may have encouraged the sergeant and satirist Jacques Sireulde to make Lhuillier the butt of a satirical play by the basoche.

[61] Le triomphe des dames (Rouen, 1599), pp. 64, 88. Attribution to Brinon rests on the handwritten inscription on the title-page of the copy at the BN: "M. Pierre Brinon Autheur."

Norman custom expressed concern about nearly every aspect of contemporary marriage. "Wives are no sooner married," he complained, "than, for failure to render them the conjugal duty, they accuse their husbands of impotence and demand to be allowed to find another partner." Godefroy's more general doubts about sexual relations, at least once the obligations of procreation had been met, are suggested by his views of second marriages: "Someone has compared [second marriages] to the toilets in a house, which are constructed out of necessity and in order to get rid of wastes and filth. In precisely the same way, second marriages are tolerated only as a remedy for the intemperance of men and women."

But for Godefroy, as for Brinon, the fundamental issues within the household were those of order, obedience, and money, for a wealthy woman was especially likely to be disagreeable and disobedient: "According to Seneca, a rich wife is an intolerable evil, . . . so that I do not at all disapprove of the laws of those who gave nothing to their daughters and demanded nothing when they themselves married. . . . This served as an obligation to make one's daughters virtuous and good housekeepers. . . ." At a later point in the commentary, he added that the custom's limitation on the size of dowries served not only "for the conservation of families, but also to prevent women from becoming more insolent because of the superfluity of their possessions."[62]

Such views were neither original to the *parlementaires* nor new to the later sixteenth century. Their significance lies not in their reflection of circumstances that were specific to the milieu, but rather in their pervasiveness as a mythology about marriage. As such they are important to our understanding of the qualities of the *parlementaire* household, as the other side of that pious affection which was the ideal of marital relations. These notions were especially relevant in the later sixteenth and early seventeenth

[62] Godefroy, *La coutume reformée*, ff. 406v, 408v, 318v, 324v.

centuries, as *parlementaire* brides became wealthier and acquired a larger control over their dowries. The fears and
tensions which contemporaries felt toward marriage gave
further coloring to the transition which starting a robe career involved. At the start of his career, the young magistrate not only assumed the widely mocked, quasi-clerical
robes of his profession; he also subjected himself to the
unpleasant constraints which marriage was popularly felt to
involve.[63] Marriage, it appears, was part of the symbolism
of age and self-restraint which surrounded the *robin* and
which, much more than any deficiency in birth, explained
the military nobility's jibes at the officials.

Thus far we have considered the ways in which marriages were formed, their economics, and the relations they
created between husbands and wives. Marriage created a
much wider set of relations, however, and marriage arrangements were often made with these wider arrangements
in mind: with an eye to the political support which wisely
chosen in-laws might supply, or with an eye to their social
prestige. Some assessment of these wider relationships is
needed. In particular, it is necessary to weigh the political
and social uses of marriage against the economic dimensions
that have concerned us thus far.

The political implications which marriage had in some
parlementaire families may be seen from the example of the
court's presidents in the years around 1600. Statistics alone
fail to convey a full sense of the closeness of the marriage
alliances that united these families, and that effectively separated them from most of their colleagues in the court. The
center of these alliances was Claude Groulart, the court's
first president. In 1602 his older son married the daughter
of Louis Bretel, one of the three presidents *à mortier*. In an
identical contract signed the same day, Bretel's older son

[63] For discussion of this mythology, see the works cited above,
note 25.

(and ultimately his successor in office) married one of Groulart's daughters. Bretel's younger son was married to one of the daughters of Charles Maignart, another president *à mortier*. Groulart's stepson Robert Le Roux (his wife's son by her first marriage) in 1601 became president of the Parlement's Chambre des Requêtes. He provided another link between Groulart and the Bretel, for Louis Bretel himself was married to the daughter of another branch of the Le Roux, and in 1602 her brother became yet another *président à mortier*.[64]

Only one of the court's presidents in these years seems to have remained entirely outside this set of marriage alliances. This was the king's attorney and later president Georges de La Porte, and his exclusion was apparently due to the fact that La Porte was a political enemy of Groulart and the families allied to him. During the League, when Groulart led the exodus of royalist magistrates to Caen, La Porte remained in Rouen and led the *ligueur* Parlement. The enmities which this choice created lost none of their force in later years, and even in his memoirs Groulart worried about "the artfulness of the president de La Porte; but I will not trust him, since he is such."[65] Marital and political alliances plainly went together, and in fact they extended beyond the confines of Rouen itself, for in 1599 Groulart married his stepson to a daughter of the chancellor Pomponne de Bellièvre. If his colleague Georges de La Porte, with his

[64] Frondeville, *Les présidents*, pp. 268, 296, 298; Hérit. 2, 17 January 1603 (marriages between Raoul Bretel and Isabeau Groulart and between Claude II Groulart and Catherine Bretel); 20 January 1610 (marriage between Madeleine Maignart and Claude Bretel, Raoul's younger brother).

[65] Claude Groulart, *Mémoires*, in Michaud and Poujolat, eds., *Nouvelle collection des mémoires pour servir à l'histoire de France*, xi (Paris, 1838), 595. La Porte's daughters married with members of the upper *noblesse d'épée*, rather than within the robe: Hérit. 2, 16 February 1602 (marriage Marie de La Porte with "le sieur baron de Pretot") and 27 February 1610 (marriage Catherine de La Porte with "noble seigneur Jacques de Durerie sieur et chastelain de Sainct Vaast Lasson et Glatigny").

ligueur connections and (as Groulart saw it) scheming ways, stood in precise opposition to Groulart's politics, Bellièvre represented Groulart's natural ally. They shared a dismay at the course of Henry IV's reign, and in particular at the disregard in which the king held their reformist views.[66]

The letters in which Groulart spilled out his indignation at the course of royal policies, however, gave expression as well to the more concrete aspects of his marriage connections. As the central figure in this nexus, Groulart had continually to beg that "we be favored with some gratification" from the chancellor and other figures at court, especially with regard to the erratic royal policies surrounding inheritance of office. When he journeyed to the royal court, about once a year, his son-in-law and stepson usually accompanied him and this provided a further occasion to seek "gratifications." "Since it is known that I have the honor of being your friend (*d'être aymé de vous*)," he wrote Bellièvre, in explanation of the demands he was making, "I cannot sometimes refuse . . . those to whom I am obliged."[67]

Few magistrates had occasion to take such frequent ad-

[66] Archives d'Esneval, Acquigny, marriage contract Robert Le Roux and Marie de Bellièvre; see also BN MS français 15898, f. 581r, letter from Groulart to Bellièvre to "assure you that the disposition of mother and child is, thanks to God, such as we could desire; I praise Him for having given us this pleasure, so needed, as an agreeable release from the continual labors and reversals that He makes us endure." On Bellièvre's politics, see the masterly discussion by Roland Mousnier, *La vénalité des offices sous Henri IV et Louis XIII* (2nd ed., Paris, 1971), pp. 234-236, 600-602; Raymond Kierstead, *Pomponne de Bellièvre: A Study of the King's Men in the Age of Henry IV* (Evanston, 1968); Edmund Dickerson, *Bellièvre and Villeroy. Power in France under Henry III and Henry IV* (Providence, 1971); and J. Russell Major, "Bellièvre, Sully and the Assembly of Notables of 1597," *Transactions of the American Philosophical Society*, LXIV, part 2 (1974) (see p. 28, for an example of cooperation between Bellièvre and the Parlement of Rouen in opposing the alienations of the royal domain).

[67] BN MS français 15898, ff. 562r, 570r. See also Groulart, *Mémoires*, 581, 587, 588.

vantage of marriage alliances as the circle around Groulart, but marriage might be important within the narrower compass of purely Rouennais affairs. Alexandre Bigot, writing in the mid-seventeenth century about the Parlement's history, recalled two sixteenth-century instances in which marriage alliances had been the crucial step for candidates seeking admission to the court. For one candidate the problem was political: his father had been hanged as a leader of the Protestant rising of 1562. For the other the problem was birth: he was the son of a tanner. Both candidates overcame the Parlement's determined unwillingness to admit them by marriage with the daughters of notable robe families, "who had many relatives and friends in the Parlement." Both candidates, however, paid in monetary terms for this political success, in the one case by accepting a dowry about half the size of those received by most of his colleagues, and in the other by allying with a family apparently nearing bankruptcy.[68]

Family alliances might thus be critical, both at the mundane level of practical assistance and at the more elevated level of political attitudes. But it is equally important to recognize the limitations which surrounded family relationships. Family alliance, in the first place, was no guarantee of frequent interchange. A letter written to Thomas Maignart in the mid-1550's suggests the distance there might be between family members. "My lord, I know the desire and affection you have for advancing your allies, among whom I am one, one of your humble relatives—and one of your friends if it pleases you, and I believe that you have no knowledge of me and have never seen me . . .": all of this introducing a demand for assistance.[69] A second and more important limitation was posed by the specific conditions of the later sixteenth century. The growing importance of eco-

[68] BM MS Martainville Y23, f. 44r; Tabel. 23 May 1583; Meubles 2, 6 April 1601. See above, note 42, for historians' discussion of misalliance.

[69] La Riv. Bourdet, 1381. Cf. Mousnier, *La vénalité*, pp. 84-85.

nomic considerations in *parlementaire* marriage alliances after 1570 left less room for extra-economic considerations. Magistrates were simply less likely to receive help in their careers from in-laws, since most of them in the late sixteenth century were outside the world of offices and politics. The declining number of joint households in this period appears to have been typical of the declining usefulness of marital connections.

Even when relations were close, an atmosphere of harsh bargaining tended to surround any questions that touched on property. Characteristic of this harshness were the relations between the Rouennais maître des comptes Gentien Thomas and his sister Margueritte. Margueritte wrote in 1614 about some properties in the neighborhood of Troyes, where the family had originated and where Margueritte continued to reside:

"By the last of your letters I see your willingness that I purchase your properties in Villegouin, and I am very sorry that I cannot content you in this matter. But I assure you, Monsieur my brother, that [what] I offered you in my last letter is all that I could possibly pay. I must therefore withdraw from the matter and give up my interest in it, since you could not be content with this sum. Please consider the small revenues which the property offers, and consider that this is a great deal of money to invest in it. I beg that you excuse my importunities. My concern was that these lands not leave our house and name."[70]

Similar negotiations, arousing equally strong emotions, developed over the transfer of offices. When Charles Maignart bought his presidency in 1600, he described the circumstances in his account book: "Monsieur de Lanquetot (Louis Bretel) offered me his position as president in the court, having broken off negotiations with Monsieur de Saint Aubin (Nicolas Le Roux), his brother in law."[71] The difficulty was simply the office's value. Le Roux had offered

---

[70] AD S-M, 10J10.   [71] La Riv. Bourdet, 2105.

38,000ł; Maignart offered 6,000ł more, and was quickly accepted. Le Roux and Bretel were not only brothers-in-law. They also formed parts of the circle which surrounded the first president Claude Groulart, and the persistence of such bargaining between them is thus especially striking. But this was not a unique situation. When Pierre Du Moucel died in 1614, for instance, he left only young children and his councillorship thus passed to his brother. But his brother received it only after paying the full market price.[72]

Here we encounter one of the essential elements for understanding the strength of the relationships which marriage created. Any generosities to one's kin or to in-laws could come only at the expense of one's own children's expectations. In this respect the family's different functions stood in some measure of conflict. The *parlementaire* family did function as an extended group of kin and in-laws, but it could not do so to the extent of cutting into the family's patrimony. In order to maintain that patrimony, magistrates tended to adopt a severely economic attitude to any but their own children. It is to this dimension of the robe family, to the relations between magistrates and their children, that we now must turn.

The *parlementaires'* eagerness to have children was most poignantly expressed by those who had none. In 1551, for instance, the president Louis Petremol passed an act before the Rouennais notaries that both expressed his dismay at having no children and sought to remedy the situation by a muted form of adoption:

"I recognize that I have had no children of my wife and companion during the eighteen years or so that I have been with her, and that without God's grace there is little hope of our having any. . . . During the past four years I have known *noble homme* Master Richard Le Pelletier, a distant relative of mine. Because of the hope I have had that his

---

[72] AD S-M, E, Fonds Bigot, unclassed: "Seigneurie de Sassetot au temps de la famille Du Moucel."

virtues and good morals will bring him to high judicial position, and also because his near relations, from an old and noble family, were my own relatives, some of them my close connections—for these reasons I have been interested in arranging a marriage between him and noble lady Jacquette Petremol, my niece, the daughter of *noble homme* Anthoine Petremol, councillor of the king and master in his Chambre des Comptes of Paris, my younger brother, if he agrees to it. [I hope] thus to have reason for a closer relationship with the said lord of Martainville, and that the civil friendship I hold for him may by his taking a son's title (*par nom de filz*) be converted to natural love; and that from a distant relative he become a close one; and that he and his bride and the children they will have will support (*conserver*) me and my wife as we enter the beginnings of old age."

With these ends in view, Petremol made a monetary gift to the couple and arranged that they reside in his household for at least the first two years of their marriage.[73]

Petremol's decision suggests several reasons for the eagerness with which children were awaited. They were to be a solace and defense in old age, their achievements were to be looked forward to, they were simply to be an object of what Petremol called "natural love."[74] Love for children, as Montchrestien's idealized portrayal of Barbe Guiffart's dying moments, cited above, had it, reflected as well love for departed spouses. Despite the strength of these sentiments, however, the *parlementaires* shared sixteenth-century assumptions about children's needs for discipline and for being kept away from the excessive warmth of their own homes.[75] No evidence survives about wet-nursing, though

[73] Tabel., 14 August 1551.

[74] For instances of fathers retiring from the management of their affairs and relying on the support of their children in old age see below, p. 301.

[75] See Montaigne's well-known comments on his own childhood and the common practices of his day: *Essais*, 3 vols. (Paris, Garnier-Flammarion, 1969), II, 8.

presumably it was as prevalent among *parlementaire* families as among the French upper classes in general. But patterns of education certainly assured that boys spent much of childhood outside the home, first at Parisian colleges, then in travels throughout France and the rest of Europe.[76] Apparently the same attitudes prevailed in the upbringing which many girls received. "We still have not in the least changed [the custom] of sending daughters to the homes of relatives or friends, in order to bring them out from under the mother's wing and to free them from that flattering doting which leaves them incapable of fear, without whose aid one works in vain to bring up young people," wrote the councillor Pierre Brinon in his satire on women.[77] And, during the years when young men were making their tour of the universities, from sixteen or so on, women from this milieu were likely to be already married off. Neither men nor women, it appears, spent more than a few years in their parents' homes, and this degree of separation from the home was part of an articulated program of child rearing, designed to prevent excessive attention and consequent spoiling of the child.

Supporting these attitudes was a stress on parents' legal and moral rights over their children. Both the Norman custom and commonly held moral views allowed children only the smallest economic claims on their parents. Except for such unusual and plainly outrageous cases as that of a father who had refused to dower his twenty-five year old daughter, the father's authority during his lifetime was to be absolute—and to admit of no challenges in the law courts.[78] When a Rouennais lawyer began a lawsuit against

[76] On the age at which university studies were normally begun, see Bernard Guenée, *Tribunaux et gens de justice dans le bailliage de Senlis à la fin du moyen âge (vers 1380-vers 1550)* (Paris, 1963), pp. 187-191.

[77] Brinon, *Le triomphe des dames*, p. 7.

[78] Thus Denis Godefroy: "our custom has considered that no affection surpasses the paternal, and therefore that it is not to be sup-

his brother in 1601, he expressed the kinds of tensions which parental authority might create. "He had done great prejudice to his rights as the oldest, to his honor, and to his wealth," so he claimed, "by having consented and agreed with his father in certain conventions and contracts, only out of pure and simple reverence for his father, and having been forced to do so, in order to have peace with his said father and for fear of being denied the necessities of life."[79] Respect for one's mother was likewise to restrain the child's assertion of his rights. In 1602 two members of the Romé family, among Rouen's wealthiest robe families, began an action against a third with the explanation that "they have not until now taken action . . . because of the respect they have for their mother and their fear of bringing on her death."[80]

The relations of *parlementaires* with their children thus combined strong affections with distance and an exercise of authority that effectively silenced potential conflicts. There was no lack of concern or affection for children in the robe family, but the normal course of families' development limited interchange between parents and children, whether affectionate or hostile. We cannot speak for the actual

---

posed that fathers do anything against their children's interests . . ." (f.319v). See also Henri Basnage, on a more specific point: "it is an unquestioned legal principle in Normandy that fathers and mothers are the absolute masters of their properties, and (that) they can change the nature and quality of these as it pleases them; they can sell their fiefs in order to buy *rotures* with the proceeds, . . . unite and divide their fiefs; and their children are obliged to divide their succession in the state they find it . . ." (*Oeuvres*, 1, 513). In other words, parents could favor their oldest son, by combining their properties into a single fief, for (as noted below) the oldest son could choose any single fief as his share in the succession—or, conversely, they could reduce his share, by investing in forms of property for which equal division was required. See also above, Chapter 4, part A, for discussion of how and how often fiefs were divided.

[79] Meubles 2, 19 March 1601.
[80] Meubles 2, 26 September 1602.

results of these practices in shaping personalities, but the intentions behind them were clearly stated. They were meant to produce personalities of some toughness and assertiveness, who were yet respectful of constituted authorities.[81]

If the psychic impact of these family patterns is uncertain, however, their implications for the course of the family's life cycle are very clear. Most important, these patterns made the father's death and the consequent inheritance of property an especially disruptive moment, one that gave occasion to a whole series of conflicts. While he lived, the father's authority was absolute, but authority ceased at death, more so under the Norman custom than others, since the Norman law so rigidly limited rights of testation. No challenges to paternal authority were allowed while the father lived, but at his death any arrangements he had made that violated his heirs' rights could be overturned in the courts. As the late-seventeenth-century Norman lawyer Basnage expressed it, echoing Montaigne, parents "have no further means of flattering their ambitions by dominating after their deaths, nor of exercising their passions, their vengeances, and their hatreds, by depriving their legitimate heirs of their inheritances."[82] The father's widow enjoyed a similar augmentation in her rights to litigate. Her properties had been largely under her husband's control, and her only recourse against mismanagement had been a virtual divorce, in which her properties were separated from those of her husband. The husband's death was the moment for her to reassert control and

[81] These at least are the aims described by Montaigne and echoed by Pierre Brinon. Although there were serious virtues and defects in this view of child-raising, it does not seem necessary either to suppose its pathological character (thus David Hunt, *Parents and Children in History*, *passim*) or to suggest that it reflected indifference to childhood or an inability to see childhood as a special period, in which children needed to be molded and guided (thus Philippe Ariès, *Centuries of Childhood*, *passim*).

[82] Basnage, *Oeuvres*, II, 180.

demand restitution of any alienations of her dowry.[83] Further, the careful efforts to place young children at some distance from the household probably made conflict at such moments more frequent and more intense, since close ties among siblings were unlikely.

It is little wonder, then, that *parlementaire* testaments often gave as their aim "leaving by this simple and naive disclosure calm and peace in my family," as the early-seventeenth-century testament of Charles Maignart expressed it.[84] In fact, the likelihood of agitation and conflict was overwhelming, and not merely because of the withdrawal of the father's absolute control. The moment of inheritance was also the moment when the family had to support some of its heaviest financial burdens, burdens which gave a particular edge to family conflicts. Most conspicuous were funeral expenses themselves. *Parlementaire* testaments often expressed a wish to be buried "without ostentation and vanity," but moderation seems to have been unusual.[85] Claude Groulart's burial, in 1607, illustrated the degree of ostentation that might be attained and its purposes. The funeral procession from his house to the church and back involved some 1,000 persons: 95 children from Rouen's four schools for the poor led the march, followed by about 300 of the city's secular and regular clergy, the bishop of Avranches (he was to perform the burial service), Groulart's own *maître d'hôtel*, 25 of his servants, the 5 priests who held the livings to which Groulart had nomination, the treasurer of the provincial Estates, the city's lawyers, its officials (including the Parlement), and, finally,

---

[83] See Bataille, *Du droit des filles*, p. 47.

[84] La Riv. Bourdet, 3344. Cf. Claude Groulart's testament: ". . . fathers are obliged, both by the commandment of God and by nature itself, to provide for their families and to cut short any difficulties that might arise after their deaths among their children, and to nourish peace and amity among them" (Meubles 2, 6 November 1613).

[85] AD S-M G6275 (testament of the councillor Jacques Voisin).

its militia.[86] The event was a vivid statement of Groulart's central importance in the life of the city and province— much as Montchrestien had described Barbe Guiffart's deathbed as the center of the city's attention; news of her death "spreads through the house, from the house to the neighborhood, and thence throughout Rouen, Rouen dissolves in tears. . . ."[87] In this as in much else, Groulart was atypical, but all robe funerals strove to convey a similar set of ideas about the magistrate's place within his own household, the parishes where he owned property, the city, and the province. The costs, spent in outfitting marchers, painting emblems, recompensing the clergy, and the like, seem to have amounted to about 3,000ł at the start of the seventeenth century, in other words about half of many *parlementaires'* yearly incomes.[88]

The costs of transmitting the family's property came to about as much. The crown levied taxes on the transfer of both offices and fiefs held directly from it, and attorneys were needed for both types of transfer. Evaluations of properties had to be drawn up, and disputes about them had to be settled. For the heirs of Jean Godart, master in the Chambre des Comptes and secretary of the king, these expenses came to just under 3,000ł, the largest expenses being the taxes on offices. This was probably more than most *parlementaire* families had to spend, especially after the Paulette eased the burdens of transferring offices. But the example of the Godart suggests the ease with which a whole year's income could be consumed by such expenses.[89]

[86] BM MS Martainville Y90, pp. 188-194.

[87] Montchrestien, *Les tragédies*, p. 366.

[88] For examples, see above, p. 223.

[89] AD S-M, 16J178. Jean Godart's death in 1601 left his family with the following expenses: funeral expenses and legacies, 3,182ł; costs of transmitting offices, 2,409ł; *debtes mobiles*, 5,600ł capital; *rentes* 998ł yearly interest; legal expenses of the succession and the accounts needed for it, 552ł; medical expenses, 553ł. In the space of a few months, in other words, the Godart estate had to support ex-

Finally, as we have already seen, there were the costs of widowhood, usually the most serious of all. A widow in Normandy had the right to a large share in the husband's properties, and could also now claim the *dot*, that part of her dowry, usually about two-thirds of it in the early seventeenth century, which was meant to be her property.

For even the wealthiest *parlementaire* families, then, the moment of inheritance was one of severe financial strain. One response, as we have seen, was marriage by the heirs themselves, for marriage offered one of the only sources of money to meet the needs thus created. But the same financial pressures provided an effective spur to litigation also—or at least to bitter conflicts within the family. Some sense of this bitterness may be gained from the deathbed testament of the *parlementaire* Jacques Voisin, in 1633. The antepenultimate clause of Voisin's testament dealt with the execution of his father's testament, written at *his* death, in 1622: "As for the execution of my late father's testament, regarding the devotions, foundations, prayers, and other pious acts, if anything remains to be executed, I desire that my children and heirs do so from my money; but this does not mean my approbation of the other clauses contained in the said testament, which might be prejudicial to my heirs. This testament was made without my knowledge, clandestinely and in hiding, by those who dominated my late father's mind, . . . even though it claims that his children consented to its provisions."[90] A decade after the elder Voisin's death, his testament remained unexecuted and a source of anger to his son, even on his own deathbed. Charles Maignart's testament, in 1621, sought to forestall conflicts of a different kind, those likely to arise between his children and his second wife. "I want . . . all my children and above all my son," he wrote, "in the name of the great

---

penditures amounting to 13,294ł—in *addition* to the various rights which Godart's widow had on it.
   [90] AD S-M, G6275.

living God, to love, honor, and respect my wife, without giving her any difficulty or reason for complaint. The faithful love which she has always had for me, the good services which she has rendered all of you, and the help which she has brought to the family—which has greatly assisted in bringing us back up, and without which I could not have so easily attained high positions, nor have enjoyed the advantages and made the expenditures that I have made—all of these are reasons that you, my son, and the rest of my family, treat her as your true mother."[91] Maignart had good reason to urge peaceful relations on his family, for his own father's death had nearly produced a lawsuit between him and his mother, over the extent of her rights. Serious conflict among family members was an expected part of the inheritance transition, not an unlikely abberation.[92]

Compared with these uncertainties and conflicts, the actual division of the inheritance among the heirs appears to have been a straightforward matter, but it probably produced the greatest impact on the family's economic position. Dividing an inheritance had such serious consequences because Norman law insisted, with only two major exceptions, that it be done equally among all sons, or among all daughters if there were no sons. One exception was

[91] La Riv. Bourdet, 3344.

[92] La Riv. Bourdet, 2147 (an agreement between Maignart and his mother, "in order to avoid a lawsuit and nourish friendship [amytie]"). For other instances of such litigation, AD S-M, E, Tabellionage de Rouen, Meubles 1ère série, 9 March 1546 (old style) (between the widow and son of the councillor René de Becdelièvre); AD S-M, B, Parlement, Registre d'Audiences, 14 June, 5 July 1575 (between the widow and son of the councillor Claude Auvray); ibid., 28 November 1577 (between the councillor Jean Benoist and his brothers); Archives d'Esneval, Acquigny (between the widow and son of the councillor Claude Le Roux); Meubles 2, 26 November 1585 (among the sons of the councillor Guillaume Auber); AD S-M, E, Fonds Restault, unclassed (between the councillor Laurent Restault and his widowed mother, discussed above, p. 215); Meubles 2, 26 September 1602 (among three brothers of the Romé family, discussed above, p. 293).

geographical. Properties in the pays de Caux, the area immediately to the north of Rouen, were to go mainly to the oldest son, with no more (and often less) than one-third to be divided among his younger brothers. The other exception concerned feudal properties. The oldest son could choose any one of the fiefs in the inheritance, instead of his normal share in an equal division; if he failed to exercise this right, it passed in turn to his younger brothers. Such provisions somewhat mitigated the effects of equal inheritance, but Norman law remained exceptionally egalitarian.[93] Under the custom of Paris, for instance, the oldest son received both an equal share in the non-feudal inheritances and a substantial share of the family's noble properties: two-thirds if there were only two children, one-half if there were more. All fief-holding families in the region of Paris were thus in some measure able to evade the fragmentation of properties at inheritance.[94]

The dangers of inheritance divisions like those practiced in Normandy are clear enough. At each generation a family's fortune was subject to dismemberment, and efforts to build up a patrimony were rendered ineffectual. Yet there is little to suggest that *parlementaire* families seriously sought to get around these inheritance laws, for instance by concentrating their properties in the pays de Caux, and there is some indication that the custom's provisions were accepted and even approved.[95] When Norman

---

[93] On these principles, see Bérault, *La coustume reformée*, pp. 245ff.; for their position within the spectrum of French jurisprudence see Le Roy Ladurie, "Système de la coutume." Cf. Jean Meyer, *La noblesse de Bretagne au XVIII*ᵉ* siècle*, 2 vols. (Paris, 1966), I, III, 126-127. Meyer argues that the Norman custom favored the concentration of property, because he considers only the case of families whose entire fortune lay in a single fief, which the oldest son might take by virtue of his preciput. This situation, however, was rare even among the *noblesse d'épée*.

[94] See Pierre Guénois, *La conférence des coustumes tant générales, que locales et particulières du Royaume de France*, 2 vols. (Paris, 1596), I, 183r, 192r.

[95] Cf. Giesey, "Rules of Inheritance and Strategies of Mobility,"

lawyers discussed the matter, they presented the advantages of equal inheritance division that compensated for at least some of its inconveniences. Equality of inheritance was a means of reducing, though not eliminating, conflicts within the family: "For [as one lawyer argued before the Parlement in 1585] if it is very useful to the Republic that families have many children, provided that they live in fraternity and amity, benefiting equally from the successions of those to whom they are equally related, who doubts that testamentary election [that is, the favoring of one child over others] would create troubles and enmities?"[96] Equality of inheritance certainly blunted the efforts of families to accumulate large fortunes, but the practice did help (so at least contemporaries believed) to maintain the delicate equilibrium of familial relationships.

In the later sixteenth century, robe families sought other mechanisms for reducing the conflicts and disruption surrounding inheritance, and at the same time for strengthening dynastic continuity. The most visible of these efforts was the growing tendency of office holding itself to become hereditary, reflecting both changes in the magistrates' own ideas about office and the changing economics of office. We gain a sense of what this change meant for family organization by considering the numbers of magistrates who had sons who followed careers in the parlements. During the Parlement's first sixty years of existence, from 1499 to 1558, this was the case for fewer than one-fourth of the lay councillors, but in the second half of the century the frequency of such cases increased quickly: to about 40

---

for stress on bourgeois families' efforts to evade the division of their properties. For *parlementaire* families' apparent acceptance of such divisions, Hérit. 2, 18 June 1567, 25 January 1599, AD S-M, B, Requêtes du Palais, Sentences, 24 October 1594. These are three attempts by parents to assure that their younger children would receive substantial shares in their property in the pays de Caux. See also Davis, "Ghosts, Kin, and Progeny," for more general discussion of the varied concerns which these decisions involved.

[96] BM MS Y202, f. 234.

percent of the councillors in the years 1559-1594, and about 50 percent in the years 1594-1618.[97]

Other changes encouraged and eased this evolution. In response to the increased frequency with which offices were inherited, for instance, the Parlement developed the institution of honorary councillorships, which allowed fathers to resign their positions to their sons while retaining the right to attend the court, participate in deliberations, and usually vote in decisions.[98] Retirement from the active management of private affairs also became more common, apparently in imitation of developments elsewhere in France. "We see this practiced every day . . . ," lamented a Parisian moralist in 1571, "poor deluded fathers giving up all their possessions in order to advance their children to the honors and high places of the world."[99] More than ambition was involved, however. There was also the wish, as the uncle of one councillor expressed it, "to live the rest of his days in tranquility of body and expense," and to make the process of inheritance a less damaging one, by settling as many issues as possible beforehand.[100]

Finally, some concern was shown in the late sixteenth century with reducing the economic impact of inheritance division. The commission of *parlementaires* who revised the Norman custom in the 1580's appears to have worked consciously in this direction. Thus, their codification eliminated the possibility that feudal properties could be divided among male heirs. Only if there were no male heirs was it possible after 1585 to divide a fief. The effect (if not necessarily the intention) was to reduce the fragmentation of properties at

[97] Calculated from Frondeville, *Les conseillers* i, *Les conseillers* ii. These figures include *all* lay councillors, not only those known to have had sons, since Frondeville and his sources in some cases fail to report sons; thus these figures substantially underestimate the importance of heredity in the early seventeenth century.

[98] See above, Chapter 1.

[99] Artus Desiré, *L'origine et source de tous les maux de ce monde* . . . (Paris, 1571), f. 11v.

[100] Tabel., 24 January 1577; Hérit. 2, 10 February 1600.

each inheritance. The attainment of some continuity between the generations became a somewhat easier matter.[101]

The threat which inheritance posed to familial fortunes and solidarity thus diminished during the later sixteenth century. Yet the principal conclusion which emerges from this examination of the *parlementaire* family remains the instability which characterized its life cycle throughout the sixteenth and early seventeenth centuries. Especially at the moment of inheritance, families were subject to drastic economic strains and internal conflicts. Efforts to alleviate these might have some effect, but they soon encountered the limits imposed by family emotions. Fraternal amity could be maintained, it was felt, by equal divisions of inheritances, and fathers were reluctant to surrender their control of family affairs. In 1610 the councillor Robert Busquet sought to overturn a retirement that he had arranged with his son, arguing that "It would not be reasonable that, during his own lifetime, his son should shamelessly despoil him of his position"; the younger Busquet replied in kind, with the claim that "all that his father purports to be doing is really with the intention of disinheriting him . . . , so as to reduce him to indigence."[102]

The wide fluctuations through which the family passed helped to determine the social and political functions it could fill. *Parlementaires* seriously pursued their relatives' interests, and their political positions might be intimately connected to the network of family alliances in which they found themselves. But few families had sufficient economic security to permit more material forms of assistance, to allow, for instance, considerations of family connection to affect business transactions: they might loan money to rela-

[101] Houard, *Dictionnaire*, II, 424. For analysis of the legal principles which informed the revision of the custom of Paris, in the early sixteenth century, see Guenée, *Tribunaux et gens de justice*, pp. 493ff.
[102] BM MS Y214, X, 475-478.

tives, but at prevailing interest rates. The family's capacity to function as a dynastic unit, steadily improving its position from one generation to the next, was similarly limited. The burdens which weighed on inheritance help to explain the pattern of family advance that was considered in Chapter 5: the tendency, that is, for families to advance by sudden and large economic gains (and to undergo losses of a similar kind), rather than by steady accumulation.

The difficulty of even preserving wealth tended to make marriage a critical event in the family's economic history. Marriage was the means by which heirs could support the cost of inheritance, and a magistrate thus tended to marry shortly after his father's death. Marriage was not for that reason a purely economic institution, nor were economic considerations all that lay behind the choice of a spouse. Circumstances in the later sixteenth century, however, tended to give marriage a greater economic importance. Higher office costs and falling revenues from the land were reflected in a rising level of *parlementaire* indebtedness in the years after 1570, and marriage choices responded to the same pressures. Marriage alliances had linked the magistrates to one another during the middle years of the sixteenth century, but after 1570 the need to find wealthy brides required most magistrates to marry brides from lower social classes, and to do without the possible advantages of more equal alliances.

Very likely this evolution added to what was the dominant quality of *parlementaire* family organization in the sixteenth and early seventeenth centuries: the family's continuing potential for instability, both economic and emotional. We have seen the real affection in which spouses and children might be held, but we have also seen the pervasiveness of anxiety and anger. Relations with siblings or more distant connections might involve similar strains. In either instance, economic issues were usually involved, visibly in the case of inheritance conflicts, somewhat less obviously in forcing magistrates into marriage or in the anxieties that the idea of a rich wife created. On occasion the *parlementaire* family might be a cohesive and powerful institution, but in the later sixteenth and early seventeenth centuries it had limited margins of either economic or psychic security.

SEVEN

CONCLUSION

WHEN Marc Bloch discussed the place of the *noblesse de robe* in French rural history, he presented the matter in clearcut terms: "This [sixteenth-century] advance by the bourgeoisie," he wrote, "followed by such rapid entrenchment, was the most decisive event in French social history, especially in its rural aspect." What was at issue, in Bloch's view, was the maintenance of the seigneurial system itself and of the aristocratic society that profited from it. In the fourteenth century the urban rich had been revolutionary opponents of the seigneurial structure. In the sixteenth century, on the contrary, they flocked into the newly created parlements and other high offices, bought up seigneurial properties, and thus became the core of a regenerated nobility. They brought with them a well-defined outlook, which Bloch summarized as "the capitalist spirit." As a result, their entry to the aristocracy was much more than just a change of personnel. Their presence changed the mentality which informed the seigneurial system, and hence changed the nobility's economic prospects and relations with other social groups.[1]

This study has been about Bloch's "decisive event," as it took place in one province. Much of what we have seen conforms to Bloch's vision of how the *noblesse de robe* formed and entrenched itself. This is true, first, with regard to the numerical importance and timing of the process itself. The development of a *noblesse de robe* at Rouen drastically changed the province's social structure. The number of large landowners increased several-fold, and they tended

[1] Marc Bloch, *French Rural History: An Essay on its Basic Characteristics*, trans. Janet Sondheimer (Berkeley, 1966), p. 125.

to fill the countryside with seigneurial institutions. By the late sixteenth century, as Bloch saw, families who had acquired high positions were establishing themselves as dynasties, and their success made the entry of new families increasingly difficult. Underlying this process of tightening, as we have seen, were a series of economic changes. The cost of both land and offices increased greatly in the late sixteenth and early seventeenth centuries; so also did the economic advantages of inheritance. In these circumstances, the magistrates' views of themselves, the monarchy, and the society around them also tended to change. Greater stress was laid on heredity, and less place was given to talent and learning. Service to the monarchy came to be less central in the magistrates' view of their role, while the importance of belonging to an order, a specific social category, increased.

In these respects the formation of a *noblesse de robe* at Rouen conformed to the pattern which Bloch and other historians have set forth. But the Rouennais experience also diverged in important ways from this pattern. This was most clearly the case with regard to the special mentality that Bloch attributed to the *noblesse de robe* and which, he believed, accounted for their success over the older nobility. We have seen that the magistrates did share a special outlook, and that their attitudes seemed alien and comical to members of the *noblesse d'épée*. Yet there was little of the "capitalist spirit" in this mentality. The magistrates' economic attitudes were those of their age: grasping and in that sense rational, but oriented to self-sufficiency and consumption, rather than to capital investment, improvement, or the like. The special qualities of the magistrates' mentality lay elsewhere. They lay in the self-restraint and conservatism which their profession demanded, and which contemporary noblemen viewed as a premature acceptance of the inhibitions of old age.

It was this difference in attitudes which underlay most conflicts between robe and sword, for their origins and careers placed most magistrates squarely within aristocratic society. A small minority of magistrates came from urban and commercial backgrounds, but many more came from the countryside, from the milieu of poor nobility and well-off peasants who clustered around the wealthy nobility and rose through seigneurial offices. Whether their origins were rural or urban, moreover, those families whose ascensions can be traced relied constantly on aristocratic patronage; and this dependence continued after they were installed in the Parlement. Far from seeking to challenge the older aristocracy, the *parlementaires* were in considerable measure recruited from the aristocracy's dependents and advanced by means of aristocratic patronage. They served the aristocracy with the means that office gave them. These facts make sense of the political as well as the social dimensions of the successes of robe families. In contrast to many Parisian families, for whom loyalty to the crown during the great political upheavals of the age was critical for success, few Rouennais families seem to have suffered from their opposition to the king in moments of political crisis. Indeed, despite their corporate dependence on the crown, many magistrates profited from their willingness to support the rebellions of the great aristocracy.

Fundamental similarities between *noblesse de robe* and *noblesse d'épée* went further still. Our examination of *parlementaire* landownership has shown that robe landowners certainly brought changes to the countryside, but that these were mainly in the direction of greater concentrations of landed property. There were few differences between robe and sword in the administration of landed properties, least of all in regard to the success of the two groups in drawing profits from sixteenth-century economic trends. In the late sixteenth century, when conditions became less favorable to large landowners, the *robins* were no more successful than others in warding off economic troubles. These difficulties were the result of fundamental problems in the rural economy, not of the landowners' insufficient concern for accumulating riches. In the same way, *parlementaires* were as likely as the older nobility to accumulate debts and even to face outright ruin because of them. Profligacy played its part in this, for the magistrates as for the older nobility, but more basic problems were also involved. With regard to incomes, there were the declining profits of both office and land; with regard to expenditures, there were above all the expenses of raising families and the difficulties of transmitting property intact from one generation to the next. Our examination of the *parlementaire* family has sought to demonstrate the seriousness of these problems and of the conflicts they might generate. It has shown also the expedients which robe families turned to in order to lessen the seriousness of these economic problems: above all, through the use of economically profitable marriages.

To what extent are the conclusions presented here of use for understanding larger problems about the nature and evolution of the French upper classes? On the one hand, it is appropriate to stress the limits within which this study has been carried out. We have been concerned here with a single region, and with a single social group within that region. In certain respects Normandy was probably well in advance of other provinces in sixteenth-century France. Its wealth was greater, and it felt more often the pressures of royal absolutism.[2] Such limitations mean that generalizations can be drawn only cautiously from the experiences of the Rouennais *noblesse de robe*. If the Rouennais example cannot simply be extended to other regions of France or to other social groups, however, it can still be of more than local use. It can suggest the kinds of forces to which the French nobilities, of the robe or the sword, were subject; conversely, it can call into question some generalizations about the dominant groups in French society during the sixteenth and early seventeenth centuries.

[2] See Edmond Esmonin, *La taille en Normandie au temps de Colbert (1661-1683)* (Paris, 1913).

Four such applications of the results of this study seem of particular importance. First, the example of the Rouennais magistrates suggests the continuing power and prosperity of the traditional aristocracy in early modern France—and in this respect the Rouennais example appears to accord closely with recent scholarship on the issue.[3] The great nobility presided over the Parlement's recruitment and regularly influenced its judgments, while the lesser nobility provided a substantial minority of the court's members. My second broad suggestion is closely related, and appears also to be in accord with at least some recent thinking about the old regime's social structure. The Rouennais example suggests that we do better to understand *noblesse de robe* and *noblesse d'épée* as components of a single, reasonably cohesive landed elite, rather than by seeing France as dominated by a pair of fundamentally hostile elites. In Normandy, we have seen, nobilities of robe and sword had similar family connections, similar economic resources, and similar ways of managing them. Conflicts between robe and sword might be intense, but they were conflicts between individuals and professional groups; they were not conflicts between alien castes or, more fundamentally, between an elite that was urban and progressive on the one side and one that was rural and backward on the other.[4]

[3] Francois Billacois, "La crise de la noblesse européenne (1550-1650): une mise au point," *Revue d'histoire moderne et contemporaine*, XXIII (April-June, 1976), 258-277, for these issues in a European context. For recent stress on the continuing wealth of the French nobility, see Jean Meyer, "Un problème mal posé: la noblesse pauvre. L'exemple breton au XVIIIe siècle," *ibid.*, XVIII (April-June, 1971), 161-188. Forthcoming studies on the nobility of the election of Bayeux and on the La Tremouille family suggest a similar conclusion: see James B. Wood, "The Decline of the Nobility in Sixteenth and Early Seventeenth-Century France: Myth or Reality?" *Journal of Modern History*, XXXXVIII, 1 (March, 1976), and William A. Weary, "The House of La Tremouille, Fifteenth through Eighteenth Centuries: Change and Adaptation in a French Noble Family," *ibid.*, IL, 1 (March, 1977).

[4] Thus Pierre Goubert, *The Ancien Regime. French Society 1600-*

Thirdly (and this appears to be somewhat less in keeping with recent historiography), the Rouennais example suggests something of the processes of movement and change within this broad landed elite. Those who have written about social mobility in old regime society have tended to stress its gradual character and its reliance on family connections: families extended their positions slowly and carefully, marshalling the resources of distant connections and *alliés* for the purpose.[5] Doubtless such analyses accord with some of the realities of old regime society, but the Rouennais example suggests another, quite different set of realities. For *parlementaire* families economic and social advancement (and decline) came in sharp, sudden bursts. Distant family connections were usually of little help in the process of advancement, for many of the same reasons. The economic circumstances of families usually were not flexible enough to permit either patient, generation by generation, accumulation of wealth or assistance to those outside the immediate family. For most robe families, the mere maintenance of a fortune was a sufficiently exacting task, one at which many failed. Serious gains in most cases had to come from outside, from a well-calculated marriage, assistance from the great aristocracy, or other good fortune. All robe families carried on their efforts to maintain and improve their position within a set of severe economic and social constraints, and the force of these constraints needs to be appreciated.

This leads to a final point. Throughout this study we have encountered the presence of economic calculations in shaping the magistrates' choices and actions: with regard to

---

1750, trans. Steve Cox (New York, 1973), 188-192; Denis Richet, *La France moderne: l'esprit des institutions* (Paris, 1973), p. 102, acknowledging the origins of this perspective in the arguments of Boris Porchnev, *Les soulèvements populaires en France de 1623 à 1648* (Paris, 1963).

[5] For instance, Roland Mousnier, *La vénalité des offices sous Henri IV et Louis XIII* (2nd ed., Paris, 1971), p. 84-85.

family, rural life, professional attachments, and so forth. These calculations often had a special character, and their terms were in fundamental ways different from modern notions of capital and investment. The Rouennais example suggests, however, that the opposite of modern monetary calculation is not simply a lack of concern with money and profit; in understanding the landed elites of the old regime, we need to look further at differences in kind in economic calculation. Historians have been quite properly concerned to avoid anachronism in dealing with the economics of sixteenth- and seventeenth-century landed society. But concern for anachronism should not lead us to contrast modern economic motives with a purely non-economic past. Our examinations of landowning and marriage have shown how carefully economic advantage might be calculated, and how necessary such calculations were to families' survival.[6]

This is not meant to suggest that economic motives and causes were the only ones shaping the magistrates' lives as a group, or that the group changed with every change in economic circumstances. Much of what we have seen here, indeed, suggests the reverse. We have seen, for instance, the degree to which the workings of the family determined the ways in which economic pressures reached and affected the magistrates; we have also seen the constant importance

[6] Again, it is Roland Mousnier and his students who have most vigorously insisted on the importance of extra-economic considerations in the individuals' and families' calculations of their interests; rather, Mousnier has argued, calculation centered on questions of honor and status. See for instance, "Les concepts d' 'ordres', d' 'états', et de 'monarchie absolue' en France de la fin du XVᵉ siècle à la fin du XVIIIᵉ," *Revue historique*, DII (April-June, 1972), 289-312. For a somewhat different view of early modern aristocracies' reluctance to calculate advantages, see Lawrence Stone, *The Crisis of the Aristocracy, 1558-1641* (Oxford, 1965), pp. 303-322. More generally, see Otto Brunner, "Das 'Ganze Haus' und die alteuropäische 'Ökonomik,' " in Brunner, *Neue Wege der Verfassungs- und Sozialgeschichte* (2nd ed., Göttingen, 1968).

of political events in shaping the magistrates' economic lives, and we have sought to understand the complexities of the mentalities in which economic facts were registered and responses formulated. There can be no question of reducing these varied phenomena to a single set of causes, economic or other. What need to be emphasized, rather, are the facts of determination and limitation themselves: the ways in which the magistrates (and other members of the landed elite of the old regime) were limited in their actions by a range of economic, political, and social circumstances. Historians of the pre-industrial peasantry and working classes have been concerned to show the ways in which the poor in early modern Europe were historical actors, not merely the objects of larger social forces.[7] For historians of the traditional wealthy, those whom I have described as the landed elite, there is an inverse and complementary need. We must understand the degree to which the rich, like the poor, were limited and changed by forces outside themselves. We must see the rich, that is, as part of the same society as peasants and artisans, not as standing outside it.

[7] See, for instance, Natalie Zemon Davis, "The Reasons of Misrule: Youth Groups and Charivaris in Sixteenth-Century France," *Past and Present*, 50 (February 1971), 41-75; "The Rites of Violence: Religious Riot in Sixteenth-Century France," *Past and Present*, 59 (May, 1973), 51-91; "Strikes and Salvation at Lyons," *Archiv für Reformationsgeschichte*, LVI, 1 (1965), 48-64; E. P. Thompson, *The Making of the English Working Class* (London, 1963).

THE *PARLEMENTAIRES* AND CRIME

ONE problem that historians interested in understanding the professional mentality of such groups as the *parlementaires* have confronted is the difficulty of following the actual work which these groups performed. Partly, this difficulty reflects the traditional separation of legal history from other branches of history; it reflects also more fundamental difficulties in relating the specific circumstances of individual lawsuits or legal doctrines to broader patterns of social and intellectual development. One aspect of the magistrates' professional activity that does allow such relationships to be seen, however, is their treatment of criminal cases. This appendix seeks to extend the analysis of *parlementaire* professional mentality offered above, in Chapter 1, by examining this aspect of judicial practice.

Treatment of criminal cases offers an especially useful approach to professional mentalities because of the very wide latitude which the court enjoyed in dealing with crime. The Parlement had the final decision in all appeals cases arising within the province; only in exceptional cases were its decisions appealed to the royal council. Seigneurial and royal jurisdictions were equally subject to this control, and by the mid-sixteenth century the church courts had been reduced to a very small role in criminal matters. Except for the crimes of simony and assaulting a cleric, the criminal jurisdiction of the church courts extended only to clerics, and then only for a few cases: heresy, blasphemy, and sorcery (Jean Imbert, *La pratique judiciaire tant civile que criminelle receue et observée par tout le royaume de France* [4th ed., revised and augmented by Pierre Guénois, Paris, 1609], pp. 668-669). Appeal cost nothing, required only that the defendant announce that he was making an appeal, and could be made at any point in the case; in criminal matters, further, there were no intermediate jurisdictions to be gone through—cases went directly to the Parlement (Laurens Bouchel, *La bibliothèque ou thrésor du droit français*, 2 vols. [Paris, 1609], 1, 790).

The advantages which the Parlement enjoyed against other jurisdictions within the province were matched by the judges' control over defendants. Criminal cases of any gravity in Normandy followed the inquisitorial procedures (described as "extraordinary procedure") derived from Roman law. The defendant remained in prison throughout his trial, with no right to consult attorneys and (in theory more than in practice) no right to speak with other prisoners. Although he might question the honesty of witnesses against him, this right was strictly limited. He might question the witnesses' honesty before he heard their testimony, and he might respond to their testimony shortly after it was given. If he failed to use these opportunities, he was assumed to have accepted their statements, and was allowed no later opportunity to object. Finally, he might be subjected to torture. An early-seventeenth-century Rouennais lawyer described the importance of torture and the way in which judges ought to make use of it. "Ordinarily the judgement of a criminal case depends on the examination of the accused and on the judge's dexterity in pulling the truth of the matter from the prisoner's mouth." When ordinary questioning failed to elicit such a confession, the judge was to recite to the prisoner "his contradictions and vacillations, which give a great and obvious and vehement presumption that he had committed the crime of which he is accused, so that he cannot evade condemnation"; now he should tell the truth, the judge was to tell him, or be forced to do so under torture (Jean Labiche, *Stile et manière de proceder* . . . [Rouen, 1609], pp. 184, 206). Such procedures were partly intended to protect those who had been unjustly accused. So much stress was placed on the defendant's confession partly because of a fear that witnesses might be biased or otherwise unfair. Stress on confession reflected also the weakness of police institutions; few existed, and their corruption and indifference were a source of frequent complaints (thus Reg. sec., 1573-1579, ff. 167-169). But such mistrust of outside sources of information tended (as Labiche's comments suggest) to leave an enormous role for the judge's own assumptions and prejudices.

Royal legislation posed equally few restrictions on the judge's freedom. In criminal as in civil law, the *parlementaires* fashioned their decisions from a group of legal traditions that included Roman law, provincial custom, and the previous decisions of the parlements themselves as well as the laws promulgated by the monarchy. During the sixteenth century, especially with the great reforming laws of the 1560's and 1570's, the monarchy's share in this mixture tended to increase, but judges retained a large measure of discretion. Thus when Pierre Guénois in the early seventeenth century sought to list the penalties attaching to different categories of crime, he cited no royal legislation dealing with the crimes of adultery and sodomy, though both were punished by death "according to the *arrêts*" of the parlements; homicide and sorcery were other crimes for which royal legislation either failed to set penalties or conflicted with other sources of law (Imbert, *La pratique judiciaire*, pp. 797-801, 790-791, 774-775). Even when clear legal dispositions existed, judges were expected to set penalties that accorded with the circumstances of the crime: "In general," wrote Laurens Bouchel, "crimes of great importance (*énormes*) are to be punished according to the full rigor of the law, and lesser ones mercifully, insofar as possible" (*La bibliothèque*, ii, 407). Under these circumstances, judges' decisions in criminal cases tended to reflect at least as much their professional mentality as the dispositions of the legal codes they applied or the facts of the cases themselves.

The present investigation is based on 574 criminal cases decided by the Parlement during the years 1548-1549, 1576, 1585-1588, and 1604-1606; these cases involved 848 defendants. This is not a scientifically selected sample, since a principal concern was to trace changes in criminal decisions over the sixteenth century, and the cases examined here represent only a small portion of those which the Parlement decided in this period. Nonetheless, these cases do suggest some important aspects of the Parlement's professional behavior and mentality. In the first place, they demonstrate the Parlement's growing influence and power within the province. In the mid-sixteenth century, appeals to the Parlement in criminal cases had come chiefly from Rouen itself and from other cities of the province. By the early seventeenth century the share of more distant and more rural districts had risen dramatically.

Table A: 1 shows one aspect of this change, the declining importance of appeals cases from Rouen and its immediate

TABLE A:1

APPEALS FROM THE BAILLIAGE OF ROUEN

	Appeals from the Lieutenant General, Bailliage of Rouen (Rouen itself)	Appeals from the Lieutenants General and Particuliers, Bailliage of Rouen (Rouen and surrounding districts)	N
1548-1549	50 (39.7% of total)	56 (44.4% of total)	126
1576	7 (10.1%)	11 (15.9%)	69
*1585-1588	28 (11.9%)	47 (20.0%)	235
*1604-1606	7 (6.9%)	13 (12.9%)	101
			531

* Cases appealed from the bailliage of Alençon have not been included in computing these percentages, since in 1548-1549 and 1576 the bailliage had been detached from the jurisdiction of the Parlement of Rouen; if the bailliage of Alençon were included, of course, the relative importance of cases from the bailliage of Rouen in 1585-1588 and 1604-1606 would be still smaller.

vicinity, the districts covered by the lieutenant general of the bailliage of Rouen and his four deputies, the *lieutenants particuliers*. More than 40 percent of the appeals which the Parlement decided in 1548-1549 originated within the bailliage of Rouen itself, and most of these had first been judged in Rouen. In the later sixteenth century the share of the bailliage as a whole had fallen to about 20 percent, and that of Rouen itself to about 10 percent.

Table A:2 shows a complementary change, the rising importance among the Parlement's criminal cases of ap-

TABLE A:2

APPEALS FROM *Hautes Justices*

	Appeals from Hautes Justices
1548-1549	1 (0.8% of total)
1576	2 (2.6%)
*1585-1588	10 (4.3%)
*1604-1606	10 (9.9%)

* Appeals from the lieutenants of the bailliage of Alençon have been excluded from these calculations.

peals from seigneurial jurisdictions. During the second half of the sixteenth century the relative importance of appeals from these jurisdictions increased more than twelvefold, from 0.8 percent of the appeals decided by the Parlement to 9.9 percent. By 1604-1606 such appeals were more numerous than those from the lieutenant general of the bailliage of Rouen. In Normandy it was only during the early seventeenth century that the situation described by Jean Imbert came to be a reality: "ordinarily . . . when the accused is condemned to corporal punishment there is an appeal" (*La pratique judiciaire*, p. 767).

Presumably this spread of the Parlement's influence to even isolated rural jurisdictions reflected the kinds of activity described above in Chapter 1. As seen there, a good deal of the magistrates' activity was devoted to controlling lesser

jurisdictions and investigating abuses that had been left un-
corrected there. The growing importance of appeals from
lesser jurisdictions seems to testify to the success of these
efforts. During the very years that monarchical authority
appeared to be breaking down, the Parlement managed to
advance considerably the process by which even isolated
parts of the province were brought into a single judicial
system.

This expansion of the court's influence within the province appears to have been partly responsible for a change in
the kinds of cases it dealt with. It is at least clear that the
same years which saw the expansion of the Parlement's
influence over the *hautes justices* also saw a striking increase
in the importance of certain kinds of crime, notably of
sorcery, crimes against sexual morality, and infanticide.
Table A:3 sets out the increasing importance of these

TABLE A:3
KINDS OF CASES HEARD BY THE PARLEMENT
(as percentages of all cases)

	Heresy	Sorcery	*Morals	Infanticide	Theft
1548-1549	7.1%	—	0.8%	1.6%	29.4%
1576	—	—	1.4%	1.4%	33.3%
1585-1588	1.9%	3.1%	4.6%	3.1%	38.9%
1604-1606	—	10.1%	10.1%	8.4%	29.4%

* Includes cases of adultery, bigamy, sodomy, and incest.

crimes, as percentages of all cases decided by the Parlement;
it also includes the percentage of all crimes which theft represented, in order to suggest the relative importance of
these crimes against morality and against the family. Sorcery, crimes against sexual morality, and infanticide rose
steadily and in close correlation during the later sixteenth
and early seventeenth centuries. Numerically insignificant
in 1548-1549 and in 1576, each represented about 10 percent
of the Parlement's criminal cases between 1604 and 1606.
During these years they formed together 28.6 percent of

the Parlement's cases: only slightly fewer than the various forms of theft (29.4 percent), and considerably more than the various forms of homicide (18.5 percent). The relationship between the Parlement's greater role within the province and the rising frequency of these crimes is difficult to document. Nonetheless, this relationship does suggest that in Normandy the late-sixteenth-century rise of sorcery was indeed (as historians have suggested more generally about France) a matter of discovery, rather than of new practices; urban magistrates were encountering and punishing "crimes" that had long prevailed in the countryside, rather than responding to a wave of new practices. Equally suggestive are the relationships among the crimes of sorcery, infanticide, and such crimes of morality as sodomy, adultery, incest, and bigamy. The fact that these three sets of crimes increased in importance at about the same pace during the later sixteenth and early seventeenth centuries suggests something of the context of Norman witchcraft prosecutions. These took place, it appears, within a set of concerns that were as much oriented to the defense of communal and familial morality as to more purely spiritual issues.

Indeed, consideration of the punishments that they applied to these crimes suggests that to the *parlementaires* communal and familial concerns may have been paramount. We may compare, for instance, the magistrates' response to infanticide with that toward sorcery. These were fundamentally similar in being nearly invisible crimes. By its nature sorcery could be detected only by indirect marks, and a royal edict of 1556 gave indirect evidence a similar importance in infanticide cases: because of the near impossibility of distinguishing between stillbirth and infanticide, mothers who had concealed their pregnancies and failed to bring their children to be baptized were now presumed to have killed them (François Isambert et al., *Recueil général des anciennes lois françaises* . . . [Paris, n.d.], XIII, 471-473). Following this measure, according to one lawyer, judges in fact ceased "to inquire very seriously (*curieusement*) as to

whether they (the children) were born alive or dead . . ."
(Iehan Papon, *Recueil d'arrestz notables des courtz souveraines de France*, f. 478r). Despite the absence of direct
evidence, however, the Parlement punished infanticide with
a consistent severity that was nearly unique. Of 20 defendants (all but 2 of them women), 18 were hanged and their
bodies burned; the 2 others were released "without absolving or condemning." In contrast, of 20 sorcery defendants
from these years 7 were executed, 6 were given various
terms in the galleys, 5 were sent into periods of banishment,
and 2 were released "without absolving or condemning;" as
striking, of the 17 cases in which both the lower courts' and
the Parlement's decisions are known, 10 were alleviated by
the Parlement. However alert the magistrates were to the
dangers of sorcery, they found infanticide still more disturbing. Such threats to the family and community, it seems,
were taken more seriously than the threat of diabolical intervention. I have suggested elsewhere the ways in which
this contrast reflected the specific political attitudes held by
the *parlementaires*—the seriousness with which, as seen in
Chapter 1, they took their task of maintaining peace and
order within the province, and the seriousness with which
they took threats to that order (see "The 'Perfect Magistrate': *Parlementaires* and Crime in Sixteenth-Century
Rouen," *Archive for Reformation History*, LXVII [1976],
284-300).

A final change which took place in the Parlement's dealings with criminal cases concerned punishment itself. The
severity of the Parlement's decisions increased markedly
during these years. Table A:4 shows one aspect of this
change, the sharp increase in the frequency with which
defendants were given capital sentences.

A similar though less clearcut movement may be seen in
the Parlement's treatment of the appeals cases which reached
it. The Parlement might revise these in any way it saw fit,
in the direction of either greater moderation or greater severity. During the later sixteenth century the number of

TABLE A:4
FREQUENCY OF CAPITAL PUNISHMENT

	Defendants Sentenced to Capital Punishment	N
1548-1549	12%	174
1576	16%	105
1585-1588	26%	397
1604-1606	24%	172

lower court sentences that it reduced tended to drop, while those which it either upheld or increased tended to grow. Table A:5 presents this change. Between 1548-1549 and 1604-1606, Table A:5 shows, the frequency with which the court either upheld or increased lower court sentences nearly doubled; the frequency with which sentences were reduced declined by about one-half.

TABLE A.5
PARLEMENT'S DECISIONS ON SENTENCES FROM LOWER COURTS
(as percentages of all defendants in appeals cases decided)

	PERCENTAGE OF DEFENDANTS' SENTENCES						
	Increased	Upheld	Total	*Upheld but Commuted	Reduced	Total	N
1548-1549	7%	23%	30%	4%	65%	69%	69
1576	3%	46%	49%	14%	37%	51%	59
1585-1588	13%	40%	53%	2%	44%	46%	268
1604-1606	11%	46%	57%	6%	37%	43%	117

* Refers to death sentences commuted to life service in the galleys.

This change had a number of causes. In part it probably reflected the greater willingness of defendants to appeal lower court judgments, whatever the likelihood of their appeals' succeeding. To a lesser degree the change probably also reflected the changes seen in Table A:3 in the kinds of criminal cases with which the Parlement dealt. The increasing number of sorcery and infanticide cases both tended to raise the number of death sentences which the Parlement gave out, and in cases of infanticide lower court sentences typically were upheld (though this was not true in sorcery cases). Changes in the *parlementaires'* own attitudes, however, appear to have been more important than these external causes. As seen in Chapter 1, in the later sixteenth century the magistrates tended to become more uncertain of their own position and more anxious about the state of their society. One result of these anxieties was an increased level of tension with the monarchy, as the magistrates (in their own view) sought to prevent the disorders which they felt royal policies would create. Tables A:4 and A:5 suggest that another manifestation of *parlementaire* anxieties in these years was an increasingly severe repression of crime of all kinds.

(SOURCE: AD S-M, B, Parlement, Tournelle, March 1547 [old style]-June 1548; September-November 1548; September-November 1549; January-July 1576; September-December 1576; July-September 1585; July-August 1586; June-July 1587; January-March 1588; April-June 1588; July-September 1588; October-December 1588; September-December 1604; January-April 1605; April-August 1605; January-March 1606.)

APPENDIX B

PARLEMENTAIRE FORTUNES

1. Guillaume Maignart, councillor 1499-1523
   Fortune inherited in 1499:
   House in Rouen: 40₶ yearly (10 percent)
   Land and *Rentes Foncières*: about 360₶ yearly (90 percent)
   Total Income: about 400₶
   SOURCE: La Riv. Bourdet, 516, 539

2. Jean Heuzé, councillor 1499-1503
   Fortune left in 1503:
   Houses in Rouen: about 2,000₶ capital (33 percent)
   Land: about 1,000₶ capital (17 percent)
   Rentes: 2,000₶ capital (33 percent)
   Tithes: 1,000₶ capital (17 percent)
   Total Worth: about 6,000₶
   SOURCE: AD S-M, G8522

3. Robert de Boislevesque, councillor 1499-1528
   Fortune inherited in 1506 (shared with brother)
   Urban Properties: none
   Land: about 340₶ yearly
   Rentes: 100₶ yearly (all set in rural parishes)
   Total Income: 440₶
   SOURCE: Tabel., 4 December 1506

4. Pierre de Montfault, avocat du roi 1522-1527, president 1527-1541
   Income from real property, ca. 1525: about 1,050₶
   SOURCE: Tabel., 9 July 1568 (widow's *douaire*)

5. Jean de Bauquemare, *father* of Jean, councillor 1533-1541

and Jacques, councillor 1543-1544, first president 1565-1584

    Fortune left in 1541:

        Houses in Rouen: about 11,500ł (14 percent)

        Fief: about 800ł yearly, or about 20,000ł (25 percent)

        Land: about 1,300ł (2 percent)

        Rentes on individuals: 46,979ł (59 percent)

        Rentes on the State: 85ł (0.1 percent)

        Total Value: 79,864ł

    Jean de Bauquemare, councillor 1533-1541

        Income from real property, ca. 1533: about 1,800ł

    SOURCE: AD S-M, 16J8

6. Guillaume Challenge, councillor 1508-1532

    Fortune left in 1535:

        Urban Properties: none

        Rentes: none

        Land: 40 *acres*, with two houses

        Total Value and Income: unknown

    SOURCE: AD S-M, Tabellionage de Rouen, Héritages, 1ère série, 19 April 1548

7. Guillaume Jubert, councillor 1504-1540

    (1) Fortune inherited in 1510:

        Urban Properties: none

        Land: two seigneuries, four other landed properties

        Rentes: 13ł, 3½ barrels wine (all set in rural parishes)

        Total Value and Income: unknown

    SOURCE: BN Carrés de d'Hozier, 358

    (2) Fortune left in 1543 [as seen in 1554]

        Urban Property: about 2,000ł (1 percent)

        Land and Fiefs: about 128,500ł (63.8 percent)

        Rentes Foncières: about 13,700ł (6.8 percent)

        Rentes on Individuals: 44,660ł (22.2 percent)

        Rentes on the State: 12,490ł (6.3 percent)

        Total Value: about 201,350ł (Note: this estimate is

based on the one share in Jubert's inheritance for which all properties can be evaluated)
   Total Income: 13,500ł
SOURCE: AD Eure, E2474

8. Nicolas Blancbaston, councillor 1543-1550
   Fortune inherited in 1547
   Houses in Dieppe: 5 houses, value unknown
   Land: 5 *acres* meadow, Arques
   Rentes on the State: 18ł yearly
   Rentes Hypothèques on Individuals: 10ł yearly
   Rentes Foncières: 12ł 6s yearly
   Total Value: Less than 7,000ł
   SOURCE: AD S-M, D350 (Ursulines de Dieppe)

9. Michel de Civille, *father* of Anthoine, councillor 1554-1568, 1576-1587
   Total Income, 1547: 2,583ł, from *rentes* and five houses in Rouen
   SOURCE: Christiane Douyère, *Une famille rouennaise d'origine espagnole à la fin du 15e et au 16e siècle: les Civille (1484-vers 1600). Schéma d'une assimilation* (Mémoire de maîtrise, Université de Paris, 1973), p. 102.

10. Nicolas Romé, *father* of Nicolas Romé, councillor 1568-1575, and Laurent, councillor 1575-1604
    Acquisitions of real property, 1526-1548:
    Houses in Rouen: 14,946ł (75 percent)
    Land: 1,033ł 8s (5 percent)
    Rentes on Individuals: none
    Rentes on the State: 3,810ł (19 percent)
    Rentes Foncières: 50ł (0.3 percent)
    Total Value: 19,839ł (yearly average of 1,526ł)
    SOURCE: Tabel., 10 April 1565 (old style)

11. Etienne Patris, councillor 1527-1548
    Fortune left in 1548:
    Urban Property: a large house in Rouen

Land and Fiefs: apparently none
Rentes on Individuals: 404ł yearly
Rentes on the State: none
Total Income: 404ł
SOURCE: Tabel., 18 September 1555

12. Jean de Bonshoms, councillor 1543-1551
Fortune left in 1551, as seen in mid-1560's:
Urban Property: none
Land: 1,109ł yearly (62 percent)
Rentes on Individuals: 540ł yearly (30 percent)
Rentes on the State: 132ł yearly (7 percent)
Total Income: 1,781ł
SOURCE: Meubles 2, 4 May 1569 (accounts from the minority of Pierre de Bonshoms)

13. Claude Jubert, councillor 1543-1559
Fortune left in 1559:
Urban Property: 1 house at Les Andelys, about 5,000ł (4 percent)
Land: about 110,000ł (81 percent)
Rentes on Individuals: 15,000ł (11 percent)
Rentes on the State: 5,100ł (4 percent)
Rentes Foncières: 360ł (0.3 percent)
Total Value: about 135,460ł

14. Isambart Busquet, councillor 1542-1560
Fortune left in 1560:
Urban Property: 2 houses worth 1,130ł, and a large residence worth about 5,000ł
Land: 149 *acres*, worth about 18,000ł
Rentes: 220ł yearly, or 2,200ł capital
Total Value: 26,330ł
SOURCE: Robert Busquet de Caumont, *Histoire économique et sociale d'une lignée de huit conseillers au Parlement de Normandie: les Busquet de Chandoissel et de Caumont* (Mémoire, D.E.S., Paris, Faculté de droit et des sciences économiques), pp. 18-19.

15. Robert Raoullin, councillor 1529-1540, 1543-1565
    Fortune left in 1565:
    Urban Property: a large house, worth about 4,000l
    Fiefs: three, two of them worth together 1,500l
    yearly
    Land: unknown
    Rentes: unknown
    Total Value: about 50,000l
    SOURCE: Tabel., 19 February 1564 (old style); Hérit. 2,
    2 May 1567

16. Pierre Dufour, councillor 1543-1569
    Fortune left in 1569:
    Urban Property: house, garden, and "empty place"
    in Rouen
    Land: 10 *acres*
    Rentes on Individuals: 68l 7s income
    Rentes Foncières: 50l yearly
    Total Value: Probably less than 5,000l (Note: Du-
    four lost much of his property during the Hu-
    guenot uprising of 1562, and his inheritance was
    accepted only *"sous bénéfice d'inventaire."*)
    SOURCE: Hérit. 2, 27 October 1570.

17. Jean de Croismare, councillor 1545-1567, president
    1567-1570
    Fortune left in 1570:
    Urban Property: 186l income (4 percent)
    Land: 1,027l income (23 percent)
    Rentes on Individuals: 2,753l income (62 percent)
    Rentes on the State: 518l income (11 percent)
    Total Income: 4,485l
    SOURCE: La Riv. Bourdet, 1796

18. Jean de La Porte, *father* of Georges de La Porte, coun-
    cillor 1568-1570, *procureur général* 1570-1597, presi-
    dent 1597-1613, and Quentin de La Porte, councillor
    1578-1579, then Master of Requests.

Fortune as divided in 1582:
   Urban Property: 1 house at Les Andelys, one-third
   of total value
   Land and *Rentes Foncières*: two-thirds of total
   value
   Total Value and Income: unknown
SOURCE: Tabel., 31 January 1582

19. Nicolas de La Place, councillor 1543-1561
   Acquisitions during his sons' minority, from the in-
   come of his estate, 1561-1583.
   Urban Property: about 4,800ł (24 percent)
   Land: none
   Rentes on Individuals: 3,300ł (17 percent)
   Rentes on the State: 11,500ł (59 percent)
   Total Value: 19,600ł, or yearly average of 891ł
SOURCE: Hérit. 2, 15 July 1583

20. Laurent Restault, councillor 1586-1641
   Fortune inherited in 1585:
   Urban Property: 2 houses at Pontaudemer (about
   10 percent)
   Lands: two major seigneuries, several other prop-
   erties (about 80 percent)
   Rentes: (about 10 percent)
   Total Net Income: 9,000ł
SOURCE: AD S-M, E, Fonds Restault.

21. Louis de La Reue, councillor 1573-1587
   Fortune left in 1587:
   Urban Property: 1 house in Rouen, about 8,000ł
   (16 percent)
   Land and Fiefs: about 40,000ł (79 percent)
   Rentes on Individuals: 2,330ł (5 percent)
   Rentes on the State: none
   Total Value: about 50,330ł
SOURCE: Hérit. 2, 28 February 1600

22. Nicolas Caillot, councillor 1572-1588
    Fortune left in 1588:
    Urban Property: 2 large houses, two adjoining small houses, and adjoining garden in suburb of Rouen
    Rentes Foncières: 100₺ capital
    Land: none
    Total Value: about 8,000₺
    SOURCE: Hérit. 2, 5 January 1591

23. Adrien de Croismare, councillor 1563-1568, first president Cour des Aides of Rouen, 1568-1589
    Fortune left in 1589:
    (1) *Propre* (Note: this represents what Adrien inherited from his father, Robert de Croismare, councillor 1529-1561, and his mother)
    Urban Property: one large residence, four rented houses, Rouen (value unknown)
    Land: 435 *acres*, about 5,000₺ revenue (57.8 percent of known income)
    Rentes Foncières: 95₺ revenue (1.1 percent of known income)
    Rentes on Individuals: 2,432₺ revenue (28.1 percent)
    Rentes on the State: 1,130₺ revenue (13.1 percent)
    Total Known Income: 8,657₺
    (2) *Conquêtes* (note: this represents Adrien's own acquisitions of real property)
    Urban Property: none
    Land: 935 *acres*, about 9,000₺ revenue (63 percent)
    Rentes Foncières: 28₺ revenue (0.2 percent)
    Rentes on Individuals: 4,815₺ revenue (33 percent)
    Rentes on the State: 545₺ revenue (4 percent)
    Total Income: 13,388₺
    SOURCE: Hérit. 2, 15 March 1595

24. Nicolas Rassent, councillor 1554-1594
    Real Income left in 1594: about 6,000₺

Source: Meubles 2, 1 March 1600 (calculated from widow's *douaire*)

25. Charles de La Roque, councillor 1581-1616
    Total Income in 1597: 2,000 *écus* (= 6,000ł)
    Source: Reg. sec., January-May, 1597, ff. 94-95

26. Robert Busquet, councillor 1578-1608
    Fortune in years 1598-1608:
       Urban Property: about 15,000ł value (9 percent)
       Land: about 135,000ł value (84 percent)
       Rentes: about 10,000ł value (6 percent)
       Total Value: 160,000ł
    Source: Busquet de Caumont, *Historie économique et sociale*, pp. 33, 36

27. Charles Maignart, president 1600-1621
    Fortune in about 1600:
       Urban Property: residence in Rouen, about 8,000ł
          (4 percent)
       Land and Fiefs: about 162,500ł (73 percent)
       Rentes on the State: 52,160ł (23 percent)
       Total Value: about 222,660ł
       Total Income: about 12,700ł
    Source: La Riv. Bourdet, 2105, 2902.

28. Jean Godart, *father* of Artus, councillor 1608-1618, and
    Jean-Baptiste, councillor 1609-1612, 1613-1640
    Fortune left in 1601:
       Urban Property: none
       Land and Fiefs: 3,500ł revenue (42 percent)
       Rentes Foncières: about 160ł revenue (2 percent)
       Rentes on Individuals: 1,515ł revenue (18 percent)
       Rentes on the State: 2,132ł (26 percent)
       "Parisis, greffes et tabellionages:" 994ł (12 percent)
       Total Income: 8,301ł
       Total Value: 119,610ł
    Source: AD S-M, 16J178

29. Marc Anthoine de Brèvedent, councillor 1600-1637
    Fortune inherited in 1603:
        Urban Property: ten houses in Rouen, including a
        large residence, 17,999ł value (45 percent)
        Rentes on Individuals: 10,100ł (25 percent)
        Rentes on the State: about 7,000ł (18 percent)
        Land and Fiefs: 28 *acres* land and meadow, and a
        small seigneurie worth roughly 5,000ł (13 per-
        cent)
        Total Value: 40,000ł
    SOURCE: Meubles 2, 5 September 1603, Hérit. 2, 27 Feb-
    ruary 1603

30. Claude Groulart, first president 1585-1607
    Fortune left in 1607:
        Urban Property: unknown (Groulart owned at
        least one large house in Rouen)
        Land and Fiefs: 13,100ł (60 percent of known
        revenues)
        Rentes: about 7,000ł income (33 percent)
        Other sources of Income: 1,600ł income (7 per-
        cent)
        Total Income: 21,700ł
        Total Value: about 375,000ł
    SOURCE: Meubles 2, 6 November 1613 (two acts on that
    date)

31. Louis de Maromme, councillor 1581-1614
    Fortune left in 1619:
        Urban Properties: about 30,000ł capital (43 per-
        cent)
        Land and *Rentes* in Rural Parishes: about 30,000ł
        (43 percent)
        Mills: two flour mills, one steel mill, about 10,000ł
        (15 percent)
        Rentes: none
        Total Value: about 70,000ł
    SOURCE: Hérit. 2, 9 November 1620

32. Pierre Puchot, councillor 1573-1619
   (1) Fathers' real fortune, 1566 (including acquisitions
       made during heirs' minority, but not including a
       substantial movable fortune):
       Urban Property: six houses at Rouen, worth about
           10,000ł (11 percent)
       Land: about 100 *acres*, worth about 10,000ł (11
           percent)
       Rentes on Individuals: 37,415ł capital (42 percent)
       Rentes on the State: 32,020ł capital (36 percent)
       Total Value: 89,935ł (note: Pierre is one of six
           heirs)
   (2) Fortune left at death, 1620:
       Urban Property: 1,760ł income (12 percent)
       Land: 7,200ł income (48 percent)
       Rentes on Individuals: 3,376ł (23 percent)
       Rentes on the State: 2,556ł income (17 percent)
       Total Income: 14,892ł
   SOURCE: Tabel., 21 September 1569, La Riv. Bourdet,
       1967, 3316

THE COSTS AND RETURNS OF OFFICE

BELOW are set out the prices of a series of royal offices at Rouen during the sixteenth and seventeenth centuries. They are presented in order to document an argument made above, concerning the complexities of the Rouennais market for offices, especially during the years before the Paulette. Whereas offices in the Parlement increased dramatically in price during the later sixteenth century, other offices increased very little or actually declined in price during the same years. Such stagnation, as noted above, characterized the office of treasurer general at Rouen: sold for 25,000ł in the mid-sixteenth century, such positions sold for between 21,300ł and 24,000ł in the 1580's, and for 30,600ł in 1602. The same pattern appears to have characterized councillorships in the *Présidial* of Rouen, which rose in value from 2,000ł to 4,500ł between 1569 and 1605, and positions as *procureur* in both the bailliage and Parlement of Rouen. The former were worth about 700ł in the early 1580's, about 1,000ł in the early 1600's, and 2,500ł in 1614; the latter actually declined in value from 2,000ł in 1586 to 1,000ł in 1601, then rose in the following decade, to about 4,500ł by 1614. It appears that only one set of offices followed the pattern set by offices in the Parlement, those in the Chancellerie of Rouen, as *notaire et secrétaire du roi*. The value of these approximately tripled between the 1550's and the late 1580's, and, after a brief decline during the League, their value continued to rise in the early seventeenth century.

Demand for each of these offices was governed by specific considerations. The number of treasurers general at Rouen was increasing steadily and rapidly during the second half of the sixteenth century, and this clearly reduced the position's appeal. The number of *procureurs* in the Parlement was apparently also increasing in these years, but above all that office was a subject of disputes between crown and Parlement which probably left its owners exceptionally insecure. Such considerations plainly affected the course of office prices, but they do not fully explain the contrast between changes in the price of offices in the Parlement and Chancellerie, on the one hand, and the price of other positions at Rouen; the crown had created numerous new positions in the Parlement itself in these years, and, as seen above in Chapter 1, there was ample reason for the *parlementaires* also to feel that the functions of their office might come under attack by the monarchy. The chief explanation for the difference, it appears, lies rather in the demands which specific categories of office might satisfy. In contrast to both treasurers general and *procureurs*, *parlementaires* and *secrétaires du roi* enjoyed high status because of their offices; in the case of the *secrétaires du roi*, indeed, this was nearly all that the office provided, for the actual functions associated with it were minimal.

It is in terms of these contrasting office prices that the economic importance of the Paulette seems most clearcut. For after 1604, when the annual tax on offices improved the ease with which positions might be inherited and encouraged speculative buying, offices whose prices had remained about constant during the late sixteenth century began to become considerably more expensive. The cost of a position as treasurer general increased by 50 percent between 1602 and 1606; that of a *procureur* in the Parlement, as noted above, quadrupled between 1601 and 1614. In contrast to the situation with regard to offices in the Parlement, for these less prestigious offices the Paulette was indeed the crucial cause of rising prices. One effect of the Paulette, in other words, was to bring a certain degree of unity to the economics of office. To a greater extent than during the sixteenth century, though still only partially, all offices in the seventeenth century followed general patterns of evolution. In this sense, at least, the *officiers* of the seventeenth century formed a group more unified in interests and experiences than their sixteenth-century predecessors.

In the case of most of these offices, full comparison with the profits which office in the Parlement offered is impossible. However, the accounts which Alexandre Du Moucel (brother of two councillors in the Parlement) kept concerning his position as *maître ordinaire* in Rouen's Chambre des Comptes do allow such comparison. Alexandre acquired the position from his father in early 1604, presented his letters to the Chambre des Comptes in October of that year, and was received in office a month later. At that time the position was worth 20,000ł (Hérit. 2, 23 September 1610). Over the following six years the average yearly income from the office was more than 2,400ł: of this total, just over 1,500ł came from "*gages et gros droitz,*" 687ł from "*épices ordinaires,*" 83ł from "*menu droits,*" and 68ł from rights to firewood. Du Moucel also enjoyed two rights in kind for which his accounts gave no monetary value: he received his salt tax-free, a right worth perhaps 50ł yearly, and he received six large wax candles yearly (La Riv. Bourdet, 2781). Someone buying the office in 1604, in other words, could expect a return of at least 12 percent on his investment. In the early seventeenth century, such a return was achieved by only the more assiduous and respected *parlementaires.* Historians have often suggested the superior profits which office in the fiscal administration offered, and this clearly was the case among Rouen's sovereign courts.

PRICES OF OFFICES

Date	Price	Source
		(1.) *Conseiller lai, Parlement de Rouen*
1543	2,000 *écus*	AD S-M, B, Parlement, Registre d'Audiences, 2 May 1543

Date	Price	Source
1551	1,500 *écus*	Tabel., 27 September 1551
		(estimate in marriage contract)
1554	5,750ł	BM MS Martainville Y23, f. 17v
1568	4,000ł	Hérit. 2, 1 January 1569
1568	6,750ł	Meubles 2, 7 May 1568
1571	3,900ł	Reg. sec. 1570-1571, f. 121v
1571	5,000ł	*Ibid.*, f. 201v
1571	2,500ł	*Ibid.*, f. 209r
1573	5,000ł	*Ibid.*, 1572-1574, f. 62v
1573	4,000ł	Hérit. 2, 31 October 1573
		(estimate in a marriage contract)
1575	5,000ł	Reg. sec., 1573-1579, ff. 453-454
1582	3,000 *écus*	Tabel., 24 May 1582
1588	3,900 *écus*	AD S-M, B, Requêtes du Palais, Contrats, "1597," 24 June 1590
1597	15,000ł	BM, MS Martainville Y24, VII, no. 26
1597	12,000ł	AD S-M, E, Fonds Bigot
1602	6,000 *écus*	Hérit. 2, 16 July 1602
1604	21,000ł	Meubles 2, 27 October 1604
1605	17,000ł	AD Eure, E1502, ff. 61-62
1608	27,300ł	Meubles 2, 19 May 1608
1619	42,000ł	*Ibid.*, 12 March 1619
1634	80,000ł	Roland Mousnier, *La vénalité des offices sous Henri IV et Louis XIII* (2nd ed., Paris, 1971), p. 360.

(2.) *Président à mortier, Parlement de Rouen*

Date	Price	Source
1555	10,000ł	BM MS Y214, V, 61
1570	6,000ł	Reg. sec., 1570-1571, ff. 1-2
1600	44,000ł	La Riv. Bourdet, 2105
1609	100,000ł	Mousnier, *La vénalité*, p. 363.
1623	120,000ł	*Ibid.*

(3.) *Trésorier général de France, Généralité de Rouen*

1557	25,000ł	Jean-Pierre Charmeil, *Les trésoriers de France à l'époque de la Fronde* (Paris, 1964), p. 33.
1570	25,000ł	*Ibid.*
1571	25,000ł	*Ibid.*
1581	24,000ł	*Ibid.*
1585	7,100 *écus*	Meubles 2, 9 September 1585
1602	10,200 *écus*	Charmeil, *Les trésoriers de France*, p. 33.
1606	45,600ł	Meubles 2, 16 November 1606
1621	65,000ł	Charmeil, *Les trésoriers de France*, p. 33.
1626	72,000ł	*Ibid.*
1627	55,200ł	*Ibid.*

(4.) *Notaire secrétaire du roi, Chancellerie de Rouen*

1551	1,500 *écus*	Tabel., 27 September 1551 (estimate in a marriage contract)
1580 (audiencier)	1,666⅔ *écus*	Meubles 2, 30 March 1580
1587 (audiencier)	3,666⅔ *écus*	Hérit. 2, 27 October 1587
1588 (contrôleur)	7,500ł	*Ibid.*, 11 January 1588
1594 (contrôleur)	1,000 *écus*	Meubles 2, 4 February 1602
1602 (contrôleur)	9,000ł	Hérit. 2, 6 December 1602
1603 (audiencier)	11,400ł	Meubles 2, 6 February 1603
1604 (audiencier)	13,300ł	Hérit. 2, 2 January 1604
1618 (contrôleur)	21,000ł	Meubles 2, 12 November 1618

Date	Price	Source

(5.) *Conseiller du roi au Bailliage et Siège Présidial de Rouen*

1569	2,000ł	Hérit. 2, 1 January 1569
1574	400 *écus*	Reg. sec., 1572-1574, f. 82v
1574	500 *écus*	*Ibid.*, f. 83r
1604	3,375ł	Hérit. 2, 3 May 1604
1605	4,500ł	Meubles 2, 5 November 1605

(6.) *Lieutenant particulier, Bailliage de Rouen*

| 1571 | 3,500ł | Reg. sec., 1570-1571, 18 May 1571 |

(7.) *Procureur commun au Bailliage,*
Siège Présidial et Vicomté de Rouen

1580	243⅓ *écus*	Meubles 2, 26 April 1580
1585	220 *écus*	*Ibid.*, 2 October 1585
1587	300 *écus*	*Ibid.*, 25 June 1587
1592	133⅓ *écus*	AD S-M, E, Tabellionage de Rouen, Meubles, 1ère série, 16 June 1592
1600	333⅓ *écus*	Meubles 2, 30 January 1600
1603	1,100ł	*Ibid.*, 9 December 1603
1614	2,500ł	Hérit. 2, 31 January 1614

(8.) *Procureur au Parlement de Rouen*

1586	2,000ł	Hérit. 2, 12 March 1587
1587	500 *écus*	Meubles 2, 9 July 1588
1601	333⅓ *écus*	*Ibid.*, 6 October 1601
1604	2,100ł	La Riv. Bourdet, 2105
1614	4,700ł	Meubles 2, 26 February 1614
1614	4,500ł	Hérit. 2, 26 February 1614

(9.) *Auditeur, Chambre des Comptes de Rouen*

1584	2,666⅔ *écus*	Hérit. 2, 14 December 1584
1585	2,000 *écus*	Meubles 2, 27 November 1585
1595	2,766⅔ *écus*	*Ibid.*, 3 November 1595
1599	2,833⅓ *écus*	*Ibid.*, 31 January 1600

(10.) *Correcteur, Chambre des Comptes de Rouen*

1580	2,400 *écus*	Meubles 2, 21 November 1600
1588	2,900 *écus*	*Ibid.*, 27 July 1588
1600	3,000 *écus*	*Ibid.*, 21 November 1600

(11.) *Maître ordinaire, Chambre des Comptes de Rouen*

1600	17,000ł	Hérit. 2, 5 January 1600
1601	19,000ł	AD S-M, 16J3, f. 2v.
1604	20,000ł	Hérit. 2, 23 September 1610

SEIGNEURIAL REVENUES IN NINE
UPPER NORMAN ESTATES

1. BOURDENY, 1507 (BAUQUEMARE)

Rentes:	150ł (34.9 percent)
Mills:	90ł (20.9 percent)
Low Justice:	10ł (2.3 percent)
Land:	180ł (41.9 percent)
	————
	430ł

2. BEUZEMOUCHEL, 1528-1537 (MOY)

Rentes:	260ł (39.9 percent)
Mill:	35ł (5.4 percent)
Land:	340ł (52.1 percent)
Treizièmes:	17ł (2.6 percent)
	————
	652ł

3. MONTIVILLIERS, 1557-1558 (CONVENT OF MONTIVILLIERS)

Rentes:	1,500ł (30.1 percent)
Mills:	500ł (10.0 percent)
Tithes:	2,350ł (47.2 percent)
Coutûmes (tax)	250ł (5.0 percent)
Land:	380ł (7.6 percent)
	————
	4,980ł

4. La Rivière Bourdet, ca. 1570 (Maignart and Pardieu)

Rentes:	246ł (11.2 percent)
Mill:	38ł (1.7 percent)
Wood:	190ł (8.7 percent)
Land:	1,720ł (78.4 percent)

2,194ł

5. Thibouville and Calletot, ca. 1570 (Maignart)

Rentes:	177ł (16.8 percent)
Mills:	40ł (3.8 percent)
Land:	836ł (79.4 percent)

1,053ł

6. Bec Crespin, 1572-1573 (Duc d'Aumale)

Rentes:	1,800ł (44.4 percent)
Mills:	350ł (8.6 percent)
Land:	1,900ł (46.9 percent)

4,050ł

7. Belbeuf, 1597 (Godart)

Rentes:	455ł (36.3 percent)
Land:	799ł (63.7 percent)

1,254ł

8. Cabot, 1597 (Godart)

Rentes:	41ł (17.0 percent)
Land:	200ł (83.0 percent)

241ł

9. Normare, 1597 (Godart)

Rentes:	131ł (24.7 percent)
Land:	400ł (75.3 percent)
	———
	531ł

Source: AD S-M, 16J8:9; La Riv. Bourdet, 865, 1772; Jacques Bottin, *Vision du monde rural à travers une seigneurie. L'abbaye de Montivilliers 1540-1660* (Unpublished Thesis, École des Chartes, 1973), pp. 95-97; AD S-M, E, Fonds Romé du Bec, Accounts, 1572-1573; Hérit. 2, 13 January 1597.

PARLEMENTAIRES AND THE LANDS
OF THE CHURCH

BEGINNING in 1563, in response both to widely expressed demands and to the financial drain of the civil wars, the French monarchy and church collaborated in the sale of a substantial amount of church property. In all there were seven sales, lasting through 1588. Few historians have suggested that these sales represented a massive transfer of property, in any way comparable to the English sales of church property in the sixteenth century or to the French and Spanish sales of the eighteenth. Historians have suggested, however, that the sales of church property might serve as guide to the groups most successful in acquiring properties during the tumultuous sixteenth century (thus Jean Jacquart, *La crise rurale en Ile de France, 1550-1670* [Paris, 1974], p. 245). In the regions where they have been studied, these sales have pointed chiefly to the successes of the *noblesse de robe*, at least insofar as the purchase of seigneurial property is concerned. For Jean Jacquart (*La crise rurale*, pp. 245-247) and Emmanuel LeRoy Ladurie (*Les paysans de Languedoc*, 2 vols. [2nd ed., Paris-The Hague, n.d.], I, 371), success in the church land sales essentially reflected the capacity of the *noblesse de robe* for dealing with the difficult economic conditions of the sixteenth century; for Victor Carrière, on the other hand, such successes resulted mainly from "the collusions everywhere to be found between the magistracy and the huguenots" (*Introduction aux études d'histoire ecclésiastique locale*, 3 vols. [Paris, 1936], III, 418).

There is thus considerable interest in analyzing the *parlementaires*' role in the sales of church property. Since the main concern here is with the transfer of larger properties, this inquiry is limited to the larger and more heavily taxed institutions, defined here as those which sold a total of more than 10,000l of property during the sales. Eleven institutions in the diocese of Rouen were thus heavily taxed: the archbishop of Rouen and the monasteries of St. Ouen, Bec Hellouin, Jumièges, St. Wandrille, Fécamp, Mortemer, St. Georges de Boscherville, Beaubec, Vallasse, and Ste. Catherine du Mont. Together their properties accounted for slightly over half of the total value of the properties sold in the diocese.

Two points should be made about these sales before we turn to the *parlementaires'* participation in them. First, in the diocese of Rouen as in other areas of France, the quantitative impact of the sales was limited. Between 1569 and 1586, all ecclesiastical institutions in the diocese were assessed a total of 350,000l; these impositions did not have to be met through the sale of land, and institutions very often simply paid cash when their assessments were sufficiently low. The first group of sales, in 1563, *did* require that all institutions sell some property, and added about 250,000l to the total imposition on the church. But institutions were given considerable opportunity to buy back properties sold in 1563, and the total imposition on the diocese during the twenty-five years over which the sales extended amounted to roughly the value of twenty substantial seigneuries.

Secondly, it is not always possible to know either who bought properties or how much property they were able to retain. The crown periodically granted the church the right to repurchase alienated properties, and these repurchases have usually not left traces in the registers of sales. And, at least in the later sales, not all purchases were made in the name of the real buyer. Thus, among the payments received after 1594 for land purchased in 1586 were payments by Claude Groulart, the Parlement's first president, and Nicolas Le Roux, president *à mortier* from 1602, both of whom

344

had purchased large properties anonymously, through agents: a practice that may have reflected the particular religious tensions of the later 1580's (AN G8 1250).

The full impact of the church land sales, then, cannot be completely known. Within the limits which the documents pose, however, it is possible to assess the gains which *parlementaires* and other officials made from the sales. In the diocese of Rouen as elsewhere in France, these groups certainly received an impressive share. The eleven most heavily taxed institutions in the diocese sold a total of 313,-466ł worth of property during the course of the sales; slightly over one-fourth of this total (85,558ł, or 27.3 percent) went to royal officials. Of the 181 separate sales made by these institutions, thirty-seven were made to officials (20.4 percent of the total); and of the forty-eight fiefs which these institutions sold, just one-third went to royal officials. The *parlementaires* themselves had an especially impressive share in these purchases. In terms of the value of properties sold, they accounted for 43 percent of the officials' total share; just under one-half of all the sales to officials (18 of 37) went to them; and they bought exactly one-half of the fiefs (8 of 16) which went to the officials.

The remaining purchasers formed a varied group. Lawyers, bourgeois, peasants, cathedral canons, and country gentlemen all received some share of the properties sold; ecclesiastical institutions themselves, such as the cathedral chapter of Rouen, also bought properties. In upper Normandy as in the region of Paris, though, the most conspicuous purchasers after the royal officials were members of the upper aristocracy. Only 8 purchases went to members of the upper aristocracy, but these accounted for 16 percent of the total value sold (50,866ł); the aristocracy bought considerably more than the value of the 18 *parlementaire* purchases (worth 36,975ł), and slightly more than the value of all purchases by members of the sovereign courts (50,435ł). Most striking, all 8 purchases by the upper aristocracy were fiefs, some of them substantial ones.

If the church land sales point to the successes which *parlementaires* and other officials enjoyed in the land market of the sixteenth century, then, they suggest equally the prosperity of the high aristocracy. It was this group, apparently, who acquired the most attractive properties which the church offered. A further consideration suggests also the limits on the *noblesse de robe*'s domination of the sales. A disproportionate share of the church lands went to the wealthiest and most powerful officials. Thus, among the 18 sales to *parlementaires*, 8 went to presidents, a group that included less than one-fifteenth of the court's membership. During the twenty-five years in which the sales were conducted, only 8 of the Parlement's councillors had any share in the church's property.

The impact of the church land sales of the later sixteenth century thus conformed closely to what has been seen above about the *parlementaires*' economic position. On the one hand, their economic role within the province was conspicuously growing during the century. On the other hand, there was a considerable distance between the most successful magistrates, notably the presidents, and the ordinary councillors; it was the former, benefiting from higher salaries and greater chances for important services to the king, whose wealth grew most dramatically during the century. Examination of the church land sales suggests, finally, the limited threat which the magistrates posed to the higher aristocracy. If the sales are an adequate indicator of economic success and failure over the century, it would appear that the wealth of the high aristocracy grew as quickly as that of the *noblesse de robe*.

Source: AN G81246, 1247, 1248, 1249, 1250.

PARLEMENTAIRE MARRIAGE

1. *Sample Documents*

THE three marriage contracts which follow (the first from 1573, the second from 1599, and the third from 1603) are intended to suggest the nature of this document and something of its evolution in the later sixteenth century, especially its evolution toward greater complexity, ostentation, and concern to protect dynastic continuity. The third contract, drawn from the high Norman aristocracy, is presented in order to suggest differences between the *noblesse de robe* and the *noblesse d'épée* in the early seventeenth century. Parental control is more prominently displayed in this contract, and the bride's dowry consists entirely of real property, suggesting the *noblesse d'épée*'s difficulties in raising funds.

16 JULY 1573

In order to achieve the marriage which, with God's pleasure, will be made and celebrated in the holy church between *noble homme* Master Nicolas Thomas, lord of Verdun and of La Fontelaye, councillor of the king and lieutenant general in the jurisdiction of the Admiralty of France in the Table de Marbre of the Palais at Rouen (and councillor in the Parlement 1576-1578, *avocat général* 1578-1602, and *président à mortier* 1602-1621), and Marie de La Haye, daughter of the late *honorable homme* Guillaume de La Haye bourgeois of this city of Rouen and of Jeanne Louis, the following agreements and promises have been made: Namely, that the said La Haye, mother of the said Marie, has promised to give and make over the day before the wedding the sum of 12,000 *livres*, of which 5,000 *livres* will be invested in 500 *livres rente* to hold the name, side, and line of the said Marie and of her heirs; and also the said La Haye has promised to give the said Marie her daughter her good dress, bed, covering, and whatever goes with it, together with her linen, all at the discretion of the said La Haye. In exchange for which the said Thomas and Marie de La Haye have given up every and any right which she might have claimed in the succession both liquid and real of the said late La Haye in favor of Georges de La Haye, brother of the said Marie—with the condition, however, that if by virtue of Marie's right to a *mariage avenant* she ought to receive more than the said sum of 12,000 *livres*, in view of the wealth and capacities of the said late La Haye, Thomas will be allowed to claim and demand it, and it will be given to him without this present contract in any way limiting his rights. And by the said Thomas has been and is established a customary jointure on all his properties and on any that may fall to him in the future. At this present *noble homme monsieur* Master Nicolas Rassent, councillor of the king our lord in his court of Parlement at Rouen, who has promised that the said Thomas owes nothing and pledges him for all debts up to this date. And also it is understood that in case repurchase is made of the said 500 *livres rente* or part of it to the said Thomas, he will be required and has obliged himself to employ the whole in a *rente* or property well and sufficiently secured, of which he remains the guarantor, to hold the name, side and line of the said Marie de La Haye and her heirs.

(The names of six witnesses and their signatures follow.)

SOURCE: Hérit. 2, 30 August 1603

20 JUNE 1599

In order to achieve the contract of marriage which, with God's pleasure, will be made and celebrated in the Catholic, apostolic, and Roman church between *noble homme* Master Gilles Anzeray, lord of Boisnormant, councillor and *avocat général* of the king in his court of Parlement at Normandy, elder son and presumptive heir of *messire* François Anzeray, lord of Courvaudon, Savery, and Duralt, councillor of the king in his *conseil privé et d'état* and president in the said court of Parlement of Normandy, and of the late *dame* Marie Damours daughter of the late *messire* Nicolas Damours, in his lifetime also councillor of the king in the said councils (*sic*) and president in the said court of Parlement, on one side; and *damoiselle* Marguerite Auber, oldest daughter and also partial heiress of the late *noble homme* Guillaume Auber, in his lifetime lord of Gouville, Claville, and Boscdurand, and of *damoiselle* Marthe Rassent, at present widow of the said *defunct* and principal guardian of the said *damoiselle* her daughter. The following agreements have been made in the presence of and by the counsel of the said lord president father and of the said lady mother and guardian and other relatives and friends named below: Namely, to marry each other in good and lawful marriage if God and our mother the holy church consent to it. In favor of which marriage the said lord president has recognized the said lord his son as his elder son and chief heir presumptive, to whom he has given and gives by advancement of succession the sum of 2,000 *livres* of revenue and promises specially to furnish and make over to the said couple good and sound *rentes* and lands, up to the value of the said 2,000 *livres* revenue each year, in the nearest and most suitable places for the profit and use of the said couple; the enjoyment of the said revenue is to begin on the day of the celebration of the said marriage. Of this sum of 2,000 *livres* of revenue there will be taken and from the present has been established and assigned, without any other demand being required, the sum of 1,000 *livres* revenue yearly as the jointure of the said *damoiselle* the bride, should this be required before the death of the said lord president and while awaiting a full jointure on his entire succession, at the said *damoiselle*'s choice (*sic*). And moreover, for the love which the said lord president has for the said couple, it has been agreed that when it pleases the lord president to let take effect, at the pleasure of the king, the letters of reversion (*survivance*) that he has obtained for his position as president in favor of the said lord of Boisnormant, his son, the said lord of Boisnormant will be required to give over and resign into the hands of the said lord president his father or to whoever pleases him, his said position as councillor and *avocat général*, for the said lord president to dispose of as he wishes, as the entire and only recompense for his said position as president—with the proviso that for the payment for the position of councillor and *avocat général* the said lord of Boisnormant has obliged himself and agreed to pay *monsieur* Paschal, who resigned the position to him, the sum of 4,000 *écus* remaining from their agreed price; and it has been agreed that if the said couple after the marriage make their residence for a year and a day or longer in the house of the said lord president, [though] at his will, there will be no community and society of property between them. And by the said *damoiselle* Marthe Rassent principal guardian of the said *damoiselle* her daughter, with the counsel, agreement, and consent of (the names of nine relatives follow), all of them present at this agreement and signed below, it has been agreed that on the day that the marriage is consummated the said couple will enter on the full possession and enjoyment of whatever part and share might belong to the said *damoiselle* in both the real and the liquid succession of the said late lord of Gouville her father, for the said couple to enjoy following the custom. And in order to support the cost of the said marriage has been granted as *don mobil* to the said groom the sum of 2,000 *écus soleil*, of which sum the said *damoiselle* mother has promised to furnish and pay the day before the wedding the sum of 1,000 *écus sol* from moneys coming from the liquid assets of the said *damoiselle* her daughter, insofar as she has the said sum by the closing up of her [daughter's] accounts. And the remaining 1,000 *écus* will be taken by the said lord groom from the debts and payments owed the said property and revenue; the said lord groom will have two-thirds of the remainder of the said debts, the other third remaining for the profit of the said *damoiselle* to be employed in *rente* or property in her name and line; these debts he will pursue as he sees fit. In addition to these agreements the said *damoiselle* mother, for the love which she has for the said couple, has promised to give and deliver to them before the said marriage the sum of 1,000 *écus* in rings and other moveables, at her discretion. By means of these donations, it has been agreed and accorded that should the said lord of Boisnormant die before the said *damoiselle* bride, she will receive before the succession is divided (*par préciput*), freely, and exempt from any debts and without diminishing her other rights, her rings and jewels or the sum of 1,000 *écus*, at her choice; and further she will receive her furnished room, clothing, and other goods that she has used. Without all of these donations, promises, agreements, and obligations the said marriage would not thus have been contracted between the said parties.

(Signatures of those present follow.)

SOURCE: Hérit. 2, 17 April 1600

5 JUNE 1603

In the contract of marriage hoped for between *messire* Adrian sire de Bréaulté, chevalier, lord of Herodeville, younger son of *hault et puissant seigneur* Adrian sire de Bréaulté, lord and castellan of Neuville, hereditary viscount of Hotot, knight of the king's order, captain of fifty men at arms of his ordonnances, colonel general of the *arrière bans* of Normandy, and of *noble et puissante dame* Suzanne de Monchy, on one side, and *damoiselle* Françoise de Roncherolles, daughter of *haut et puissant seigneur messire* Pierre de Roncherolles, lord and baron of Pont St. Pierre, also a knight of the king's order, captain of fifty men at arms of his ordonnances, seneschal and governor of Ponthieu, and of *noble et puissante dame* Charlotte de Moy, on the other, the following agreements have been made: Namely, that the said Adrian sire de Bréaulté, lord of Herodeville, and the said Françoise de Roncherolles, with the advice, counsel, and consent of the said lords and ladies their fathers and mothers, have promised to wed each other according to the laws of the Catholic, apostolic, and Roman church, at the convenience (*à la commodité*) of the said lords and ladies. In favor of this marriage the said lord of Bréaulté and of Neuville has recognized the said lord of Herodeville, the groom, as his younger son and heir to succeed him according to the customs of the places [where his properties are situated], in what remains to him of property at the time of his death. And at present, in the form of an advancement of succession, the said lord of Bréaulté has given the said lord of Herodeville his son the property and enjoyment of the properties and seigneuries of La Muldraguiere, Conteville, Dorville, St. Martin, Le Valpain, La Gazelliere, Dame Philippes, and Le Valdery, in their entirety, the whole exempt from any obligations or debts; these properties, however, the said lord of Herodeville cannot sell or mortgage during the lifetime of the said lord of Bréaulté without his consent. Also the said lady of Bréaulté has similarly recognized the said groom as her younger son and presumptive heir for whatever may belong to her according to the customs and for the possessions she will leave at her death. And the said lord of Herodeville has granted to the said *damoiselle*, bride, a full jointure after the death of the said lord and lady of Bréaulté, set on whatever would fall to him of their successions. And while awaiting her full jointure she will have, and her jointure has been limited to, 2,000 *livres* yearly, which the said lord of Bréaulté father has obliged himself to furnish, make good, and guarantee to the said *damoiselle* from the day of the said groom's decease, without her having to make more specific demand or action; she will have also her residence in the principal house (*maison, manoir et pourprie*) of the said seigneurie of Valdery. And on the part of the said lord and lady of Pont St.

Pierre, the said lady duly authorized by the said lord her husband, has been given to the said couple, in favor of the said marriage, the property and seigneurie of Corbon, with its patronage and all its circumstances and dependencies, free of all debts, as the part and share which the said *damoiselle* may claim in their successions; in exchange, she has renounced these in favor of *messire* Pierre de Roncherolles, chevalier, lord of Bouchevillier, her older brother, and his heirs: with the provision that if he should die without children, the said successions will be divided between the said bride and her younger sister, according to the customs, the bride having returned to the succession what she has been given in marriage. The said lord and lady of Pont St. Pierre have retained for themselves and the said lord of Bouchevillier their son the right of reclaiming the property and seigneurie of Corbon within five years from the celebration of the marriage by paying the said couple the sum of 60,000 *livres*. From this property the said lord and lady of Pont St. Pierre have agreed that the said lord of Herodeville receive as *don mobil* 15,000 *livres*; and should its repurchase take place the remainder, amounting to 45,000 *livres*, is from the present time constituted and assigned as a *rente* on all the properties of the said lords of Bréaulté and Herodeville, with each fully responsible for it. And the said lord and lady of Pont St. Pierre have promised to give the said *damoiselle* their daughter clothing suited to her station. These clothes, as well as her rings, jewels and other articles in her personal use, with her furnished room, carriage, and horses she will receive and take for her profit before the succession is divided (*par préciput*) and free of any obligations and debts in the event that the said lord of Herodeville dies before her, without restricting the *damoiselle* in the other rights which the custom gives wives over the possessions of their deceased husbands. And because the said property of Corbon is of the *propre* of the said lady of Pont St. Pierre, the said baron, her husband, has granted and from the present grants her replacement of the sum of 40,000 *livres* on all his possessions, lands, and seigneuries. For the remainder the said lady, authorized as above by the said lord her husband, has made a gift of it to the said couple, as is said above. And the said lord and lady of Pont St. Pierre have promised to secure consent to the present contract from the said lord of Boucheviller their son. The whole done in the presence and with the consent of . . . (nine names follow) all close relatives and friends of the said couple.

(Signatures follow.)

SOURCE: Hérit. 2, 5 June 1603.

2. *Marriages of* Parlementaires *and their Daughters*
(*Asterisks indicate presidents or other* gens du roi.)

a. *Marriages between* parlementaires *and* parlementaire
daughters

Date	Future Husband/ Future Bride	Source
1528	Estienne Bernard Marie Feu*	Tabel., 9 July 1528
1535	Jacques Centsols Barbe Quesnel	*Ibid.*, 24 April 1540
1541	Jean de Bonshoms Françoise de Becdelièvre	*Ibid.*, 30 April 1542
1549	Louis Thibault Florymonde Feu*	*Ibid.*, 18 July 1549
1549	Jean de Quièvremont Marie Le Roux	*Ibid.*, 3 April 1565 (old style)
1553	Jean Bouchard Marie Bigot*	*Ibid.*, 24 October 1553
1555	Anthoine de Civille Françoise Quesnel	Hérit. 2, 1 January 1554 (old style)
1559	Pierre Charles Marthe de Croismare*	Tabel., 19 November 1572

354

1568   Jean Paul Le Conte*   *Ibid.*, 15 August 1569
        Madallaine de Croismare* (baptized 31 January 1552:
            AD S-M, Parish Registers, St. Laurent, Rouen)
1570   François Anzeray*   Hérit. 2, 23 June 1571
        Marie Damours*
1572   Romain de Boivin   Meubles 2, 17 June 1602
        Anne Péricard*
1589   Louis Garin   Hérit. 2, 12 February 1589
        Margueritte Paixdecoeur (baptized 29 December
            1566: AD S-M, Parish Registers, St. Laurent,
            Rouen)
1597   Jacques de Civille   Hérit. 2, 25 February 1597
        Marie Duval
1602   Alfonce Jubert   Hérit. 2, 31 January 1603
            (baptized 21 April 1578: AD S-M, Parish
            Registers, St. Laurent, Rouen)
        Marie Maignart* (born 1586: inscription, Église
            Collégiale, Vernon)
1602   Raoul Bretel*   Hérit. 2, 17 January 1603
        Isabeau Groulart* (born 1 November 1586: BM MS
            Martainville Y24, 1, f. 26)
1602   Claude Groulart   Hérit. 2, 17 January 1603
            (born 1580: BM MS Martainville Y24, 1, f. 26)
        Catherine Bretel*
1608   Jean Hallé   Hérit. 2, 23 April 1608
        Marguerite
        Groulart*
1609   Jean Baptiste Le Brun   Hérit. 2, 29 January 1610
        Catherine de Bauquemare (baptized 3 July 1587: AD
            S-M, Parish Registers St. Lô, Rouen)

b. *Other* parlementaire *marriages*

1500   Louis de   Tabel., 23 December 1503
            Quièvremont
        Katherine Auber
1505   Pierre Le Lieur   AD Eure, E2474
        Lucque Jubert

Date	Future Husband/ Future Bride	Source
1513	René de Becdelièvre Marie Osmont	BN, Carrés de d'Hozier, 77
1529	Nicole Le Sueur Françoise de Coursillon	Tabel., 28 April 1534
1529	Pierre Dufour Marie Dubosc	*Ibid.*, 27 September 1551
1531	Louis Petremol* Claude du Buisson	*Ibid.*, 27 April 1540
1536	Jean de Croismare* Marie Gombault	*Ibid.*, 29 November 1536
1538	René de Becdelièvre Marguerite de Bonshoms	*Ibid.*, 21 September 1538
1542	Jean Dubosc Katherine Guyot	*Ibid.*, 22 April 1542
1548	Claude Auvray Catherine Deschamps	Contrôle Normand, 1607, ff. 722-725
1548	Nicolas de La Place Louise Thiboust	AN, Y 495, ff. 413-414
1552	Charles Le Verrier Claude Roger	Tabel., 22 February 1580
1552	François de Villy Jeanne Duval	*Ibid.*, 31 March 1582
1553	Robert Le Roux Madeleine de Valles	Hérit. 2, 31 May 1557; Archives d'Esneval, Acquigny
1557	Pierre Le Jumel* Madeleine Eude	Hérit. 2, 5 May 1598
1563	Jean Busquet Marthe Le Roux	Tabel., 4 January 1578
1567	Nicolas Romé Isabeau de Hanivel	Hérit. 2, 26 January 1613
1569	Claude Hédiart Jeanne Le Seigneur	Tabel., 15 October 1570
1570	Adrien Toustain Françoise de Hanivel	Hérit. 2, 12 May 1571

1570	Robert Tourmente Barbe Lefebvre	Hérit. 2, 6 March 1573
1570	Guillaume de Pinchemont Jeanne Osmont	Tabel., 20 May 1570
1570	Louis Le Masson	*Ibid.*, 23 October 1570

1570   Marie de Bauquemare (baptized 2 December 1554: AD S-M, Parish Registers, St. Laurent, Rouen)

1571	Georges de La Porte* Marie Dufour	Tabel., 22 September 1571
1572	Nicolas Caillot Catherine Deschamps	*Ibid.*, 28 September 1572
1573	Nicolas Thomas* Marie de La Haye	Hérit. 2, 30 August 1603
1573	Louis de La Reue Anne Piedeleu	*Ibid.*, 28 February 1600
1576	Robert Le Roux Barbe Guiffart	Archives d'Esneval, Acquigny
1576	Laurent Romé	Hérit. 2, 10 April 1577

(born 1 July 1551: AD S-M, 1F39, pp. 38-39)
Marguerite Halley

1578	Anthoine Caradas Madeleine Lefebvre	Hérit. 2, 7 January 1579
1579	Pierre Puchot Jeanne Labbé	Tabel., 14 June 1579
1580	Quentin de La Porte Madeleine Asselin	La Riv. Bourdet, 2065
1581	Jean Cavelier Marie Margas	Hérit. 2, 19 April 1602
1582	Charles de Grouchet Catherine Jubert	Tabel., 23 May 1582
1582	Charles Maignart*	Hérit. 2, 22 May 1583

(born 31 November 1562: BM MS Martainville Y24, 1, f. 82)
Madeleine Voisin

1584	Laurent Godefroy Marie Lefebvre	Hérit. 2, 12 May 1584

Date	Future Husband/ Future Bride	Source
1584	Claude Groulart* (born 1551: BM MS Martainville Y24, I, f. 26) Barbe Guiffart	*Ibid.*, 2 January 1587
1584	Jacques Dyel Marie Dujardin	Hérit. 2, 15 January 1595
1586	Nicolas Le Roux* Catherine Olivier	AN, Minutier Central, XXIV, 165, 10 February 1586
1586	Baptiste Le Chandelier Marie de Bailleul	Hérit. 2, 20 September 1586
1589	Laurent Romé Marguerite Burguet	*Ibid.*, 20 July 1601, 6 October 1604
1594	Gallien de Bethencourt Marie Ygou	*Ibid.*, 10 September 1598
1597	Charles Maignart* Catherine de Gouel	*Ibid.*, 19 April 1597
1597	Jean Le Cornu Madeleine de Restault	*Ibid.*, 6 October 1597
1599	Gilles Anzeray* Marguerite Auber	*Ibid.*, 17 April 1600
1599	Robert Le Roux (born 1572: BM MS Martainville Y24, II, 2, f. 42) Marie de Bellièvre	Archives d'Esneval, Acquigny
1601	Robert Le Prévost Marguerite Mustel	AD S-M, B, Requêtes du Palais, Contrats, 20 September 1601
1604	Jacques Rocque Catherine Le Blanc	Hérit. 2, 24 February 1604
1604	Marc Anthoine de Brèvedent Jeanne Le Blanc	*Ibid.*, 23 October 1604

1605	Mathurin de Blays Marie Tirel	*Ibid.*, 20 July 1605
1605	Pierre de Brinon Anthoinette Restault	Meubles 2, 23 November 1605
1606	Alexandre Bouchard Rachel Du Moucel	Hérit. 2, 14 February 1606
1608	Charles Baudry Madeleine d'Ambray	*Ibid.*, 25 November 1608
1608	Isambart Busquet Barbe Bauldry	AD S-M, Contrôle Normand, 1608
1608	Robert Toustain Anne Mariage	AD S-M, E, Tabellionage de Rouen, Mariages, Minutier Meslé, 1500-1600 (*sic*), 12 December 1608
1609	Nicolas Grimoult Marie Le Goix	Hérit. 2, 18 September 1610
1609	Artus Godart Isabeau de Vymont	*Ibid.*, 18 July 1609
1610	Emery de Guéribout Isabel de Challon	AD Eure, E827

c. *Other marriages of* parlementaires' *daughters*

Date	Future Bride/ Future Husband	Source
1479	Anthoinette Toustain Jean Erquemboure	Tabel., 3 May 1480
1493	Catherine Destain François de Lombelon	AD Eure, E796
1507	Laurente Toustain Mathieu Aubert	Tabel., 27 April 1507
1507	Anne de Croismare Guillaume Toustain	BN, Carrés de d'Hozier, 214
1512	Jeanne Boislevesque Noel Le Barge	Tabel., 7 May 1513

Date	Future Bride/ Future Husband	Source
1521	Barbe Caradas* Jacques de Quincarnon	AD S-M, E, Tabellionage de Rouen, Meubles, 1ère série, 6 February 1546
1524	Florence Bordel* Louis Roussel	Tabel., 28 May 1526
1530	Geneviève Le Lieur Jacques Le Grant	Ibid., 16 August 1530
1537	Anne Becdelièvre Jacques Vastel	Ibid., 20 October 1537
1540	Marguerite Patris Charles Le Paulmier	Ibid., 8 May 1542
1548	Marguerite de Croismare Michel de Mesnildo	Hérit. 2, 11 July 1548
1549	Marie Mesnage Simon de Moustiers	Tabel., 25 January 1575
1551	Anne Dufour Guillaume de La Mare	Ibid., 27 September 1551
1554	Marie de Cormeilles* François de Montgomery	Ibid., 19 August 1569
1554	Anne Lefebvre François de La Place	Hérit. 2, 9 January 1554 (old style)
1555	Marie de Croismare Jean de Tournebu	Tabel., 11 August 1555
1557	Marie Jubert Jean Du Moucel	Ibid., 20 April 1558
1557	Marie de Croismare* Jean Maignart	La Riv. Bourdet, 1430
1566	Héleine Auvray Richard Le Gras	AD S-M, Contrôle Normand, 1607, ff. 722-725
1572	Catherine Toustain (baptized 19 May 1552: AD S-M, Parish Registers, St. Laurent, Rouen) Jean Duquesne	Hérit. 2, 16 July 1572

1573	Catherine Cavelier Robert de Felius	AD Eure, E1324, f. 394
1574	Anne Jubert Jacques Dubosc	Hérit. 2, 25 October 1581
1575	Catherine de Bauquemare* François de Saussay	Ibid., 2 September 1575
1575	Marthe Rassent Guillaume Auber	Ibid., 5 May 1577
1575	Anne Cavelier André Le Sens	Ibid., 11 February 1587
1579	Anne Dufay Pierre Deschamps	Ibid., 3 March 1584
1579	Madeleine Jubert Jean Dufay	Tabel., 7 February 1582
1581	Catherine Le Prévost Pierre de Fry	Hérit. 2, 6 August 1581
1583	Charlotte de Bauquemare* (baptized 15 April 1563: AD S-M, Parish Registers, St. Laurent, Rouen) Mathurin Gillain	Ibid., 8 January 1584
1588	Marie Dufay André de Faicterau	Hérit. 2, 24 May 1588
1588	Hélène Bouchard Philippe de Chefderue	Ibid., 1 February 1589
1589	Marie Jubert Barthélémy du Thuict	Ibid., 27 February 1595
1593	Katherine Toustain Anthoine de Mesniel	Ibid., 7 May 1593
1594	Marie Romé (baptized 6 April 1574: ibid., pp. 59-62) Hugues d'Athenous	AD S-M, 1F39, p. 60, n.2
1594	Marguerite Le Jumel* Gabriel de Grieu	Hérit. 2, 17 January 1598

Date	Future Bride/ Future Husband	Source
1595	Marguerite Le Masson Pierre Lhermitte	*Ibid.*, 22 July 1595
1595	Madeleine Cavelier Guillaume Hue	*Ibid.*, 26 May 1598; AD Eure, E1438, f. 402
1596	Marie Bretel* Jean Le Seigneur	Hérit. 2, 1 March 1601
1597	Barbe Jubert (baptized 12 May 1576: AD S-M, Parish Registers, St. Laurent, Rouen) Isaac de Bellehache	Hérit. 2, 10 June 1597
1597	Isabeau Romé (baptized 19 September 1597: AD S-M, 1F39, pp. 59-62) Georges de La Haye	Hérit. 2, 24 January 1598
1598	Victoire le Jumel* Anthoine Le Marinier	Hérit. 2, bound 8 April 1601
1599	Marie Le Conte Charles de Bonenffant	*Ibid.*, 25 November 1599
1600	Claude Busquet Charles de Recusson	*Ibid.*, 22 November 1600
1601	Madeleine Le Prévost Jean de Lampérière	AD Eure, E1466, ff. 268-269
1601	Marie de La Porte* le baron de Pretot	Hérit. 2, 16 February 1602
1602	Marguerite Romé Jean Auffrye	Meubles 2, 26 February 1604
1602	Marie Groulart* (born 1587: BM MS Martainville Y24, 1, f. 26) Nicolas de Servian	Hérit. 2, 16 December 1602

1603	Marie Busquet Anthoine de Bellemare	Hérit. 2, 28 August 1603
1604	Catherine de Grouchet Robert Le Barge	*Ibid.*, 29 November 1604
1604	Isabeau Le Prévost Robert Le Clerc	*Ibid.*, 22 November 1604
1605	Marie Diane Romé (baptized 19 March 1583: AD S-M, 1F39, pp. 59-62) Anthoine de Calmesnil	*Ibid.*, 25 September 1606
1606	Madeleine Romé François de Brèvedent	Hérit. 2, 23 December 1609
1607	Françoise Voisin Georges Duhamel	*Ibid.*, 15 September 1607
1608	Marguerite Garin Denis de Vandes	*Ibid.*, 12 February 1608
1608	Madeleine Romé François de Rely	*Ibid.*, 28 July 1608
1608	Marthe Busquet Charles Le Pesant	*Ibid.*, 25 August 1608
1609	Marie de Boislevesque Jacques Godart	*Ibid.*, 25 April 1609
1609	Marguerite Pipperey Constant de Malhortye	*Ibid.*, 2 December 1609
1610	Madeleine Maignart* (born 6 February 1595: BM MS Martainville Y24, 1, f. 82) Claude Bretel	*Ibid.*, 20 January 1610
1610	Catherine de La Porte* (baptized 20 August 1585: AD S-M, Parish Registers, St. Laurent, Rouen) Jacques de Durerie	Hérit. 2, 27 February 1610

Date	Future Bride/ Future Husband	Source
1610	Marie Le Brun (baptized 8 January 1588: AD S-M, Parish Registers, St. Lô, Rouen) Gilles Charles	Hérit. 2, 4 April 1610

BIBLIOGRAPHY

I. Manuscript Sources

Archives Départementales, Seine-Maritime (Rouen)

Series B: Parlement, Registres Secrets, Registres d'Audiences, Registres d'Arrêts, Registres de la Tournelle (all of these are classified only by the date of the register); Tutelles.

Series B: Requêtes du Palais, Sentences, Contrats (only a few registers of each, classified by date).

Series D350: Ursulines of Dieppe.

Series E, Notarial Series: Tabellionage de Dieppe, Tabellionage du Pont St. Pierre (both only isolated registers); Tabellionage de Rouen; Tabellionage de Rouen, Héritages 1ère and 2ème séries, Meubles 1ère and 2ème séries (classified only by date). With these are manuscript inventories of marriage contracts, inheritance divisions, testaments, and sales of land, houses, and offices; these were apparently compiled in the mid-seventeenth century. Together the series which make up the Tabellionage of Rouen include at least sixteen large volumes of contracts for each year in the early seventeenth century, and only slightly fewer during the sixteenth century; it is only with the aid of these inventories that the individual researcher is able to deal with the series.

Series E, Seigneurial Papers: Fonds Baronnie du Pont St. Pierre.

Series E, Family Papers: Fonds Bigot, Caillot de Coquéraumont, Poerier d'Amfreville, Restault, Romé. Both seigneurial and family papers are entirely unclassified; however, a manuscript guide compiled by M. Georges Mouradian, formerly Archiviste Adjoint, greatly facilitates their use.

Series F, Parish Registers: Berville sur Seine, La Neuville Chantdoisel; St. Laurent, St. Lô, St. Patrice, Rouen.

Series F, Local Studies: 1F39: Abbé Maurice, *Les Romé de Fresquiennes*; 6F: notes of Charles Robillard de Beaurepaire.

Series G, Secular Clergy: G3431, 3442 (testaments of cathedral cannons); G6275 (testaments, St. André of Rouen); G6827 (foundations, St. Laurent of Rouen); G6852 (parish of Sahurs).

Series H, Regular Clergy: 14H102, 14H104 (accounts of the kitchen of the Abbey of St. Ouen); 32H, unclassified (accounts of the Carmelites of Rouen).

Series J: Chartrier de la Rivière Bourdet; 10J, Chartrier de Bosmelet; 16J, Chartrier de Belbeuf; J57, History of the Chambre des Comptes, Rouen.

Archives Départementales, Eure (Évreux)

Series E: E3, "Rôle des fiefs. . . ."

E1224, 1229, 1235, 1242, 1247, 1252, 1259, 1260, 1261, 1295, Tabellionages, Pont St. Pierre.

E1324, 1428, 1435, 1438, 1465, 1466, 1499, 1502, 1523, Tabellionage de Vernon.

E796, Fonds Lombellon.

E827, Fonds Guéribout.

E2474, Fonds Jubert.

E3207, 3208, 3212, Seigneurie de Thibermesnil.

Archives Nationales, Paris

G8 1246, 1247, 1248, 1249, 1250, Alienations of church property, diocese of Rouen.

P265¹, Register of homages, bailliage of Rouen.

U 754, "Extraicts des registres des deliberations secretes du Parlement de Normandie."

Y 153, 495, Insinuations, Châtelet de Paris.

Minutier Central, xxiv, 165.

Bibliothèque Municipale, Dieppe

MS 63, Inventaire après décès, Claude Groulart.

Bibliothèque Municipale, Rouen

Y 17, Chants royaux, Puy de la Conception, Rouen.

Y 94, Denis Godefroy, La Coutume reformée du pais et duché de Normandie.

Y111, Compte du receveur général de Rouen des rentes payées pour l'année 1578.

Y 186, Registre d'inscriptions pour les associés du Puy de l'immaculée conception de la sainte Vierge. . . .

Y 202, Recueil de pièces autographes de Claude Groulart.

Y 214, *De divers registres de la cour de parlement de Rouen.*

Martainville Y 2, Magistrates' Tombstones.

Martainville Y 23, Alexandre Bigot de Monville, *Traité de l'Eschiquier et Parlement de Normandie.*

Martainville Y 24, Alexandre Bigot de Monville, *Recueil des présidents, conseillers et autres officiers du parlement de Rouen.* . . .

Martainville Y 55, *Recueil sur les livres et lieux communs de monsieur maître Jean Lefebvre.*

Martainville Y 90, *D'un registre . . . contenant plusieurs cérémonies et délibérations de ladite cour.* . . .

Martainville Y 96, *Extraict des registres des mercuriales du parlement de Rouen.*

G 247⁸, *inventaire après décès,* Adrien de Croismare.

m 254, *Livre de comptes de Louis Dubosc.* . . .

Bibliothèque Nationale, Paris

Genealogical Collections:

Pièces Originales, 227 (Bauquemare), 503 (Bretel), 1596 (Jubert), 1794 (Maignart), 2557 (Romé).

Carrés de d'Hozier, 70 (Bauquemare), 77 (Becdelièvre), 214 (Croismare), 358 (Jubert), 489 (Péricard).

Cabinet de d'Hozier, 301 (Le Roux).

Letter Collections:

MS français 15547, 15551, 15898, 15903, 15905, 20532, 20533, 20538, 20541, 20542, 20649.

Fonds Clairambault, 348.

Fonds Dupuy, 712, 802.

Other Manuscripts:

MS français 5346, Register of Testaments, St. André, Rouen.

MS français 5348, *Recueil par M. Caillot de diverses consultations faictes au parlement de Normandie.*

MS français 5351, *Dénombrement de fiefs.* . . .

MS français 32318, *Observations Extraits ou abregé historique du parlement.* . . .

Fonds Dupuy 498, *Extraict des registres de la court du parlement.*

Cinq Cents Colbert 16, *Extraict des registres de la Court de Parlement.*

Cinq Cents Colbert 488, Satirical poems.

Private Archives

Archives of the Baronnie d'Esneval, Acquigny, Eure.
Archives of the family Busquet de Caumont, consulted at the residence of the Comte de Caumont, Versailles.

II. Printed Sources and Works Published Before 1800

André, Louis, ed., *Cardinal de Richelieu, Testament politique.* Paris, 1947.

Angot des Retours, J., ed., "Épitaphier des Vauquelin," *Bulletin, Société des Antiquaires de Normandie,* xi (1933).

Aubert, Abbé, "Notes extraits de trois livres de raison de 1473 à 1550. Comptes d'une famille de gentilshommes campagnards normands," *Bulletin historique et philologique du Comité des travaux historique,* 1898, pp. 447-499.

Auvray, Jean, *Le banquet des Muses, ou Les divers satires du Sieur Auvray.* . . . Rouen, 1628.

Basnage, Henri, *Oeuvres,* 2 vols. 4th ed. Rouen, 1778.

Bérault, Josias, *La Coustume Reformée du Pays et Duché de Normandie.* 4th ed. Rouen, 1632.

Blangy, A. de, ed., *Journal de Gilles de Gouberville pour les années 1549, 1550, 1551, 1552. Mémoires de la Société des Antiquaires de Normandie,* xxii. Caen, 1895.

———, ed., "Tutelle de René du Parc, baron d'Ingrande, 1579-1585," *Bulletin de la Société des Antiquaires de Normandie,* xxv (1906).

Bouchel, Laurens, *La bibliothèque ou thrésor du droict françoys* . . . , 2 vols. Paris, 1615.

Bouquet, F., ed., *Hercule Grisel, Les fastes de Rouen,* 4 vols. Rouen, 1866-1868.

———, ed., *Mémoires de Pierre Thomas, Sieur du Fossé,* 4 vols. Rouen, 1876.

———, ed., *La Parthénie, ou Banquet des Palinods de Rouen en 1546. Poème latin du XVIe siècle par Baptiste Le Chandelier.* Rouen, 1883.

Bourgueville, Charles de, *Les recherches et antiquitez de la province de Neustrie, à présent de Normandie.* . . . Caen, 1833; first published 1588.

Brinon, Pierre, *Le triomphe des dames.* Rouen, 1599.

Castiglione, B., *The Courtier*. Trans. Charles Singleton. Garden City, 1959.

Chéruel, M., ed., *Le journal d'Olivier Lefèvre d'Ormesson* . . . , 2 vols. Paris, 1860.

Desiré, Artus, *L'origine et source de tous les maux de ce monde par l'incorrection des peres et meres envers leurs enfans.* . . . Paris, 1571.

D'Orléans, Louis, *Les ouvertures du parlement*. Paris, 1607.

Esmonin, Edmond, ed., *Voysin de la Noiraye. Mémoire sur la généralité de Rouen (1665)*. Paris, 1913.

Estienne, Charles, *La grand guide pour aller et venir par tout le royaume de France*. . . . Rouen, 1600.

Estienne, Olivier, *Nouveau traité des hypothèques.* . . . Rouen, 1705.

Estienne, Robert, *Dictionnaire Francoislatin, autrement dict Les mots Francois, avec la maniere duser diceulx, tournez en Latin.* Paris, 1549.

Ferrière, Claude-Joseph de, *Histoire du droit romain*. Nouvelle édition. Paris, 1738.

Foisil, Madeleine, ed., *Mémoires du Président Alexandre Bigot de Monville: le Parlement de Rouen, 1640-1643*. Paris, 1976.

Fontanon, Anthoine, *Les édicts et ordonnances des rois de France*, 4 vols. 2nd ed. Paris, 1611.

Groulart, Claude, *Mémoires*, in Michaud and Poujolat, eds., *Nouvelle collection des mémoires pour servir à l'histoire de France*, XI, 549-598.

Guénois, Pierre, *La conférence des ordonnances royaux.* . . . Nouvelle édition. Paris, 1596.

————, *La conférence des coustumes tant générales, que locales et particulières du Royaume de France*, 2 vols. Paris, 1596.

Histoire de l'église cathédrale de Rouen, métropolitaine et primatiale de Normandie. . . . Rouen, 1686.

Hotman, François, *Francogallia*, ed. Ralph Giesey and J.H.M. Salmon. Cambridge, 1972.

Houard, Maître, *Dictionnaire analytique, historique, étymologique et interprétatif de la coutume de Normandie*, 4 vols. Rouen, 1780.

Imbert, Jean, *La pratique judiciaire tant civile que criminelle, receue et observée par tout le royaume de France.* 4th ed. Paris, 1609.

Isambert, François et al., *Recueil général des anciennes lois françaises.* . . . Paris, n.d.

Kinser, Samuel, and Isabelle Cazeaux, eds., *The Memoirs of Philippe de Commynes*, 2 vols. Columbia, South Carolina, 1969.

Labiche, Jean, *Stile et forme de proceder. Ou sont contenues les formes de toutes matieres Civilles et Criminelles.* . . . Paris, 1609.

La Noue, François de, *Discours politiques et militaires*, ed. F. E. Sutcliffe. Geneva, 1967.

La Roche Flavin, Bernard de, *Treze livres des Parlemens de France.* . . . Bordeaux, 1617.

La Tournerie, Maître de, *Traité des fiefs à l'usage de la province de Normandie.* Paris, 1763.

Le Charpentier, H., and Alfred Fitan, eds., *La ligue dans le Vexin normand. Journal d'un bourgeois de Gisors.* . . . Paris, 1878.

Lefèvre, Louis-Raymond, ed., *Journal de L'Estoile pour le règne de Henri IV*, 3 vols. Paris, 1948.

Loyseau, Charles, *Oeuvres.* Paris, 1701.

Meyer, Jean, ed., "Un témoignage exceptionel sur la noblesse de province à l'orée du XVII⁰ siècle: les 'advis moraux' de René Fleuriot," *Annales de Bretagne*, LXXIX, 2 (June, 1972).

Monluc, Blaise de, *Commentaires, 1521-1576.* Paris, Bibliothèque de la Pléiade, 1964.

Montaigne, Michel de, *Essais*, 3 vols. Paris, Garnier-Flammarion, 1969.

Montchrestien, Anthoine de, Sieur de Vasteville, *Les tragédies.* Rouen, 1627.

Mousnier, Roland, ed., *Lettres et mémoires adressés au chancelier Séguier (1633-1649)*, 2 vols. Paris, 1964.

Ordonnances des rois de France. Règne de François Iᵉʳ, V. Paris, 1936.

Panel, Gustave, *Documents concernants les pauvres de Rouen extraits des archives de l'Hôtel de ville*, 2 vols. Paris and Rouen, 1917.

Papon, Iehan, *Recueil d'arrestz notables des courtz souveraines de France.* . . . Paris, 1566.

Paschal, Charles, *Christianarum precum libri duo.* Caen, 1592.

Pasquier, Estienne, *Les mémoires et recherches de la France, Livre premier et second*. . . . Paris, 1594.

Porée, Chanoine, *DuBuisson-Aubenay, Itinéraire de Normandie*. Paris-Rouen, 1911.

Prévost, G.-A., ed., "Documents sur le ban et l'arrière ban, et les fiefs de la vicomté de Rouen en 1594 et 1560, et sur la noblesse du bailliage de Gisors en 1703," *Mélanges, Société de l'histoire de Normandie*, 3rd series (1895), pp. 231-423.

———, ed., *Notes du premier président Pellot sur la Normandie. Clergé, gentilshommes et terres principales, officiers de justice.* Paris, 1915.

Robillard de Beaurepaire, Charles de, ed., *Cahiers des États de Normandie sous le règne de Henri III*, 2 vols. Rouen, 1888.

———, ed., "Les harangues prononcées par le président de Bauquemare aux États de la province de Normandie, de 1556 à 1583," ext. *Précis des Travaux de l'Académie des Sciences, Belles Lettres et Arts de Rouen*, 1871-1872.

Seyssel, Claude de, *La monarchie de France*, ed. Jacques Poujol. Paris, 1961.

Sireulde, Jacques, *Les abus et superfluitez du Monde*. . . . Rouen, n.d.

Souillet, Louis de, *Histoire de la ville de Rouen*, 6 vols. 3rd ed. Rouen, 1731.

Taillepied, Noel, *Recueil des antiquitez et singularitez de la ville de Rouen*. Rouen, 1610; first publ. 1587.

Toustain-Richebourg, Charles Gaspard, *Famille de Toustain-Frontebosc*. N.p., 1799.

III. Secondary Works

Abel, Wilhelm. *Geschichte des deutschen Landwirtschaft von frühen Mittelalter bis zum 19. Jahrhundert*. 2nd ed. Stuttgart, 1967.

D'Arandel de Condé, G. "Les anciennes mesures agraires de Haute-Normandie," *Annales de Normandie*, xviii, 1 (March, 1968), 3-60.

———. "Les anciennes mesures de capacité pour les grains en Seine-Maritime au XVIIIe siècle," *Revue d'histoire économique et sociale*, xlviii, 3 (1970), 305-352.

Ariès, Philippe. *Centuries of Childhood. A Social History of Family Life*, tr. Robert Baldick. New York, 1962.

Bardet, Jean-Pierre. "La maison rouennaise aux XVII⁰ et XVIII⁰ siècles, économie et comportement," in Bardet et al., eds., *Le bâtiment. Enquête d'histoire économique, XIVᵉ-XIXᵉ siècles*. Paris-The Hague, 1971, pp. 313-518.

Bataille, Roger. *Du droit des filles dans la succession de leurs parents en Normandie*. Paris, 1927.

Baulant, M. and J. Meuvret. *Prix des céréales extraits de la Mercuriale de Paris, 1520-1698*, 2 vols. Paris, 1960.

Beik, William. "Magistrates and Popular Uprisings in France before the Fronde: The Case of Toulouse," *Journal of Modern History*, XLVI, 4 (December, 1974), 585-608.

Benedict, Philip. "Catholics and Huguenots in Sixteenth-Century Rouen: The Demographic Effects of the Religious Wars," *French Historical Studies*, IX, 2 (Fall, 1975), 209-234.

Bercé, Yves Marie. *Histoire des Croquants. Étude des soulèvements populaires au XVIIᵉ siècle dans le sud-ouest de la France*, 2 vols. Geneva, 1975.

Berkner, Lutz K. "The Stem Family and the Developmental Cycle of the Peasant Household: An Eighteenth-Century Austrian Example," *The American Historical Review*, LXXVII, 2 (April, 1972), 398-418.

Bezard, Yvonne. *La vie rurale dans le sud de la région parisienne de 1450 à 1560*. Paris, 1929.

Billacois, François. "La crise de la noblesse européenne (1550-1650): Une mise au point," *Revue d'histoire moderne et contemporaine*, XXIII (April-June, 1976), 258-277.

Bitton, Davis. *The French Nobility in Crisis, 1560-1640*. Stanford, 1969.

Bloch, Jean-Richard. *L'anoblissement en France au temps de François Iᵉʳ*. Paris, 1934.

Bloch, Marc. *French Rural History: An Essay on its Basic Characteristics*, tr. Janet Sondheimer. Berkeley and Los Angeles, 1966.

Bluche, François. *Les magistrats du parlement de Paris au XVIIIᵉ siècle (1715-1771)*. Paris, 1960.

——, and Pierre Durye, *L'anoblissement par charges avant 1789*, 2 vols. La Roche sur Yon, 1962.

Bois, Guy. "Le prix de froment à Rouen au XVe siècle," *Annales. Économies, Sociétés, Civilisations*, XXIII, 6 (Nov.-Dec., 1968), 1262-1282.

——. *Crise du féodalisme. Économie rurale et démographie en Normandie orientale du début du 14e siècle au milieu du 16e siècle*. Paris, 1976.

Bouard, Michel de, ed. *Histoire de la Normandie*. Toulouse 1970.

Bourel, M. *La commune de Limésy. Souvenirs du passé*. Rouen, 1899.

Boutruche, Robert, ed. *Bordeaux de 1453 à 1715*. Bordeaux, 1966.

Bouwsma, William. "Lawyers and Early Modern Culture," *The American Historical Review*, LXXVIII, 2 (April, 1973), 303-327.

Braudel, Fernand. *The Mediterranean and the Mediterranean World in the Age of Philip II*, 2 vols., tr. Sian Reynolds. New York, 1972-1973.

Brenner, Robert. "Agrarian Class Structure and Economic Development in Pre-Industrial Europe," *Past and Present*, 70 (February, 1976), 30-75.

Brunner, Otto. "Das 'Ganze Haus' und die alteuropäische Ökonomik," in Brunner, *Neue Wege der Verfassungs- und Sozialgeschichte*. 2nd ed. Göttingen, 1968.

Brunot, Ferdinand. *Histoire de la langue française*, 13 vols. 2nd ed. Paris, 1966.

Buisseret, David. *Sully and the Growth of Centralized Government in France*. London, 1968.

Busquet de Caumont, Robert. *Histoire économique et sociale d'une lignée de huit conseillers au parlement de Normandie: les Busquet de Chandoissel et de Caumont*. Mémoire, D.E.S., Paris, Faculté de droit et des sciences économiques.

Cerné, A. "Les hôtels des Bigot à Rouen," *Bulletin de la Société d'Émulation de la Seine-Inférieure*, XXXIX (1934), 205-226.

Charmeil, Jean-Pierre. *Les trésoriers de France à l'époque de la Fronde*. Paris, 1964.

Charpillon, M., and Abbé Caresme. *Dictionnaire historique de toutes les communes du département de l'Eure*. Les Andelys, 1868-1879.

Chartier, Roger, Marie-Madeleine Compère, and Dominique Julia. *L'éducation en France du XVIe au XVIIIe siècle*. Paris, 1976.

373

Chateaubriand, F.-R. de, *Mémoires d'outre tombe*, 2 vols. Paris, Bibliothèque de la Pléiade, 1946-1948.

Chaunu, Pierre. "Sur la fin des sorciers au XVIIe siècle," *Annales. Économies, Sociétés, Civilisations*, xxiv, 4 (July-August, 1969), 895-911.

Church, William F. *Constitutional Thought in Sixteenth-Century France*. Cambridge, Mass., 1941.

Cobban, Alfred. *The Social Interpretation of The French Revolution*. Cambridge, 1964.

Constant, Jean-Marie. "L'enquête de noblesse de 1667 et les seigneurs de Beauce," *Revue d'histoire moderne et contemporaine*, xxi (October-December, 1974), 548-566.

Couturier, Marcel. *Recherches sur les structures sociales de Châteaudun, 1525-1789*. Paris, 1969.

Curzon, Alfred de. *L'enseignement du droit français dans les universités de France aux XVIIe et XVIIIe siècles*. Paris, 1920.

Dahm, Georg. *Zur Rezeption des römisch-italienischen Rechts*. Darmstadt, 1960.

Dalloz, V.A.D. *Répertoire de droit civil*. 2nd ed. Paris, 1973—

Daumard, A., and F. Furet. *Structures et relations sociales à Paris au milieu du XVIIIe siècle. Cahiers des Annales*, xviii (1961).

Davis, Natalie Zemon. "Sixteenth-Century French Arithmetics on the Business Life," *Journal of the History of Ideas*, xxi, 1 (January-March, 1960), 18-48.

———. "Strikes and Salvation at Lyons," *Archiv für Reformationsgeschichte*, lvi, 1 (1965), 48-64.

———. "Poor Relief, Humanism, and Heresy in Lyon," *Studies in Medieval and Renaissance History*, v (1968), 215-275.

———. "The Reasons of Misrule: Youth Groups and Charivaris in Sixteenth-Century France," *Past and Present*, 50 (February, 1971), 41-75.

———. "The Rites of Violence: Religious Riot in Sixteenth-Century France," *Past and Present*, 59 (May, 1973), 51-91.

———. "Ghosts, Kin, and Progeny: Some Features of Family Life in Early Modern France," *Daedalus*, cvi, 2 (Spring, 1977), 87-114.

Dawson, John P. *The Oracles of the Law*. Ann Arbor, 1968.

Delisle, Leopold. *Études sur la condition de la classe agricole et l'état de l'agriculture en Normandie au moyen âge*. Évreux, 1851; repr. New York, n.d.

Dent, Julian. Review of Davis Bitton, *The French Nobility in Crisis*, *Renaissance Quarterly*, XXIV, 2 (Summer, 1971), 244-247.

Dessert, Daniel. Review of J.-P. Labatut, *Les ducs et pairs*, *Annales. Économies, Sociétés, Civilisations*, XXXI, 4 (July-August, 1976), 850-851.

Dewald, Jonathan. "Magistracy and Political Opposition at Rouen: A Social Context," *The Sixteenth Century Journal*, V, 2 (October, 1974), 66-78.

———. "The 'Perfect Magistrate': *Parlementaires* and Crime in Sixteenth-Century Rouen," *Archive for Reformation History*, LXVII (1976), 284-300.

Deyon, Pierre. "À propos des rapports entre la noblesse française et la monarchie absolue pendant la première moitié du XVIIe siècle," *Revue historique*, CCXXXI (April-June, 1964), 341-356.

———. *Amiens, capitale provinciale: Étude sur la société urbaine au XVIIe siècle*. Paris, 1967.

Didot, Firmin. *Nouvelle biographie générale*. Paris, 1858.

Doucet, R. *Les institutions de la France au XVIe siècle*, 2 vols. Paris, 1948.

Douyère, Christiane. *Une famille rouennaise d'origine espagnole à la fin du 15e et au 16e siècle: les Civille (1484-vers 1600). Schéma d'une assimilation*. Mémoire de Maîtrise, Université de Paris, 1973.

Drouot, Henri. *Mayenne et la Bourgogne. Étude sur la Ligue (1587-1596)*, 2 vols. Paris, 1937.

Duby, Georges. *La société au XIe et XIIe siècles dans la région maconnaise*. 2nd ed. Paris, 1971.

———. "Lignage, noblesse et chevalerie au XIIe siècle dans la région maconnaise," *Annales. Économies, Sociétés, Civilisations*, XXVII, 4-5 (July-October, 1972), 803-823.

Edwards, A. L. *Statistical Methods*. 2nd ed. New York, 1967.

Esmein, A. *Histoire de la procédure criminelle en France*. Paris, 1882.

Esmonin, Edmond. *La taille en Normandie au temps de Colbert*. Paris, 1913.

Esneval, le baron d', "Une famille parlementaire de Normandie: Les Bretel de Grémonville," *Revue catholique de Normandie*, XXXIII-XXIV (1924).

375

Estaintot, Robert d'. *La Ligue en Normandie, 1588-1594.* Paris, Rouen, Caen, 1862.

———. *Recherches sur les hautes justices féodales existant dans les limites du département de la Seine-Inférieure.* Rouen, 1892.

Favier, Jean. "Un terrier Cauchois au début du XIV⁰ siècle: le domaine de Longueil," *Annales de Normandie*, xiii, 3 (October, 1963).

Febvre, Lucien. *Philippe II et la Franche-Comté.* 2nd ed. Paris, 1970.

Fédou, René. *Les hommes de loi lyonnais à la fin du moyen âge.* Paris, 1964.

Finley, M. I. *The Ancient Economy.* Berkeley and Los Angeles, 1973.

Flandrin, Jean-Louis. *Les amours paysannes. Amour et sexualité dans les campagnes de l'ancienne France (XVI⁰-XIX⁰ siècle).* Paris, 1975.

Floquet, A. *Histoire du Parlement de Normandie,* 7 vols. Rouen, 1840-1842.

Ford, Franklin. *Robe and Sword: The Regrouping of the French Aristocracy after Louis XIV.* Cambridge, Mass., 1953.

Forster, Robert. *The Nobility of Toulouse in the Eighteenth Century: A Social and Economic Study.* Baltimore, 1960.

———. *The House of Saulx-Tavanes: Versailles and Burgundy, 1700-1830.* Baltimore, 1971.

Fourquin, Guy. *Les campagnes de la région parisienne à la fin du moyen âge, du milieu du XIII⁰ siècle au début du XVI⁰ siècle.* Paris, 1964.

Franklin, Julian. *Jean Bodin and the Sixteenth-Century Revolution in the Methodology of Law and History.* New York, 1963.

Frêche, Georges. *Toulouse et la région Midi-Pyrénées au siècle des lumières (vers 1670-1789).* Paris, 1974.

Frondeville, Henri de. *Les présidents du Parlement de Normandie (1499-1790).* Paris and Rouen, 1953.

———. *Les conseillers du Parlement de Normandie au seizième siècle (1499-1594).* Paris and Rouen, 1960.

———. *Les conseillers du Parlement de Normandie sous Henri IV et sous Louis XIII (1594-1640).* Paris and Rouen, 1964.

Fruit, J.-P. *Vexin normand ou Vexin parisienne? Contribution à l'étude géographique de l'espace.* Paris, 1974.

Gately, Michael O., A. Lloyd Moote, John E. Willis. "Seventeenth-Century Peasant 'Furies.' Some Problems of Comparative History," *Past and Present*, 51 (May, 1971), 63-80.

Giesey, Ralph. "Rules of Inheritance and Strategies of Mobility in Prerevolutionary France," *The American Historical Review*, LXXXII, 2 (April, 1977), 271-289.

Godelier, Maurice. *Rationalité et irrationalité en économie.* Paris, 1968.

——. *Horizons, trajets marxistes en anthropologie.* Paris, 1973.

Göhring, Martin. *Die Ämterkäuflichkeit im Ancien Regime.* Berlin, 1938.

Goldthwaite, Richard. *Private Wealth in Renaissance Florence. A Study of Four Families.* Princeton, 1968.

Gosselin, E. *Recherches sur les origines et l'histoire du théâtre à Rouen avant Pierre Corneille.* Rouen, 1868.

Goubert, Pierre. *Beauvais et le Beauvaisis de 1600 à 1730: Contribution à l'histoire sociale de la France au XVIIᵉ siècle*, 2 vols. Paris, 1960.

——. "Recent Theories and Research in French Population between 1500 and 1700," in D. V. Glass and D.E.C. Eversley, eds., *Population in History. Essays in Historical Demography.* Chicago, 1965.

——. *L'ancien régime*, 2 vols. Paris, 1969-1973.

Grenier, le baron. *Traité des hypothèques* . . . , 2 vols. 2nd ed. Clermont-Ferrand, 1829.

Guenée, Bernard. *Tribunaux et gens de justice dans le bailliage de Senlis à la fin du moyen âge (vers 1380-vers 1550).* Paris, 1963.

Habakuk, H. J. "The Price of Land in England, 1500-1700," in W. Abel et al., eds., *Wirtschaft, Geschichte, und Wirtschaftsgeschichte: Festschrift zum 65. Geburtstag von Friedrich Lütge.* Stuttgart, 1966.

Harris, B. J. "Landlords and Tenants in England in the Later Middle Ages," *Past and Present*, 43 (1969), 146-150.

Harvey, Howard Graham. *The Theatre of the Basoche. The Contribution of the Law Societies to French Medieval Comedy.* Cambridge, Mass., 1941.

Hunt, David. *Parents and Children in History. The Psychology of Family Life in Early Modern France.* New York, 1970.

Huppert, George. *The Idea of Perfect History: Historical Eru-*

dition and Historical Philosophy in Renaissance France. Urbana, 1970.

———. *Les Bourgeois Gentilshommes: An Essay on the Definition of Elites in Renaissance France.* Chicago, 1977.

Hurt, John. "Les offices au Parlement de Bretagne sous le règne de Louis XIV: aspects financiers," *Revue d'histoire moderne et contemporaine,* xxiii (January-March, 1976), 3-31.

Jacquart, Jean. *La crise rurale en Île de France 1550-1670.* Paris, 1974.

Kelley, Donald. *Foundations of Modern Historical Scholarship: Language, Law, and History in the French Renaissance.* New York, 1970.

———. *François Hotman. A Revolutionary's Ordeal.* Princeton, 1973.

———. "History, English Law and the Renaissance," *Past and Present,* 65 (November, 1974), 24-51.

Kerridge, Eric. *The Agricultural Revolution.* London, 1967.

Kettering, Sharon. *Judicial Politics and Urban Revolt in Seventeenth-Century France. The Parlement of Aix, 1629-1659.* Princeton, 1978.

Kierstead, Raymond. *Pomponne de Bellièvre: A Study of the King's Men in the Age of Henry IV.* Evanston, 1968.

Labatut, Jean-Pierre. *Les ducs et pairs de France au XVIIe siècle Étude sociale.* Paris, 1972.

Labrousse, Ernest, et al., eds. *Histoire économique et sociale de la France, II:1660-1789.* Paris, 1970.

Langbein, John. *Prosecuting Crime in the Renaissance: England, Germany, France.* Cambridge, Mass., 1974.

Lapeyre, Henri. *Une famille de marchands: Les Ruiz.* Paris, 1955.

Laslett, Peter. *The World We Have Lost.* New York, 1965.

LeChevalier, A. *Notice historique sur les barons et la baronnie du Bec.* Paris, 1898.

Le Mercier, Pierre. *Les justices seigneuriales de la région parisienne de 1580 à 1789.* Paris, 1933.

Le Roy Ladurie, Emmanuel. *Les paysans de Languedoc,* 2 vols. 2nd ed. Paris-The Hague, n.d.

———. "Système de la coutume. Structures familiales et coutume d'héritage en France au XVIe siècle," *Annales. Économies, Sociétés, Civilisations,* xxvii, 4-5 (July-October, 1972), 825-846.

———. "La verdeur du bocage," introduction to Abbé Tollemer, *Un sire de Gouberville, gentilhomme campagnard au Cotentin de 1553 à 1562.* Paris-The Hague, 1972.

———, and Joseph Goy. *Les fluctuations du produit de la dîme: conjoncture décimale et domaniale de la fin du Moyen Âge au XVIIIᵉ siècle.* Paris-The Hague, 1972.

Le Verdier, P. *Une famille de robe. Histoire de la famille de Pipperey.* Rouen, 1929.

Lougee, Carolyn. *Le Paradis des Femmes. Women, Salons, and Social Stratification in Seventeenth-Century France.* Princeton, 1976.

Macfarlane, Alan. *Witchcraft in Tudor and Stuart England. A Regional and Comparative Study.* New York, 1970.

Mandrou, Robert. *Introduction à la France moderne (1500-1640). Essai de psychologie historique.* 2nd ed. Paris, 1974.

———. "Vingt ans après, les révoltes populaires dans l'historiographie française du XVIIᵉ siècle," *Revue historique,* ccxlii (1969), 29-40.

———. *La France aux XVIIᵉ et XVIIIᵉ siècles.* 3rd ed. Paris, 1974.

Major, J. Russell. "The Crown and the Aristocracy in Renaissance France," *The American Historical Review,* lxix, 3 (April, 1964).

———. "Bellièvre, Sully and the Assembly of Notables of 1597," *Transactions of the American Philosophical Society,* lxiv, part 2 (1974).

Maugis, Édouard. *Histoire du Parlement de Paris de l'avènement des rois Valois à la mort d'Henri IV,* 3 vols. Paris, 1914; repr. New York, 1967.

Merle, Louis. *La métairie et l'évolution agraire de la Gâtine poitevine de la fin du Moyen Âge à la Révolution.* Paris, 1958.

Meuvret, Jean. *Études d'histoire économique. Recueil d'articles. Cahiers des Annales,* xxxii. Paris, 1971.

Meyer, Jean. *La noblesse de Bretagne au XVIIIᵉ siècle,* 2 vols. Paris, 1966.

———. "Un problème mal posé: La noblesse pauvre. L'exemple breton au XVIIIᵉ siècle," *Revue d'histoire moderne et contemporaine,* xviii (April-June, 1971), 161-188.

Michaud, J.-Fr. *Biographie universelle ancienne et moderne.* Paris, 1854.

Mollat, Michel. *Le commerce maritime normand à la fin du Moyen Âge.* Paris, 1952.

Mougel, François-Charles. "La fortune des princes de Bourbon-Conty: revenus et gestion, 1655-1791," *Revue d'histoire moderne et contemporaine,* XVIII (January-March, 1971), 30-49.

Monter, E. William. *Witchcraft in France and Switzerland. The Borderlands during the Reformation.* Ithaca, 1976.

Moote, A. Lloyd, *The Revolt of the Judges: The Parlement of Paris and the Fronde, 1643-1652.* Princeton, 1971.

Morineau, Michel. *Les faux-semblants d'un démarrage économique: agriculture et démographie en France au XVIIIe siècle. Cahiers des Annales,* XXX. Paris, 1970.

Moroney, M. J. *Facts from Figures.* London, 1951.

Mousnier, Roland. *L'assassinat d'Henri IV.* Paris, 1964.

————, et al. *Problèmes de stratification sociale: deux cahiers de la noblesse pour les États généraux de 1649-1651.* Paris, 1965.

————. "Trevor-Roper's 'General Crisis': Symposium," in Trevor Aston, ed., *Crisis in Europe, 1560-1660.* Garden City, 1967, pp. 103-111.

————. *La plume, la faucille et le marteau. Institutions et société en France du Moyen Âge à la Révolution.* Paris, 1970.

————. *Peasant Uprisings in Seventeenth-Century France, Russia, and China,* tr. Brian Pearce. New York, 1970.

————. *Le conseil du roi de Louis XII à la Révolution.* Paris, 1970.

————. "The Fronde," in Robert Forster and Jack Greene, eds., *Preconditions of Revolution in Early Modern Europe.* Baltimore, 1970.

————. *La vénalité des offices sous Henri IV et Louis XIII.* 2nd ed. Paris, 1971.

————. "Les concepts d' 'ordres,' d' 'états' et de 'monarchie absolue' en France de la fin du XVe siècle à la fin du XVIIIe," *Revue historique,* DII (April-June, 1972), 289-312.

————. *Les institutions de la France sous la monarchie absolue, 1598-1789, I.* Paris, 1975.

————. "Les survivances médiévales dans la France du XVIIe siècle," *XVIIe Siècle,* no. 106-107 (1975).

Newton, W. R., and J. M. Ultee. "The Minutier Central: A Research Note," *French Historical Studies*, VIII, 3 (Spring, 1974), 489-493.

Permezel, Jacques. *La politique financière de Sully dans la généralité de Lyon.* Lyon, 1935.

Perroy, Edouard. "Social Mobility among the French *Noblesse* in the Later Middle Ages," *Past and Present*, 21 (April, 1962), pp. 25-38.

Plaisse, André. *La baronnie de Neubourg: essai d'histoire agraire, économique et sociale.* Paris, 1961.

Poli, Oscar de. "Les seigneurs de la Rivière Bourdet," *Revue nobiliare historique et biographique*, nouvelle série, IV (1868), 97-108, 207-233, 261-275.

Pocock, J.G.A. *The Feudal Law and the Ancient Constitution. A Study of English Historical Thought in the Seventeenth Century.* Cambridge, 1957.

Porchnev, Boris. *Les soulèvements populaires en France de 1623 à 1648.* Paris, 1963.

Porée, Chanoine, *Histoire de l'abbaye du Bec*, 2 vols. Evreux, 1901.

Prentout, Henri. *Les états provinciaux de Normandie*, 3 vols. Paris, 1925-1927.

Procacci, Giuliano. *Classi sociali e monarchia assoluta nella Francia della prima metà del secolo XVI.* Turin, 1955.

Quenedey, Raymond. *L'habitation rouennaise: étude d'histoire, de géographie et d'archéologie urbaines.* Rouen, 1926.

Richet, Denis. *La France moderne: l'esprit des institutions.* Paris, 1973.

Robinne, Paul-Édouard. *Les magistrats du parlement de Normandie à la fin du XVIIIᵉ siècle (1774-1790): Essai d'étude économique et sociale. . . .* 2 vols. Thesis, typescript, École des Chartes, 1967. (AD S-M, F86).

Roupnel, Gaston. *La ville et la campagne au XVIIᵉ siècle, étude sur les populations du pays dijonnais.* 2nd ed. Paris, 1955.

Saint Jacob, Pierre de. *Les paysans de la Bourgogne du Nord au dernier siècle de l'ancien régime.* Paris, 1960.

Salmon, J.H.M. "Venal Office and Popular Sedition in Seventeenth-Century France: A Review of a Controversy," *Past and Present*, 37 (July, 1967), 21-43.

381

Salmon, J.H.M. "The Paris Sixteen, 1584-1594: The Social Analysis of a Revolutionary Movement," *Journal of Modern History*, XLIV, 4 (December, 1972), 540-576.

Schalk, Ellery. "The Appearance and Reality of Nobility in France during the Wars of Religion: An Example of How Collective Attitudes Can Change," *Journal of Modern History*, XLVIII, 1 (March, 1976), 19-31.

Schnapper, Bernard. *Les rentes au XVIe siècle: Histoire d'un instrument de crédit.* Paris, 1957.

Schramm, Percy. *Der König von Frankreich. Das Wesen der Monarchie vom 9. zum 16. Jahrhundert*, 2 vols. Weimar, 1960.

Shennan, J. H. *The Parlement of Paris.* London, 1968.

Sion, Jules. *Les paysans de la Normandie orientale: Pays de Caux, Bray, Vexin Normand, Vallée de la Seine. Étude géographique.* Paris, 1909.

Snyders, Georges. *La pédagogie en France au XVIIe et XVIIIe siècles.* Paris, 1965.

Stocker, Christopher. "The Politics of the Parlement of Paris in 1525," *French Historical Studies*, VIII, 2 (Fall, 1973), 191-212.

Stone, Lawrence. *The Crisis of the Aristocracy, 1558-1641.* Oxford, 1965.

Strayer, J. R. "Normandy and Languedoc," repr. in *Medieval Statecraft and the Perspectives of History.* Princeton, 1971.

Tapié, V.-L. "Les officiers seigneuriaux dans la société provinciale du XVIIe siècle," *XVIIe Siècle*, 42-43 (1959), 118-140.

Thompson, E. P. *The Making of the English Working Class.* London, 1963.

———. "The Moral Economy of the English Crowd," *Past and Present*, 50 (February, 1971), pp. 76-136.

Thurow, Lester C. *Generating Inequality. Mechanisms of Distribution in the U.S. Economy.* New York, 1975.

Tollemer, Abbé. *Un sire de Gouberville.* 2nd ed. Paris-The Hague, 1972.

Viollet, Paul. *Histoire du droit civil français.* Paris, 1905; repr. Darmstadt, 1966.

Weary, William A. "The House of La Tremouille, Fifteenth through Eighteenth Centuries: Change and Adaptation in a French Noble Family," *Journal of Modern History*, IL, 1 (March, 1977).

Wheaton, Robert. "Family and Kinship in Western Europe: The Problem of the Joint Family Household," *Journal of Interdisciplinary History*, v, 4 (Spring, 1975), 601-628.

Wolfe, Martin. *The Fiscal System of Renaissance France*. New Haven, 1972.

Wolff, Philippe. *Commerces et marchands de Toulouse (vers 1350-vers 1450)*. Paris, 1954.

Wood, James B. "La structure sociale de la noblesse dans le bailliage de Caen et ses modifications (1463-1666)," *Annales de Normandie*, xxii, 4 (December, 1972), 331-335.

———. "The Decline of the Nobility in Sixteenth and Early Seventeenth-Century France: Myth or Reality?" *Journal of Modern History*, xxxxviii, 1 (March, 1976).

———. "Demographic Pressures and Social Mobility among the Nobility of the Election of Bayeux, 1463-1666," *The Sixteenth Century Journal*, viii, 1 (April, 1977), 3-16.

INDEX

Library of Congress Cataloging in Publication Data

Dewald, Jonathan.
The formation of a provincial nobility.

A revision of the author's thesis, University of California,
Berkeley, 1974.
1. Nobility—France—Normandy—History—16th century.
2. France. Parlement de Normandie.
I. Title.
HT653.F7D48   1979   301.44′2   79-83986
ISBN 0-691-05283-2